"DEAREST GEORG"

LOVE, LITERATURE, AND POWER IN DARK TIMES

ELIAS AND VEZA CANETTI

"DEAREST GEORG"

LOVE, LITERATURE, AND POWER IN DARK TIMES

The Letters of Elias, Veza, and Georges Canetti, 1933–1948

edited by
Karen Lauer and Kristian Wachinger

translated from the German by
David Dollenmayer

OTHER PRESS
NEW YORK

Production Editor: Yvonne E. Cárdenas

Book design: Simon M. Sullivan

This book was set in 11.5 pt Fournier by
Alpha Design & Composition of Pittsfield, NH.

10 9 8 7 6 5 4 3 2 1

 Printed in the United States of America on acid-free paper. For information write to Other Press LLC, 2 Park Avenue, 24th Floor, New York, NY 10016.
Or visit our Web site: www.otherpress.com

Library of Congress Cataloging-in-Publication Data
Canetti, Veza, 1897–1963.
[Briefe an Georges. English]
Dearest Georg : love, literature, and power in dark times : the letters of Elias, Veza, and Georges Canetti, 1933–1948 / Elias and Veza Canetti ; edited by Karen Lauer and Kristian Wachinger ; translated by David Dollenmayer.
p. cm.
Includes bibliographical references and index.
ISBN 978-1-59051-297-5 — ISBN 978-1-59051-366-8 (E-BOOK)
1. Canetti, Veza, 1897–1963—Correspondence. 2. Canetti, Elias, 1905–1994—Correspondence. 3. Canetti, Georg, 1911– —Correspondence. 4. Authors, Austrian—20th century—Correspondence. I. Canetti, Elias, 1905–1994. II. Lauer, Karen. III. Wachinger, Kristian. IV. Dollenmayer, David B. V. Title.
PT2605.A588Z4813 2009
833'.912—dc22 [B] 2009023467

CONTENTS

ABOUT THIS TRANSLATION

Elias Canetti's younger brother Georges Canetti lived in France from 1931 until his death in 1971. Among his papers was a large packet of letters from Elias and his wife Veza. They had been stored in a steamer trunk in a damp basement and had absorbed quite a lot of moisture. Some of the letters were still in their envelopes and tied in bundles, others stuffed haphazardly into the trunk. An initial sorting by sender and date revealed that the letters from Georges's brother and sister-in-law were almost complete for the years 1933–1938 and 1944–1948. These letters, along with the surviving ones Georges wrote in return, were first published by Hanser Verlag, Munich, in 2006 and now appear in English translation.

Elias's letters are all handwritten, mostly in pencil. In the early years, his handwriting was much larger and more expansive than in the second half of his life. Despite Veza's physical handicap—she was born without a left hand—she typed most of her letters and emended them by hand.

During the latter part of the Second World War and continuing into the early postwar years, British censors required that letters to France be written in English. Thus Veza wrote all her letters from May 18, 1940, through February 25, 1947, in English (exceptions are the letter to Georges of October 4, 1945—in German except for a postscript in English—and the letter to Elias of August 1946). The frequently idiosyncratic spelling, diction, grammar, and punctuation of her English letters have been faithfully reproduced with the following exceptions: missing apostrophes in possessives and contractions have been added, as well as periods after the titles "Mr." and "Mrs." and in such place names as St. Hilaire to conform to American usage. Locutions with underlying German syntax such as "Maudy is divorced since a long time" and "the Comedy is unique what concerns imagination" are clear enough not to require annotation. It is not known how Elias managed to continue to write his letters in German during this time. There is some evidence that he sent them via New Zealand for this purpose.

The editors' and translator's annotations identify persons, explain references and allusions, gloss non-English words and phrases, and supply the reader with background information where necessary. In the nature of things, there are occasional passages that remain obscure.

The original letters were discovered in the Fonds Jacques Canetti in Suresnes, near Paris. After the German edition appeared, they were given to the Zentralbibliothek in Zurich (ZB), which houses the largest collection of Elias Canetti's literary remains. The two final letters of 1959 are in the archives of the Institut Pasteur in Paris.

> It is a coincidence that the two gods I acknowledge, the artist and the doctor, are brothers, and it could be a happy coincidence except that the arrival of the doctor has split my love.
>
> VEZA TO GEORGES, *September 24, 1937*

Vienna–Paris, June 1933

VENETIANA TAUBNER-CALDERON, thirty-five, born in Vienna on November 21, 1897; under the pseudonym Veza Magd, the author of stories published in various Viennese newspapers, including the *Arbeiter-Zeitung*, the organ of the Social Democratic Party; for the past eight years in a relationship with . . .

ELIAS CANETTI, twenty-seven, the oldest of three brothers; born in Rustschuk, Bulgaria, on the lower reaches of the Danube, on July 25, 1905; spent his youth in Manchester, Vienna, Zurich, and Frankfurt; holder of a doctorate in chemistry from the University of Vienna and author of an unpublished novel.

GEORG CANETTI, twenty-two, the youngest Canetti brother, born in Rustschuk on January 23, 1911; medical student, living in Paris for the past two years, also home to his mother Mathilde and the middle brother Nissim; recently naturalized as a French citizen under the name Georges.

In the fall of 1938, after being driven out of their apartment in Vienna, Veza and Elias Canetti will flee via Paris to London. Unlike Elias, who destroys the letters from his wife and brother, Georges Canetti will carefully save the letters from his brother and sister-in-law (as well as a few drafts of his own letters to them). Thus, despite what is lost, this epistolary account of a triangular relationship has been preserved.

The Letters of Elias, Veza, and Georges Canetti, *1933–1948*

Georges Canetti in the 1930s

Georges to Veza (*draft*) · *June 10, 1933*

Paris, June 10, 1933

My dearest Veza,

Your[1] letter has just arrived and I have to tell you it's almost incomprehensible—although I understand it very well. One thing alone is crystal clear, namely, of the four of us (you, Elias, Mama, and me), I am the only halfway normal person. You misunderstood my letter in a way that makes my hair stand on end; you've read all sorts of things between, below, and beside the lines and responded only to them—and anyway, who asked for your opinion about the trouble between Mama and Elias in the first place? Just because I wrote you about it doesn't mean I ascribe even the slightest role in it to you. You had a role, of course, but only a passive one. You were just a pretext, providing fresh fuel to the utterly predictable conflict between Mama and Elias. It could have found similar nourishment in a hundred other places, just as it has in the past. I wrote you about it the same way one discusses some especially sad preoccupation with a friend, hoping to obtain advice and encouragement, the way it's good just to be able to talk about things from time to time. And what did you do? You misunderstood what I said, misunderstood it with a passion that is lovely, to be sure, but in this case completely inappropriate. You mistook a token of my trust (one of the highest there is, namely, to discuss anything about my mother with anyone—even with you) as God only knows what—some sort of cryptic accusation, which then, if it had been justified at all, necessarily seemed just as fruitless as it was absurd in reality. Haven't you grasped the fact yet, Veza, that I never pursue a goal without saying what it is, or rather, that the only person I don't tell is the person who will benefit when I achieve it? You may consider this evidence of my shameless arrogance, but that's just the way it is. And what could have been the goal of my letter? At the most, to show you the damage Elias has done to other people—to his own mother!—and thereby to somehow make the weight, the unbearable weight of your relationship with him more bearable—but how wrong it would be to think so! For isn't it precisely the consciousness of one's own loneliness that is the most precious thing left in such cases—most precious at least for worthwhile human beings? In any event, I have nothing to reproach myself with, because I wasn't trying to achieve anything. —As you can see, no trace of an "outrageous" attack remains, unless the counterattack can be called outrageous. How can you seriously think that I would know anything at all about some idiotic gossip—and if I did, that I wouldn't write you *directly* about it instead of "*par faits interposé*," as they say. What's more, how can you think that my mother is the source of it! I give you my word of honor she is not. And finally, how can you think that her voice speaks through my letters! That really makes me laugh, and it must make you laugh too, because you know my independence of mind and could only have forgotten it in the heat of your passion. My dear, good Veza, let's leave the misery of our surroundings out of our letters: I'm a *participant* in that misery and wanted to tell you about it, but you *suffer* from it and in your suffering, you think that[2]

Georges to Veza (*draft*) · *October 25, 1933*

Paris, October 25, '33

My dear Veza,

Well, the three days of grace you granted me once my examination was over have stretched into fourteen. As for the first few days, it's easy to understand why, and I don't have to explain to you how much one's nerves need relaxation—or rather, application of a different kind—after such enormous stress. But more important, I have to admit, was my difficulty in picking up the thread again. Not that there's a dropped stitch between us that needs to be picked up, is there? Let's just say that a lot of knots have developed that both bind us together and trouble us in equal measure. Now, one could just slice right through them like one of those "blond Teutons" who crop up with such remarkable frequency in your letters (this just in passing). I'm a different sort of person, and so first of all, I must inform you that since Friday, your Canetti has not been in Paris, but in Strasbourg.[3] His visit here lasted a month and a half. There's a lot I could tell you about it, even though we didn't see much of each other and were never able to establish a truly lasting cordiality because of the quite unpleasant atmosphere that was mostly the doing of Nissim's fiancée.[4] But other things were also to blame. Elias is doubtless the sort of person who needs a very special lens, a particular camera angle and lighting level to appear to his best advantage, and all these things he definitely lacked in Paris. In his case, the undeniable discrepancy between the poet and the rest of the person must not be too harshly illuminated, which is only possible if the poet is overpowering and casts everything else into shadow. But that was of necessity impossible in Paris, and thus many things about Elias were not as they should have been. But by no means must you think that, due to these circumstances, I came to judge Elias in a different way. I only wanted to explain to you that since he senses such things immediately, he felt uncomfortable here and, despite many pleasant memories of specific details, could not help but come away with an overall impression of unpleasantness. It's simply that we always like it best where we are best liked, no matter by whom. God knows that's true for the species "poet."

Georges to Elias (*draft*) · *November 26, 1933*

November 26, 1933

My dear brother Elias,

Today I feel a special urge to write you, so I shall.

For over a month, my life has been turned away completely from all the things that had filled it up before: I am reading my way through stacks of books and as I read, I have a growing appetite to let their echoes become louder and louder. I'm like an insect shedding its chrysalis; under the massive stress of studying for my internship exam

(I still ought to be feeling stress about the oral exam, but it is a matter of utter indifference to me)—under the unbearable pressure of the last few months, a dam has suddenly burst and an unstoppable flood surges through me, filling me with the endless riches of real life. At least for the time being, these riches find expression in—or rather, after reading—books written by others. And for that very reason I'm so sad you are not here now; for if we had been attuned to each other when you were here, much of the mutual alienation we were not always able to overcome with the best will in the world would have disappeared. Precisely because it would have been temporary, our mutual attunement (yours organic and lasting, but mine functional and contingent) would have been all the more deep and powerful. Perhaps this letter can at least hint at all the things that would have been possible: not consonance, of course, for that doesn't exist, but assonance, or at least not my derisive intolerance of the richness of your inner experience, an intolerance with which I reacted time after time, taking offense at ill-chosen phrases—epiphenomena of the fact that you are only twenty-eight. Instead, I could have reacted with joyful anticipation of seeing many things work their way up into that world of expression that you now have access to in the written word, if not yet in demeanor and gesture. That is the world, whatever form it take, in which two richly endowed human beings will always find mutual recognition and support. But because it wasn't in the same location in you as in me, I did not seriously seek to find it. Absurdly enough, I forgot that you are a poet. I ascribed to that word only the meaning "counterfeiter" without realizing how much more important the compulsion to counterfeit is for you than the skill with which it is done. I failed to recognize the peculiar essence of a counterfeit (and it *is* a counterfeit, despite everything): a deep compulsion forces one to aspire to make the counterfeit as genuine as possible, and only those who long for it the most are spared from its poison. For poetry must be regarded as the embodiment of just such a principle, one that carries its own contradiction within itself as its ultimate wisdom. Thus, I was unfair and resolve not to be so in the future, as long as

Veza Taubner, about 1934

my clear-sightedness is not clouded by the frictions of daily life when we are together. The latter would probably have continued to prevent this other insight.

A wonderful book has helped me in my resolve: *Wolf Solent*,[5] by John Cowper Powys. I think it is the book you once told me was so great, at least that's how it surfaced in my memory when I happened to see it in a bookstall on the quays, so I bought it.

VEZA TO GEORGES · *December 16, 1933*

Mr. Georg Canetti
9, rue du Pavillon
Boulogne sur Seine
France

Dec. 16

Dearest Georg,

Your letter was terribly, terribly clever and beautiful, but I'm not going to answer it for a long time. I'm going to make *you* wait *at least* as long as you made me wait.

Instead, I'm sending you with this mail a story from a novella cycle called *Die Gelbe Strasse*.[6] It will be finished in January. The fourth novella tells the story of your cousin Mathilde.[7] The first one, the one I'm sending you, still has many flaws; each story that follows is of course more mature. But this time, I must ask you to *return* the copy since I need it for the volume. The fourth one, the one about your cousin, will follow in a few days and you can keep it. Canetti will soon be having nothing but resounding triumphs.[8] On starvation rations he soldiers bravely on. I'm starting to learn patience. Please do *not* show my novella to the *A*'s[9] what's the matter with you, you didn't write anything about that.

Affectionately,
Veza

Georges to Elias (*fragment*) · *February 10, 1934*

February 10, 1934

My dear Elias,

Today I would finally have begun writing you a "real" letter—a long one—if I hadn't been interrupted by a piece of news that forces me to write as quickly as possible. So this will be a short letter. I've heard that you plan to marry Veza, that the banns have been posted in the Temple, already proclaimed once, and that it will all be over after the third proclamation. I cannot believe that anyone could be so ill-disposed to you as to invent and spread such a blatant lie. Consequently, I must regard the news as true, just as I have until now always refused to take at all seriously anything on this topic that could be interpreted as a silly rumor.

I don't have the slightest intention of influencing your course of action and in any case, I don't even know if it's still possible. Don't think I'm being a hypocrite when I say I don't want to interfere, because it's obvious that you already know everything you will read here. Thus, it would be possible for you to judge *on your own* whether there's the slightest connection between what you *know* and what you're about to *do*. So let me just refresh your memory. I have the right to, for you know how highly I regard Veza, how much I like her, and on the other hand, as an honest—if uncommunicative—person, how much I wish only the best for her precisely because I regard and like her. Thus, I'm writing this only *for you* and not *against her*. You are about to do the stupidest thing you could possibly do. However one looks at it, there is no other conclusion. I leave aside any question of material advantage, for I can't believe material things would have the slightest influence on you, and if you were to mention them nevertheless in the absence of other justification, I would consider it only a cynical pose and not a cynical deed. In any event, for such things marriage is completely unnecessary. Thus, only more worthwhile motives remain. You want to help Veza secure her place in your circle, lend her positive prestige as someone forever attached to you and your rise to fame—for even if you should separate some day, she would still remain what she once was in relation to all that. And at the same time, by this marriage you hope to facilitate her life in the Sephardic circle she can't seem to free herself from. But the question is not just whether you will be able to achieve all that (and thus provide Veza with some quite trifling conveniences), but first and foremost what you will inevitably, necessarily also achieve: you will bring her enormous misfortune.

ELIAS TO GEORGES · *March 2, 1934*

Vienna, March 2, 1934

My dear Georg,

I understand that you are piqued by your absurd and accidental bad luck in the oral examination,[10] but when one thinks it over at this distance, one can't help but be glad about it. You're still damn young, and the experience you have acquired this year can only be useful to you. At the same time, the increase in idiotically mechanical learning you had to slog through just for the exam is unavoidable if you seriously want to accomplish anything in the sciences. The more things you plant in yourself and the deeper you let them take root, the better the fruit they will bear. Not that you suffer from a dearth of seedlings, but you've had too little time to propagate them. Overall, I'm not worried about you—at least to the extent that one doesn't need to worry about the world. You possess such a fortunate mixture of artistic and scholarly qualities, and since your recent encounter with John Cowper Powys, I see the day approaching—after significant scholarly achievements—when it will be you and not your brother who astonishes the world with a great novel. There are three Powys brothers,[11] all three of them writers, and the greatest was the last to become an artist. Previously, he was exclusively a philosopher.[12] I hope you appreciate the honor I do you by this remark.

Carlo liked you very much. He wrote me an enthusiastic letter and thinks I didn't exaggerate at all when I told him about you.

As for my "strange wedding": I don't know in what idiotic form the news reached you. What I write you now is the truth that only Renée[13] and a few of my closest friends know. I shall let you decide whether to tell Mama about it, too.[14] What concerns me there is that the truth might trickle back to Vienna by some circuitous route, where it would *inevitably* injure us considerably. Veza has just made it through some very nasty months. In January, as a Yugoslav citizen and contributor to a certain Viennese newspaper,[15] she was already being threatened with deportation to Yugoslavia. You can well imagine how they handle such cases there. So it was *my* brilliant idea to *marry* her. Since my status is that of a stateless person,[16] she has lost her Yugoslav citizenship by marrying me and if she is deported, can decide for herself which country she wants to go to. My plan was easier said than done. With the papers I have, a civil marriage was impossible; only in the Sephardic Temple are they sufficiently slapdash about such things. Since it was a big risk (for a while it even looked like mortal danger—you have to bear in mind what a delicate and sensitive person Veza is), we both bit the bullet and played the role the Sephardim expected of us to the hilt. So now we are legally married and both *stateless* according to the official marriage certificate. That is an advantage for me, too, since my statelessness was always a shaky affair and any additional official documentation will make it easier for me to gain citizenship somewhere else in the future.

The marriage changes nothing in my relationship to Veza. She is my warmest and most selfless friend (and yours as well, which you have obviously forgotten: you never write to her although you know she's been expecting a letter from you for *months*!); actually she is now my *mother*. If I ever wanted to really get married, which is highly unlikely, she would of course agree to an official divorce immediately. This wedding has absolutely *no* effect on anything in

Elias Canetti in the 1930s

our current state of affairs. I had hoped you would figure all this out for yourself without need for explanation. But since you live in our family, you can't help taking weddings more seriously. Members of the artistic community have always regarded Veza as my wife, and in the beautiful intellectual and spiritual sense in which these people mean it, she really is. You and she, the two of you, will always be the people I love the most, and it is my firm intention *always* to spend a part of the year with her (and with you as well, I hope).

I have no wish to write about local events.[17] You can well imagine all the varieties of beastly behavior on display here in their quaint Viennese manifestations. I hope to tell you about them personally and describe them *exhaustively* in a book at a later date. My personal prospects are as bad as can be. Even before this, there had been no more talk of my novel.[18] It is now with a new publisher in Switzerland. My comedy[19] caused a huge stir locally and a production, to be directed by Reinhardt in the Josefstadt[20] in April, seemed all but certain. But so far those people have prudently avoided signing a contract. Since these latest incidents, it all seems to be up in the air. Maybe I'm more gloomy than necessary about the fate of the comedy, but from now on, I intend to count only on what is *certain*, and most important, to give *you* a clear picture. Following the advice you gave me in the fall, I've been keeping quite busy otherwise. For a Viennese writer I deeply despise I fleshed out a film script (it's called "helping him"), under the proviso that my name not appear.[21] (So no one knows about it, and you must *not* mention it to *either Nissim or Mama.*) This man now writes from London that the prospects are excellent that the film will be accepted, and promises a definite decision in the next three weeks. I must tell you that I did this work on speculation, that is, without pay. If the film is picked up, my worries will be over for the next two years.

Moreover, I have an unbelievably good friend in Dr. Cohn in Strasbourg, who does his utmost to help me. For months, he has been making careful, quiet preparations to give me a job in Strasbourg that would employ me part time but support me full time. He is as reliable as humanly possible; I consider him even more reliable than you, which is saying something. And everyone tells me he loves me more than if I were his own child. So probably something will come of it. Whether I'm the right person for the job he's creating for me is another question. It requires fluent *written* French, and you are the only person who could help me acquire that. Thus if I hear from Dr. Cohn that I've got the job, I'll come to Paris for a month or two and you'll teach me what I need to know. The passport difficulties would be taken care of from Strasbourg (I hope).

In the course of the coming week, a woman named Dea Gombrich[22] will arrive in Paris. She's a wonderful violinist, the best in Vienna for modern music (and the only person in the world who plays certain pieces by Berg,[23] Křenek, Webern). She is incomparably more accomplished than Erika and is an especially sweet and unpretentious person. Moreover, she's one of Veza's and my *closest* friends. She is going to play a radio concert in Strasbourg and again in Paris, where she will play with an orchestra (Festival Autrichien on March 15). The cousin she's staying with is the secretary of a very important man in Parisian theater whose name I can't recall. She's taking along a copy of my comedy and will pull out all the stops for me. I've asked her to call you up as soon as she arrives. I don't need to tell you to take good care of her; it will be a pleasure for you to show Paris to a woman who is so sensitive and truly noble and charming in the bargain. Please tell Nissim to do something for her at his company[24]—besides modern things, she also plays classical pieces she has rediscovered *herself* and almost no one else knows about. Nissim should definitely have her play for him; I will be doing him a favor for a change instead of him doing me one, since she is an artist of the *highest* caliber. —Enough for today. Write back soon and at length. Reassure Mama. If you think it's a good idea to tell her the reason I got married, then at least impress upon her the need for absolute secrecy, otherwise she could put us in great danger. Greetings to everyone. And for yourself the most *heartfelt* embrace from your

Elias.

Georges to Veza (*draft*) · *April 4, 1934*

April 4, 1934

My dear Veza,

When I have to stop writing, I shall send this off to you no matter what shape it's in. It's the fifth letter since July. Above all, I want to tell you that the few lines I received via Renée made me very happy. Not because a sad Veza spoke from them, but only because it was Veza speaking. Why don't you write more often? Because I don't reply? I almost always do, but then I never think what I've written is good enough. Accordingly, you can easily imagine for yourself what I'm writing and then reply to that.

You are mistaken to think I attach too much importance (as you call it) to formalities. I merely wanted to know if it had really taken place. And I'm certain that a contract, a piece of paper—especially one issued by a Jewish temple—will change nothing in a relationship as beautiful and pure as yours, with all its mutual support and loyalty despite more than occasional aggravation. I know very well how easily one can chafe against bonds that are much looser than those of a real marriage, which is exactly why one so resolutely imposes them on oneself. But you know that as well as I do.

Elias to Georges · *July 1, 1934*

Zurich, July 1

My dear Georg,

So here I am, armed with all my visas, hope in my heart and sadness in my head, on my way to Paris, where you are all expecting me with such overflowing affection. I just wish you still had your old apartment! I don't know your new address and am writing to your old one. Surely they will forward your mail. Please write me as soon as you get this letter and tell me where to reach you—write to Strasbourg. Because on Wednesday I'm leaving Zurich (where I'm negotiating with the theater about my comedy) and going on to Strasbourg, where I'll spend one or two days. So I'll be in Paris by the end of next week. Although it is also possible that I'll extend my stay here by two or three days.

In any case, write care of Dr. Cohn, rue Schwilgué 16, Strasbourg.

I can hardly wait to see you despite your cool letter and beg you to keep the next few weeks a *bit* more open. Scherchen's workshop[25] will last the whole month of July and you should attend now and then, if only to see the curious people who congregate at such an event.

If Mama happens to still be in Paris, give her my greetings. It's lucky that Paris is so vast and spread out. Otherwise, the anticipation of having to run the gauntlet of all our relatives could almost drive me to commit suicide. It's a good thing I'm coming by myself.

In the meantime, an embrace from your brother Elias (who is not trying to get something *out* of you—please don't forget that).

ELIAS TO GEORGES · *August 18, 1934*

Strasbourg, Aug. 18

Dear Georg,

Just imagine my good fortune: they've given me the key to all the tricky little locked doors we passed in the cathedral and now I can wander around every day to my heart's content. You have no idea how happy it makes me. I've put it right at the beginning of my letter, even though it's not the reason I'm writing you.

Then why am I writing? Of course, as always, for money. I think if someone collected all my letters to you, I would look like the world's filthiest highwayman. However, let me assure you I'm not. Well now:

very soon, my expenses will increase, namely, by 100 francs for a new *récépissé*.[26] Dr. Cohn has undertaken the necessary steps to obtain a year's residency permit and for the time being things look quite promising. Your money had hardly arrived when I had to spend 35 francs on laundry. You can do the math: I have 25 francs left on hand.

But what's worse, the Cohns are going to Karlsbad next week and their maid has vacation. I'll probably be allowed to stay and look after the house, but I have to pay for my own breakfast and for the three or four suppers per week that I usually eat at home. They will be gone until at least mid-September. I really don't know how I'm going to manage. For now, I shall see if I can postpone paying for the *récépissé* for a while. In any case, as soon as you get this letter send me *at least* 200 francs. For if they do demand the 100 francs right away, I can't very well say no and thereby put everything in jeopardy. And please give a thought to other ways to find another 300 francs for me for the first half of September. The sale of the piece of jewelry is certain; it's only a matter of a few weeks. But it's also certain that something will turn up for me here in Strasbourg. It's just that it won't happen until summer is over, because it is difficult to start anything in the summer, as you can imagine.

For my part, I've been quite busy since coming to Strasbourg. I'm reading the medieval *Strasbourg Chronicle* (by Königshofen)[27] in the original and it's one of the most exciting things I've ever come across. It contains detailed descriptions of the plague, the pogroms, the flagellants. More and more, I'm feeling my way back into fourteenth-century life, which *really* presages our own time. Now, it seems to me very difficult to present the coming war in Europe[28] in such a way that one is fully cognizant of its scale, its terrible scale, for even if that were technically possible, it wouldn't be plausible. After all, the most precisely imagined future is the least plausible, because furthest removed from present reality. All depictions of the war to come have something utopian about them. That is a misfortune, for actually, war is already here and there's nothing utopian about it. Thus the relatively small, medieval town (tightly circumscribed, everyone knows one another, and the lanes squeeze their way between the houses rather than the houses bordering the streets) provides an opportunity to depict everything, the same situation, but in reduced scale. The city of Strasbourg in the fourteenth century will be something like my *map* of present reality. So I'm not using the olden times as in a historical novel—as empty learned trappings—but rather as the network of meridians and concentric circles that I need for the reduction in size. —By the way, I'd be very happy to get a volume of Proust, but I would like it to be the *first* volume, so that I can read the whole thing in order. Please write a good long letter. But send some of the money (200 francs) *at once*. Affectionately, your brother Elias

ELIAS TO GEORGES · *September 13, 1934*

Strasbourg, September 13, 1934

My dear Georg,

I just received *Die Fackel*.[29] Veza was on vacation and couldn't send it to me any sooner. I can't believe my eyes. I had heard the most unbelievable things about it from various sources; of course, your letter had already made a strong impression on me, since I know you are circumspect in condemnation and tenacious in love. But I never would have expected this—this thing I spent all night reading. I'm ashamed of ever having been influenced by such a monster. I'm ashamed of the enormous and decisive impression he made on me with his earlier campaign against Schober following the events of July fifteenth.[30] I fear there are traces of his influence in my plays and I want to expunge whatever is reminiscent of him in any work of mine and in my own self. Although he is so frail, I wish I could administer *corporal* punishment. What a Thersites![31] What a Goebbels of the spirit! How is it possible that for this "sensitive" man who is so tortured by the suffering of all creatures, blood is suddenly no longer blood, women no longer women, children no longer children? What made the strongest impression on him in Germany was the threat to sexual intercourse between Jews and

Aryans. Germany alone is the devil, so everyone else is an angel. I have to say that his is a personal worldview that makes me tremble for my own, to the extent that it is also personal. Karl Kraus expresses support for the survivors of the dead policemen! Karl Kraus explains and makes excuses for "war." War is war!—thus argues the man who taught us everlasting hatred of war. How he disavows the consequences of his own actions! How he *apologizes* for his campaign against the regime and his animosity toward Schober following the fifteenth of July. Above all, how he himself is precisely what he accuses the Social Democrats (with some justification) of being: *irresponsible*. This man with his great sense of responsibility for commas, periods, and hyphens!—but why am I telling you all this. You know it all just as well as I do, in fact, even better. There's only one thing I fear: that you will identify too much with the way he was *before* he toppled from his pedestal. It seems to me more important and healthier to examine the curious inner resistance one felt toward him even before, but didn't dare admit out of a sense of gratitude and loyalty; to picture our relation to this man psychologically, as in a novel. One would come to remarkable conclusions: Karl Kraus is a master of the *phrase*; he was something like a Hitler for intellectuals. He was able to mold them into a mass of believers and, astonishingly enough, by the same means—the moral slogan.

We must sit down sometime and have a long talk about him. As much as I welcome your newly awakened delight in giving *form* to things, as happy as it would make me to see you join the company of doctors who are also major writers, as much as I would like to replace the false analogy of the van Gogh brothers[32] with the more accurate one of the Goncourts,[33] and as much as I think you capable of anything (for you contain a multitude of possibilities and have kept yourself both intellectually and spiritually *pure* for an enormously long time), still and even more important, I beg you to destroy within yourself the false idol named Kraus. Do not try to become what he should have remained. Do not write things like "about whom no one can contradict my French, not even Paul Valéry," for that could have been written by Karl Kraus—and not just in its form and diction.

Don't go down the path of *his* self-assertion, for you have your own path, and above all, don't forget that most of what Kraus fought for in the German language is already a matter of course in French, so there's nothing left for you to do.

It's good that you are giving your break with him a formal structure; but is it good that you are structuring it in *his* form? Don't you agree that one of his regal charms is that he permits people to speak to him only in his own language? Any attempt to address him without "Your Majesty" and the rhetorical flourishes with which he is accustomed to pronounce his own edicts is doomed to failure. Ah Georg, you are too *fine* a person, too French, for this bugaboo with delusions of grandeur. Perhaps you can wound him by attacking him in French; he's incredibly vain and thus has a parvenu's inner respect for anything he doesn't understand. You can see for yourself how tangled up I'm getting. I can't help it: I'm so pained by this sudden, irreversible, fatal plunge of my last remaining demigod (I had no full gods left). Georg, I think that in these times, if we don't inwardly cling to each other, we will perish. And when I say "we" I don't mean us. I mean the significance we can have for others. You see, every little sentence you utter that expresses the feelings of my own heart and could have come from my own mouth (e.g., the one about your colleagues and the next war) literally gives me the strength to continue to exist and not suffocate, for I know I have a real brother. How many other people have that? The few who have decided to exist, on their own, for the sake of everyone else, *are* alone and are not strong enough to bear it. —But it makes no sense for me to moan and groan to you now, when your test is coming up. I ask only one thing of you: don't preach at me and don't be petty. That's the only thing that still keeps us a bit apart. I would never withhold from you what I possess—and that's not just a Platonic phrase, for some lucky accident might make me rich just as well as the next person. So you ought not to make my already not very pleasant situation even more difficult by philistine admonishments, admonishments that must strike you as laughable the moment you've written them down. You can see I'm *still* in Strasbourg, although it is a city for spending weeks in and not years, living in a lonely state that is *unbearable*. You are lonely too; you, however, can simply lock away what is of value to you, whereas I have to *dissimulate*. Surrounded by idiots and corpses—and, it's a crying shame, also by my beloved lunatics (although I am at their disposal)—I have to *dissimulate*, play the lamb of Jewish misfortune although that's not at all who I am; it makes me puke! And then this "good and gentle man" (as we thought) is in actuality as insidiously *tactless* as Edith,[34] but in her case it was forgivable because of her lack of education.

All these heartless people trampling around on my enormous heart as if my art were any of *their* business should be sent to Veza for a half-day of remedial education. —But you can see that I'm still here, in fact, completely by myself until the end of the month. I must wait until the fall in any case, because I won't know until October if there is the chance of a job. It would be possible for me to get a *récépissé* for the *carte d'identité*, which would ensure that I could stay here in the meantime. It costs about 100 francs, which I don't have. You must send me 300 francs at once: 100 for the *récépissé* and 200 for living expenses until the end of the month. I have no money left at all. The sum I'm asking for is the pitiful minimum I need for existence, and the only reason I didn't ask for it before was that the sale of the jewelry I told you about seemed certain to take place this week. Now it may take another two weeks. Please don't make me wait; if it's not possible to send it all, you can send 200 first and then 100 in another week. *Please* write even though you have to study.

Veza to Georges · *December 20, 1934*

Dec. 20

Dearest Georg,

Well, my mother had to die[35] for you to write me, and then in addition to that you have unhealthy lungs and that's why you look so awful in the photo I haven't torn up yet. Canetti is profoundly sad today. The little fellow is quite sorrowful. He's running around aimlessly, doing nothing, and hopes to see you in February. Because he should be going to Switzerland in a week, where he and the composer Vogel[36] are going to stay in the house of a patron and compose (or in Canetti's case, write) an opera.[37] After that, he intends to come to Paris on your account, so he can see you. He yearns for you.

I yearn even more but it does me no good and don't worry, I'm not going to write any more about it!! On the night of the 17th, I dreamed that I was with you and kissing you a lot and it made me so happy that it helped me over the *taedium vitae* of my waking life. For I am indeed weary of life. I told Elias the dream, too, and I think it's simply wonderful, like everything about you. Don't worry, I'm already telling myself to stop. Because you don't want to hear any of this. I'm tired of life. I am. Because my mother was a really good person and she was my good fool; she let me torture her and she idolized me. Now I'm all alone.

But you, you'll soon be well again and the next letter I get from you will be on my deathbed. If I could only come to you and kiss you on the mouth and swallow your germs, that would give me a reason to live. But it is not to be! Canetti is already a full-blown, egotistical pest, very spoiled and independent. He'll muddle along quite well without me. He loves me, but he loves Anna[38] more and who wouldn't? I too have fallen completely under her spell and how strange fate is! *She* loves *me* and not Canetti and if she wants to see me, she has to pay for it. I make her grant Canetti a rendezvous, but for heaven's sake, don't tell him that, Georg, because he loves her and her alone. And she is intoxicating and a fairy tale and Canetti calls her a "beam of light" and I call her my "beloved sin."

This whole time I really ought to be writing that I'm sad. Because you're sick, because you're in the hospital, because . . . because . . . But I am not sad. I'm quite happy that you have those tubercles. Maybe I'll come to France after all and then I'll say I have to kiss you so you don't think you have tubercles and then I'll *finally* be able to kiss you. But

Anna Mahler, about 1935

perhaps I'll commit suicide instead. For as I said, I miss my mother terribly. I often cursed her, always ridiculed her, mostly tormented her. And now I weep and talk out loud to her and plead with her to stay here with me and I'm happy when I see her in my dreams and sometimes I think there really is a soul and sometimes I don't believe it and am in despair that nothing, nothing of her remains, and so I often think of turning on the gas. For no one shows me any affection, Georg, no one. There are a few here who would, but Canetti drives them off and returns home early in the morning instead, assuring me that I am a good mother to him and a poetess to boot. And I am a poetess. I've written two plays.[39] One of them, a comedy, will earn us some money; the other, a drama, will earn me fame. *You* play a major role in the latter. You have no name, you're simply "the young doctor."

Well, the last thing you should have to worry about is us. You are now our favorite child and can't escape. If I write you one love letter after another, it's only because you're sick and can't protest against it. I'll write again next week. Perhaps you will keep in mind that I would like to know how you are and perhaps you will write me after all.

Although your little letter to me was formal and written only to be polite, I hid it from Canetti. That's what I'm going to do from now on. I'll keep every one of your letters a secret. Yes, that's just what I'll do. You know why? Because then I can persuade myself it's a love letter, even though you write that *everyone* must be in love with me and other equally cruel dilutions of that amiable word. I can also tell you I'm going to keep your letters a secret because I intend always to tell you the unvarnished truth about him, about his facile, lovable, thoughtless, unadmirable character. Yes, I can tell you about it, and then you can make dutiful excuses for it. By the way, I won't have to keep anything hidden. Because he won't be here.

But it's also possible that your next letter won't reach me. On account of the soul's mortality, etc. Because sometimes, I just can't go on. But if you would only send me one letter after another! ~~Or if you~~

~~called me to come to you! But that's over. And I'm old and too unhappy. And I would have come only to kiss away your germs or whatever you might have. Maybe a lot of kissing would make them go away. I would have loved you, that's all~~. There! That's my revenge!

I've been writing and writing and it's like writing to a stone. Enough, no more. Well, you don't have to worry about us. We have friends here who help us out financially and know their money is well invested in us. So, Mr. Moneybags, write me a postcard and tell me how you are. Don't leave me in suspense! I must know how you are. That's plausible, isn't it? And never again write to Canetti that you will help him. If he ever accepted help from you, I would despise him for the first time in my life. And that would wound him. He won't accept anything from you. Doesn't need it anyway.

Tomorrow he's going to read his marvelous comedy[40] for Alban Berg, Alma Mahler,[41] Anna (who will meanwhile be drinking in the glances of long-nosed men, but not his, no, not his), and twenty other famous men. I baked vanilla crescents for the occasion, but I burned them. I'm writing a little crazy, I know. Canetti is starting to work hard. He wrote a film for Forster[42] which Forster then wasn't allowed to make. Couldn't your brother do something to promote this excellent film? Of course, he must not find out that I worked on it too, because he and I can't stand each other. But why do *you* always complain about me to Renée and Aunt Bellina?[43] We like each other, don't we?

Now I must see to the housekeeping, urge the maid to be thrifty, and take charge of the keys. In between, I'm invited to palaces and great painters are *especially* eager for the boon of being allowed to paint my portrait. It's true: my portrait, not Anna's. Even though you too would instantly desert me for her if you came here. And even though I . . . ah, I'm not going to say what. Perhaps I'll send you a photo of the portrait, should my soul find the strength to drag itself before the easel. The soul is the stupidest thing mankind has ever invented. That's what I thought as I lay awake in the night with my dead mother. I wish I was just an animal. How good that would be. How bearable.

That's that. I'll bring this to an end. I think Canetti will also come to see his mother. It's just that he's ashamed to talk to her because he hasn't had any successes yet. As if he won't achieve the most by working as he does. A successful Canetti would be a spoiled Canetti. It's true that he's been shattered by Anna. Perhaps the trip will prove helpful. I'm glad he's going, poor fellow. He will see you. He definitely intends to. He loves you like a fiancée. He's in love with you.

Renée is coming now and will write you a bone-picking letter.[44] She loves you too. As for me, in a week I'll send my finished play to you in the hospital, perhaps in *three* weeks. It may take that much time to copy it. Please let me know if you move to a new place, out of respect for my work, if not out of—after all, Georg, you must let people know when you have a new address, and the status of your lungs!!!!!!!!!!

This was a pretty demure letter, wasn't it? At least for me?

I'm so glad you're sick. Perhaps now the women will leave you alone!

Veza

Canetti will write separately.

ELIAS TO GEORGES · *Turn of the year 1934–1935*

Monday, Comologno

My dear, dear Georg,

Your letter horrified and frightened me, sending me into such despair it took several days to halfway recover. You poor dear fellow, what could have reduced you to such a state? I'm sure you weren't eating enough and picked up an infection in the hospital. I made inquiries everywhere about a "pneumothorax"[45] and found out to my—let's call it—relief that a pneumothorax is completely curable. And to keep myself from senseless yammering, I would like to enumerate the great advantages of this illness (I really mean it): at last you will be able to get a few months of decent rest. With the best will in the world, you won't be able to race around as much as usual up there.[46] Possibly you will escape military service. You will have time for yourself and in that time, you will become a better writer than your brother. And the most beautiful thing for that brother is that he will visit you up there, will be with you, and as soon as you have taken your examination, he can exchange wonderful, real, long, intelligent letters with you. Seriously Georg, please do everything you can to get completely well again. A guy like you, with such a well-furnished and extensively cultivated mind, has obligations: large obligations to everyone, smaller ones to the individuals who love him and expect great things from him. Don't let your energy slacken, cling fast to your goals, don't lower your expectations. Nothing is more dangerous than a supposed catastrophe that has *time*. Veza really loves you and you know that I love you, and if the unconditional, unshakable, and undying affection of two possibly exceptional individuals were the only thing you ever earned in your life, it would already be quite an accomplishment. Ah Georg, I myself find everything I'm able to tell you here quite inadequate and petty, but you must sense *why* I want to say it, and that alone might convince you.

Since receiving your letter, I've come closer to you in a spatial sense as well, and here is how it happened: Wladimir Vogel, whom you know, wants to write an opera with me, in a completely new form, of course, and for Russia. He suggested we spend January together in Ticino, where a house has been put at our disposal for the purpose. I didn't like the plan at first, because I didn't want to leave Veza alone. Since her mother's death, she has not been in good shape at all. Moreover, our financial situation is quite precarious and I didn't really know where I could scare up the travel money. But once I had your letter in my hand, I decided to come see you soon and combine my intention to do so with this other job.

The plan was delayed a few days by difficulties with money and my passport, but they have been resolved. Today, I'm here at last. Along with Vogel and our hosts, I've settled in at *your* altitude (3,600

Elias Canetti in Comologno, 1935

feet), Alps all around me, twenty miles from Locarno, right on the border with Italy and not so very far from you. We're in an enchanting old castle in Louis XVI style, and although it's so beautiful here, I'm looking forward to seeing you in February. I intend to go to Strasbourg for about ten days at the end of January and on to Paris in February, when you have your exam (without disturbing you, of course). Anyway, write me *as soon as* you receive this letter. Neither of us has any more excuses. You have more than enough time to spare, and I promise to answer just as promptly. I want the most *detailed* reports about you, the state of your health, the course of your day, and I want them immediately. The most loving and tender hugs and kisses from your brother Elias.

The postman is here, so I must close.

Dr. Canetti "La Barca"
Comologno sopra Locarno / Ticino / Switzerland

ELIAS TO GEORGES · *January 22, 1935*

Zurich, January 22, 1935

My dear, dear Georg,

I'm desperate because I've had no news from you at all, and neither has Veza or anyone else. I've forgotten Nissim's address, so I can't even ask him about you. About three weeks ago I wrote you from Ticino and you must have received the letter. It was sent to the address you gave me. There are two possible explanations. You may have been insulted that I waited ten days before answering your letter, and since that would be a weighty indictment which, if true, nothing could excuse, you must believe the facts of the case this one time—I *implore* you: as soon as I read your letter, my decision to travel was made *so that I could see you* (everything else was only incidental). I must tell you that Veza's and my outward circumstances are really catastrophic (however, that need be absolutely no concern of yours at present), and for that reason, in the days following your letter, I was preoccupied with raising money, running around on account of my passport, and finally with the trip itself. The journey to Comologno is more complicated than one might think. But quite apart from that, I wanted to write you from closer *proximity*. Please understand this feeling of almost physical fraternity. All of us who love its contents want to protect the body now causing you difficulties; so I would be happy to serve as a donor if you have need of blood.

But perhaps you're not insulted at all. Perhaps you are not doing well. But you see, Georg, you must realize that nothing in the whole wide world (and you know how wide my world is) interests, involves, tortures me as much as your well-being, and that's why you will write me at once. Please don't punish me now for all my former sins; they were small, measured against the love I had for you then and have for you now and forever, more and more. Georg, I *must* know when you will be in Paris, since I'm planning the whole rest of my trip around that. Day after tomorrow, on Thursday, I'm traveling from here to Strasbourg, where I would like to work about two more weeks with Vogel. (He has to go back to Strasbourg now.) I was thinking about coming to see you in Paris sometime in February. When I come depends entirely on your exam. Since Veza is not in very good spirits when alone, I don't want to leave her by herself for too long. I have to go back to Vienna by the end of February or beginning of March. So write me immediately, but not at Cohn's address, since I absolutely do not wish to stay there again, but rather to:

Canetti c/o Wladimir Vogel
chez Mathis
rue Wimpheling 2
Strasbourg.

I have a fairly remarkable visa for France (a general visa for any number of entries and exits, valid until the end of May 1935). Having not yet made use of this visa, I'm a bit skeptical of it, as I would be of anything that is *too* beautiful.

Here in Zurich, I'm staying with Dr. Rosenbaum,[47] the foremost lawyer in Switzerland, a wonderful and brilliant man who has become my friend for life. On Sunday there was a big reading from my works,[48] attended by James Joyce, among others. (He lives in Zurich part of the time. A local specialist has restored the sight in one of his eyes; Joyce had been blind for a long time.) I think the reading was a success. There would now be an audience for my books in Zurich. But that's of no interest to me until I have news from you. You are going to receive a whole lot of books from me for your birthday. Write *immediately*, even if only three words,

to your brother Elias,
who loves you above all else.

VEZA TO GEORGES · *January 27, 1935*

Georg Canetti
Sanatorium des étudiants
St. Hilaire du Touvet
près Grenoble
Départ. Isère
Frankreich

II.
Ferdinandstr. 29/5
Vienne

Dear Georg,

I am appalled that you don't write. Canetti is in despair about it. Please send news.

Veza

He is in Strasbourg c/o Cohn, rue Schwilgué 16.

Elias to Georges · *March 4, 1935*

Paris, March 4, 1935

My dear Georg,

At first I was very upset at your silence. But now at least Mama and Nissim have news of you. And you seem to be feeling halfway better as far as your health is concerned. I really need Veza's play back,[49] since I'm leaving for Zurich today (that is, I'm going to Strasbourg first). Please send it to Zurich by registered mail. I'll be there by Thursday at the latest.

Canetti c/o Dr. Rosenbaum
Stadelhoferstrasse 26 / Zurich

Unfortunately, this time I cannot stay with Rosenbaum, or only for a very short time, because all their larger guest rooms are occupied. So I'm staying in Zurich for only a week *at most*, but probably less, and that's why I need to have the play there waiting for me. So please don't wait any longer but send it off as soon as you get this letter.

I really got a lot accomplished here, for the most part with the help of Mathilde Camhi,[50] who really ran herself ragged for me and was utterly charming in general. If you need anything special, feel free to turn to her. In her, as in all my friends, you have a reliable friend yourself. I got as far as the owner of the Théâtre de l'Œuvre.[51] The *Hochzeit* at least interested him enough that he wants to read it for himself. The content and the way it's realized appeal to him; I think I have a good chance there.

I'm not going to tell you about everything I did, only what has to do with you. Uncle Josef[52] got me together with that young Arié from Paramount who is so intensely interested in my film script. Since Nissim had the goodness not to be interested in it, I'm going to try my luck with Arié. You have the script with you. Probably the best thing would be for you to translate it into the clearest possible French, but it must be *good,* too. I think you could get it done comfortably in one good week without undue effort. If something came of it here in Paris, I would of course share the profit with you. If there's a typewriter up there, you can dictate the manuscript to somebody. If not, then send it to the office and Uncle Josef will have it copied. In any case, write me in Zurich and tell me if you will do it. I think it an easy and pleasant task that would cost you hardly any effort, but if your doctors don't agree, then of course you mustn't do it.

Please write a proper letter to me in Zurich if you can. I'm in a big hurry now and so I'll say adieu. The most heartfelt embrace from your brother

Elias.

RENÉE AND VEZA TO GEORGES · *Postmarked March 6, 1935*

M.
Georg Canetti
Sanatorium des Étudiants, St. Hilaire
du Touvet près
Grenoble
(Dep. Isère) France

II Ferdinandstr.

Dear Georg,

Congratulations on your new title of doctor,[53] a great accomplishment.

Renée.

Dear Georg,

Why did Renée blush so much when she wrote you? I'm very proud of your accomplishment Doctor and very angry that you don't write despite my "young doctor." I'm writing this in bed, sick with the flu, and my good foster daughter Renée is taking care of me.*

Write me!
This instant!
Veza

*She's actually a bad foster daughter because she's going to leave her sick mother for two weeks of skiing.

GEORGES TO ELIAS (*draft*) · *April 14, 1935*

St. Hilaire, April 14, 1935

My dear Elias,

Don't be angry that it has taken me so long to write. Perhaps I could have written sooner—but there was almost never any real incentive to do so. I didn't want to write about inconsequential or "interesting" things, and there isn't much else here. The first thing you probably want to know is how I am. I am feeling much better. Improvement began with my trip to Paris, and during the first weeks was progressing by leaps and bounds. Now the tempo has slowed somewhat, but the turn for the better continues. The spitting has stopped almost completely, although I probably still have germs—but many fewer than before. My fever is completely gone. The x-ray shows the cavern[54] to be almost entirely closed up, and lastly, my weight has improved as well: I've gained six and a half pounds. You can't achieve much more than that in six weeks. A complete recovery now seems possible, even in the foreseeable future. Thus I hardly think a second winter in the mountains will be necessary. If things continue to look up, I shall return to Paris at the end of September and then move into an apartment with Mama again. It's the only possible solution for both of us, since Mama certainly cannot be left alone any more—it was only the loneliness of the last few months that put her into the state you saw her in—and, on the other hand, because I must take very good care of myself if I am not to suffer a relapse as soon as I begin working again. For the next four or five years, the sword of Damocles will be hanging over me—an incentive to keep on living that is not to be sneezed at.

I'm not going to write what you've probably been hoping to hear about the sanatorium. Whether it's the French, or just me, or the mendacity of those who have previously written about sanatoriums—whatever the cause, in our sanatorium there's no excitement at all. There's certainly not enough going on for a novel—barely enough for a diary. Amazing how little pathos you find where you seek it most—probably because pathos, as the discrepancy between what is sought and what is found—can only be found when it is not sought.

VEZA TO GEORGES · *Postmarked June 25, 1935*

Mr.
Georg Canetti
Sanatorium des Étudiants
près Grenobles
St. Hilaire du Touvet
France

6/25

Dear Georg,

I'm only writing so you can make your mother happy by telling her that Canetti's book will be published by a new, well-respected publishing house here in Vienna, thanks to the mediation of Stefan Zweig.[55] In my opinion, the book is going to cause a stir. There is also interest in America. I have nothing more to tell you.

Veza

Canetti has long been *planning* to write his mother. I hope *you* understand . . .

ELIAS TO GEORGES · *August 8 and 13, 1935*

August 8, 1935

My dear Georg,

It has now been a month since we spent those lovely days together in Strasbourg, and since then, you've had no news from me. Now you are going to get some from quite close by: I am in Beauvais, less than fifty miles away. I don't know whether you're familiar with Beauvais, but in any event, you know Rouen, where we will be tomorrow. I'm traveling with Mme. Cohn[56] and her sister, Frau Prof. Hamm. We've come this far in two days. The first day was Strasbourg—Metz (delightful drive through Lorraine)—Verdun—St. Ménéhould—Reims. The battlefields we drove through yesterday and today are so depressing that one feels like throwing oneself in front of the next passing car. Town after town between Laon and Compiègne has been newly rebuilt. No house, not even one from 10,000 B.C., makes such a ruinous impression as these brand spanking new little brick ones. Noyon with its marvelous new old cathedral looks like the second day of creation, but God did poor work here. In Beauvais, one is glad to be out of the battle zone and ashamed not to have fallen there in the first place. In Verdun, there's an honor roll of all the French soldiers who were in Verdun during the war. In this book, the names of the French dead who could be identified to date number 93,000. In the streets, tiny children, beautiful and ugly ones, are playing. The men lie with their womenfolk, the women give birth, and tomorrow morning there will be war again

Well, that was the beginning of a letter I wrote you at night in Beauvais. Since then, even more has happened. I've seen so much that it has literally given me a headache; if I had to describe in detail the intervening days up to today, the 13th, it would take me a few months and I still wouldn't be finished. France is marvelous; it breaks my heart to see huge stretches of it devastated. They should have left Reims Cathedral in ruins and driven everyone on earth there in big buses: *Ici vous voyez . . . Ci gît la guerre.*[57] If such a gravestone ever really existed somewhere—I would happily die for such a fatherland, but not for any other. I don't know if you've ever been to Verdun. For every inhabitant today there are sixty who fell in the fighting here (550,000 of them Germans).

Perhaps one remembers it all even more intensely today because we're on the brink of a new war[58] since nothing has changed, since Russia alone, and precisely because it is alone, is supplying us the material for new wars, whether it intends to or not.

Actually, it is quite pointless for me to be writing you about such things. Perhaps I do it only out of a sense of shame, for despite all these horrors—or probably even because of them—I've thrown myself all the more into everything else, for example, after Beauvais: Rouen, which you know and love. It's something like a French Strasbourg, much richer in its details, but on the whole not the uniformly ancient city Strasbourg represents. By the way, do you know the old cemetery next to St. Maclou with its curious, vivid insignia of death? After Rouen came Normandy as *countryside*. We were guests on a large farm (250 acres, 100 cows, 100 calves, hundreds of chickens, 21 children, a divine fertility that flies in the face of every war). In Dieppe the sea, the sea again after such a long, long time. It seems so deeply in the blood of all of us that at the seaside, we're on the edge of our homeland. I am more and more convinced that the sea is the greatest and most extensive symbol of the *mass*. On the return trip we were in Senlis and Meaux; at some point between them we were only twenty-two miles from Paris, about as far as the Germans at the beginning of the war. I would have loved very much to visit you and take you with us for a stretch. But Frau Madeleine seems to be quite fearful of driving in Paris and so she stubbornly ignored my hints. I'm sure you are familiar with Senlis. It was one of my strongest impressions from the trip. Via the Marne valley—Épernay—Châlons sur Marne—Vitry-le-François—St. Dizier—continuing via

Toul—Nancy (Place Stanislas!) we finally reached home again. This dry *itinéraire* sounds pretty pitiful. But I don't want to start in on even a halfway detailed description. There was one quite disagreeable thing about the trip for me: we slept and dined in the most expensive hotels, where my traveling companions always paid for me—such was our agreement. In return of course—because of my time in Strasbourg if nothing else—I had to pay for the lunches, so the tour cost me the substantial trifle of 500 francs. I cannot successfully sell the piece of jewelry I told you about until the beginning of September. I had borrowed money for the intervening time, in addition to the 200 francs from you. It's impossible for me to borrow money a second time; it would make the worst possible impression. So somehow or other, you have to scrape together 500 francs and lend them to me so I can make it to the middle of September. Please rest assured that you will get back the 700 francs, and before the end of September. When you get this letter, please send me what you can spare *at once, with the next mail*, even if only 100 francs, since I now possess a total of F 2.70 and cannot go out to eat either today or tomorrow. Then send me the rest as soon as possible. I'd also like to have Mama's *exact* address so I can write her a long letter. A letter from you would be a joyful event. But if you can't write one this minute, please send one with the second sum of money. Don't forget to reply to Veza. She feels very lonely in Vienna. And you must write to *Renée*.

A hug from
your brother Elias.

ELIAS TO GEORGES · *October 11 and 15, 1935*

Vienna, October 11, 1935

My dear Georg,

Veza and I are really somewhat bitter that neither of us has heard a word from you. I don't even know if you are still in your sanatorium up there above Grenoble. Many months ago, a journal was sent to me anonymously and it seemed curious in many respects. I searched through it for an article by you, but apparently my ability to recognize an individual style in French is still very limited: I didn't find one.

Not a day passes that we don't think of you or talk about you. Don't suppose that I'm unable to imagine how you're faring. Despite your silence, I sense you are improving. I imagine you're back to hitting the books in preparation for your exam, working much more than you should, thinking of taking the exam again soon, and therefore haven't found much opportunity to devote yourself to *my* profession, writing, which I think is so important for you to do as well. Moreover, you are very angry at me because I haven't written to Mama for so long. Well, let me explain that to you right away: I have held to the resolution I felt *compelled* to make after the way you all treated me in Paris. A certain subtle contempt for someone who calls himself a writer but hasn't published anything, yet acts proud even if he doesn't have 50 francs to his name—a trace of that contempt was audible even in your voice, but resoundingly loud in the others', and I just couldn't take it anymore. Veza is the only person who's *never* had it, you *relatively* infrequently. All in all, what I was forced to undergo in Paris in February was a reprise of the events in the Radetzkystrasse ten years ago.[59]

I therefore decided to treat you all as you deserve and to regale you worshipers of facts with nothing but *faits accomplis*. Now it's difficult to make facts credible when one has lied as often and with such joyful abandon as I have. All one can do is produce the proof in proverbial black and white. That's why you and Mama received those printed invitations to my reading, which was sold out, by the way. And now (it's taken five months, unfortunately) comes a novel, also in black and white, entitled *Die Blendung*, a book in which you will recognize a man named Kien (whose name has been changed from "Kant"). I have thereby discharged my obligation to the facts. Or rather, I still ought to provide proof that since June—i.e., for the last five months—I have been living on the advance I received for the novel. But I don't really know how I can prove it. Perhaps the smallness of the sum involved will persuade you: 2,000 schillings. It isn't much, but given current conditions, it amounts to a miracle that they paid me any advance at all.

October 15, 1935

So much for bitterness. You can hardly imagine what it means to finally see a manuscript published that has been lying fallow for four years (it really has been that long). One's feelings are not all pleasant by any means; one is so far removed from the work and now must be its advocate before the public. You feel like a swindler, because there are only parts of the work that still please you, some things you don't like at all, and even though I deleted the twenty weakest pages, I can't even consider a serious reworking, because then not a single sentence would remain atop another.

You will also be glad to hear there is great interest in the novel in America. One of the most influential publishers[60] wrote a positively enthusiastic letter about it and I believe (but it's not a certainty yet) that there will be a contract from America in the coming weeks.

As for "copies" of the novel: I only get a few (10) free copies from the publisher and have to send some of them to other writers. For the time being, I will send Mama one at Nissim's address, since I don't know where she's currently living. I will hold on to two copies—one for you and one for Nissim—for the time being, in the secret hope that you will both buy your own and I won't have to send them to you. Since the book will most likely be banned in Germany[61] and any prospects for continued support from this publisher depend on the first printing selling quickly, it would obviously be very significant if there is a lot of demand for the book in Paris, too. Georg, please make sure that all of "our people"—even the shabbiest of our relatives—ask for the book at all the German bookstores in Paris and *purchase* it as well. In Paris alone, at least fifty copies must be sold. You're probably laughing at my calculations, right? But when you think about how daring it has become these days for a non-German publisher to publish a book in German, and how furious those people are if they lose a lot of money by doing so, you'll understand my concern. Because at this very moment, with the greatest temerity in the world, I'm trying to convince the man to publish my *Komödie der Eitelkeit*—this coming spring, of course.[62]

Now for another piece of news from my personal life that means almost as much to me: I have a marvelous place to live in Grinzing,[63] in what is probably the most beautiful spot in Vienna, quite high up, with a view of vineyards, vineyards, and more vineyards and as peaceful as paradise. It consists of a garden that is essentially an entire mountainside, a marvelous studio plus balcony as a study, a small boudoir for Veza, a small attic bedroom for me, and kitchen and bath. By a lucky accident, this whole apartment costs us only 100 schillings a month—exactly the same as our abominable place in town,[64] except that heat in the winter will be pretty expensive. If we live very frugally, without a cleaning lady, and not counting any clothes we buy, we can get by on 400 schillings a month. (That's about 1,200 francs.) Isn't that wonderful? One can work here like a god and take marvelous walks. It's *much* more beautiful than the Hagenberggasse.[65] What's more, the building is half empty and our own apartment actually has even more room than I described, so you can rent yourself a lovely south-facing room anytime and live awfully cheaply with us in Vienna. You know how much that would delight both of us, Veza and me. On Sundays we always have guests who are very special indeed: some of the most interesting and important people in Vienna frequent our house. I think you would very much enjoy spending a sort of "posttreatment" convalescence here.

Well, my dear, dear fellow, I expect a long letter from you telling me absolutely *everything*, really *posthaste*, and only if you are *truly* still in the middle of your exams will you be allowed to put me off with just a postcard, but I *must* have news. A thousand hundred thousand embraces

from your brother Elias
Please give Nissim and Edith my best

This letter has been lying here for eleven days already. Forgive me. But I've been ill with the flu in the meantime.

Elias to Georges · *November 18 and December 5, 1935*

Vienna, November 18, 1935

My dear, dear Georg,

In recent weeks not exactly devoid of joy, your letter was the greatest joy of all. I certainly can't complain about not having much incoming mail. Some other time I shall describe the lovely and comical things one gets to read. But even what Thomas Mann had to say about my novel[66] didn't make me as happy and excited as your letter. To be sure, secondhand sources kept me informed of your progress, so I knew that you were improving, and some lung specialists I've had frequent contact with since returning to Vienna have led me to believe that you will recover completely. For instance, there is a country doctor I was introduced to with a practice that is physically quite taxing. Twelve years ago he had a pneumothorax, and since then, he's gotten married and fathered three children. He looks like an allegory of good health and his children like they've stepped out of a painting by Rubens. So I wasn't really so worried about your *physical* health anymore, but still feared for the course of your *psychological* recovery (you surely know *The Magic Mountain* as well as I do, a book I value but don't admire[67]) and I really panicked at the thought of you taking up your old life with Mama again. You see, Georg, despite your somewhat childish threats and attempts to blackmail me, I really will write Mama more often now. And you are very mistaken if you doubt my profound and positively dangerous love for Mama. It's less tender but more *obsessive* than yours. It has the character of a paranoid relationship, but as such, it's a love more intense than any other in my life. To put it more concretely: what Mama thinks of me, what she expects of me, whether she is proud or contemptuous of me—these things are probably more important to me than anything else, even though in individual instances I'm seldom conscious of it. But her physical presence is deadly for me. If I had to live in the same room with her, I would suffocate or hang myself, and that's not just a turn of phrase. The deeper reason is that there is no way I can possibly close myself off from her. Whatever she thinks flows immediately over into me with undiminished strength. I am as much at her mercy as many others are at mine, and what she is in her life—a mesmerizing spider (I use that word because of her *web*; it's not meant to be derogatory at all)—I am in my books. Well, now I can admit to you that I saw you as a *hopeless* victim in her web. That has changed fundamentally. You have become doubly healthy: physically, and by discovering the possibility of closing your inner self off from Mama. It is vitally important that you do so. Today you are still plagued by a bad conscience about it; three-quarters of your letter was self-defense without your wanting to admit it. As far as I'm concerned, however, you don't need to feign a strength on a field where you cannot possibly *have* it yet. In different ways, Mama is both my fate and yours. It was Veza, as interesting a person as Mama but also a better one, who saved me; your illness has saved you. These things are very curious. If I were a teleologist, I would say that's why you got sick. Your suitability for the *divine* profession you have taken up was developed in reaction to Mama. Your illness, not the *concours*,[68] was the final examination. As a poet, I can read between the lines of your letter that you passed it with flying colors. And for the life that awaits you, I would gladly surrender the immortality I'm striving so desperately to achieve. I can't pay anyone a higher tribute than that.

But don't think I mean to disparage Mama with all this. On the contrary, I am convinced that only two things can benefit her. First:

great public achievements by all three of us, e.g. this business with my book. Such things validate and strengthen her life in exactly the appropriate direction: the direction of her pride and enormous ambition. But secondly, and perhaps more important in the long run, there is now some feeling of uncertainty in her hypochondriacal system. As long as the system included you, she could remain placidly within it; now that you have removed yourself from it, it will necessarily be in her interest—to the extent possible—to mobilize all her psychological forces to get well. Maybe that seems superficial to you, but that's only because I'm giving you a mere outline. Think about it in more detail and you'll admit that I'm right. Through your *love*, you've given so very much to Mama and really served her faithfully, but through your indulgence for the construction of her system, you've harmed her a bit, too.

Dec. 5, 1935

Two weeks have passed since I started this letter to you. Perhaps I only left it unfinished because I wasn't pleased with the tone I had set. It's just that I can't tell you how happy and excited your double recovery makes me. Nor do I have any desire to talk about your experience up there in the mountains. I was so shaken by your illness that I would have liked to squeeze your hand tightly and tell you: Georg, you are even more of a brother. Now you are my brother forever, for you know what death is and will no longer smile at my rabid tirades against it. I would love to be with you. In the next two years, I shall be working on the most daring book ever written; it is a book against death that I've been thinking about for eight years or more.[69] I would have loved to write it while living with you, because I love you so much and half a year ago was trembling for your sake. But I fear it won't be possible. Perhaps, if I'm lucky (I mean material luck—some dough), I can really come visit you for a month. Otherwise, you've got to come to Vienna.

What you have to say in general about my (latest) book is very wise. You have completely grasped the essence of the automatism

I intended to portray. In fact, of all the readers who have commented upon it, you are the sharpest. But you have underestimated the lucid consciousness with which I did it. Naturally, it is only for the sake of the automatism that I turned to the psychotics. In a letter I wrote to Thomas Mann four years ago,[70] I explained my plan to base a "*comédie humaine*" on psychotics, and used literally the identical wording you use in your letter. (With the one difference that at the time, Joyce was only a name to me. My notion of his work was extremely vague, so I couldn't measure my project against his.) —But you are *mistaken* in the details: you could only have formed the impression of excessive erudition because you were anticipating the final chapter, especially the great debate between the two brothers. No doubt part one and part three contain too much erudition when placed immediately side by side. But for the average reader, the longer part two stands between them and leads very far away from all that erudite ballast. Besides, there's something particularly attractive about clarifying the structure of madness with the help of learned, foreign, quasi-objective building blocks. The "automatism" becomes clearer; it has something of the advantages of a puzzle or a chemical formula that you memorize in the same way. —I myself am disturbed by the frequent scenes of beatings. I'm sure they disturb you even more. They stand for something other than beatings: perhaps for all hurtful words, perhaps (and this seems even more likely to me) for the hundreds of thousands of attempted murders everyone alive is constantly exposed to. —In one point, however, your misunderstanding is much more profound: perhaps the most important thing about the book for me is the way the characters talk past each other. It may seem exaggerated sometimes, but that is only because old, bad novels have gotten us used to people understanding each other. That, however, is one of our silliest illusions. In reality, no one understands anyone else. It amounts to a miracle if once in a great while it happens after all. The nonstop mutual understanding that goes on in old-fashioned novels is kitsch. When I differentiate my characters, even in their speech, so sharply from each other, all I'm doing is raising an utterly normal element of our lives as individuals to an aesthetic principle.

The reviews have been excellent so far. I sent Mama one from the *Neue Freie Presse*[71] and I'm sure she has shown it to you too. But perhaps with the exception of Thomas Mann and two local writers, Dr. Sonne and Dr. Sapper[72] (and you of course), I can say that hardly anyone has really *understood* the book. It makes an enormous impression on people. It impacts them in about the same way as someone hitting them over the head with a club. Some of the reviews seem to be written by people who have been drugged. But what does it matter? The fact remains: since the publication of *Die Blendung*, everyone who reads it considers me one of the most important writers of our time, and I admit that, given the enormity of my craving for fame, I am not indifferent to this. Maybe it's unwise of me to say it out loud, but you know me well enough in any event: *I do not want to die*, and fame is for me only one of the most obvious paths to immortality. —It may interest you to know what Thomas Mann said about *Die Blendung*. In a long, handwritten letter, he says that my novel and a book by his brother[73] have preoccupied him more than any other new books this year. After going into great detail, he summarizes his impression as follows: "I'm really struck and very positively impressed by its eccentric abundance, overflowing imagination, a certain embittered grandiosity of its plan, its poetic courageousness, its mournfulness, and its daring. It is a book that can stand beside the works of the greatest talents of other literary cultures, in contrast to the stuffy mediocrity common in Germany today." —In this judgment, you have to make allowances for Thomas Mann's natural reserve and somewhat dry disposition. He is so completely and utterly lacking in effusiveness that the words above can almost be taken as effusive. And that is how all the experts take them. I hope you are not annoyed at this long gush of self-congratulation. I've written you this to spare you the somewhat silly reviews, however much they may sing my praises. I won't send you any unless they are intelligent enough to take halfway seriously.

47

Veza to Georges · *January 1936*

January

Dear Georg,

Renée has an odd request she asked me to pass on to you. She knows a nice young man who's currently in Paris and, in fact, used to be *engaged* to her. Discretion is called for! However, he has decided to—join the clergy. From his letters and conversation, she can tell that he wouldn't be any good as a Catholic *priest*, because he thinks clearly and doesn't believe in miracles. Renée thinks that would qualify him to be a Protes. clergyman (and the poor child's secret thought is that they could still get married then). And her question (I wouldn't dare be so presumptuous as to ask you such a thing for myself) is whether you would be willing to meet with the young man for an hour in Paris and clarify his thinking for him without his being aware of it, because he himself says that his mind is in chaos. He loves Renée.

Where we live is utterly beautiful. We have a south-facing room for you with a balcony and fragrant breezes. And yes, I even think that as early as Easter, one or the other of us, either Canetti or I, will have some success in business, so we will be able to offer you not only a *room* as we do now, but all the other amenities as well. I can't tell you how much I look forward to that.

If you would rather not do anything about Renée's request, let me know *in such a way* that I can show it to her; and so Canetti "awoke one morning and found himself famous."[74]

Veza

I just got the flu, that's why my handwriting looks this way.

Dear Georg,

Ignore the above request, since the young ascetic is coming to Vienna and Canetti is going to work him over. But it's good that you read this letter anyway. —There are some farmers living in our building, too, so fresh eggs every day and milk still warm from the cow. Doesn't that sound tempting?

Elias to Georges · *January 21, 1936*

January 21, 1936[75]

My dear, dear Georg,

In the meantime, weeks and weeks have passed and this letter is still lying here. I'm going to send it to you now just as it is. Mama sent me a letter that—forgive my sentimentality—I found deeply moving and very upsetting. I think that we are patching up our relationship at the place where it was destined to tear apart. It is sad that it took the external evidence of success to give Mama an idea of the work I do. If she had read the completed manuscript 4 (?) years ago, things would have turned out differently between us. But I am *enormously happy* that it has happened at last. It was always bitter for me to have to live with Mama's disregard when I regard her so highly. Nevertheless, I take back nothing of the objective things I wrote in the first pages of my previous letter. On the contrary: I think the course of Mama's development in the last two or three months only proves what I said. I will write to her more often now, of course, and would like awfully much to see her soon.

But I want to give you a quick report on recent events in my life. Perhaps most important is the contract for the English and American editions of my book.[76] Two of the leading publishing houses are interested. I can very likely expect an advance by the beginning of March. In addition, two big German publishers have approached me about acquiring my next book. Obviously, I mustn't be hasty in negotiations, and especially never show how desperately I need the money. But here's how things are with us: I don't have a single complete suit of clothes left and don't know what we're going to live on until February. You absolutely have to send me 500 francs right away. If you don't have it, borrow it from someone. Somehow or other you must scare that much up; I'm relying on you. Then I can at least count on paying the rent and utilities. In addition, I have the following request: give some *very serious* thought to whether I could approach our uncles for 3,000–4,000 francs, first to get myself outfitted again to some extent, and second to survive the two months or so it could take to finally get my finances in order. Since they have "seen" something now, namely the book and its reception, I don't think it would be either <embarrassing>[77] or difficult. Maybe it would help if I played it as "Grandpa's inheritance" or something like that. In any case, take this very seriously and think it over carefully. It would be unforgivably stupid of me to put in jeopardy all future <?>[77] because of a momentary shortage of cash. Don't forget: 500 francs *at once*.

And don't be angry that I have nothing better to write on your birthday and about your *concours*.

Most affectionately,
Elias

Elias to Georges · *February 20, 1936*

February 20, 1936

My dear, dear Georg,

Your news is terribly worrisome, not because it has any real importance, but because it affects you so much. I have long been convinced that an internship would be the absolute *wrong* path for you to take. You belong with people and not stuck in an institute. And it is by no means a prerequisite for academic work that you be an intern. I have gathered very precise information about this from informed sources. I can imagine two things that could be seriously rankling you. One is the enormous erudition you have assembled for the express purpose of taking the *concours*. Well, as far as that's concerned, I am convinced that there cannot be too much of anything for people like you and me; everything is to our advantage. For my part, I don't even regret having taken those idiotic examinations in chemistry[78] so many long years ago, which had absolutely no connection to my actual goals. What seems to me of essential importance to the intellectual development of a modern man is the *amount* of associative material he amasses, and part of it should be in at least *one* field of modern scientific practice that he can encompass, look at from all sides, and acquire exhaustive knowledge of. God knows you have done quite enough of that, and to top it all off, in a field that is eminently practical for you. You have lost nothing by doing so. Joyce can speak who knows how many languages. You have now mastered German, French, and the language of medicine. I mean that literally, not as a jejune metaphor. This is how an intellect fills itself up for an unknown destiny. Each combination is new and unique. Its only task is to *fill* itself. And so, my dear, brave brother, I would like to express my respect once again that you continually fill your mind and never slow down, but remain alive and wide awake. Anything else is trivial and stupid and not worth our attention.

Here is the other thing you ought to consider: the same applies to the abominable injustice that was done to you (whether it will turn into a scandal or not) that applied to me for four years. For four years the manuscript of *Die Blendung* just lay around the house, either unknown or despised, and ineffectual. Today they're singing its praises as the devil only knows what kind of major work of art. Well, it doesn't seem such a major work to me, and I attribute such emphatic declarations of its importance to the earlier injustice of its rejection. Yes, just think, I believe in the *immanent* retroactivity of injustice, not from some form of higher, divine intervention, but quite simply for straightforward psychological reasons I will explain to you at length sometime. Not so many years ago, Fritz Wotruba, Austria's greatest sculptor,[79] was kicked out of the Academy for having no talent. Today he's 30. Now gray-haired dignitaries, seventy-year-old idiots from the Academy, doff their slouch hats in his honor.

Ah Georg, I want you not to take all this superficial foolishness with the *concours* as seriously as a Frenchman would. Go ahead and be a Frenchman if you like, but not in this regard. And so I'm going to ask you the following favor. Please direct your attention in the next few days to a person whom Veza and I love as much as we love you. Anna Mahler, Zsolnay's former wife and the daughter of Gustav Mahler, is coming to Paris for a few days. I've told you a lot about her already; she's that very talented sculptor whose work you've seen in photographs. You should call her up this Sunday, February 23, at 2:00 o'clock after lunch, at the Hotel Majestic. Ask for Frau von Zsolnay. If they don't understand you, add: the daughter of Frau Werfel-Mahler (her mother and Werfel[80] often stay there as well). Anna knows Paris well, but even so she'll be pleased to have your company. You must be *especially tactful* and not let on you know all the things I've told you about her, except for her sculpture. Be clever and charming and don't embarrass me. She's one of the most magnificent and wonderful women of our time; for heaven's sake do not let her come into contact with *anyone* from our family (not even Mathilde Camhi).

Many many hugs from Elias

You won't be getting a "business letter" until tomorrow. By then I'll have the reviews you need.

Veza to Georges · *February 1936*

Dearest Georg,

Today I posted a letter from Canetti to you that was supposed to have been in your possession by tomorrow but won't be because of Canetti's procrastination. Now I fear that you could misunderstand it. I haven't read it, but it says that you should call up Anna on Sunday, and when the letter doesn't get there in time, perhaps you'll be reluctant to try her on some other day. Anna will certainly stay 5–6 days in

Paris (Hotel Majestic, I think, Anna *Mahler*) and since she is my favorite person after the two Canettis, it means a lot to me that you see her (and when you do, you'll see what a compliment I'm paying you). By this point, you're starting to get scared of me, but all I can say is: would I show you *Anna* if I weren't so resigned, so white-haired, so toothless, so opulent (but more from rice pudding than from capons)?

Well, we have at most two more difficult months, and even the foehn weather can't cast a shadow on my confidence. I'm sitting on our balcony (your balcony, come Easter), wearing a light blouse, and writing. Canetti has a dozen very good and brilliant reviews. He'll send them to you soon; we ordered more copies.

What do you need those examinations for? You're the great doctor of France just as you are and someday you will write a wonderful novel. As you can see, I'm more of a believer in you than you are in me (as far as *I'm* concerned) and someday you'll be biting your tongue, trying not to laugh.

I'll see to your copy of the erstwhile K. K.'s[81] *Fackel.* Please be sure to have Anna show you photos of her sculptures. It will please her and what's more, she's really talented.

Don't forget! Call Anna!

Terribly excited about Easter,

Veza

ELIAS TO GEORGES · *MARCH 4, 1936*

March 4, 1936

My dear, dear Georg,

So now you have met Anna, plus mother and Werfel. Anna is already back and has given me a report about you even before I've received yours about her and her family. According to her, you look very well, even a bit stout, completely healthy (another reason your meeting them was so important to me). The entire clan found you especially congenial. There was no time for more than that. They searched in vain for physical similarities between the two of us. I'm sorry you had so little time with Anna alone; she is as marvelous as her mother and Werfel are loathsome. But I don't want to anticipate your judgment of them. You must *absolutely* come see us for a few weeks at Easter. We're all counting on it. It would make Anna happy, too. You will stay with us in the most beautiful house with the most beautiful garden in Vienna. And it will surely do you good to meet some of Vienna's most significant and important inhabitants as well. Take your time getting used to the idea. Easter is on April 12. The best thing would be for you to come at the beginning of April; we (Veza and I) will be quite angry at you if you don't arrange to make the trip. Staying here will cost you nothing, of course. We eat out, to the extent that we eat at all. Figure on about 5 schillings per day. You'll hardly need more, except for the theater and concerts. The air is marvelous; a divine, peaceful landscape; long walks; a part of Vienna we were completely unfamiliar with, astonishingly enough. You will find it just as salutary as the mountains of France.

This much as an introduction and reminder to make prompt arrangements for the trip. What follows is the business letter I promised you. I need to write you in detail about these things because I trust you completely. Please pay close attention to everything below. I can't write like this to Nissim, and it would be an unmitigated disaster if he made any mistakes.

I once sent you a piece of paper with excerpts from selected reviews of *Die Blendung*. You may use *anything* on that page for publicity. At the top of the page is *the* sentence from Thomas Mann. He himself meant for it to be published. Since the publisher uses these reviews himself to peddle the book (please excuse the harsh term) and I am not personally *allowed* to interfere with his activities in this regard, there is no reason why Nissim can't use some of them as well. In case he needs a translation, I'm asking you to do a very precise one, especially of Thomas Mann's sentence. Of course, there are many other reviews at our disposal. For the moment, I'm sending you only three newspaper clippings, since I haven't received the others yet. There are about twenty newspaper articles in all. We've ordered copies, but they haven't arrived yet. —The one review, from the *Presse*, would be especially appropriate for idiots. Nissim should definitely use that one. The second, written by Hermann Hesse for the *Neue Zürcher Zeitung*,[82] struck me as insultingly simpleminded; when I compare them, it's actually the worst I've seen yet. My publisher was of a completely different opinion. He was positively ecstatic about the words "thriller," "highly suspenseful," and "virtuoso performance," and strangely enough, success proved him right. Three days after the piece appeared, he received an inquiry from Mondadori, the biggest publisher in Italy, referring specifically to Hesse's review, and now they're negotiating an Italian edition.[83] So I leave it to Nissim to decide for himself if it makes sense to use this review. And finally, an interview,[84] just to show you how quickly *Die Blendung* has made me "popular." I've already thrown out four interviewers. I couldn't throw this one out for personal reasons (he came warmly recommended by some very good friends). It ended up being terribly serious for an interview—just imagine such a thing in an ordinary illustrated weekly! The effect of this interview was unbelievable. I get letters about it every day, more than I do about the book itself, even though the idiot really botched my poor sentences, to say nothing of the picture he took of me! Forgive me for sending you this rubbish, but maybe Nissim will find it useful.

And now to get down to business. If Nissim really plans to do something, then I'm very grateful to him. Especially in France, it's supposed to be very difficult to market foreign novels. Yet my book is particularly suitable for France. But we must bear one very important thing in mind: most critics have compared the novel to Céline, Joyce, and Döblin, i.e., it's seen exclusively as a *serious work of literature and it should be sold only as such.* I have some anxiety that Nissim, precisely because he's my brother, is not the appropriate person for the job. Of course you mustn't say that to him. I have absolutely no wish to offend him. But make it clear to him that the book must be presented as something extremely literary and exceptional. So he should base his marketing especially on Thomas Mann's statement and Fischauer's review.[85]

Grasset has had the book for a few weeks now, where it came highly recommended.[86] Nissim should intervene there only if he has *serious* influence through a respected literary friend, but otherwise not, for it would cheapen the whole thing and look like nepotism. Grasset would be outstanding (Julien Green). We should also try the *Nouvelle Revue Française*. I have no contacts there, and Nissim should only try it if he knows someone there who is taken seriously in literary circles. He should always stress that I am *Viennois* and not an emigrant. I've heard the French are fed up with émigré writers. Lastly, it's worth a try at Denoël and Steele, Céline's publishers.—Under no circumstances may the book be abridged. If it reaches the point of negotiations, please write me promptly regarding the matter of a translator. (I know of a young, talented French writer[87] who is very familiar with Vienna, speaks excellent German, has already done a lot of translating, and is the one who advocated for my book at Grasset—I would trust him to do the translation. Under no circumstances should Mathilde Camhi get her hands on the translation; don't say anything about it to her.) The book could be a gigantic financial success in France as well. In America, where it is very likely to appear by late fall, they're all predicting similar success. Please, Georg, make sure Nissim doesn't do anything stupid!

Now for the other matter that is even more important at the moment. Please don't be alarmed, but you have to scare up at least 4,000.00 francs for me. Because 1,000 francs a month is the *minimum* I need for living expenses for March, April, and May, and in addition another 1,000 francs for *clothes. You see, I don't have a single complete suit to my name, and no overcoat,* not one pair of good shoes, and almost all my underwear has holes. It's just impossible to go around like this, especially now. Before, I was able to halfway conceal the desperate state my clothes are in, but I can't keep it up any longer. There is no source of income I can count on for *certain* in the next few months, despite the assured prospect of larger sums later. It would be simplest if you would speak to Nissim first about this. He should send me (and now he will surely have more confidence in my abilities) 1,500 francs right away, 1,500 francs at the beginning of April, and 1,000 francs at the beginning of May, and deduct them from the advance for the French edition. Please talk to him about it very seriously and objectively. If he doesn't want to do it, you must go right to Uncle Josef and describe the situation to him as *an official request from me personally*: I beseech the family to help me get over the next two or three months. They can also do it in three installments. You don't need to be ashamed; what I'm doing can only bring honor to the family, and their little bit of help will be repaid a hundredfold. Somehow or other *it has to happen*, Georg. It's not necessary to break out in moans and groans. It should be handled as discreetly as possible. Tell Uncle Josef that I've been living on the advance for my book since last summer, that's three-quarters of a year. But don't tell him the amount. And believe me, there is no reason, absolutely no reason to be ashamed about it. If you think it's wiser to approach Uncle Joe first, then write me directly. Respond *at once*.

Most affectionately, your brother Elias.

And get ready for your *Easter visit*.

It all has to happen right away, Georg, since I'm in desperate need of money. Please don't be a coward.

ELIAS TO GEORGES · *March 23, 1936*

March 23, 1936

My dear Georg,

I would gladly be patient, if only I could, but I just can't! It is *urgent* that you do something *right away*. Our situation has taken an unexpected turn for the worse. Veza has fallen quite ill and is in the sanatorium. I hope she'll be allowed to come home in a few days, but you can imagine how much new debt I have incurred because of this. I already owe the 1,500 francs for March which I asked you for, and this time I *must* pay them off. Please, Georg, don't delay any longer. I have the feeling that you're ashamed to speak to Nissim and our uncles. There is not the slightest reason to be. Even from their point of view, my name will be good business for them, especially when my book is published in France. If they had the slightest bit of respect—respect for intellectual achievement or even, for all I care, for the filthy success they worship—they would set up a little annuity for me for the next year or two and would offer to pay for it of their own accord, without me having to ask for it. But it's probably smarter for you not to scare the daylights out of any of them by suggesting such a thing. Stick to what I told you and I'll at least be able to pay these latest sanatorium bills and survive the next two months. But *hurry*; I don't know what I'm going to do. —Please also tell me how Nissim has reacted to the various reviews and if he really intends to do anything on my behalf. —A letter from Mama just arrived. She says you will move in together again in April. That seems to me the worst plan there could possibly be for the two of you. You're coming here for Easter, aren't you, so we can talk it over? You're coming for sure!

Affectionately,
Your brother Elias

It's high time you wrote about yourself, exams, your impressions of Anna, etc.

VEZA TO GEORGES · *May 13, 1936*

5/13

Dearest Georg,

Your letter was very sweet. Please tell me if we owe you a lot of money. I can't travel around on account of Murkl.[88] He's terribly depressed. I don't know how we're going to get through this. Sometimes I think I will drop dead. Can't you write us something apodictic? Everything you say is so agreeably indefinite, friendly, and naive. And we can't go on. My heart will not endure it.

And you'll see for yourself the psychological state Murkl is in.

Or will you? Will we? It seems strange to me to be planning, hoping, intending to do anything. That's it: I'm going to stop hoping for anything. I have been burned in all three degrees.

Murkl is worried because you didn't take a rest at Easter. He thinks it will do you harm. You will become debilitated. Very nice of you to worry me as well. Murkl tried to poke out both his eyes with a file yesterday. You probably think I'm crazy. Unfortunately, despite everything, I am not. It's just that my heart doesn't seem to want to beat right. It's so wise. Love and best wishes,

Veza

VEZA TO GEORGES · *September 16, 1936*

Sept. 16

Dearest Georg,

The terrible news apparently hit me harder than "his sister," for I've been distraught the last two days and only now able to write to that small, heroic woman.[89] We would be very grateful if you wrote us *what* poor Hans said to you in his confusion. We would be interested in even the least scrap of a sentence about it.

The thought expressed in your letter, that Canetti could be blaming himself, has reconciled me a bit to the thoughts in your previous letter. He was in fact terribly unhappy about this undoubtedly inevitable suicide and told me *he* was the murderer. As for the thoughts in your next-to-last letter, I shall assume you never thought them. Otherwise, I could not respect you. I love you as always, but I won't respect you if you persist in a single one of those ideas.

Your brother, who has the kindest and most noble character I know, was unable to sleep for three nights. Then he calmed down and wanted me to write you that he had never received the letter because *I* had confiscated it. Because he did not want *you* to lose *your* best friend.

As for *his* letters, I would like to state categorically that it wasn't money he wanted, but help. Money is not the word for what we needed. We were starving. We had no coal. We were sick and didn't have a schilling to our name—for a long, long time. My brother,[90] a poor shopkeeper in Surrey, paid our rent. Then he couldn't do it any longer and we didn't have rent money either.

I'm telling you this because our situation has improved and should get even better in a few weeks. "With a likelihood of seventy percent," says the director who acquired Canetti's film. It's a movie in which the violinist Huberman[91] plays the main character. *This last is a secret* and it could *harm us very much* if you were to reveal it. It's seventy percent certain that the film will be made. As you can see, I've become very cautious and speak in percentages.

As for Canetti, although we were starving and had no help from anywhere (the doctor paid for the cost of my operation by performing it for free), he kept expecting *you* to *come*. I will never forget him waiting for you to arrive this Easter. He didn't leave the house, ran after the postman, and finally stopped expecting you, but hoped for at least a letter from you, and in the end he even would have been happy if your brother Nissim had come. But you didn't so much as bother to let us know you weren't coming.

And all this after I wrote you a letter about what you mean to me. I never confessed to Canetti that I wrote you that letter because I was so ashamed of your "answer." But not ashamed of my letter, for he already knows how much I love you.

As for your beautiful mother, if you are not superstitious about it, I would like you to exaggerate the state of her health in your letters to Canetti (for you are going to write him a heartfelt letter). Canetti always wants to wait for a moment of inspiration to write to her and the poor woman is waiting to hear from him. I press him to do it, but to no avail. Please give him an added incentive. And again, please write more about Hans Asriel and his mother.

The grateful adoptive parents of the patient whose "life you saved" were very nice. They talked of you just as I've always pictured you and that broke the ice. I ought to say, it broke the *iron*, because your letter was like a dagger to the heart.

Veza.

VEZA TO GEORGES · *Postmarked November 10, 1936*

Dr. Georg Canetti
85, rue de la Convention
Paris

Oct. 10[92]

Dear Georg,

Toward the end of this month, a young lady will arrive in Paris to join her husband there. She will tell you his remarkable story herself. We want you to give her some helpful *suggestions*. She has a Ph.D. and is looking for possible au pair jobs. Although she has friends in Paris, we would like you to look after her a little. She is charming.

Please tell us how your mother is. Elias is going to send her a little surprise soon. How are *you?* I just read Aubry's *Napoleon*[93] and recommend it highly. Please write.*

Most affectionately,
Veza

*Also tell us if the young lady can come.

61

Veza to Georges · *May 25, 1937*

5/25

Dear Georg,

You wrote Canetti a postcard from Germany that made him very happy. He carries it around with him all the time, and if he hasn't answered it yet, it's for the following reason: he's been invited to a writers' conference[94] in Paris and thought he would surprise you, and especially your mother, with a visit. He assured me that he had great hopes it would do your mother good, for we've heard that she's been feeling weak and depressed. That's probably due primarily to the vile foehn weather that makes me sick too, so sick I'm almost always in bed. We heard the news of your mother from Mathilde,[95] of course. Well, things don't always go according to plan. Canetti was invited to read on Prague radio and also give a lecture at the Urania.[96] Both were great successes, but he is still in Prague, being feted.[97] Although he is a dilatory correspondent, however (and you are not one bit better), he did ask me to inform you of all this. For he will be back here in two or three days, but then comes the difficult business of getting a visa. The invitation to the conference will probably facilitate it, but nevertheless, the process can often take a stateless person weeks to wrap up. By the way, isn't there something you can do from your end to help things along? The conference begins at the end of June, but Canetti wants to get there sooner. He has meetings beforehand, which is one reason why he won't stay with you. Don't think that his renting separate quarters is just a waste of money. He has to receive conference participants, there are late-night discussions, and he needs a separate place so he doesn't have to tone down his voice. So first off, Georg, what can you do to expedite the granting of a visa? Second, where can you find a room for him? He has had all sorts of success which he will describe in detail when he reaches Paris. To be honest, he can hardly wait to burst out with everything, for in his boundless ambition he especially wants to impress his mother and steal her heart from you, so to speak (for he's quite jealous). Of course, he wants to give you his in return, because he loves you and always will. (Do you deserve it?) Enclosed a clipping from a Prague daily. He will bring much better reviews himself. I'm just enclosing the interview.

Please see to it that his mother is positively disposed toward him, for he is just bursting with experiences and events and has a burning desire to lay them all at her feet. He would be terribly hurt if she didn't accept them in the same spirit. There can't be anyone he loves as much as her. Please excuse my somewhat wobbly handwriting. But my heart is not quite in order and I just got furiously annoyed at the French consulate because they're dragging their feet. I should have written you this letter two weeks ago, so please don't betray me to Canetti. There were so many things going on. And now, best wishes and help out a bit with the administrative details.

Veza

Please confirm receipt of this letter at once, since I'm not sure the address is correct.

ELIAS TO GEORGES · *June 1, 1937*

Vienna, June 1, 1937

My dear Georg,

Yesterday I returned from a lecture tour in Czechoslovakia. As Veza wrote you a while ago, I had intended to continue on immediately to Paris for a writers' conference I've been invited to. It doesn't begin for two or three weeks, but it was very important to me to participate in the conference preparations. I would also have liked to spend my free time with you and Mama—for I wouldn't have had much opportunity for that once the conference was under way.

Well, today I was at the Fr. consulate in Vienna and they are causing me the same old problems; they sent a telegram to the French Foreign Ministry's department for regulation of foreigners. As the reason for my hasty decision to travel, I gave my desire to visit my sick mother, whom I haven't seen in more than two years. Please don't hold this against me; after all, I really am coming to see Mama. The conference is such a good opportunity to do it. If I give the conference as the reason, they'll take forever to approve the trip. So now I'm waiting for a telegraphic reply from the Foreign Ministry in Paris. The insolent people in the consulate here told me it could take one or two weeks. So it would be good if Nissim could go to the Foreign Ministry on Thursday, find the official in charge of my application, and expedite its approval. I gave Nissim in Paris and Hoepffner[98] in Strasbourg as references.

Please let me know immediately what you can do. The most heartfelt greetings to Mama, Nissim, and you.

From your Elias

The trip to Prague was a huge success!

VEZA TO GEORGES · *June 7, 1937*

June 7th

Dear Georg,

Please pass this letter on. I am delighted that your mother is feeling better. Unfortunately, Canetti is somewhat ill. He still has a touch of bronchitis and as always, heart problems, stomachaches, and acne. As always, he's a laggard and doesn't meet even his most *pressing* obligations. For instance, it is *urgent* that he send an interview to Prague, because he's world-famous in Prague. Please take this burden off my shoulders a bit and ask him every day, "What about that interview?" so that he will send it off before the end of the year at least. Also keep asking him if he's written to me. I always take care of his correspondence, but I can't very well write to myself. If your mother is feeling better now, won't you come visit us? We have a heavenly apartment.

Most affectionately,
Veza

Veza to Georges · *June 19, 1937*

June 19th

Beloved Georg,

I didn't love Elias or you, I loved your mother. I was in thrall to her. And so I don't know how to comfort you.[99]

I have only one thing to ask: please be considerate of us, because you mean *the world* to me and Elias. Stay well for us. *We cannot be without you.* You are our happiness and our fruit. I received a letter about you today and I am going to put it in safekeeping. Someday it will please you and convince you.

It's a comfort to me that you were so good to that marvelous woman.

Georg, please keep well for us; we deserve it.

Veza.

Elias to Georges · *End of June 1937*[100]

Georg,

Just now, after the meal and an hour after speaking with you on the telephone, I had the conversation I had been dreading with Nissim. It went much worse than I could ever have imagined. You should not have done this to me, Georg. You are so thoughtful to everyone, but you've caused me the deepest humiliation I have suffered since my last visit to Paris two and a half years ago. I followed Nissim into the next room and asked him to advance me a thousand francs. That was all; the other

Mathilde Canetti

things you and I talked about briefly weren't mentioned at all. His initial reaction was, "You must be crazy. I have no intention of lending you money. Why would I?" I said that you had discussed it with him. No, he claimed, he had come to an agreement with you to give me 100 francs every four days, and I could have them now. I was foolish enough to tell him I wanted to send 500 francs to Veza to pay our rent on July 1 (which is true, because if she pays the rent on the first, she'll have no money left) and needed 500 more for myself. He replied in the lowest, coarsest way you can imagine. Up to that moment, we had been speaking to each other in such a friendly tone—almost tenderly—that I was so taken aback I didn't end the conversation right there, which would certainly have been the smartest thing to do. He said there was no money, it had all been spent on the burial, and they[101] never send any money from Palestine or England—or if they did, one never knew when it was coming. He was no banker, he said. He had plenty of money at home, but he would never consider giving me any. *His* money belonged to *him*. If I wanted 100 francs of *his* money every four days, I was welcome to it. It was a disgrace that someone as old as I couldn't support himself, etc. etc. He finally agreed to give me 500 francs for Veza, but that was all.

This conversation lasted about twenty minutes and has killed all the feelings for Nissim I had taken so much trouble to rekindle. I did not speak harshly to him. I remained calm and amicable, because I had promised Mama three days before she died that I would never again fight with any of you, not even with Nissim. I took this promise so seriously that I was *seeing* Nissim in a completely different light—as a funny, charming fellow, as a father, etc. In actuality, he's the same old person. Not even this enormous event we're experiencing together, which has filled me with tenderness and love for him, could change him. Of course, I will accept nothing from him, not even the 500 francs for Veza. I gave him my hand and said a few amicable words in farewell. I never want to see him again. I want to leave here immediately. I have absolutely no money. I can't even get out of Paris. Ah, Georg, I knew why I was so afraid to have that conversation. I wanted to avoid everything. I wanted to have a brotherly relationship with him. Nissim has destroyed everything on account of 1,000 francs, an amount he does possess. What shall I do now? I would have *murdered* any other person for speaking to me that way. Veza must never find out about this. She already had so much anxiety about it. He was just as mean as ever. He repeated several times, "What do I care about sentimentalities?" Georg, Georg, at your most desperate you didn't neglect to help Vernier,[102] but you have exposed me to the most unmitigated humiliation.

Elias

ELIAS TO GEORGES · *July 15 and 25, 1937*[103]

Paris, July 15, 1937

Dear Georg,

What very good news. I have decided to believe it, because I do not think you would break the solemn oath you made me in the car on the way to the train station. So you are not sick. When I read that, I literally jumped for joy. Imagine how graceful that must have looked. I wanted to write you immediately after your departure on Sunday morning. But then it seemed to me more "humane" to save my brilliant warnings (man, you have no idea of the admonitory tanks and large-bore cannon I was ready to deploy against you!) until I had heard from you. But now, in all seriousness, Georg, it's your damn duty to Veza and me, but especially to your own profession, not to do anything that could worsen your condition. First of all, stay up there as long as possible, at least two weeks. Second, divide up your work so that you can take frequent vacations. You *must* come to Vienna at the beginning of October, if only for just two weeks. Veza cried all night after our telephone conversation because she figured out we were lying to her. She realized you have no intention of coming to Vienna. Since then, I've sent her two telegrams, written two letters, and had a telephone conversation in which I *assured* her of the opposite. I told her that you had promised to come "at the end of the year" and that you really do intend to come in October. You must write to Veza *at once*. She knows that you've been in St. Hilaire[104] for a few days already. You have to reassure her about everything, but especially about that. I would also be very grateful if you would encourage her to hire a housemaid, if only *so she has more time to write*. Please mention that you read her long novella.[105]

Basel, July 25

Dear Georg,

This is a letter I began ten days ago and have been carrying around with me ever since. Perhaps you've already written to Veza in the meantime, hopefully in the way we discussed. If not, please do so right away. And please make a copy of your aphorisms for both of us and send them as soon as possible.

I took the following books of yours along with me for Veza. Of course you'll get them back when you come to Vienna:

4 volumes of Jules Romains
2 volumes of Proust (*Du côté de chez Swann*).
Stendhal: *Lucien Leuwen*, 2 vols.
Valéry: *Variété* I.
Gide: *Congo. Tchad. Pages du Journal.*

A total of twelve volumes, only one of them for me (Valéry). I left behind at Nissim's the Goncourts' diaries and the volume *Rhumbs*.[106] Send Lévy-Brühl[107] and the two Champions[108] directly to me in Vienna, this week if possible, because in August we're going to the mountains. But you can also hang on to the Champions if you like them. In any case, keep the Metalnikov,[109] because I've bought a copy for myself.

From Tuesday to yesterday, I was in Strasbourg. I had a very cordial visit with my old friends, including the Cohns. Yesterday I left Strasbourg to surprise Veza on my birthday. The train was late, and in Basel I missed the express train to Vienna by a hair, so I had to stay here overnight. Luckily, I still had some Swiss francs. But I'm feeling awful, with a high fever. Devil knows how I caught it. The train to Vienna leaves in an hour. A sorry sort of birthday, what?

By chance, I met a Viennese doctor in Paris, *Dr. Sommer*, who had to leave Vienna and lives in abject poverty in Paris. He has a wife and two children in Vienna who are, like him, starving to death. I was only able to give him a little money, not enough to redeem the medical equipment he had pawned for 220 francs. He has submitted a monograph on the yogurt bacillus to the Pasteur Institute.[110] I gave him your address. He will write to you. *Please, Georg, see him right away*. Be tactful with him—he's very sensitive—and try to help him in any way you can. I think that you, as a doctor, will be the best judge of what he's capable of. He's quite distraught at his misfortune. He hasn't slept in a bed for weeks. But avoid any political discussion with him; you can never be sure whom you're dealing with.

Elias

Please write and tell me what you think about Dr. Sommer and what you can do for him.

ELIAS AND VEZA TO GEORGES · *August 10, 1937*[111]

Gersbergalpe, Salzburg 11

August 10, 1937

My dear little Georg,

It has been exactly a month since we parted. I've had *one* letter from you and Veza not a single blasted syllable. I really can't understand why you don't write, and it upsets me especially because you had made a solemn promise to get in touch with Veza, and what reason could you possibly have not to? I'm beginning to fear that you're sick, but Nissim would surely let me know if you were. Then I try to reassure myself that you've been too preoccupied with the move and getting used to your new job,[112] but that's not a very happy thought, either. In any event, I urge you to send us news *immediately* and in detail. If you really have no time at all, then we insist on at least a card.

When I received your letter from St. Hilaire, I began to answer it right away, but then didn't finish it until my mournful, feverish birthday in Basel. At the last moment, as my train was departing, I realized it was still in my pocket and I gave it to a Swiss newspaper vendor to mail. She assured me that she had often mailed letters for passengers in a hurry. Recalling all the honest "daughters" from our wonderful days in Zurich, I had complete confidence that you would get the letter. But that seems not to be the case. Perhaps you never got my answer and that's the reason you are mad at me. In any case, don't keep me guessing any longer and do write *immediately*.

I arrived in Vienna suffering from bad angina and was in bed quite a long time. Veza isn't all that well either. For the last few days, we've been on the Gersberg alp near Salzburg, where we were all together five years ago. It is indescribably marvelous and it's a shame you can't be here. Maybe you can come after all. We will definitely be staying for all of August. At the end of the month, Herr Hoepffner from Strasbourg is going to visit us. Since he cannot come before the 26th and will stay to the 30th, we're tied down here in any case. In the meantime, however, we may pay a two- or three-day visit to the fledgling couple Renée-Blatt[113] in Fusch. —And now I have something wonderfully remarkable to tell you: the view I have from here is precisely in the direction of Reichenhall. I can see the mountains in the immediate vicinity of Reichenhall: the Hochstaufen, the Zwiesel, and the Predigtstuhl. The last time I was with Mama in Reichenhall,[114] we had a view of the Staufen and the Zwiesel. It's less than fifteen miles from here to there. Surrounded by those mountains, continuously in haze and hidden behind some low hills, lies Reichenhall. The air above *Nonn*[115] wafts over to me today. The rain comes from that direction as well. That first visit to Reichenhall (in 1916, when we joined you later in Rheinfelden)[116] was the time of my most passionate attachment to Mama. I threatened to box the ears of the professor[117] who was there too. I didn't realize why I wanted to come to the Gersberg alp—it just happened of its own accord. Now I know exactly what drew me here. And so, for all three of us, I have paid my respects to Nonn, and in a much nicer way than if I were there: by always having it *in view* and feeling its breezes. You can tell Nissim about it, if you think it's the right thing to do and if you can speak to him alone.

Many many embraces from your brother Elias
and write at once.

Elias sometimes misspeaks and calls me Georg and that always makes me happy. *Write* to me!!

I have *never* gotten a letter from you.

Veza

And please send the aphorisms you promised us, soon!!

VEZA TO GEORGES · *August 16, 1937*

8/16

Dear Georg,

I can't understand your silence in response to Canetti's affectionate letters. It has caused him to have a psychotic episode. Unfortunately, I am not exaggerating. The actual gravity of this outbreak is the reason for this letter.

His previous big attack happened last summer with the failure of the film project.[118] That time, he groped his way through the apartment with twitching eyelids. He was blind and said I was intending to kill him with a dagger. When he came to himself, he said the groping had been the wish to find an exit, fleeing from me because I wanted to stab him!

Last night he was fantasizing about a woman *you* were alienating from him, whom *you* intended to marry against your mother's last wishes. I began to doubt the complete truthfulness of his statements when he said that I was a great beauty but an evil person. Since grief has ravaged my features, I didn't take the second part of his assertion to heart, either. What I do take to heart is his attack.

As for my life with him, I would not call it being caught between Scylla and Charybdis, but rather fluctuating between madness and suicide. The constant allowances I make for his quirks and propensities demand a degree of self-control that puts my own health at risk. My despair at the prospect of him suffering Hölderlin's fate[119] points to suicide as my only escape. When he is off on a trip, I gradually rediscover myself. I open up and begin to shine. I am seized with yearning for an unencumbered life of health and freedom. I would like to leave—leave him. When he returns, I'm so overcome with compassion and stand in such awe of his *genius* and his *boundless goodness* that I lapse back into my old habits.

I'm writing all this so that you will help me. I would like to tell you everything about him and then perhaps you as a doctor will know a solution. He says you are one of the most erudite men alive and now he writes only about you. If you knew a possible way to avert this terrible disaster, he would cooperate himself, for he is aware of his condition.

When he wrote me about you in the summer and I heard your voice, I felt a great longing for you. I was repeatedly seized by the passionate desire to write you and call you up. I did not do it. But I am writing now. You must come in October, or whenever you are able. Fearfully, he insisted that you would not be coming. And because I almost fear it myself when I see your indifference to his love, I'm writing you now. I beg you to tear up this letter at once. No document that gives access to Canetti's inmost being must be allowed to survive.

I don't pretend to be a saint, because I'm not one by any means. I am too tortured, too bad-tempered. Again and again, I struggle against all his weaknesses—noble weaknesses he simply cannot afford to have because he's poor in pocket and strength. Again and again, I've tormented him about all his weaknesses. Of course, it's our former dire straits that have made me so hard.

I'm asking you please to answer his letters at once. Please confirm receipt of this letter by adding in a footnote "Cordial greetings to Veza." You cannot write me directly until after Sept. 5, when we'll be back in Vienna, where I handle the mail. But there's little point. I need a doctor here, one who is extraordinarily smart and can work wonders.

Veza.

VEZA TO GEORGES · *August 18, 1937*

8/18

Beloved Georg,

Today, before my very eyes, the postman on the alp took my letter to you from the mailbox and handed me yours. And I had to let it go without softening its contents. I cannot weaken anything I said in it. Emboldened by your letter, I can only confess that I am enraptured at the prospect of seeing you again.

What you wrote is very wise and good and I would like to send the same back to you. When Elias wrote from Paris, describing how you looked, a wild tempest blew the ashes from my heart. But you have nothing to fear: they stuck relentlessly to my head.

I cannot revise anything in my letter about Canetti. I can only repeat that he is in more danger than I can put into words, that you were wrong to doubt it, that I love him as only a mother can love, but that I am at his service in every respect and without reservation—and that I am tortured by that service. It reminds me of the sacrifices you made for your mother. That's why I'm telling you about it, and even this comparison is presumptuous—you did more. And my hair stands on end at the thought that you aren't singing your own praises every single day for what *you* did. We are singing them.

I think of you constantly. And I know a thousand tricks to hide the fact from Murkl, for he clings to my skirt as he once did to his mother's and won't allow me—as he wouldn't allow her—to remarry. He even wants to armor-plate my dreams. And all day long, he gives me food for thought about how many possessions and how much energy, imagination, and time he is wasting. And yet I should be circumspect, like the hairdresser of the Empress Elisabeth. Woe to her if a hair fell from her head. Oh! I've torn many a hair from his head.

Look at my picture and you can see how tough I've become. And that's after the photographer, thinking I was a star, powdered away my wrinkles. But what can one do! I had to shout at the man who brings us our breakfast, "What? You can't even change a hundred schillings? Then be off with you!" so he wouldn't find out that we don't have a single schilling to our name. That's how tough I've become.

I am in *despair* to hear that you're rushing around like a bicycle racer! I will send a favorite book from Vienna. Hoepffner made me a present of it: *La Princesse de Clève* of Mme. de Lafayette.[120]

We're expecting Hoepffner in a week. And then we'll return to Vienna. If you intend to write me, then preferably not until we're back in Vienna. But I fear if you write you won't come. It would be best for you to acknowledge receipt of this letter with a postcard to us here. Saying that is a big concession for me, because although you write wonderfully, it's a wonder how infrequently you do it, and in that respect, you have nothing to complain about vis-à-vis Canetti.

You ask if Canetti is working. Beloved Georg, you don't know the extent of his derangement. I tremble to write about it. You must come!

Veza.

My letter is so banal compared to yours, but I wanted to answer quickly quickly.

Veza to Georges · *August 22 and 23, 1937*

8/22

A terrible thing has happened. If genius is "the ability to endure unending suffering,"[121] then I am a genius. Yesterday, Canetti suffered his first major psychotic episode. I was the catalyst, because I lost control of myself. It was about his wastefulness again, especially how he wastes his time with the dumbest, most inane girls. I tried to approach the problem pedagogically and <wanted to . . . Anna>[122] who has great admiration for him. It was the worst thing I could have done to him, but I told you, I'm no longer in control of myself. Indulging him means allowing him to squander himself completely. And that means complete disintegration. To know him is to drive him to madness. That is what I did yesterday.

At home, he began to laugh in a terrifying way. I was quite frightened, but he told us that's how *you* had laughed when your mother died, and so I thought it was just an attack of nerves and would pass. He asked for tea and I calmly handed him a cup. But he made me exchange it for my cup, because his was poisoned. I've been hearing this for 12 years so it made no impression, although I was horrified by the look on his face. I drank his poisoned tea and he lay down. His face was very red. And then he hallucinated that he was in an insane asylum: the musician L. was an attendant I had secretly hired; the beautician (one of those silly geese of his) was also an attendant; I myself was very very evil and had driven him mad three weeks ago (he shifted our scene back three weeks). This went on for an hour. I was so horrified that I started to shiver and called to him for help in my misery. Weeping in despair, he now declared that I had poisoned myself with the poison tea that had been meant for him. I turned ice cold, and he thought I was your dead mother. I don't know how I summoned the strength to make myself go into a feverish flush, so that he then quieted down. Then I spoke about Hoepffner and suddenly it all fell away from him and he became calm again. The attack had passed. Today we talked through everything that happened, for he is not confident that the attack won't recur. We will try and see if I can be his nurse. Implicitly, that's what I've been for a long time, but to be exhorted daily, hourly, to whisper in a soundproofed room (because everyone can hear), not to do or say certain things, to accept everything that is *destroying* him—I don't know if I will be able to do it. In that case, he intends to "treat himself," as he calls it. He thinks I am his misfortune. For he can't live without me and he can't live with me. I think he's right. I'm no longer the good, fine person I was. I am distraught, domineering, hard.

He strictly forbade me to write you. You would tell Nissim—who would gloat, for it would justify his previous bad behavior. I think he's right to fear that and I require you to remain silent as a tomb, just as I have done for years and years. I'm asking for your help. Since he won't go to a doctor and I can't bring one to him, can you tell me if there is some medicine I could give him when he feels an attack coming on? Write to me in Vienna and send the letter so it gets there by Sept. 5. Write *circumspectly* and tell *me* to keep it a secret. He won't see the letter, but just in case, I want you to exercise extreme caution and the greatest possible sensitivity in handling this noblest of men. Please tell me if you know of a book that describes this type of mania, and if it's curable. If it is (but I would have to see it in a book), then I'm ready to put up with anything. If it isn't, then there's only one thing left for me to do.

For I, too, live in a delirium. Isn't it delirium when for years and years, a celebrated and much-envied woman sees no other way out but suicide? I, who despite my age, despite looking like an old crone, despite my white hair, am wooed by the most important men? They're the ones who will tell you the best things about me. The women, of course, who only hear how I *economize*, how I *control*, how I keep Canetti "*prisoner*"—the women will tell you it's all my fault. That doesn't bother me at all, not at all, but if I were to tell you about my hellish life, you would not believe it. You would weep as I am weeping.

I'm asking you now for your advice as a doctor. If you come, he must not guess what I've told you. I want to gradually get him to tell you himself. Perhaps his extraordinary intellect and yours can help find the right thing to do. I could not survive his insanity. I am ready for an *immediate* separation if that would be good for him, but he assures me that he can't live without me and would be lost, "although you are so evil, such a bad person." Now he is quite despondent and so good, so good. He confessed to me that he only sought out this stupid circle of female acquaintances and only kept running off to Salzburg because he always has visions of his dead mother. He can hardly write a line without seeing her lying there dead and hearing *you* laugh. Please write me in Vienna, but I don't know if I'll ever see you, for if he has a new outbreak—helpless as I am—my own system will begin to function: eternal, longed-for peace. On Tuesday, an admirer of his from Prague may visit (the director of the Urania) and Hoepffner comes on Thursday. He will surely find that absorbing enough so that he'll recover. I hope so. I intend to keep everything secret as long as possible. He must *never* be sent to a mental institution. He must *never* be declared incompetent and assigned a legal guardian. And he must only be seen by a doctor if he is calm and does not know it is a doctor (unless you persuade him to go to one voluntarily).

Forgive me. But I have committed my life to protecting Canetti. I'm no genius in Carlyle's sense, for I *cannot* go on. *He* carries the whole world's suffering within himself. I myself believe that I am only doing him harm, for I have lost control. I am unrestrained, not always patient—short-tempered even—loud, nervous, peevish, tortured—I do him harm.

What should I do?

Veza

I implore you, keep this secret!

He says *himself* that his attack was very serious this time, because he even turned back the time of our quarrel. He fears a recurrence. If you do *not* hear from me, things have quieted down for now.

See over!

8/23/37

Dearest Georg,

There has not been another attack, but he is unfortunately very irritable and has a red face. Everything I say annoys him beyond measure. I am really very harmful to him, for I am too impatient to acquiesce gracefully. Hoepffner is coming on Thursday and looks forward to seeing us. If I am friendly to him, Canetti will get suspicious. If I'm indifferent, then we run the risk of losing our best friend and patron. Hoepffner thinks a lot of my writing and I fear he will say so. That could really irritate him in his present condition.

We have decided to leave the alp tomorrow and move down into the valley because the weather is so bad. Canetti asks you to wait until Sept. and send the money to Vienna, because we don't know what our address here will be. The postman will forward any letters to us. Write him! I live in great fear and worry. How quickly I had to destroy the beautiful image you have formed of me. Write me in Vienna and if there's any hope, let me hear about it! But don't lie! I need books!

I shall write again soon. You write as well and stay just as you are! It is so much!

Yours,
Veza

VEZA TO GEORGES · *September 15, 1937*

Sept. 15

Dear Georg,

Canetti seems to be the only patient to whom your famous conscientiousness doesn't apply. I've been waiting for your orders: what should I do if the blood rushes to his head? if he feels that terrible pressure that presages an attack? He had a third attack 2 weeks ago.

He collapsed on the street. Here in Grinzing, he feels better. I let him have his way in everything. His condition also depends on my behavior and condition.

By the way, he submits voluntarily to a certain routine and occasionally works. I don't like the look of his eyes. I know what's coming, but I hang on defiantly. I will not abandon this marvelous person. I hope I will still have the strength if I see him suffering. Recently he slept fifteen hours straight. Should I let him sleep so long? Please write 2 letters and put them into *one* envelope: one for him and one with rules for how I should behave. Even in the latter, be very careful to write of his "*melancholy*." Don't use any other word. I get the letters first, but I have to be very much on my guard, because I'm his only support.

It was an ordeal to keep all this hidden from Herr Hoepffner in Salzburg. He is one of the most charming old gentlemen under the sun and developed a crush on me. He made me a correspondent for his newspaper[123] and admires my work more than he does Canetti's. What a fate! Even Canetti's friends fail to recognize his genius! His brothers will get rich on his works, his nieces and nephews even more so, but he goes to rack and ruin because for two years he had to run from one pawnshop to the next and could never work in peace.

We were both so worried about you before your news arrived* and we're still worried that you have taken on such a huge burden of work. *And when are you coming to visit?* You don't have to fear seeing me tearful or weak. Life has made a heroine of me. News soon, please.

Your unhappy
Veza

He calls his condition paranoia.[124]

Please take care of yourself and don't drive too fast. *Promise me!!!!*

*Along with the 800 francs, for which Canetti thanks you very much.

VEZA TO GEORGES · *September 24, 1937*

Sept. 24, 37

Dearest Georg,

Your letter was somewhat reassuring, but it also reminded me strongly of the scene between Kien and Georg.[125] As a child, I lived with a paranoiac[126] who was institutionalized in Vienna for ten years. But just as I believe in the brother who is a genius, I believe in the one who is a doctor, and when you talk about yourself as "the likes of us," I see only the concealed pride with which you justifiably put yourself on a par with the artist. It is a coincidence that the two gods I acknowledge, the artist and the doctor, are brothers, and it could be a happy coincidence except that the arrival of the doctor has split my love.

As for the symptoms you won't acknowledge: why did the youthful Elias ten years ago refuse candy because it was poisoned? Back then, there were no external reasons why he should have attacks. Similar occurrences have become more and more frequent over the years. To be sure, as you so rightly say, they are related to his fate. How do you explain his tendency to tell outrageous lies? We have been through terrible things which I am certainly not going to describe to you, but why didn't he tell you about them instead of inventing an ailment I didn't have at all? I've had seven other operations[127] that were much harder on me psychologically. And in that condition, I had to ask a doctor for help who had been passionately pursuing me for a long time. And soon thereafter, I saw no other possibility for Canetti except to risk my life.

And why does he boast to you, but doesn't tell you that he's loved Anna for years, completely hopelessly and unhappily (her attraction to him soon vanished), and that I fueled his passion, for I too was enchanted by Anna, and I too loved you!

How would you treat his persecution complex? My paranoiac in Inzersdorf always made me listen to the diatribes against him on the radio. What do you say to his penchant for intrigue? Well, I'm not trying to talk you into anything and I'd be happy if you talked me out of things, for I believe in you alone and haven't consulted any local doctors.

You didn't write a word about coming to visit. I would love to take care of you when you have the flu, I would like to know about it if you don't look well, and I want to admire you and ask you a lot of questions, because your field of science is the only one that fires me up.

In case you're afraid of me—I'll only allow myself to kiss you when you have germs on your lips. Yet in spite of that, I wish you health!!

Your brilliant observation in Canetti's letter that the poor become suspicious when a doctor won't take their money is used by Broch in an unpublished novel.[128]

Your flu is nothing to trifle with; you should take it very seriously. Since you icily refuse to be my Benjamin, I will love you but not tell you about it. I'm actually happy that your cousin[129] is making too much fuss over you, but I'm also very *jealous.*

I have—written back so quickly only because I owe you a report: Canetti is feeling better. Every day he locks himself in a room with your mother's picture. As for my lack of concern, dear Georg, Canetti always had his attacks at times when I was suspicious and acting tough because I thought his symptoms were just playacting. I'm ashamed to admit it. Now I'm not going to write again for a long time, and if you don't come see us, I won't write at all.

With much unhappy love,
your
Veza

Please write me!
Keep in mind <*arrow to "unhappy"*>

He knows *nothing* about your letter to me!

ELIAS TO GEORG · *October 2, 1937*[130]

Vienna, October 2, 1937

My dear Georg,

It's such a strange feeling to be writing to you; it seems like a stupid, inept sham. I talk with you so often, about all sorts of things, and you always answer wisely and in your own way. And that is a real joy, for if we had to rely on our letters, we would both be in deep trouble. Writing is so superficial. It's as if someone would suddenly call to us and say we should draw up a contract for our relationship. That's how vapid and downright juridical our letters are compared to what's really going on between us. —Nevertheless, I think we must both *force* ourselves to write more often. It's better for our letters, too. The more that's in them, the sooner one can write them. Perhaps we'll get further than before if we have a definite *schedule*. I suggest we write each other every two weeks—so, twice a month. My next letter will be due in mid-October. First, however, about the 10th or 12th, I have to receive one from you. Let's really stick to that. In my current work, I see how much good it does me to follow a schedule. And you are the personification of orderliness, so it won't be difficult at all for you to carry this out once we've agreed on it.

I envy you your profession more and more. There's no doubt it's the only possible one to have. It allows you to live a particularly well-tempered life, equidistant from delusions of grandeur and defeatism. Only doctors live in "reality" all the time. What the mercenary creatures who completely dominate Paris think is "reality" is a totally fictitious entity with strongly paranoid features; money, the only building block of their system, recommends itself by its numerical certainty and symbolic comprehensibility. This is an inexhaustible topic. But for now, I'm only concerned with doctors. The atmosphere in which they live is the *most intense* because it's most endangered. They live continuously within death, that is, within the essential surrender of our humanity. Of necessity, they are constantly *failing*, which deprives them of grandiose words (one cannot imagine a good doctor becoming a dictator). They must make the attempt again and again, however, and even though *all* diseases have been classified and schematized beforehand (the great Achilles' heel of medicine, in my opinion)—each patient is still *new* for them. The doctor who is really a doctor *cannot* escape reality; the artist must do so much too often. His self-esteem is a dangerous and abhorrent affair from the first; there is nothing more arrogant and inhumane than an artist. The world makes them into oracles just as it makes doctors into miracle workers. If people don't succeed in inflating artists (who by nature are often meek and quiet) into celebrities, they just throw them onto the manure pile. In my case, my natural delusions of grandeur meet the world halfway. It's the one concession I was born with; otherwise, I make no concessions. It is to *this alone* I owe my success at such a young age. For who could have had such success through his *achievements*?! Artistic success! But I am sick of it, nauseated by it. I will only count it as success when I have struck a first decisive blow against death. If death is the enemy, one is even permitted to act like the Japanese.[131]

By the way, you never told me what kind of impression Metalnikov's book made on you. I'd like to hear what you have to say about it as a scientist. You absolutely must read Carrel's *L'homme cet inconnu*.[132] There are positively magnificent passages; its psychology is of course shallow, but otherwise the most exciting and thought-provoking book I've read in years. If you will not be able to come to Vienna before the end of October, please send me Levy-Brühl and the two volumes by Pierre Champion. Then you can have them back. Currently, I need anything that has to do with the history of medieval cities. I hope you haven't forgotten that you are to come to Vienna very soon. To be sure, you've already missed the most beautiful time of year: a heavenly September with almost French air. But October has its own charms: the grape harvest is in two weeks. Then Grinzing[133] will be even more attractive because you see more than just the drunks; you also see people working hard for their living. Give it serious consideration: wouldn't a little two-week getaway do you good in mind and body? Maybe you even *need* one. I certainly hope you haven't used up your vacation substituting for another doctor! That would be really irresponsible, Georg! Anyway, you can tell me in your next letter what you think about a vacation in Vienna. There would be *one* great advantage if you could come *before* October 20: on that day, Josef Blatt[134] will conduct Mahler's *Das Lied von der Erde* in the main auditorium of the Musikverein. I must tell you that on Thursday, he ventured his first concert in Vienna, this time in the Ehrbar-Saal, which has only 400 seats. On the program were Mozart, Janaček (the greatest Czech composer), a violin concerto of his own, and finally the Brahms Fourth. He exceeded all my expectations. He's a wonderful conductor, a powerful talent of the first order, sensitive and supple and intense, with an uncanny memory. He conducts everything by heart, even the most difficult modern things. Thanks to his interpretation, by the way, for the first time in my life even Brahms made a strong impression on me. It was an enormous success with both the audience and the critics. Renée's parents and the whole rest of her tribe are finally reassured about their daughter's "mésalliance" (he comes from a very poor family). And it took an eighty-pound load off my mind because I had gone so far out on a limb for him that a bad performance would have made me almost more laughable than him. And now his greatest undertaking will be on Oct. 20. The auditorium of the Musikverein seats 2,000 people. *Das Lied von der Erde* is an uncommonly difficult work. —What I see is only this: there is no such thing as believing in someone too intensely and passionately. Who knows? Perhaps one could impel *any* individual (to say nothing of such a great talent) to rare achievements. Basically, Mama's educational method was nothing more than that—in her case, it arose from her uncanny and almost violent pride. Dear, dear Georg, write to me in a week *at the latest*, as we have now agreed to do. I have saved a lot of important things for my next letter. See to it that you come to Vienna. It will do you good and will please us here immensely. Most cordial greetings from Veza.

I embrace you a hundred thousand times,

Elias.

VEZA TO GEORGES · *October 8, 1937*

Vienna, Oct. 8, 1937

Dearest Georg,

Today I'm also mailing you my favorite book in French. When Herr Hoepffner heard it was my favorite, he sent me this beautiful edition, but I'm happy to betray him by giving it away to you. If you should find that it is not your favorite book, then please bring it back to me when you come to Vienna. I'm terribly happy to give it to you and will be terribly happy to get it back again. In Vienna, you'll get more beautiful books from me, but I think I must have written this one here, *La princesse de Clève*, in a previous life.

I have good news to tell you about Canetti. He's been working peacefully in his beautiful room, which his admirers call Faust's chamber. He is very, very sad, but calm and serious. And I've even done him an injustice: I really did have the operation he told you about. He was babbling so many things this summer that I had the impression he was telling you things that weren't true, such as that I was sick; I'm quite well, of course. Which is not to say that he's a fanatic truth teller. He especially likes to lie to the two of us and then after a while, gets real pleasure from revealing to me all the outrageous fibs he's told. I need a good memory for his lies when I'm out in society.

Georg! I've put up five pounds of wild cherries for you, two pounds of quinces, and I bought real wildflower honey for your lungs. Canetti is childishly happy at the prospect of your visit and assures me and everyone else that of the three of you, you're the most distinguished, but you'll be the last to become famous "because you're so exacting." He wrote you recently, and since you are my Benjamin, I'm writing you today. Will it be bad for you if our hall is cold? Could you catch a chill there? I can install a heater. Please, a telegram with your arrival date, and read my book right away.

Affectionately,
Veza

How *are* you??

Veza to Georges · *October 15, 1937*

Oct. 15

Dearest Docteur Canetti (this in anticipation of your future fame),

We have received your disappointing letter. (letter!) Right away, I looked to see if there were a hug in it for me. There was one, but now I have to make do with this paper embrace until Christmas. If you don't come then, however, I will have an insatiable yearning for my brother and will come to him in Paris. Hear it and tremble!

We thank you very much for the thousand francs. I have learned that you're loaning them to us on my account. This pains me, so I hereby declare that I would take money from anyone at all for Canetti, except from you. Because you are not completely healthy and we will not let you work for us. Never! You will take back the money or I will be forced to hate myself and become distraught. You will also get back the sum we owe you from much earlier.

Because you are my Benjamin.

Canetti's Czech agent forced him to give her your address; unfortunately, I was telling her about you. She will call you, but you should feel free to tell her you're too busy. Canetti has *no* interest in you meeting her. She's nice enough, but uninteresting and not pretty.

I write you letter after letter. For although you're rude and thoughtless, you are charming. And then, you are my favorite son. If you don't come for a long time, however, you'll be my grandson. And that doesn't sit well with me.

Canetti works and suffers bouts of deep depression. And if you were right, you're a god.

Go ahead and become thin and pale, breathe poor air, go to bed late, don't eat regularly, save the lives of people who aren't worth your little toe, but I'm telling you: I'll disown you!

Veza

What about *La princesse de Clève*?

VEZA TO GEORGES · *Postmarked October 29, 1937*

Dr. Georg Canetti
rue Nungesser et Coli N° 24
Paris 16e

Thurs.

Dearest Georg,

Renée Blatt and her talented spouse arrive in Paris on Sunday evening and will call you as soon as they do. Will you please let us know where you can be found (they will call Nissim's), because the two of them are embarking for NY, as early as Tuesday, I think. They are supposed to give us a report about the things you won't tell us, e.g., how you look and how you're feeling. They are both very nice and very happy he had two big concerts here that were a great success. We also need a *letter* from you that they will tell you about. I'm writing this in a hurry on the streetcar. You've forgotten about me—my imminent renown will put you to shame.

Veza

VEZA TO GEORGES · *November 29, 1937*

Nov. 29

Sweet Georg,

Now you've made a discovery, on top of everything else![135] If only you weren't so handsome! And your voice alone would be enough! I'm so afraid of you, that is, of myself, that for my protection I've ordered the Baroness Birgitte Eleonore von Klenau[136] to come to Vienna for you. You can read it for yourself. She's as svelte as I am fat and as young as I am old, and she's pretty as a picture and elegant to boot. It requires much self-denial from me to allow her to come—20 years old and 40 pounds thinner than me. But you are my Benjamin.

Don't labor too much over your discovery. I swear you'll get the Nobel Prize someday. I swear that you're the only person I respect in the whole world, because you've achieved something real.

We had a good laugh at Blatt's "catastrophic" exterior. We orchestrated him, stage-managed him, etc. I intended to write you at once, for although you turn a cold shoulder to me, I send you a warm heart—and you should know that we worry about you every day—but that Canetti fellow wanted to write—he intends to, he will, he promises. He is better, but he tyrannizes me beyond human endurance. I'm not even allowed to go up to the editorial offices of my newspaper[137] because there's a young manager who's a bit of an admirer, despite my being 40 pounds overweight. I weigh 155 pounds and look 45. I still have some scrap of charm left—but what did Kirkegaard say—"Spice is the last thing to go." So, now at least you won't be too startled when you see me. My aunt wrote about a photo I had sent her, "Look at you, so fat and ugly. You look thirty years older than you are. What's happened to you? You're not my beautiful Veza anymore."

Nevertheless, I'm not allowed to go up to the editorial offices, and yet I only go because they treat me like a writer, with respect and courtesy, and I'm already trembling to think what will happen when I put a large piece of cake on your plate, because you're so delicate (but not skinny, thank God, just a little pale, according to reports).

We confirm prompt receipt of the money and thank you for it. There now. And now you'll keep right on not writing us. But just wait, Canetti is very famous and it will get into his biography. Yesterday there was a discussion of his book on the radio. Physically he's *somewhat* better, but he torments me a lot.

Much love, Georg Canetti!
Veza

There's a cow in our yard and fresh eggs.

Elias to Georges · *December 27, 1937*[138]

Vienna, December 27, 1937

Dear Georg,

Christmas is over now. I had still hoped that your last letter was a joke and you would suddenly come walking up our hill on Christmas Eve (like that time at the Yalta).[139] We had everything ready for you. Our apartment has quite a large number of empty rooms and we keep a very pretty one nicely furnished and reserved for you "at your option." We stayed home on Christmas Eve. Not one of the approximately 365 invitations could tempt us away: you would surely be arriving on the night train. It was curious how Veza shared my anticipation without us having really discussed it. I'll dispense with a detailed description of her disappointment. We certainly no longer expect that you still might come. That's why I'm writing now, to let you know once and for all that your behavior is abominable. You allow yourself things I wouldn't forgive anyone else but you. As far as I'm concerned, it's not so important; I'm already used to your attitude that swings between the greatest tenderness and extreme unkindness.

As much as it wounds me every time, it has become part of our relationship. Perhaps it's a compensation for the many things about me you don't like. But the way you treat Veza is utterly *impossible*, positively *criminal*. There are very few people whom Veza really likes; she's actually quite conservative in her feelings (just as you are yourself), but the few people she loves, she really loves—loves them like a mother, so your behavior is simply killing her. Last summer, by mutual agreement, we already caused her great disappointment. For four months now, she's been living for this Christmas, making preparations, getting the apartment ready, getting me ready, and suddenly you let the whole plan drop without so much as a by-your-leave. You can gauge how utterly impossible it seemed to us that you would not come by the fact that we didn't take your last letter seriously, not even for a moment. We were completely convinced that you were having us on and were going to surprise us.

Now Veza is very unhappy, depressed, and in despair. She thinks that you're just making a fool of her and have no intention of ever coming to Vienna. You know the dangers of her melancholy disposition. Any new blow can reawaken her old craving to commit suicide. Since Christmas, she's suddenly begun to repeat that she's a catastrophe for me; that because of her, I'm destitute; that your behavior shows that you agree; that she must finally surrender her place to a rich young woman—in short, this is a train of thought I've heard for years and which always presages her melancholy attempts at suicide. In order to cut it short in time, you must do the following *at once*: write that you were not at all satisfied with your holiday. You would much rather have been with us. You didn't want to frighten us and that's why you didn't write to say that your holiday visit to St. Hilaire was *on your doctor's orders*. You were unfortunately a little overworked, but now you will certainly be more careful and will spend an entire month convalescing with us at Easter time. Georg, please, do it right away and just as I said. Your lungs are the only argument she can believe now, and she'll be too worried to bear you a grudge. She doesn't know I'm writing this letter to you. Pretend you haven't heard from me this whole time. If possible, make money the ostensible reason for your letter. If not, you have to invent some other reason. Best would be something you need (a book? a letter? a recommendation? a piece of information? You'll think of something). In any event, it has to happen *right away*, before her melancholy has time to spread. Then once you've complained about me not writing, you will receive an official letter from me.

So please, don't put off writing. You don't know Veza and you have no idea the extent of the danger all this can cause.

Affectionately,
Elias

VEZA TO GEORGES · *January 5, 1938*

January 5

Dear Benjamin,

Your letter was a sham from *A* to *Y*. The only thing I believed was *Z*, about the Princesse de Clève, and I read that passage of your letter again and again. Since you are my son, I am just glad you are well, and you should stay healthy and feel well even if I am never permitted to see you again. I would very much like to watch over you in place of your dear mother, and I do so even from afar. Sometimes I have one of those beautiful visions of your mother and I could scream that she is no longer alive.

Canetti had *another* disappointment around Christmastime, and I'll tell you about it later. He grew increasingly quiet and sad and his eyes glazed over. An American publisher[140] asked for a copy of *Die Blendung*. He wrapped one up and I gave him the accompanying letter to sign. He starts to sign it and suddenly says, "I've forgotten my name." I calmly reply, "Go to my bookcase, take down your book, and read the name." He really does so and copies the name. Then he's completely normal again. That evening, he comes home and starts to work. At 4:30 a.m., I hear these terrifying words: "Elias, prophet: burglars!" Canetti is on the telephone with the police emergency response squad. I jump out of bed and try to wrestle the telephone from him. Too late. He hangs up and rushes wild-eyed into his room. He listens at the door where he hears the burglars. I see immediately what's going on: there's nothing to hear. I plead with him to tell me why he did that. He says, "Say nothing more or I shall collapse." So at 4:30 a.m., scared to death, I have to make a plan with him and discuss what we're going to tell the police so they won't become suspicious. The police arrive, seven men strong, with rifles slung over their shoulders. They search the apartment, the garden, the entire building. Canetti is mortified, but bravely keeps up appearances, and the policemen tell him straight out he was imagining things, a case of nerves. This incident could have turned out very badly if I hadn't claimed to have heard the burglars as well.

Please keep this letter with my others. I'm incapable of writing all this down again, and I shall need it someday. I have to believe what I see, and I see a terrifying change in Canetti's eyes. I see the flush at his temples, his testiness when an attack is imminent, and the attacks recur periodically. I talked everything over with him afterward, and he himself thinks it is a paranoia he can *combat*, but that's exactly what I doubt. Canetti would never have called the police if he was in his right mind. Not even if there was a murderer in the house.

It was before Christmas. He was feeling much better, working on his novel,[141] when a letter arrived just after you'd told us you wouldn't be coming. It was from the Blatts in N.Y., declining in the most polite way to send him the monthly sum of money they had led him to expect. Those Blatts, who only exist thanks to us (he owes every word of his good reviews to Canetti's influence. In fact, it's thanks to us they're still alive), are now leaving him in the lurch. So he had to interrupt his magnificent work and be grateful that a Bulgarian writer brought him a bad novel to proofread. The work cost him a month's time and much more than that psychologically, and the pay is laughable. And if we didn't have you, we would now be at our wits' end.

So that's how I spent Christmas, I who would like to live in the atmosphere of the Princesse de Clève. And I won't even describe to you the other details of how I live. Sometimes I think I will cast everything off and flee from Canetti, from all the Canettis, including Benjamin Canetti. I hope you can see nothing else to worry about in Canetti. But if that is not the case, then I don't know how I can communicate with you *on this topic*. For you can't write to me here. He's taken possession of the key to the mailbox and watches over me like Othello. But if you think it necessary to consult a doctor or wish to advise me yourself, then add the footnote "Happy New Year" to your next letter and I will give you the address of a friend of mine, a woman to whom you can write about his condition. I would not be so frightened if he hadn't had such a completely feebleminded expression on his face for minutes on end during his previous attacks, contorting his face and babbling. I ask you again to save this letter. Why did you betray me to Canetti, that arch-traitor, plotter, and liar par excellence?

I'll send you the Lichtenberg. Such serious reading material so late at night? Your mother really had wonderful children!

Veza

Paint a white raven[142] black, because what good is a white raven?

Our address is Vienna XIX, Himmel Str. 30.

ELIAS TO GEORGES · *January 21 and 31, 1938*[143]

My dear Georg,

You've earned this letter on your birthday,[144] so much so that I'm no longer angry with you for your failure to come at Christmastime. Because your letter to Veza came really quickly and was very charming. And you even made very original use of the opportunity to take a swipe at me. I'm just happy to know you already have a Lichtenberg, so I can keep mine. Officially, in front of Veza, I mailed it off; actually, it's well hidden in my library. Or are you carrying this successful playacting to such extremes that you really want the Lichtenberg? —In any event, Veza is reassured. Her concern about your condition, which has turned out not to be so dangerous after all, has blown away all her anger and disappointment. That's how easily a person can be turned inside out. Now she's looking forward to Easter, as if you hadn't already disappointed us 64 times, and I, the initiator of this whole well-meaning farce, I'm looking forward to it as well.

January 31

My dear Georg,

This birthday letter I began for you has been lying here for ten days now. For inexplicable reasons, it didn't get finished. I'm sending you its brief beginning so you can at least see my good intentions. Don't think I want to get out of sending you a birthday present. I only want to force you to pick it up in Vienna. Here you will find a library that, although for my purposes small, is select. You can take anything you want from it that strikes your fancy. For now, there's only one thing I ask of you: keep a list of books you want, keep adding to it, and when it's a mile long, then there will be nothing for it but to come to Vienna. You may also think up lists of other things you need so that you have time to get used to the notion that you're going to spend four weeks in Vienna at Easter time. Don't forget that you will be able to work here as nowhere else, in complete quiet. Once you have the material for your thesis[145] halfway collected, you can get down to the actual writing here. With this goal in mind, you will have to take a proper vacation sometime soon in any case. For I can't imagine how you can begin work on a thesis of such scope in addition to all the practical, everyday work you must perform in Paris. Perhaps you can take an even longer vacation for precisely this purpose.

The very best thing would be if you could be in Vienna by March 3, when the Werkbund has invited me to give a big public lecture on the topic "Saving the Theater" (or the title may be The Apparent Death of the Theater).[146] It is a great honor for many reasons. You should know that the Werkbund is actually an association of modern architects in Vienna, but they also have people such as the painter Oskar Kokoschka[147] and the art historian Tietze[148] on their board. The Werkbund has a glorious avant-garde tradition. A few years ago, there was a schism: the reactionary members (anti-Semites, nativists) who had been infected by the new political currents resigned and almost everyone else in Vienna who tries to maintain freedom of thought stayed together in the "Old Werkbund": all the Leftists and all the independents, too, who don't subscribe to any political program. Last year, Robert Musil gave a lecture "On Stupidity." You can imagine how many idiots attended, all elevated far above the stupidity of others. The title and topic of my lecture are of course not anywhere near as big an attraction, but will be more programmatic. It's beginning to get around that there is a dramatist by the name of Canetti, even though no one performs his work.—How nice it would be if you could be here! But perhaps you'll be able to read the lecture in printed form; a very interesting writer on philosophical and sociological topics named Erich Kahler[149] (a large work of his entitled *On the German Character in European History* has just been published) has invited me to be a correspondent for the journal *Mass und Wert*,[150] which Thomas Mann publishes in Zurich. I agreed, on the condition that they publish longer, complete pieces of mine (e.g., a lecture like this one), but that I will not write specifically for the journal. In a word: I would like to be able to speak in the journal without having to make any concessions, and it looks like they will agree to this stipulation.

Ah, Georg! I had so many things planned! So many new and revolutionary ideas have come to me during these months, mostly in connection with my novel—among other things a "Treatise on

Shadows."[151] (You have no idea how many psychological and aesthetic problems allow of a solution via a thoroughgoing meditation on shadows, especially their *mutability* in the course of a day.) Then a new hypothesis about the source of musical rhythm[152] that will especially delight you as a physiologist. Further, an attempt to lead anthropology out of the fruitless dead end of racial theory and put it onto a firm scientific footing—a solution of striking simplicity, by the way, that makes me laugh every time I think about it. And so many, many other things! It has also become clear to me during these months that I will end up with persecution mania, and that the time remaining to me for my work is limited. It is precisely this time, however, already standing in the grim shadow of my end, that *must be used*. I can see my powers of synthesis growing bolder and stronger the closer I know the final syndrome to be, from which there will be no more escape. And in this brief grace period, I am forced to suffocate under external worries. Jo[153] was here. You've probably spoken to him already. He said that there was still no prospect of getting our money from Aunt Rachel.[154] She would have to sell her orange groves at a loss to pay off her debts. Of course, I don't want to put pressure on her to do that just for our sake. But couldn't Nissim suggest that she send small monthly stipends of 20 pounds? That would at least help me over the worst months, until a good buyer for her orange groves can be found. Jo gave all sorts of excuses why he couldn't advance me any larger sums from the estate. But he is willing to send me 1,000 francs a month for the next three months if necessary. Together with your 1,000 francs (which I didn't mention to him), at least ⅔ of our monthly budget would be covered. As it has up to now, the balance must remain a debt that gets harder and harder to carry. Enclosed, a letter to Jo, which you should send to his office *right away*. I'm not sure if the address is correct. Please be so good as to send your 1,000 francs immediately if at all possible. For we can't even pay the rent at the moment and I fear that Jo will not be as punctual as necessary in keeping his promise. Forgive this awful money business, but there's no avoiding it.

Most affectionate hugs from
Elias.

Veza to Georges · *February 12, 1938*

2/12

Dear Sir Georg,

Your letter arrived today as if from heaven. We thought you were sick, unable to write, pale, coughing, with circles under your eyes, fever—it was terrible. I decided right away not to outlive you. Yes, it's serious.

Because three days ago, I had a beautiful dream about you.

Well, your note is unpleasant. It tortures us to think of how overworked you are. You're destroying us!

Won't you please confirm receipt of Canetti's letter? He sent it to you ten days ago. He enclosed a letter to his Uncle Joe because he doesn't know his address. He was in a fever waiting for an answer. None came.

I have good things to report about him. For one thing, Thomas Mann had the journal *Mass und Wert* ask him to be a contributor. They pay about ten schillings per page, and since an essay of Canetti's is at least thirty pages, and he writes wonderful essays, this is welcome news. It heartened him so much that he has grown *stingy with his time and tight with his money*—you wouldn't believe it—and is completely transformed, although still very sad. He's been invited to give a lecture on "drama" at the Werkbund on March 3. This essay will probably be immediately submitted to *Mass und Wert*.

I just reread *Madame Bovary*. Oh, it's so beautiful! I also love

Minuit by Julien Green very much, and *Eugenie Grandet* by Balzac is my favorite book.

So, now *please don't leave us guessing* whether the two letters arrived safely and whether you forwarded the one to Uncle Joe (Uncle Joe and Canetti had talked about Canetti writing him if things got desperate. It's just that Canetti couldn't find his address). Just send us two lines about it, please. It's important.

Your *enemy*,[155]
my handsome enemy.
Veza

We live in Vienna XIX, damn it!

VEZA TO GEORGES · *March 2, 1938*

3/2

Dear Enemy,

We were both very happy with your letter. You probably think it's because you're such a sweet fellow and we needed a little happiness so badly. But you won't be so happy to learn that we're taking you at your word! At Easter time we'll both be here and expecting you! We won't let you escape! Of course, Canetti will have to do some business traveling, but business in Austria is conducted with that cozy lack of hurry that's so calming to one's nerves. One has plenty of time. One has to think things over. One isn't even close to packing one's bags yet. Especially not me. I don't like to travel.

Seeing you would be so beautiful, it scares me.

Canetti will courageously give his lecture, even though, as you know, he is not a good speaker. It was postponed until the 17th; he hadn't finished it yet.

I would love to read what you've been writing. And when I think of you and look at the Canetti who's here, or even when I think of the two of you, I am filled with bitter sorrow that your mother can't be here to see you. Most of the time, I'd prefer to be under the ground, but the two of you are magnificent. And she can no longer see you. I almost don't deserve it. I can't do anything for you. She did so much merely by being alive.

Your uncle has kept his word, although tardily, and has also promised to do the same this month. He's a somewhat unsteady character, however, but not like Hamlet was. Very nice, but somewhat of a buffoon, the one people laugh at.

Thank you very much for going to the movies. It's therapy. It's more than that. The only thing that worries me in your case is that people in France smoke in the movies. That's not good for your health.

Please let me know if I should have the cow in our yard examined by a veterinarian so you can drink milk warm from the cow.

It's a good thing I know what a treacherous enemy you are. Otherwise, I would sit right down and write you a love letter at the address of that Italian girlfriend. But I am shrewd, and besides, *you're* the one I hate, not her. I imagine it must be Ruth, but since she gave me a different address, we can't figure it out.

We've had an exciting time here because we're Jews, and it looked as though Hitler would "lay his heavy hand on Austria," as the newspapers put it. You must have read about it as well. We very much fear it, and think it's only a matter of time. We have a good chancellor,[156] but it's well known that those madmen have enormous power.

Canetti says he sent you the volume of Lichtenberg.[157] I should have been more suspicious, for does he ever actually do what he says? But there is a space on his bookshelf where it used to be.

I can't stand Chamberlain.[158]

Many thanks from both of us for your dear little letter. Canetti will probably go to Switzerland first, since Thomas Mann is there and he will really get him launched. Mann's best friend, Herr Kahler (who just wrote a hugely learned book about Germany), is crazy about him. About Canetti, that is. But that's still a long way off, because now we have it in writing that you're coming!

Here in Grinzing, we live in the land of milk and honey. And they don't like Hitler here, either, because of the tourist business. In Grinzing, they call Seis-Inquart Scheiss-Inquart.[159] I'm writing to you because you are so svelte, fine, distinguished, elegant, fragrant, well-groomed, soigné, sensitive, slim, aristocratic, and pallid. Ah, that will make you lose your composure!

With love,
Veza

I'll send the Lichtenberg again.

VEZA TO GEORGES · *Postmarked March 31, 1938*[160]

Dr. Georg Canetti
24, rue Nungesser et Coli
Paris 16e

3/31

Dearest Georg,

I was overjoyed when I saw your dear handwriting on the envelope today. Because the first thing that always occurs to us is that you're sick; you're lying in bed instead of going from bed to bed in your white lab coat. Sweet Georg, I dream of you every night, and last night, I dreamed you were finally, finally coming. I was on my way to the station to pick you up when I woke up. Ah, why did I have to wake up? You must know that we've heard almost nothing from you for a month. Once, 320 francs were sent from Paris, but no letter or any other kind of mailing. Unfortunately, you've got our address wrong. It's XIX, Himmel*strasse* 30. The poetic "Am Himmel 30" is wrong.[161] Take note: Vienna XIX, *not* XVIII. Please pass this on to Uncle Joe and the others. Write the address correctly, for we are in desperate need of letters. Our telephone number is B 16-2-59, but you should not call me up. I'm so agitated when I only have 3 minutes to talk, and when I hear your voice, I'm seized with such desperation and longing that I'd rather not talk unless you have some real scoop, such as that you've won the lottery jackpot. In four days you're going to get a gigantic long letter from me. I can't write it until Sunday, for that's my day off. Professor Moll[162] was just here, a famous painter and nationalist. He wanted to prove to us that he has great respect for respectable Jews.

All the love in the world,
Veza

VEZA TO GEORGES · *MARCH 31, 1938*

3/31

Dearest Giorgio,

Forgive me for writing in pencil, but it's the only way I can quickly conceal the letter in my ample bosom when I hear the approaching footsteps of my spouse, who must not get hold of this love letter. Well, if my respectable brother in Surrey[163] knew that I was writing you love letters, he would be shocked to the depths of his pure, good soul, for he has character. He speaks five languages, would have liked to be an engineer, dreams of a gigantic park where elephants, polar bears, gazelles (like you), hedgehogs, and piglets amble peacefully about and eat from his hand. He would like to cultivate the park himself and would only allow his little son to watch from time to time. But if the boy dared to plant so much as a violet by himself, he would fight with him. That's my little brother, a shopkeeper in Surrey. It has often heightened my prestige to be able to say that my brother is a shopkeeper in Surrey. I wonder if people expected a cavalier, a person who only thinks noble thoughts and is completely amazed and horrified that there are other kinds of thoughts, too. His little son, my nephew and my pride and joy, is a big, blond boy, half Aryan. Perhaps this word surprises you, but here, people are classified as

Aryan, half-Aryans?, Aryans?, Aryans, dogs, and Jews. The Humane Society looks after the dogs. So you can imagine, how happy we are to get letters from you or from my little brother and to see that you're worrying about us. No, you can't imagine it until you've experienced it for yourself. Please, sweet Giorgio, don't grieve me by doctoring up a storm and making *yourself* sick! You have made great discoveries and you have great achievements ahead of you. Save yourself for this greatness (and for your little mother in Vienna) and above all, remember: the people whose lives you are now saving by risking the flower of your youth will later throw stones at you!! This the fruit of my own proud experience. For I'd rather break than bend. I'm breaking all day long.

We received your letter with the notification of a pleasant visitor *today*. I hope it isn't the same one who got in touch with us *yesterday* on the recommendation of your brother. He was very unpleasant and made stupid suggestions to Hatschu.[164] Hatschu was very reserved; he didn't like the little shmuck.

You've developed a labyrinthine style. Please get out of the habit again and write simply. Because people are very suspicious of stilted writing. Every letter arrives with the stamp "Opened by customs"! We gather from that that someone in Paris sent us money, and certainly also our dear friend in Strasbourg,[165] money that we didn't receive, however. Please send money *only* in the prescribed way, including marks. I don't know what is permitted, for we're not allowed to sit in the streetcar if an Aryan is standing. We had some money here from Bucka,[166] but it was "requisitioned." For such are the methods of the Bolsheviks here. They exploit the upheaval to go "requisitioning" in Jewish homes. If one is able to call the police, they intervene immediately and fairly, but the telephone lines have usually been cut. I've always hated the Bolsheviks.

People out here—and this is the truth—behave charmingly to us and bow deeply to us. My brother would be happy to learn that I inherited something good from my mother, namely, the gift of commanding respect. All hatred melts away before me and people love me dearly. Of course, no one is safe from slander.

My little brother, the shopkeeper in Surrey who doesn't even have time to breathe, is racking his brains and his legs for us. First, he wrote comforting words, and I won't ever forget that. He always writes very clearly and it's better that way, for no one would expect lepers to feel good on a desert island. One can go ahead and admit that one would like to get away. I did *not* write to my friend, the attendant with the beautiful name, because I don't have the time to.

We need money. Just enough for the next few weeks and a possible holiday trip. We have seven serious invitations, mostly from Aryans. Oh, if only you would come see us! Can I wish for that? No!! For our landlady is about to evict us, now that she's getting renters who will pay more. That, in addition to all our other guesswork. We don't know what to do, what to think, what to write.

From a social point of view, much is being done for the workers here. The German soldiers are nice: if they see a crowd taunting an old Jew who has to wash the street, they break up the crowd. Again, I want to emphasize that we were *not politically active in any way*. We didn't even allow ourselves to *think*. Scotland Yard has nothing on us. But one is never safe from malicious slanderers, and that's what we fear. Where there's much light there's also much shadow.

People here are terribly angry that in other countries, voices are raised and demonstrations organized for the downtrodden, the crushed, the humiliated. That's why one must proceed politely when intervening, because otherwise it does more harm than good.

If you have sent money other than the 320 francs, see if you can expedite it, because we haven't received *anything*. And let me know about it, too. And let me know, too, if letters have gone astray: we haven't heard from anyone in France since your last note (*one* line long). *Our* letters abroad also usually arrive opened.

That aunt of yours[167] is a good person but a congenital fool. We can't discuss anything with her because in her good-heartedness, she gets everything mixed up and gossips about it and that does us more harm than good. There's not much sense turning to her. Here there are demagogue-sniffers, agents provocateurs, S.A., S.S., S.C., S.D., the entire alphabet. There are all sorts of colors, too: first red, then black, then brown.[168] Many people are iridescently tricolored. Even Goering has an upset stomach from all the denunciations. He spoke about it very humanely.

The only consolation for us Jews is the sentence we heard someone say: they're not allowed to kill us. The Führer alone reigns over life and death. If that isn't balm in Gilead![169] —Oh, I won't call you *du*.[170] That will cost you ten kisses. Anytime I want them. Good thing my brother doesn't read anything.

Please acknowledge this letter at once.
Don't refer to anything in it.
I feverishly await your answer.

Veza to Georges · *1938*

Dearest Georg,

A day *before* your letter arrived a gentleman called up who claimed to be a friend of your brother N. At first, we were delighted, for we are now very much alone. Everyone has left and someone from abroad is a welcome event. But when Murkl met him, this person acted like such a boor that Murkl got the impression he was some fan trying to meet a "star," as often happens. He didn't know you at all and didn't even know that your brother is married. So Murkl acted very reserved and dismissive and had the worst possible opinion of the gentleman.

The next day, of course, your letter arrived and then we were sorry that Murkl had been so gruff. We were just about in despair, although what you say in your letter doesn't fit at all with the description of this man. He was not at all nice and well educated, but a real boor. It was quite distressing. If you're going to send us a sympathetic person, why don't you give us enough advanced notice? Why do you write so seldom, anyway? Why do you treat complete strangers and neglect us? Because we're Jewish? That's the worst illness of all.

Please *do not send us any money. No one should send us money.* By the way, they renewed my passport, but it does me *no good* because I need confirmation from the tax office if I want to travel. People all over the world are inviting us to come, disguising it in obscure mystifications. What's the point? The papers are full of the news that they want the Jews gone. Who can blame us if we want to oblige?

Of course you can feel free to come for a visit. But it's not possible, first of all because it would be too beautiful for me and beauty is not my lot, and second we have nothing, nothing to offer. All the big names have either left or are doing time. I'm talking about Jews. What would you do here? Our garden is wonderful, but that's all.

Murkl says he's known me now for 14 years and he's awfully tired of me. He says he's going to foist me off on you without your noticing it. He wants to get rid of me. He says you have a lot of sympathy for old women and he can con you into taking me. You'll think he's doing you a favor, that's how sly he'll be. Will you really take me? I don't cost anything at all. I make a good nut cake, slatko,[171] ham and noodles, vanilla cookies, brown eggs, linzer torte, and muesli.* I'm not asking for a salary, just a movie once a week. If you'll sit next to me, the film doesn't even have to be running.

My little brother is sure to show you my letter if he comes to P.

And now, clear everything up for me and write more often and love me some, you brute, and don't get more and more pallid, and don't make the sick well, it's not worth it.

Nothing is worth it. If I don't see you for an eternity, nothing is worth anything. And God knows how disappointed I'll be when I do see you. (Sour grapes!)

Türmchen[172]

*I'm a good typist too. I can type your research papers—5 copies. On my little machine.

VEZA TO GEORGES · *April 11, 1938*

4/11

Madame,

Ayez l'obligence de passer cette lettre le plus tôt possible au Docteur. Merci bien.[173]

Dear Nephew,

Your letter made me very happy and scared me at the same time. I'm afraid that you will cause me great expense with the anthology. I'm prepared to sacrifice up to 500 marks, but only if I *can pay them from here*, for I cannot incur any debts, dear Nephew. I am old, and it's difficult to get ahead. So I definitely want to pay from here, because I'm not permitted to take anything along, and where am I supposed to get the money to pay you? So please don't run up too many expenses, and above all, see to it that *my photograph is definitely in with the other things*,[174] otherwise there's no point in the whole business. Don't forget: I have to be in with the other things! (I'm not going to sacrifice for nothing.)

As for my trip, I have mixed feelings about it. By the way, I see that you took my joke seriously and really believe I would put up at your house. But I won't. For even if a proud old aristocratic tree like me must leave the palace of my fathers, I cannot accept charity. I shall only pass through on the way to one of my ancestral estates. I have enough invitations, for in one respect (but only one) the aristocracy and the Jews are alike—they stick together.

Very nice of you to ask if I need money. I need no money, but I don't want any debts, either. I'll cover all the travel expenses myself. As I said, the only thing I need is the *documentation* of my racial purity. I'm racking my brains about the right way to do it: I'm accustomed to a soft bed—all wool blankets and down pillows—and would like to take with me at least mattresses, bed linens, and tableware, so I don't have to put a stranger's spoon into my mouth or cover myself with a stranger's blanket. One may have to give up many things, but must remain true to oneself. What do you advise? But please don't mention this letter. Your aunt is very fearful and doesn't want me to write you openly. I don't know what it is I have to hide, but old people are simply childish unless they're from the same sturdy stock as your uncle. Give me your point of view about all my questions, and right away, so I know you understand me well and don't despise me, for that would grieve me. Advise me: should I take along some of my possessions? Or do you think they won't be considerate of an old gentleman? I beg you again not to act young and hot-blooded, and don't cause me any expenses, or if you can't avoid them, I want to settle them up here, for our motto is: Keep your table clean.[175]

Although I'm an aristocrat, I have not been mistreated here in any way. There's real law and order and everything they report in your newspapers is a lie. Things are done for the people and the people have things to talk about. It's been going on like this for quite some time. I want to leave the country only in amicable agreement with the authorities, not precipitously. For that can only be harmful when one wants to return to one's beloved fatherland. And I'd like the chance to see the Belvedère[176] once more before I die. Nothing must be rushed, although as an old man, I'm more than a little frightened, even though I act composed in front of your aunt. But I'm really frightened all the time. Always frightened. Once I'm gone, the fear will be over and my yearning for the fatherland will remain. But what can one do? *You do not need to worry* about my getting away from here. *I will* not *be living in dependency for long. I have connections in high places and have my wits about me.*

You inherited that from me and I'm really proud of you. Yes, you will achieve great things for science. I have no desire to desecrate it by the meditations of my old brain. I shall read and be astonished.

Now please answer all my questions and put my mind at ease on all counts. Your friend here can't do anything with her maid's pass.[177] Your brother will have to have someone compose a waltz. Thus one always returns to the old melodies and in art they are achieving outstanding things here. Enclosed, an example of genuine poetry.[178] A great poet here at present.

So have no fear, dear Nephew, that I might really come to stay with you. That was only a joke. I have 7 invitations. I'll only come to you for a few days. Should I put up in a hotel? What do you recommend? Please answer soon—no, at once, but as if I hadn't written.

Uncle Bodo.

Forgive the handwriting. *Tel maitre tel valet.*[179]

Many thanks for your efforts and counsels and hopefully you won't make fun of your old uncle and make Count Bobby jokes[180] about his letters. Again, many thanks. I was really happy that the man was not a relative of ours, for they are cut from a different cloth. Stay well, and it's good to have wonderful work but overwork is poison.

What pain to leave here and what fear to remain.

Addendum

One more important thing: some people could get in touch with you and misuse my good name to say that I have debts and you should pay them. That is not true, so do nothing of the kind. If you see Aunt Bucka, do not return the favor, for her gift was shabby and I will return an equally shabby favor (pay her back in kind) *right here*. Please do just as I say: no paying for me. My name is being shamefully misused.

It's terrible work getting the documentation from all 4 grandparents together. I spent a whole week at the parish office.

Veza to Georges · *April (?) 13, 1938*

<4>/13[181]

Dearest Georg,

I must emphatically repeat that you absolutely have to include a photo of me in the review, otherwise it's of no benefit to Murkl. He doesn't want me to wait, and it won't work the way I thought.[182]

Dear boy, if I come, then only to see you at last. But as far as I'm concerned, you'll be running around in tatters for a long time yet, for I have no intention of sewing for you. I would only travel via Paris to visit you and then I'll deliver myself into my brother's custody. I'll pull off another button for you. (Gladly.) I'll stay a few days. Murkl is welcome at my brother's, but he doesn't want to go there.

You can hardly imagine how grateful we are to you. If only we traveled more. Here we don't go out at all, for everything costs huge amounts of money and is uncertain.

The spider has it good, for it doesn't matter if the thread tears from which it dangles. But it matters to us!

I'm very sorry that your aunt was such a disappointment. Ah well, but I am coming (hopefully, touch wood, unbidden) and we're bringing with us a beautiful portrait of me painted by Merkel.[183] Murkl loves it more than he loves me. It will be good for you to see something beautiful, too, for your mother had a monopoly on beauty and you inherited it from her and didn't leave much for the rest of her family. I'm sort of salvaging beauty in the family (but only in Merkel's portrait).

I can't say anything about us. I just can't.

Stay well. I won't even kiss you, I've become so serious.

Will I see you?

Türmchen

Veza to Georges · *May 23, 1939*[184]

5/23

Sweet Georg,

So many exciting things written with such bacteriological calm! Did the *trip do you*[185] *any harm*??? Will you send me the 19 printed

PREVIOUS PAGE

Family gathering on Rosh Hashanah. Suresnes, France. September 1938.

From left to right, back row:
Regine Béhar-Ova (cousin), Claire Canetti (Salomon's daughter-in-law), Mony Canetti (Claire's daughter), Nissim Jacques Canetti (brother), Edith Canetti (Nissim's wife), Georges Canetti, Marianne Canetti (Cousin Elias's wife), Elias Canetti, Marguerite (Guite) Canetti (Joseph's wife), Elias Canetti (cousin).

Middle row:
Jacqueline Canetti (Joseph's daughter), unidentified girl standing between the back row and the middle row, Salomon Canetti (uncle), Mathilde Canetti (Salomon's wife), Joseph Canetti (uncle).

Front row:
Claudine Canetti (Joseph's daughter), Marcel Canetti (Cousin Elias's son), Ruth Canetti (Cousin Elias's daughter).

pages?? I will read every word three times and look after the notebook for you. Please, don't be so snooty; you have such a beautiful nose. I'm terribly in awe of you, for in contrast to your brother, you have the habit of not making much of yourself and playing your cards close to your chest. How lovely that is!

But with all your riches, you have a miserable character, "you dirty scoundrel!" (quotation). If we hadn't had the bright idea to call up Auntie and your cousin[186] on Saturday, we would have died of fear.

Murkl has definitely decided to accept the Vandsburgers'[187] invitation and to go *by himself.* He's enjoying a good phase right now and should make the most of this opportunity. So reply at once, saying when he should come and if he's also welcome if he's there alone. He really is ready now.

I shall be eternally grateful that you came. I shall never get over it that you left again. But that you didn't write a letter right away quick—I shall avenge.

Are you reading Dante's *Divine Comedy*? A few beautiful pages are missing. Murkl knows them by heart.

We got an invitation from Scherchen. Murkl didn't even let me thank him and watched me like a hawk. I don't know where Scherchen is at the moment, but if you find out from the papers and have time in between two inflammations in two lungs, write him a thank-you card for us. We ask an awful lot of you, but I will reward you for it.

Please write explicitly if *I* must also come along. He prefers to travel alone, and I—oh how happy I would be. Also send Aunt Vandsburger's address and if possible, that of a cheap hotel in the center of town as well.

I dreamed that my mother was carrying me in her arms out of a dark room and put me down in front of a door. I was indescribably happy, woke up, and thought of—you.

Please send some definite news about the state of your health. Your health in danger in addition to everything else—that makes the romance complete, lovely knight. (You really were.)

Your enemy,
Veza

Veza to Georges · *May 18, 1940*[188]

19, South Hill Park Grds NW3

Saturday Mai 18th 1940

Dearest George,

I shall have finished my translation[189] in the middle of June and therefore wanted you to come only in 4 weeks. But considering your shattered health I implore you, to come at once and enjoy the fresh air. Our flat is situated as beautifully as that one of 3 years ago, and the rooms are nice and cosy. You shall have my room and splendid air coming from Hampstead Heath. *I* promise it and so no fear this time.

I am writing in bed, because I feel sick reading about you to day, that you are coughing. I am terribly worried. So please do come to this beautiful country and to the two persons, to whom you are dearer than to anybody in the world. You need not worry about food: I have an electrical kitchen and shall do the cooking for you with Friedl.[190] Anna comes to see us every day. She loves you. Kay[191]—is our English friend—to say that she came out of a picture of Van Eyk »the singing angels«,[192] would be doing her wrong. She is more. She lives opposite us; you will have the nicest people. Do come, I write it for your sake. Personally: do you know »la Parure« par Maupassant?[193] I am Madame Choiseul *at the end of her life*.

Murkl is worried about you and does not deserve your challenge. I want you two to live in peace and like each other. I shall not sever you. I am too abstracted by thoughts and mysteries, nobody can solve for me.

It is awfully kind of you, that you are helping me again. I hope you addressed that letter to my new place, if not let me know and also the name of the second person. If it is your brother's name it is all right. I must know exactly each Christian name not only the family name of each sender. I want that help of yours badly, and am extremely grateful to you. But if you send me money without writing *at once*, it is like giving a gold ring to a mother whose child died. I *am* Madame Choisel, but why let me feel it?

All my love,
Veza

Once more I repeat: I am ten years older since last year and enthusiasm left me altogether. So if I tell you, be my guest, I know what I say. You'll only have the expences for your dinner. Nothing more. We managed to live all the time and now everything can be so nice and easy in this beautiful surroundings. I have an electric kitchen. We all love you so much, do come at once.

V.

How is Nissim?

VEZA AND ELIAS TO GEORGES · *OCTOBER 27, 1944*

Dr. Georges Canetti
21 Boulevard Jourdan
Paris 14e

Canetti
Durris Stubbs Wood
Chesham Bois (Bucks)[194]

Oct. 27

Dear Georg,

We just learned that you are O.K. but would like direct news to the above address. We were overjoyed. Much love, do write at once. We are all right.

Elias's book is soon coming out in English. Write about yourself and about all our relations.

Love,
Veza and Elias

VEZA TO GEORGES · *January 6, 1945*

Mrs. Canetti
1, Grimsdells Corner
Amersham, Bucks, England

January 6th 1945

Dearest George,

We got two post cards up to now, one from Nov. and one Dec. We are very proud of you and your work amidst a chaotic atmosphere. It's quite like you. And I am going to call you Big Ben, from now on.

Your brother longs for the day when he can tell you, how much he admires and loves you. He tore your first postcard in two and kept one half in his wallet and I was presented with the other half. It came on Xmas day and that *was* a Xmas present. He has not been idle and will write to you himself about his work. We have no financial troubles and shall not have any. I live at the above address which is safer for letters now, your brother lives ten minutes away from here,[195] for we cannot find a flat big enough for two though we pay an exorbitant rent. How is Nissim and Edith??? We are much concerned about them. Answer at once and write a lot about yourself.

I wrote a novel in English two years ago.[196] Of course you were the hero, and of course you were a prominent physician, and of course you saved hundreds of lives and of course all women were after you. It was not quite up to the mark in spite or because of that grand personallity and I did not revise it. I am working on a play (in English)[197] which Elias will have no difficulty to place, since his influence is growing. The difficulty is—I shall not be able to finish it. I am very ill. As to my physic, you would not recognize me in the street, but as to my psychic disposition, that is worse and I have been to a London hospital twice last month. The last six years were too much for me and my mind is incapable of conceiving gas chambers and similar inventions. So you will probably not meet me in the street and by pass me. For if I should regain any strength (which is doubtful) I would set out on a trip. In order to investigate. I would investigate and find out. All those that are responsible for the murder of Alice and her innocent daughter.[198] I would bring them before justice, all of them, I would trace them all; but the last one, the murderer I would handle myself. So you see what has become of me.

We live in a fine place in the country an hour away from London. Your brother goes to London regularly twice a week. He has a miserable life with me and sometimes calls me V3.[199] Which is putting it mildly considering what he went through with me. You are his only bright ray. He has many nice friends, and it is not easy with this proud and reserved people to achieve. They are more shy than reserved and very kind and fair, the English. Do write about yourself, that's all that matters. Your brother will write himself.

All my love,
Veza

VEZA TO GEORGES · *January 19, 1945*

Mrs. Canetti
1 Grimsdells Corner
Amersham Bucks.

Jan. 19th 1945

Dear George,

We got two postcards of yours but you never mentioned Nissim and it worries us. We are very proud of you, you are a shining star in darkness. So is your brother. He is a star that unfortunately for him fell down and finds no place in a gloomy world like this one. And I can't help him anymore, I have been maybe a little too brave in some occasions but now I give up. Reality has no attraction for me anymore and slipping away from it is too near insanity. So you must help him. His outward position is settled. It will soon even be glorious (just as yours). What he wants is someone to love him. You are everything to him, the apple of his eye and you should requite his affection. He has many friends but not one close friend and the girl that followed him from Paris (F.)[200] is a menace and disgrace and he cannot in his kindness of heart find a radical way of ridding himself of her much as he would like to (though he does it *gradually*). A nice voice in the radio just sings: Good men and bad men lying in their grave—which was the good man and which was the knave. Yes, which *was* the good one. I wish we had more news from you.

Wishing you everything nice and beautiful,

Veza

VEZA TO GEORGES · *January 27, 1945*

Mrs. Canetti
1 Grimsdells Corner
Amersham, Bucks.

Jan. 27th

Dear George,

You will be glad to learn that cousin Mathilde[201] has been hiding from the Nazis in the Vatican all the time, and is now living in Rome. We shall send her some money, as soon as we are allowed to. What about you? Are you o.k. with money? We are allowed to send some to Paris.

Your brother has done good work and his publisher[202] is anxiously waiting for him to finish his Psychology on Power,[203] a vast proportion of which is piled up on his desk. Also thousands of pages with aphorisms and thoughts. He is working at the other address and there

Friedl Benedikt

he has most of his manuscripts and onethousandfivehundred English books, acquired these last five years. The library we brought over is also here with a friend up here in Amersham. You should know all this, being our only son and heir. Your brother's translater[204] is one of the greatest historiographers and thinks the world of him. But he has only one wish. To see you and talk about *his* work and *your* work, and tell you, how dear you are to him.

What concerns your friend E. and the girl F. who followed him in this country, she developed very bad habits, such as are not consistent with the law of any country and your poor friend, a spotless character, tries hard to get rid of so unhappy a union. He'll probably tell you about it himself, but if he does not, find out yourself.

For I shall not see you to tell you. I shall go to Switzerland, as soon as I can, much as I regret leaving this country and these kind people who with a divine smile for me, often saved me from despair. The climate kills me. And then I don't want anybody to see me, who knew me once. I should never go back to Central Europe, and share the distress of the Nazis who by then will all have Jewish passports, I guess. Let them perish. Let them go through Hell. I went through Hell. Let them be destroyed. I am destroyed. And I have done a lot of kindness to a lot of rotten muck. Yes, I am done for.

My Chemist[205] read your book, at least he tried to, I can't vouch for his French. And we shall be very glad and proud to get your new book. I shall swank with it, I love swanking with you two. You make up for a hundred Nazis, but who is going to make up for the millions that still exist? How is Nissim? Do write, no answer to a telegramm, that we sent you in December. We both send you all our love and long for news from you.

Love,
Veza

Write to the above address.

VEZA TO GEORGES · *March 24, 1945*

Mrs. Canetti, »Durris«,
Stubbs Wood, Chesham-Bois,
Bucks, England

March 24. 1945.

Dear George,

I sent you a tiny sum of money some time ago, that is your brother wanted me to, but it came back. Your brother is worried at your not having enough food, but the censor[206] did not see his point. Also they gave in the paper, that we can send soap. That, too, came back. We are very sorry, and we are not allowed to send food. But I shall try and approach the French consulate. We were delighted with your last letter, but since I had to write three, till you wrote one, I shall strike and be very short this time. I am very much against your having a lot of visitors, they bore you, they take away your strength and leave you with a blank. I very nearly moved to London, but did not get the flat and have to move out here. This is my tragic fate since 1938. My address for the moment would be the above, your brother's, where I go until I find accommodations.

Though I have much to tell you I close now, to punish you, but want to tell you one of the jokes during the Blitz in London. »There is one good thing about the Blitz,« said a charwoman to a warden, while they were clearing away debris. »It makes you forget the War.« That's the spirit how they took it. They were marvellous during the Blitz. I enclose the end of the letter, that the censor returned. Much love, and do write about you and send your book as soon as it is out. Your brother intends to write to you, of course . . . *He* is in London to day, and nearly every day now, which is a strain on my nerves.

Write!!

Love,
Veza

Once[207] when I went to St. James Palace where the Red Cross is stationed, to inquire about you and Nissim, there sat a lady, well over fifty years old but of extreme beauty, her divine smile evincing, that she had never had a sad day in all her life. I gazed at her, lost in admiration, I could not take away my eyes from her. She seemed to conceive the oposite opinion regarding me, for when I gave Nissim's age as 36, she looked at me with a noble mien and said: »They are your sons, arn't they.«

To forget this century I plunged myself with infinite pleasure into the memoirs of the Duc de Saint Simon,[208] a shortened edition of about a thousand pages. It is tenthousand pages too short for me.

Write at once.
All our Love,
Veza.

The next soap parcel is for Edith[209] and Regine.

VEZA TO GEORGES · *April 16, 1945*

Mrs. Canetti »Durris«
STUBBS-WOOD
Chesham-Bois, Bucks

April 16th

Dear George,

Edith wrote that you are going to have an operation towards the end ot the month and we *are* worried. I wish I could have it for you and in stead of you. I shall be brave and try to get over it. Your brother is not in the best of health, a dry cough since months and his heart very weak. There were two shamrocks* fixed at your photo at the time of the Nazi invasion of France[210] and they worked. This one will work, too. Do let us know at once and if you can't write at once, Edith, we hope will tell us. Do write!!! Good luck, son. All my love,

Veza

*I hope the censor does not drop it.

Veza to Georges · *June 6, 1945*

Mrs. Canetti »Durris«
Stubbs-Wood Chesham-Bois
Bucks

June 6th

Dear George,

As soon as we got your (by the way very charming letter full of ésprit) we went to an English doctor to inform about your case, because we feared, that Daniels' report[211] might be reassuring on purpose. The explanations of the Amersham Doc was so favourable, that we could believe every word Dan. told us, because they gave the same explanation. Since I went through a dozen operations myself in my life, I am not anxious but do hope Edith sends a wire. For not alarmed and happy, are two different things. Canetti will go to see you, as soon as they let him go to France, to help you pass your time during convalescence. When I read your lovely note, I felt the more sad at what has become of me. Shall I tell you the most cruel facts! Well, I go to the pictures three times a week, and when there is a love scene, I keep thinking, isn't she beautiful and isn't he handsome, but why on earth are they passing all their time spooning and courting how dull! Does *that* convince you, that I am lost!

Sweet George, the other day we went to see Daniels and I bought a toy, which in this country costs a minor fortune and then I thought there are two kids and sacrificed our sweet ration of this month and bought milk chocolate, too. Your friend expressly invited us for after eight, that is he wanted nine p.m. but Canetti pointed out to him, that I am not too healthy and can't go as late as that. So after eight we went, fully aware, that we would not have to expect a high tea which indeed we did not want, since our president of the Pen club, Robert Neumann[212] had invited us to a nice supper. What you get after eight is a cup of tea and a biscuit or two, even when you go to see your charwoman.

Well, we arrived to find, that Mrs. Daniels had gone out. Your friend was very busy working on his immortal work[213] and the kids were asleep. Your friend sat at the edge of his bed in the most disagreeable, nasty, cold, filthy room I have seen, and I have come across very dreary rooms in this country. When I unpacked the toy and the choc, he felt ashamed, and asked, should he make coffee for us, at which we protested, vehemently, for the prospect of staying a minute longer than nessessary to put our questions, froze our bones. We stayed not thirty minutes, only talking about George and then we left, like chased by a lion, no, a guttersnipe, and though not hungry, we dropped in at the first restaurant we came across, only to forget the gloomy atmosphere, the reception and the room and Daniels looking like a detective, whom burglars had robbed of his whole fortune. He did not even have a proper photo of his kids I think he is too filthy to waste paper on them.

At the restaurant we ordered a whole big dinner each and left everything because we were not hungry and I was blazing, because it was bad and cost a guinea, but your brother said, when you have been at Daniels, you've got to throw some money out of the window, you just have to. That was so convincing, that I forgot my bad temper. And that bloke had the impertinence to tell to all Manchester, what a bad character Canetti is, Canetti, the nicest and most generous chap in the world, who should not sit near the like of him. That about your friend.

About us there is much to tell. But there is still a censor and I am fed up with everybody reading what I write and so I'll wait. Why we have that censor, nobody knows, probably they fear I might tell you to dig out Hitler and stuff him. You know that I have *one* gratification in my rotten life—Ernst.[214]

How could I ever have thought you are thrifty, when you have kept us for such a long time. What would we have done without you! I am not going to be sentimental, but shall write a long very personal letter, as soon as the operation is over. How brave you are, never complaining and never swanking. I think Edith is in love with you too, the way she writes about you.

Elias says he is going to write you a long letter, and he will, one day. God knows when. We are arguing the whole day, he good natured, I like a fury. We cannot live together in the same house, and I lost my flat and you, it's easier to find diamonds in the street than a flat with a kitchen, not even if you pay much, unless you buy a house. We live in a nice villa—the description of our landlord and landlady[215] will one day be published in a Viennese paper or anthology.

And we are all bored stiff: no War, no doodle bugs,[216] no bombs, no ambulances and sirens, it gets you down nothing happening and even the Nazi leaders all caught. Anna said to me the other day, she does not know why, but since Ve-day she feels depressed.

Much love, you'll find me very foolish, I asure you, I am worse than that.

We adore you.

Veza

Veza to Georges · *June 30, 1945*

Mrs. Canetti »Durris«
Stubbs-Wood Chesham-Bois
Bucks

June 30th 1945

Dear George,

I must tell you that I am constantly in a very dangerous state of mind, and that it was cruel to leave us without news. When I saw your envelop I was exultant, thinking the operation over. We are quite happy though, for if the doctors hesitate, it means that the operation is a mere trifle. Still. Don't insist, I am convinced, if you can get much good food (can you?) and fruit, that you'll be well without operation and it would be such a blessing to us.

I appreciate your having written to me on the 15th of June,[217] but must tell you, that your brother said to me: »I wish he would not be operated round that date, for he'll be very sad on the 15th and that might impair his will to resist.« I tell it you that you should see how you misjudge your brother. I could not help showing him your letter, but I crossed out three lines . . .*

What you hint in them is the practice of dreamers, artists, writers and fools and not your invention. It was my practice long before old age and contempt for most partners (would be partners) made it my own resort. There are variations. I create my actors myself and I am not the third person but usually the man. It is much nicer to create *yourself* and be independent of others.

I shall soon write the six pages about us and a lot of six pages. I am a bit unsettled, not having a flat, that's why I can't concentrate. We live in a villa of a wealthy country parson and pay a lot of rent. He has the main qualities of the père Grandet,[218] but of a dry one. We have the nessessary, but what I would want at my age, with my ardent wishes and with my past record (of ten years privations, shattered dreams, shattered hopes . . . with all masts broken) is luxurious comfort. That I have not.

This is intirely my own fault. For instead of taking chances in London, I shut myself up in the country for six years, so that your brother should be in comparative safety during doodle-bugs and other heavenly surprises. Well, I succeded, and am dissatisfied with myself now, *about* myself.

Your brother had to interrupt his work and is working hard on the revisal of the translation of the Blendung. His translator is a very well known historiographer and she is a great admirer of your brother. But of course it is hard to translate the Blendung and there are cases when she writes: er giftet sich—he poisoned himself.[219] Useless to say, that I have a spot of work, for I read the German version and then we compare.

You know Dea?[220] She married the director of the British museum. Her story wants six pages description which I shall send you one day. Anna is married to a conductor,[221] who, being the greatest blockhead and a mediocre musician, is a great success in this country. Besides a lot of friends who are anxious to make the acquaintance of the handsome brother, you'll have a lot more curious people to face here—once the Blendung is published. The translator for inst. is in love with Georges Kien[222] and the chapter »madhouse« is thrilling to her. What concerns myself, I am very biting, I warn you, Georges Kien, but shall insist on getting my sweets tasted by you, as was my habit. Yes, you'll have to get the foretaste—if— ever I see you again. This is very doubtful, as I told you before, in previous letters. My parson is going to bed so I have to stop writing, but shall send another note in a few days. I am afraid you won't find this one 18th century—it's 20 century alright.

I shall never forget that you wrote to me on the 15th of June. Up to now I did nothing to deserve this privilege!! You two brothers *are* noble!! How I wish I could thank you! Your description of your life in the SANA!!! *YOU* ARE going to write *the* great »Magic Mountain« one day.

Good luck and do write at once and Edith should write—it is dangerous to leave me in suspense!!

Veza.

All our *Love*.

*I have 3 lines crossed out in that letter now, which ennoys me.

About E. Fisher[223] next time.

I'll write again in a few days for your letters are delightful and I want to intice you to answer.

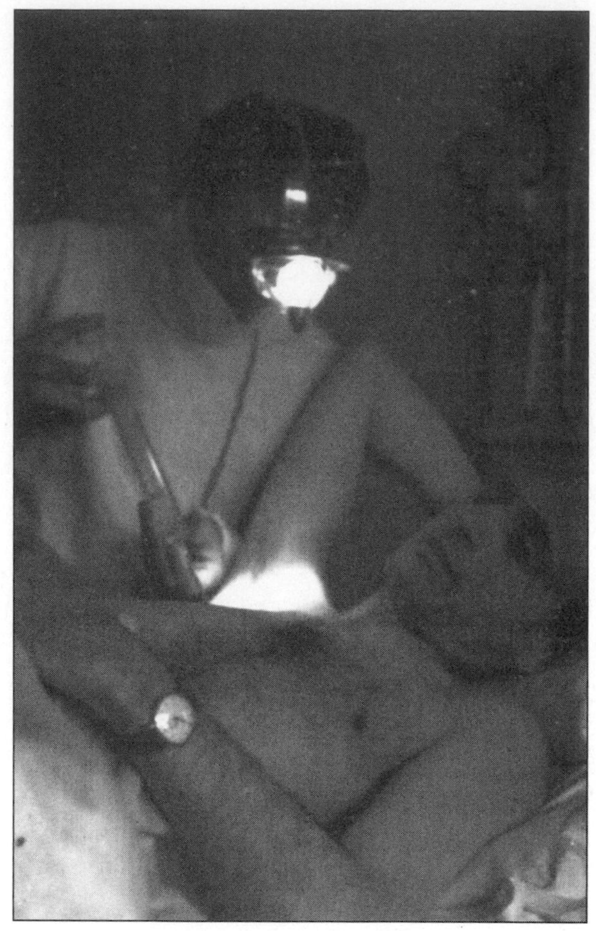

Georges Canetti undergoing an operation around 1947

Veza to Georges · *July 22, 1945*

Mrs. Canetti DURRIS
STUBBS-WOOD
CHESHAM-BOIS, BUCKS

July 22nd

DEAREST,

We were overjoyed and embraced each other when we read the first lines. But what is a »retemps«[224] I could not understand the word and shall be terribly worried until I know. We fear it means another, minor operation in »aout« (August), which thought is insupportable. Do write at once about it. At once!!! What about PENICILLIN?[225]

What a charming letter to write in the midst of your pains. How brave you are. We keep thinking of you and I try like a magnetic steel to take the pain away, we keep telling each other, that if we think of you all the time, and feel with you it will help. Did you notice any effect?

What concerns the fact that you are not going to have any deformation—this of course is the most important statement. Before you reassured us in this respect your brother and I kept telling each other, that we will have to—well, not exactly cancel our acquaintance with you—if there should be one, but at least we would cool off towards you and certainly change our will to your disadvantage. So now we don't have to.

If Edith admits in court, that she wants to marry again and therefore divorces her husband, you will of course get May Collette.[226] But if she states, what *you* gave for her reason and claims, she wanted more children but . . . *she* wins. If I know one thing of her fiancé, it is, that being a Viennese solicitor he is bound to be shrewd and therefore you'll have to take the best solicitor in the land to get the child. Of course I shall not mention a word to her, your brother was well pleased, he said Nissim should marry a »merry widow« pretty, young and rich and at the thought he got so envious, that I offered for the 12th time to divorce him. Where upon he implored me, not to, since there are two women[227] waiting for such an event and to tear him to pieces. So this sums up my function in his life. Beside having to find the adequate terms for his English version of the »Blendung« (for which we can't find an English title) I keep the tigers away.

I very *nearly* finished my second play written in English,[228] but it will last a few months till it is in the right hands and seriously considered. It is a charming comedy, witty and sharp.

A lady doctor here cannot wait any longer for your work. She was very much interested in what little we know of it and I suspect also in your person. Even your brother said *you* are going to write »the« novel one day. He seriously believes that he is going to write you soon. Excuse my rotten hand writing, but I must not type when he is at home, and hélas I can't get a flat of my own.

I don't see why I should let you have the address of Daniels. It revolts me, to write it. I feel I should charge him for the ink wasted on it. I feel my letter gets invalid with his address on it—but here you are.

47 PARK HILL rd
London NW3

I'll write again in a few days but skip back into the 18th century. I am fed up with reality. And that's even *one* reality—varnished and perfumed—it's what *we* call reality God knows what the real reality is like. Chamfort?[229] Your brother wrote *thousands* of aphorisms—each the »Regent« compared with Chamfort. It's a job to get him publish his things!!!

All my Love,
Veza

VEZA TO GEORGES · *August 1, 1945*

Mrs. Canetti Durris
Stubbs Wood Chesham-Bois
Bucks

August 1. 1945

Dear Benjamin,

There is *another** letter which is a great concession, for I can never typewrite more than three pages a day and our correspondence thus delays my »work«. You don't take my illnesses a bit seriously, so I will tell you what I have got. No, I better tell you, what I have *not* got, it's shorter. I have *not* got tuberculosis, because I read your book and keep drinking unboiled milk, though they tell us in the paper we should not, on account of the high percentage of T.B. germs in milk. Yet I, a fanatical believer in your theory risk tuberculosis, which by the bye could not do me much harm. In fact, I dont know *where* I could get it. I am so ill, that there would not be room for one more disease. The doctors pulled out half my teeth, when they thought it's the kidneys, they kept pressing my legs, when they thought it was Bright's disease,[230] and though I told them it was potatoes, that's all we got during the Blitz, they still waited for the water to go down my legs and I am as fat as a hog and still think it's potatoes. Then they started treating my nerves, for what with one illness or another and so many at a time, I forgot, that a cloth begins to burn, when you throw it on an open gasfire, and even when I saw it burning I did not think much of taking it away slowly and looking at it, reflecting what to do. My former landlady does not know, how narrow she escaped being burnt alive with three kids and her portly husband, who is very fat and would have burnt quickly—when your first letter from Paris came. I had just lit the oil stove, but forgot to put the lid on when I saw your letter, and it stood near an armchair, the flames rising high, it's a good thing I have a too big nose, smelling things, when I forget them.

Otherwise I kept my brain pretty clear, which you have, when you are a slave driver. You would think there are no slaves anymore maybe there are no slaves, but I sure am a slave driver, with your brother neglecting the trivial things in life, and never wanting to give finishing touches to the last chapters, so that I can have his book out and live in the fat of the land. And that we can fulfil our lifelong obligations to you, which he is fully aware that he has. With it he is so generous and so dammed kind hearted, that you don't use your whip, and I decided to leave the job to you and hand him to you, work and all. To convince you however, that I am very very ill, note the following conversation between him and myself. I: »I am glad George can't see me, ill as I look, bitter and worn.« He: »Why, George is such a kind chap, so affectionate, why should not he like you even if you look our grandmother. I like you, though you are my grandma.«

Yes, I want to send him to you and have a break—he is a marvelous worker and has thousands of pages finished, but I have to get a nervous breakdown before I get him to dictate things to me, he wants to work on and on, the real man of science, but meanwhile even *his* original ideas get stale and I have no nerves anymore to break down. You'll have to watch out also for his company, that girl I mentioned has bad habits, very bad indeed, I'll say more when I am sure that you alone read the letters and please don't mention a word about it in your answer. Since he is a spotless character, noble minded and kind to a fault, he likes sometimes to mix with just the opposite people, which of course can become dangerous to his life and his work. And I shan't always be here to protect him. That's why I write this letter to you, I might not be there, Benjamin and you must take care of him. Take away as much money of him as you can (he is very generous) I do that, and keep it for him for a rainy day.

I do hope your pains have ceased. Do write about that. Our admiration for you is unbound, you never complain, you write letters plein d'esprit[231] and we love you so. It's like a wonderful dream having you and at times, when we are disappointed at one thing or other we tell each other: but we have George. If we had all the success and all the richess in the world, what would it be without George. —He would be miserable if he thought I complained about him, I did not mean to, what I want is to give you instructions, in case one of my many illnesses getting the better of me. He would think I interfere with you two, he said I used to (I never meant to) he said he loves you most in the world and I should not take away from him the most precious possession he has got. You.

We had at the moment no disappointments on the contrary the very thrilling experience of the great labour victory,[232] you can imagine how we feel, everything that we fought for and thought lost seems to come forth anew, but what sacrifices. All those people young and hopeful who had to die and those that are left behind . . . oh how we feel it! I am a bloody fool and though terribly glad about labour victory, I felt sorry for Churchill, a unanimous feeling in this country, everybody loves him and is grateful, yet, have you ever seen such a grand people! They love him, they are fully aware of what he has done for the world and still they refuse his party (conservatives) and the methods during the election campaign. I only hope the labour leaders will be up to their task. —I am reading for the 5th time Tolstoy's great novels now—and your brother despises me beyond description, because in the morning I have the privilege of reading the »Blendung« to him, while he corrects the translation, and in the evening—Tolstoy, after Canetti . . . what a fall! That lady doctor here chucked her fiancé out and is waiting for you. When once you are quite healthy again, I would wish you to have a grandchild for me with a nice girl. You need not get married, I just want the baby, and I pester your brother to do the same. I want grand children. He would say great grand children. This is a letter End of XIX century. Gradually I'll grope back to the XVIII and meet you there.

All our love,

Veza

*I wrote one last week.

!! Do write *at once*.

VEZA TO GEORGES · *August 15, 1945*

Mrs. Canetti »Durris«
Stubbs-Wood Chesham Bois, Bucks

PEACE WITH JAPAN[233]
Mind *above address* and don't misspell it.
PEACE
<Individual letters in a descending vertical column on the left margin:>
! PEACE ! PEACE ! ! ! ! !

August 15th

Dearest George,

We got your letter to-day very quick and I answer at once, though this is not *the* letter, but just a quick note and *the* letter follows. You can imagine that we were thrilled at the thought that there might not be another operation and that you would be fit without it. You seem much too fit for me, going to pictures with beautiful nurses and all the consequences. I am prepared to let you go, since I can't prevent it, but do you have to rub it in to me! I'm of course jealous.

You'll get honey from New-Zealand, if our friend,[234] whom we asked to send you some, can get it through, we hope it's possible from N-Z. As to myself, I keep looking at two pounds of orange marmalade and a pound of best tea, we saved it for you but up to now could not send it and I kept the registered envelop and lids of parcels that came back.

Your brother is in a strange mood, as only a poet can be—about the atomic bomb.[235] In fact he was so downhearted, that he refused to eat and nearly to live on, considering that the A-bomb is going to interfere between his immortallity and even—who knows mortallity. It was a serious crisis, but I saved his life when I told him—strange George demanding your Comedy,[236] but never asking as much as to read *my* immortal play written in English a second nearly finished. At which remark he got so happy, telling me, that I am one of the seven world wonders, bothering about such trifles (with trifles he did *not* mean my comedy) that he begins to get used to the atomic bomb. As to my plays he swore they'll be performed here, the sterling being better value than francs (ecco). Next I intreated him to let me send you his comedy, at which he has the following objections: First: the atomic bomb being so overwhelming that it darkens the overwhelming effect of even this great work. Second: He cannot let you have it without telling you, that he would not let Nissim treat it at his pleasure, curtail it, take out the idea etc. Third: he cannot write to you about it nor send it, since he has not written before. He has got to wait, till he writes a brotherly letter and then business. —It reminded me of the fact, that this comedy might have been produced by Reinhard, but your brother said, Reinhard is not great enough, and never answering Stephan Zweig's letter who suggested praising it to Reinhardt. And of another fact, that a friend of ours and in the »book branch,« asked for it three years ago, she is in New-York, but your brother said they would steal the idea, and did not let me send it. But this time I'll insist. If he does not send it in a few days, I *will*. It's a persiflage of all that happened under Hitler, with keen foresight and poetical construction I even prefer it to the »Blendung«.

Your letter with the charming description of Elias[237] turning up and all the other most interesting details deserves an adequate answer for which I must gather strength. Of which, what little I possessed, was absorbed by your brother and his atom splitting. It takes a boxer to hammer it out of his brain. At last I convinced him, that there'll be a commission watching over its use, and that *he* will be member for Austria, of that commission. It has an excellent effect on his work,[238] which he seems to hurry up now, fearing that it might never appear. He races with the atom now and I am well pleased. But these *were* hard days. —As to our labour victory, take it from me, nobody expected it, least the labour party. The conservatives were sure of a big majority, the liberals of a big increase and labour prayed and hoped for just one M.P. more than the Tories. So you can imagine how we feel. —Which *is* your permanent address when you leave the Sana? For New Zeal. I gave Nungesser, but is that a safe address? Write about it. You'll have to come over as soon as you can, to recuperate here, with the food shortage in France. We'll send what we can as soon as we can, but you better come here. Let me know how the prospect is about your travelling. I fear it won't be possible before spring (so Daniels thinks). Which will find us still in Amersham, a fine country place, with very good air they say. Well in spring it's not too damp. Amersham is a big garden and an hour away from London. The place where we live is very much like our place and gigantic garden in Grinzing. Are my letters censored?[239] Yours are not, as far as I can see. What concerns my health, my nerves are the worst trouble and as for the climate, I don't see how I can stay in this country, though we have all prospects here, all chances, lots of friends and good connections and a genuine love for the people, with their divine smile, that left an atom of myself unsplit.

Much love, you scoundrel, and dare not write again about pretty nurses and all your charm and irresistability—your brother was shocked that I wrote that about the Regent and Chamfort, and said, »probably *he* is writing the aphorisms of the modern Chamfort« (but don't write that to him, he added). So of course I write it. Much love and please news at once! You have two nice cousins, Maudy and Cissy,[240] I got quite attached to them and they want me to find them husbands. So I'll have to use your brother's charms to fulfil their wish, which charm has not diminished and you'll probably like his head.

It may interest you to learn that I might contemplate using »George Brand« as my pseudonym, since I'll have to use an English pseudonym. But if you send me a photo with two nurses kissing you—I will call myself Nissim. Sounds like the name of a slave in Bagdad who has been turned into a dog by a magician.

All my love,
Veza

Veza to Georges · *August 30, 1945*

Mrs. Canetti »Durris«
Stubbs-Wood Chesham-Bois
Bucks

August 30th 1945

Dearest George,

I must tell you a thing that you undoubtedly know, namely that your handwriting is practically illegible and I cannot decipher the name and address of your English soldier friend in Paris and therefore cannot write to him. Can you repeat his address? And is he really as decent as you seem to think? Answer at once.

What concerns the »Komödie« of your brother, it is locked up in a small suitcase, to which I have no key, and it will cost me a few heart attacks to make him open that case and give it me for me to send it to you. I would break it open, but it's the only case we can lock and there is not the locksmith available to repair it for me, labour being still very short. Also I must save my strength to get him finish the revision of his novel, so that he can go on with his main work. All these efforts WERE in the long run of years too straining for me, and I begin to consider Edith's action a good idea and I do not deny, that I fancy myself much rather alone and living carefree, than worrying all the time about all the neglects of a »Dichter[241] par excellence«.

We want your advice: suppose you pass a booksellers and see the following titles: »Autodafé« *or* »The Maze« *or* »The Pyre« which title would entice you most? We are still trying to find the right title for the »Blendung«. What the first title means you know. »The Maze« is a labyrinth. »The Pyre« is a heap of burning books. Your brother is for the first title, I for the second. Tell us swiftly, we think much of your opinion. —*How are you?* When is your book coming out? What about the »retemps«? My nephew[242] was in Africa in the army and had malaria and dissenterie. After that he got so depressed, that the doctors said he must go home, which he refused to do, thinking it is a cowardly action to leave the army, as long as there is a war on. He stayed on, got worse and since a year is now under treatment in an asylum, and I have not seen him yet. Your brother considers his case pretty serious (he forgets how to spell his name, can't *read* and when told to dance with a girl he says, who would dance with an ugly fellow like him, and he is definitely handsome, tall and good looking). His health is otherwise good. He gets electric treatment now, after a long sleeping cure. I wish you'd tell me what you think of it.

Still going to the pictures with fine girls? Right you are. I bet they are all in love with you. Who is not. Do write at once and answer all the questions. One day I shall send you a description of all that we went through during the Blitz. Of all? No. Of one day. One day would be twelve pages. We were in London during the worst part of course. At that time, we were very poor (we are not, now) and I went to the market every day, half an hour away from home, to save three or four pennies. There was an undertaker in the street near the market place who had so many orders for coffins, that he had to spread them in the street, the pavement full of coffins, fifty sixty, they were for *us*, for us in Hampstead, and I looked at them with a queer feeling and also telling myself, that they were much too long and to narrow for me. One night we had fifty incendiaries on the Heath. We were all in the street to put them out, there were boys of fifteen, brave kids, there were the Wardens, lots of women wardens, all pretty and young and brave amid the deadly shells and bombs, they had crept out from under the earth, silent we were, in the dark, putting out bombs, a Norwegian asked me something in a language, he thought was English, there was Babel—excitement love—everybody was kind and neighbourly—oh how I miss that war!

All my love,
Veza

VEZA TO GEORGES · *August 31, 1945*

Mrs. Canetti Durris
Stubbs Wood Chesham Bois
Bucks

12 o'clock p.m. August 31st 1945

Dearest George,

I just got your delightful letter, when I came home from London, tired and disappointed. If you ask me why disappointed, I could not tell you, I just went to see my friend Anna Mahler because her stepfather Werfel has died. She was not a bit upset, I am glad to say and there was no reason to be melancholy, still, here I am, and when I saw your handwriting I was thrilled and still more when I read your most fascinating letter. I shall never see you again, for I am terribly afraid, hard hearted as I became, callous, cynical, wicked and derisive, I shall not be proof against your charms and fall for your bald head. And thus I shall never see you again and when you come here, I9ll (there is your birthday again)[243] sneak away and hide myself. Come you must, because you must recuperate here. You'll be in time to read the reviews on your brother's book. You are his guest, of course and this time we mean it.—What concerns his Comedia, I shall break open his suitcase, the only one we have been able to lock up from the indiscrete eyes of our landlord. For without landlord or landlady or either, we never seem to be able to manage. The apartment-question is disastrous, since so much has been destroyed by raids. Yes, I shall break open his suitcase and the only thing I don't know is, whether we may send German manuscripts to France, without censor, we may have them censored, but then this would last two more months. No, I shall not joke about the name of your brother, if it hurts you and am prepared to think he is very gifted. Being the brother of you two, how could it be otherwise. I was not thinking of Brand of Ibsen,[244] but of the German meaning of the word (the English meaning is irrelevant) since—though my will is dead, there is still a flame burning in my heart, it has no place, no food no lustre, but there it is and therefore Brand. Actually I thought of Adam Brand, but if your letters continue as they are now, I'll have to usurp your name—cherishing the assimilation. I shall not retake my German pseudonym of yore,[245] no—for all my friendship with the Viennese government.[246] I cannot forget. I cannot forget how their faces changed and how friends had to see us at night, for fear of being caught going to see Jews. —A negro entered my compartment to-night and asked very humbly, would we mind if he came in. »Certainly *not*« I blurted out, for the lady, to whom he addressed himself, smiled meekly, she was old and withered and did not understand what was behind his question, what suffering, what degredation. A pastor in the train fell in love with me an account of my vigorous affirmative, and carried the negroe's luggage out of the coach, himself, at his destination. —What people! Never, never could have happened here, what happened elsewhere. Now, since the election we know. Shall I ever forget how they behaved in the Blitz. Shall I ever forget! Shall I ever smile, sigh a sigh of relief, wonder, love? No. I am hard and bitter. —On my way to the market—beside the coffins, there was a big block of houses in ruins . . . in the debris buried lay thirteen corpses . . . they could not dig them out and you had to pass these ruins every day with the thirteen people buried and you could not help thinking one of them might be in a hole, not dead, but buried alive and living for days. —And that child, that was brought to hospital—dying and was asked by nurse—what on earth she wished—she should utter a wish, whatever it was, nurse was ready to get it for her—and she said »a lemonade with a straw«—that was her last wish, and there was no lemon in the whole country but they got a substitute, Ersatz lemonade, and an innkeeper opened his public house at night, because he remembered he had a straw somewhere and found the straw for the child . . . How can I forget, son!

I wrote this letter last night—and your brother coming home from London at two in the morning, learned *your* letter by heart—and honestly, truly, said—a thing he never says—he *is* gifted—what a letter—

he is a writer himself (of which there is no doubt). I am dotting this down in the train, going to London, a cousin of mine is there, of Manchester—Maudy is divorced since a long time, the whole family is very nice.

I have got to show your letters to your brother. He is so longing for every line from you, so devoted to you, I just have not the heart not to. He also likes Nissim, don't worry, that War has changed us a lot. He is more sensible, kinder still, full of affection—I am the opposite in every respect or to put it short—*old.*

No. Not much will be changed on the Continent, but it does you good to live among a people, who could not be bribed, by Churchill's great qualities, by his appeal to them, by his grandious eloquence and personality and by his elaborate propaganda.

I close now, but this is no answer. I am going to pour letters into the Isère,[247] only to get them from you!! How you cheered me up, last night!! What stimulant, what source of life ésprit[248] and brilliant clever thinking is! What treasure you are to me, to us, of whom we speak as of our son!

All my love Benjamin,
Veza

Hoepffner is O.K. back at his Newspaper in Strassbourg. How *are you*?

VEZA TO GEORGES · *September 11, 1945*

Mrs. Canetti Durris
Stubbs-Wood Chesham-Bois, Bucks

Sept 11th

Darling George,

To-morrow is the day and we think of you incessantly and I have no words to express my admiration for you. Writing this grand letter before that operation!

Your brother read your letter about his »Blendung« with great delight, but I cannot comment on it, in fact I cannot write properly before I have your note, that you are O.K. and doing everything to recover quickly thinking all the time, that we depend on your life, being interwoven with you.

Bless you, and as soon as you can write—»O.K.«—on one little piece of paper and tell nurse to post it at once. But examine the address, I am capable of writing it all wrong, when excited. Every good wish, son, we are with you!!

We'll find a way about food.

Veza and
Elias

I too found Blendung a rotten title.

You see! how I began the address on envelop!!

Veza to Georges · *September 21, 1945*

Mrs. Canetti c/o Mrs. Fistoulari[249]
21 Campden Hill Court, Campden Hill rd, London W8

September 21.

Dearest Georges,

No, this is not my address, it's Anna's, Anna Mahler's, I put it on top, because we are supposed to give our address and I don't want this letter to come back, for reasons you'll soon understand. In this country they are so courtious as to open your letter at the P.O. and returning it without reading it, to the address on top. In an envelop »on your majesty's service.«[250]

I just got your telegramm and this inspires me to write you a long letter—up to now I could not, and you can imagine how downcast we were, when the op. was postponed. So now, I can enjoy the magnificant letter that came in the morning, and that we read twice. Your brother *will* be happy to see the telegr. to-night when back from London. We knew it is a slight operation, but what operation *is* light. And above all, your magnanimity in writing and even cheering us up and being brave as *you* are brave. Write *at once* how you feel. Pains??

How long do you think you'll have to stay in the sana? Don't forget to thank Regine for the wire. And answer sober questions, not only the great ones. How long? Because for your physic it may be good but for your psychic Paris is surely the better place. Also send me a list of the things you can't get in Paris, food, I mean. Don't forget, a whole list*, we don't know here, we live in the lap of luxury concerning food, compared to Belsen,[251] of course, for everything can only be taken relatively. We get plenty to eat, as much as we like, but always the same monotonous things—I am sick and tired of bacon, cheese, roast lamb, biscuits and dried eggs. Owing to good connections of your brother to a baroness,[252] we get shell eggs now and then, but a lady here said the other day to me: this is my shell egg of 1945. She gets one a year.

I9ll (there it is and I was so careful it should not come forth, I seem to be a spiritualistic medium, things coming forth against my will, ectoplasm forming 9 9 9, no 1911. It just shows. Even though nearly dead, very nearly, I manifest my affection for G.C. Which I tell you, because my old age, decay and despair, I am a clinic case for despair, a melancholy maniac, shall not destroy our ties, by which word I don't mean cravats. Nothing shall destroy the afinity between us three, E.C. included. Not even I shall destroy it.) I'll—*was* I careful—tell you now, why I'm going to move to a boarding house soon from here, not a London one, but here, near your brother, who remains at the usual, dry address that I usually give you . . . Durris . . . brr. The whole address is stingy, miserly, mean, filthy, as the owners are.[253] I suffered two years during the Blitz, not wanting your brother to go back to London. Oh, how we had to fight to get the exorbitant rent. When I washed a pair of stockings all in secret, they *would* find it out, for they are religious people, the man being a retired country parson. His wife was 58, when they met, he at that time being 68. They lived in all innocence together in their bed, if that disturbs you. For they are pious people and, kind of saintly. So saintly, that they drove me out of my wits, telling us every week we would have to leave, because the Germans may invade and then they would get killed for harbouring Jews. Only when there was a bomb on Amersham, they grew mild for a while, because they feared the wrath of the Lord even more than the Germans. Oh how I prayed for bombs! For when they stopped they did fear God much, but the Germans more. At last I was half mad and moved into the house of a proletarian, a woman who could neither read nor write. —»I go to the dance every night«—she told me apologetically, and I felt this was the chance of my life, a room with the landlady out all night and I having some peaceful hours. —Well, what shall I tell you, she was a prostitute and if I say, I answered the door to the whole eighth army, I am not giving away a vital secret anymore, but at that time I could have told you the movements of the troups like anything. At noon we had a parade overhead, American planes flying very low to wave to us, it *was* a treat when the whole day and night you had nothing but enemy planes. Her love letters to the various boys—I wrote, I typed them and her trade florished. She could not sign her name, pretty Mrs. Lancaster, but she could find five men a day and make her husband believe in her innocence. Useless to say that I wrote a musical play about her,[254] which they think charming, who read it (she used to sing a lot and very correctly which replaced, as your brother says, books to her).

In the end there were so many applicants, that I had to move out, because some moved in, and I went to a respectable house, the Chemist's place, his wife having been partly a show girl, and partly, as she styled it »in drapery business,« walking about in riding costumes at Selfridges,[255] where middle aged wives came with their husbands to buy fur coats. She is extremely tall and good looking and has now a big bank account. Though »she *was* innocent when she got married, her husband knows, he had to *fight* for it . . . « I quote, if you'll pardon me. She is only one small episode in my play, for she chucked me out for greedy reasons, a lady from Nigeria came with a big trunk and offered her ten pounds of chocolate, twenty pounds of tea thirty pounds of almond for my flat—off I went, back to . . . where I am now, but my saints found out that I smoke (which I do) and your poor brother will pay an enormous amount for me in a boarding house, but I am so tired of struggling, I don't care.

Listen, dear Georges, you can't promise things to me, and disappoint me. My heart is set now on your plan about the Comedie der Eitelkeiten and Cape[256] (the Publishers) is posting it to you tomorrow, we not being allowed to post German ms. —I tell you, it's grandios. Everything that happened is anticipated in that work and in what way! And Georges, what about »Die Hochzeit«?[257] You know that that work too, is anticipating everything that happened in the Blitz. It is of course much easier to perform and just as good in quality as the other. I'll send that too but later (no I9ll, no, that must be rare manifestations). Though the Comedy is unique what concerns imagination. He has a good working period, your brother has, and if I die before seeing the day, tell him, I knew he would be famous and shall enjoy it in my grave. For that he will be. Yes, I want you two to stick together, for frankly, he likes a lot of people but he only *loves* you and confessed it to me once, that he is also »in love« with you, because you are so attractive. »You are telling me,« I replied. Listen Georges, if the ms is not in your hands in about at most a week, write at once, for then he did not give it to Cape. I can't go round telling his backers that he is unreliable, a dreamer, a good for nothing, a poet—in a word. And that he might have thought, he should wait now, because after your operation you can't be bothered. Whereas I think, here is my chance. Back in PARIS, with all those usherettes or midinettes[258] as you call them there, you'll forget us.

No. *He* sent the telegram, and was asked to put his second name, were you? Oh, if I would only learn that these works are being performed I could die with less resentment. A propos my death—your brother wants to publish my letters after my death, so keep them, please (with your kind permission of course). I had to write that to New Zealand, too, a friend there[259] is thrilled by them. She left

England and went as far as N.Z. for unrequited love. Who did not requite it. Your brother.

He says of course Nissim must be upset, if a woman *dares* to leave a Canetti. —Now this *is* a long letter and you'll answer at once and get a much longer one. Your brother took your letter of to-day with him, I think he has a faint notion he helps you with his warm body, when he carries your letter, or something unspoken, undefined and ridiculously sentimental, but genuine. So I may not have answered questions, for though I kept everything in your letter, I would not keep a question, having never been able to answer any in my whole life, never pretending to hope that I shall be able to. At which deep sentence I close and send you all my love and all my surplus love and all my eternal love and even the one that will disperse in the Atom.

Veza

All your relatives in Sofia are O.K. I write Georges now, because of a superstition. Without the »s« that would be 13 letters. Yes I am a fool. I know.

Love from a
Bloody Fool.

*I'll do my best to find a way, legal of course!

Was glad about old Merckel. Hoepffner is alive and all my cousins in Sofia.

!!! I just got news: Alice is alive[260] and on her way back to Paris.

Veza to Georges · *October 4, 1945*[261]

No word from you since the 21st, you scoundrel!! And I can't send you anything, I'm running my feet off (except via New Zealand).

Write immediately—immediately, or you'll be getting telegrams! Your brother is beside himself.

Veza

The Red Cross advised me to write to the customs office . . . petition, etc.

P.S.

We just got a letter from Harry Arditti,[262] he spoke on the telephone with Nissim, who asked for Canetti's play. So there can't be nothing wrong about you except that you are a scoundrel! The play was sent to *you* (St. Hilaire) 2 weeks ago.

Write at once whether you got it.

Veza to Georges · *October 5, 1945*

Mrs. Canetti Durris
Stubbs-Wood Chesham-Bois
Bucks

Oktober 5th 1945

Dearest,

This is a strictly business letter for you deserve no other. But for that telephone call of Nissim we would be mad by now, leaving us without news. There are two letters on way, one with insults.

I want to repeat, that Cape, Publishers, Bedford Square, no, not the publishers, I remember now, Miss Wedgwood, the reader there and translater of Canetti's, had it sent you via the Time & Tide,[263] and it should be in your possession. The play is grandios, but in case your brother cannot afford to bring it at the moment, his other play »Die Hochzeit« is as good in quality, is much shorter, has no expensive scenery, is very simple as to the construction and very deep and »genial« (German word)[264] as to the contents and easy to translate into any language.

The contents: All floors of a house are shown, all flats and the inmates of the flats and their habits. There is a wedding going to be celebrated, at the flat of the owner of the house, who at the same time is the architect. The guests are all futile, heartless and vicious. Except one man, Horch, who sees through them, and seems to have a premonition, for he suggests the following game:[265] »Let us pretend, that there is an earthquake. Everybody will tell me now, which his last wish were, if there *were* an earthquake.« Needless to say, that the last wish of most of them is as shallow as they are, and the whole is a masterly characteristic of each guest *in* their last wish. As soon as each has pronounced his or her last wish—there *is*—an earthquake and the house begins to fall into ruins. They are all crazy now, the guests at the wedding party and the owner of the house stands himself before the entrance and allows nobody to escape, repeating in his frenzy, that *his* house can't crumble—because he . . . *he* . . . built it. Oberbaurat[266] Segenreich. I get excited when I think, that this has been written ten years ago, no more, and has happened every day in this country during the Blitz . . . when dance halls, clubs etc. were hit. I strongly recommend you to read it and during your convalescence *you* could translate it, of course your brother would offer to share any royalities with you. I suggest it, because Daniels thinks you'll have to stay in St. Hilaire for a few months. I wish it were not true, though, and have you been informing about the possibilities of coming here? We shall of course do all necessary steps here, but shall achieve nothing before Canetti's book is published, which we hope will be in Febr. or March, the paper shortage being acute. By that time I hope to be installed in London, by a miracle, which in this country like in no other is performed by the powerful, the Lords and Ladies, who even sway their wand over the unholy unglorious and dark and gloomy head of a »foreigner«.

If I am still pressing at your heart, who is doing it with mine. I feel a heavy weight like the poor old king of Heine,[267] who had a young wife. Sein Herz war schwer, sein Haar war grau, der arme alte König, er nahm eine junge Frau[268] . . . But of course, there is also a young page, and the poor old king with *my* heart is left alone. I do hope when you come, that you'll live up to your maximes and let me have morphia, to forget my heart and my head, that tension in my head, which drives me *insane*, nerves, is the polite impression, will you help me? It's sure better to be a drug addict than not to be at all, and there have been lots of opium eaters among the writers in this country and among the good writers, too. Where do you take your patience from, that angelic attitude, that fortitude? Probably from the feeling that you gave and will give the world so much benefit, as can only be rewarded with the satisfaction that you feel (the noble Prize?). »We'll both get the noble prize, Georges and I, you'll see,« is, what Canetti told me yesterday, and he would kill me, if he knew, that I suggested, you should translate his play. He thinks my attitude to you is not respectful enough, though I have more than respect, I have unbound admiration.

At the red cross they told me, I could only send you medical supplies through them. So I thought you might not want those. On second thought—are they of any help—and *what* would you want. And don't forget the list about food, I read you are going to have plenty of sugar so soon, which seems miraculous to us, who these last five years have never any sugar the last two days of the month. I wish you'd also let me know how you sleep, eat, and what, how you dream, and what, but not in terms that are delightful but mysterious, rather bluntly I want it, as a grandmother that I am, wants to know about Benjamin.

The Jewish pioneer soldiers that come back from the continent tell us, that there are still most of the Nazis living peacefully and in high positions in the English and American zones.[269] Not with the Russians but they on the other hand vie with the Anglican allies in setting into the world little Nazis of big German women, who are much stronger than a Tommy or a Muschik.[270] My friend in the Austrian government[271] is much disputed by the Anglican part, but has succeeded in introducing a lot of social reforms, also reforms in Art, and *he* will understand no nonsense about Nazis. He is very much pro Jewish and we always fought each other. —I was *against* the Jews and he *for* them. Well, I paid it back to him in a way that enabled him to become minister. And he won't remain minister, he'll be Chancellor in good time. Write about yourself, Benjamin, your words are as sweet as your voice and moisten the burning heat, that the gassed victims of Belsen have left in mine.

Veza.

I passed a house every day, during the Blitz, that is, what *was* a house. A big block of houses, to be exact. Thirteen victims were buried there and could not be extricated. You passed it, saw the ruins, ah, your thoughts—and knew, they were there. A refugee and his wife lived there too, and that night, when the bomb fell, they decided not to go to the shelter (we were tired of going to the shelter, lie on damp floors in the cold, incapable of sleeping). But then his wife said: it's Friday the thirteens, to-day, better let us go. They went and escaped.

We liked to shelter in churches at daytime, a superstition, a crazy hope, for churches is, what Jerry liked to chose as targets, together with hospitals. One day we had a bomb *near* the church, it was clear, that we were the target. The next hit the hospital, because it had a red cross flag pleading commiseration! Commiseration from German pilots!

Dear Georges, Canetti was blazing when I told him that I had written about the »Hochzeit«. He says Nissim disliked it, and »The Comedy« is still more phantastic and highbrow. Forget it, please.

I told him I won't post the letter.

Auto da Fé is already announced in Book lists.

VEZA TO GEORGES · *OCTOBER 15 AND 16, 1945*

Mrs. Canetti Durris
Stubbs-Wood Chesham-Bois
Bucks

Oct. 15th

No, not dearest Georges,

After having waited for three days now for an answer to your brother's telegram, in agony, a letter came to-day dated from the sixth, slipped in quietly, and with a quiet contempt, whereas we are raving mad. I was so upset, that I did not feel quite happy about the letter, still looking for a yellow envelop, thinking there should be a telegram. You are not getting away with it, I warn you. I've been fretting quite enough and shall not do so anymore and shall *not* correspond with you anymore unless strictly business relating your brother's plays. No. I shall *not* correspond so as not to have to *fear*. My face is nothing but fear. My eyes stare in fear. I have had fear since 1938 incessantly, and I shall get rid of you two buggers and leave you one to another and cancel our acquaintance. I am fed up, I am. —Through not writing you missed a lot of stories happening meanwhile, which will get lost to posterity. Suffice it, that we even sacrificed our vehical, no not a car—for whereas your brother, the director, has two cars, and *you* probably have a giant car instead of that nice tiny one, all that *we* could achieve was a bycicle, a 12 guinea bycicle, war time quality, which your brother lost a week ago. That is to say, he left it somewhere, forgot where, and since he is terribly afraid of going to a police station, he kept the whole thing dark from me, for fear that he would have to go to the police. When he revealed it to me, we were so worried about your not writing, that we resolved to sacrifice the byke, as a gift to the merciless Gods—to get a letter from you. Since we decided this, up turned the byke, at which we were both more dismayed than glad, not having any news of you and of course thinking the envious Gods did not accept the sacrifice. *How* we recovered it, you'll never learn, since you won't get any nice letters anymore. Well, there is your letter now, and if your brother has not lost his byke on his way to the station to day, we have *you* and the byke. Will *he* be glad when he comes home to-night and sees your handwriting. He wanted to wire a letter of about fourty words, but since the P.O. does not accept 40 words I pretended to write them down and shortened his message to 15 words. He thinks cabling 40 words makes up for his letter. He may offer a thanks-giving gift to the Gods and *write* a letter to you now. If my machine jumps, it is, because *I* jump. I cannot quite read everything in your note and fear there are some more complications or trying »retemps« for you, but hope I may be wrong, however shall not know till E. comes home.

Your brother anyhow feels very much like a hero now, for when he *got* his byke, he *had* to go to the sub-station and was amazed, that they did not arrest him, came home like a superman and declares now he is »vorbestraft«[272] because his byke had been lost.

How can you think I would write a short note about Alice.[273] Her blasted niece, my cousin, in Mc[274] wrote *one sentence*, namely the one sentence that the Red Cross had sent her, and I got the letter when I had finished yours. She herself is wondering about Nuni, I begged her to let me know more, but apparently she does not know more. She is madly in love with you, on account of all that Alice and Daniels told her about you, but I'm afraid you won't requite her love, she is not your type (nor anyone else's neither, I am afraid). —The title up to now is Autodafé, the translater and Canetti being in love with that word. I would never read a book with that title. But the »Blendung«, as you very rightly remarked, was a rotten title, too.

You are responsible for my not being able to finish my second play[275] this week, though it is urgently wanted by a good producer (my first play[276] is being read by two producers at the moment) and why, because I was too nervous to finish it. It wants two days' work and God knows when I shall have the peace of mind, with two ungrateful, prodigal sons, that I have, and I shall not call you Benjamin, I'll call you Cain, and worse, if a worse name comes into my mind. Yes, I am considering Barrabas.[277] —When are you coming over? I ask, because I9ll escape to Switzerland (and that 9 is unvoluntarily). About Autodafé I9ll send you a catalogue where it is announced for the beginning of 1946.

Well, whatever you say, we *are* worrying about you and it *is* necessary for you to write more often, and we do love you, though we shall carefully hide it, and mind you . . . I am a *clinical* case of depression and hysteria, sorry, this is no joke, the result of the last eight years and of having two sons like you. If you make more jokes, you'll risk getting my funeral speech, which your brother undoubtedly will form, express, and even *write down* in a magnificent style.

My nephew is much better, and there is much hope of recovery.

Shall I send the »Hochzeit«, just in case? It is a grand play, I would send it secretely.

Much Love, angry Love,
Veza

I saved two pounds of tea for you and you'll get it somehow.

Sorry, I ordered honey from New Zealand.

Oct 16.

Dearest, at 12 o'cl. last night your brother read your letter to me and we were a bit upset about that »sac«[278] merely, because we don't want you to undergo all that torture. Why don't they apply that new serum,[279] the one recently discovered, *not* penicilin. This new serum works marvels. It's not a question of money—is it—if so, let me know at once. You are like me, banished to the country, I am, where I belong, whereas you, young and handsome should be in Paris. Though your brother says, that's the only good news, since you won't be allowed to work in St. H. —Considering that you wrote such a nice letter about such an unsatisfactory result, I made up my mind to continue my series of

»posterity« letters—that is, if you think they'll brighten up St. Hilaire a bit. Yours certainly brighten up *my* life—they are the *essence*. Is it possible for you to send me your pamphlet on the Jews?[280] When that »Autodafé«—is published we shall have a good periodical at our disposal, ready to accept good articles and I might translate it. You would have to send it to me typewritten. —We adore you.

VEZA TO GEORGES · *October 29, 1945*

Durris
STUBBS-Wood   Chesham-Bois
Bucks

Oct 29

Dearest Georges,

No answer to a telegramm—and your last letter, which came after 4 days of agony—dated from the 6th inst. So more than 3 weeks no letter.

Of course I would not write either, were it not, that I fear you might be fretting for having to stay on in St. Hilaire. Here a gentleman (I know his granddaughter) had exactly your complaint, he is *eighty*, always since his early youth had one lung out of action, and got married, and felt fine. As I say, I know his *grand*daughter. What you want is patience.

Not me! If I don't get a note soon, and others more often (Regine might write) I shall cancel our acquaintance. I am sick and tired of your brother reproaching me, that I probably annoyed you with something—and actually wanting to PERUSE—actually to »censure« my letters to you!!!! Of course I write them in his absence and post them at once.

Much love yours
Disgustedly,
Veza Canetti

VEZA TO GEORGES · *November 27, 1945*

Post Office: if undelivered do *NOT* return letter
Mrs. Canetti
7 Chestnut Lane, Amersham, Bucks

November 27. 1945

Dearest George,

I did not answer your fine letter at once, because I thought, if you find a letter with an English stamp every day, you'll not look out for it. But after a week there were obstacles and I'll not do that again. For why should I deprive you of good literature. In fact I want to send you some, namely the letters of Walpole,[281] which range right after mine in quality, and are far more interesting as to matter.

The obstacle was a nice one, meet me at the above address, ten minutes away from Canetti, and for the first time a nice flat, id est, a large very bright and cosy room and a kitchen of my own. It is my 27th removal since Grinzing, twenty seventh, and when Canetti had carried everything for me to this place (no vehicles available in time) and arranged everything in my drawers for me and switched the electric stove on for my feet to get warm, and lit my cigarette for me, I sitting in a huge armchair—I started crying. I cried and cried for over an hour, C. pacing the room in despair, for he does for me whatever is in his power, his nice face got quite wrinkled, he bit his lips, he did not know what to say, he was worried, it was cruel to cry, I tried not to, but then I started again, and he said if I cry I should for God's sake not cry out aloud, the landlady must not hear me, for she would turn me out at once, you've got to be cheerful, when you want a nice flat, you've got to pay a lot, and you've got to clean it out incessantly. *She* may have a mess in her kitchen, you must cook without even a trace of such an ugly thing being done. You've got to clean and polish—*polish*, that word!—your soul out, till you get a new soul, that makes you polish minded, till you think of nothing else, and when you have a visitor you hate him, because he left a trace on the polish and you've got to sink to your knees and wipe it away and pray to God and your landlady to pardon. And since my joy of life has been scrubbed away long since, I cried. And unless I get a flat of my own or a charwoman, to polish for me, I shall never smile again. How blasphemous I was in Paris, when I said I am Madame Choisel of la parure by Maupassant.[282] For now I am.

But this time it pays, I have a nice flat. At the other place, where your brother still stays on, having a large room and comparative quiet, they were rich people (90,000 pounds, and a gorgeous place, I walked on carpets, not one less than a hundred pounds). But the proprietress, the wife of the worthy parson, when she took her luke warm hot water bottle down in the morning, poured the water into the kettle to make tea with it and save money. For it was still warm. This one of a thousand characteristics of these people,[283] another funny one being, that *he* suffers from cleptomania and steals. He only steels trifles, nails, oil from your oil tin, very little, too. But he steals. You'll read quite a lot about them, so I close this chapter interrupting myself only for a minute to put some lovely scent on my grey hair, the nicest perfume I have had since many years, I would have to pay for it five guineas in the black market, which I don't, but my son sent it to me from France. That was a nice day when I met Daniels. It was pitch dark at half past four, there being fog, that London fog, that your brother and all great poets find so thrilling, and that minor contemporaries find depressing, taking your breath away, tiresome and unhealthy. We went to a nasty little café no other being near, and I said at the outset that I am twenty years older and that D. is my guest, but no, he paid! I was alone, poor C. waiting at another Café, to get the news about you right after my quitting him, I thought alone he might be nicer, which he was, he tried to be nice and told a lot about you far too little, though. I wanted him to give a parcel to Benjamin, but was embarrassed to ask, for I thought if he wanted to, he would offer it himself, knowing how much I want Big Ben to have my parcels, so I only ventured a pound of tea, would he carry it to his place. He said he would on Saturday, so I posted a pound of tea to him on Thursday (21st of Nov) morning, express and registered, Sainsburie's best tea, he must have had it in the afternoon, next day *at latest*, and we agreed if he does not get it in time his wife let's him have a pound and he carries it to Ben and keeps mine, which I would not like, since his wife is sure to get a brand twopence cheaper and no good. Of course I'd like to know, if Ben got it, I'm sure he'll write at once, for I can reclaim at the p.o.

I've hundreds of things to tell you, funny once, sad once, the disappointment about Austria,[284] election, and I don't even know yet if my friend has been reinstated.[285] It is all for the Russians having looted a lot in the towns, I can't blame them, they want to restore their homes in Russia.

I asked Daniels if by any chance you owe him money which I could repay, since we owe a lot to you, but he would not hear of it, he must be a mind-reader and maybe read my description of him, to you in a previous letter. I wanted of course to get the book for you through Cape, but he says you've got it. The translator of Cape, Miss Wedgwood, sent me a bunch of roses, because I corrected *her* English in Canetti's Autodafé, she being English, I being Austrian, and I made valuable suggestions as to style. Had she made my acquaintance, she would probably have sent me a dozen handkerchief, because I am dressed in rags, and I don't want to meet her, until the restrictions about clothing[286] are withdrawn and I can dress properly. It is essential in this country. That was lovely in Austria, you could dress as you liked, what was inside was essential. Though I am glad we did not accept the high positions offered to us. We would have to be schoolteachers now. Oh—your description of your life in the sana! Better than Thomas Mann. Though probably intended to be fiction for what Daniels told me. First he said, you are o.k. and that wound is very likely to heal without operation. Then he said two of your books[287] are coming out now. Then he said you are a great personality, and everybody considers it an honour to talk to you. (So I feel honoured, it does me good to know you, after having polished the kitchen, will you greet me in the street?) Then he said you are in a posh place, renowned for its luxury, comfort and high minded, educated, famous inhabitants in all France!!! So don't ask me to be sorry for you, I am not. And your brother said, good for him to be there, he can do his intellectual work which is more important to the world, than hospital work.

Haunted by my own defeat in life (when I cried I said to your brother, I don't believe him, what he promised that I'll sit in a box next year and see my play performed in London, for a person who has been thus degraded by landladies, cannot rise to any hights, there are no such examples in literature), haunted by a heap of burned bodies in Belsen, and by the living skeletons eating part of the carcasses, and by the presence and the future of the world, I consider it an honour if anybody talks to me. The archduke of Austria[288] could talk to me, Hess[289] could, he had a bodyguard of thirty people here, and ate chicken every day. The trial? I am a great hater, but once the enemy at my feet, I cannot triumph.

Do write. I shan't write before I get a long letter from you. Write to the above address, but since it may go to Durris Stubbs wood (before I inform the p.o. which I will only after a month, after seeing that my landlady is condescending to keep me) be careful what you write though you can write that you love me. For you'll never say so anymore, but before you see me again, you might think you do. Report of a dream on this subject next time.

Thank you for your present. I cherish it. I love it! I use it like a miser! I get transformed with it.

Veza

Did you get parcel by Kae Hursthouse? She posted end of October.

How did you know that I longed for scent?

Elias to Georges · *November 28, 1945*[290]

Wednesday

My beloved Georg,

Your books have finally arrived and you can hardly imagine the general excitement that has seized everyone here. You look marvelous, both pleasant and serious. I'm so proud of your accomplishment and the honor this publication has earned you that I can't think of anything more to say. I've read the two introductions, which are *masterfully* written, with a stylistic clarity, concision, and wisdom I envy you. What language! And how you wield it! It makes me extremely happy to think that *both of us* have produced works in completely different languages, works which, apart from their content, make use of these languages with total authority. I also like the generous way you approach your problems. I would never have thought that one could remain so *sovereign* in such a specialized enterprise. You are a brilliant fellow. You are a genuine intellect, and you've finally brought me to the point where I can take off my hat to you, honestly and proudly, without reservation. I intend to study both volumes closely. I'm afraid there is much I won't understand, but you will be able to explain it to me easily. This letter is only a quick, initial confirmation of receipt. In two or three days, I will write you at length. Please don't misunderstand Veza's behavior. She will definitely visit you; she talks about it constantly. It's just that everything has been postponed because of external circumstances. She has just been through weeks of agitation. Her landlady in Amersham suddenly behaved like a low-down dog and put her out on the street. With the greatest difficulty, I've finally found her something provisional in London, and she moved the day before yesterday. She could not even think of traveling in her terrible state of mind. Now, she will soon calm down and can make the necessary preparations. Oh, if only you would live in Paris again soon and we could take turns visiting you! For now, an embrace and admiration and congratulations from your terribly happy brother,

Elias

Elias to Georges · *December 3, 1945*

Monday, Dec. 3, 1945

My dear, dearest brother,

Your telegram just arrived, and Veza went out a moment ago to send you an answer. I'm lying in bed with influenza and feel an irresistible urge to write you. A letter from Veza is on its way—actually, you ought to have it by now. In the meantime, she has moved into a dwelling somewhat more fit for human habitation, and she likes it. Here at my place, she didn't even have a kitchen. The latter part of her silence was due to the move, which was fairly exciting. The earlier part was probably punishment for some imagined slight or other. Perhaps you didn't answer her right away. She sometimes thinks she's been insulted, and then—although otherwise the best human being in the world—she can suddenly turn cruel and hard. Because of Veza's culpability, I myself seem almost exculpated. That's why I'm talking about it so much.

You will find it difficult to understand why it was so hard for me to write to you. How often I have begun and simply couldn't continue. I would so much like to have *seen*, *heard*, and *spoken to* you beforehand. There was so terribly much I had to tell you. How can one even begin to write it in a letter! I would have liked to find a point in the external world equidistant from both of us; then we could have built everything else up around it. Most of all, I would have liked to be with you for a half year or longer, to be sick myself, so I could share your illness and thus make it easier for you. This war, this world has made us a thousand times more loving. I used to contradict you sometimes when you said that it all depends on how much one loves people, not on their moral or intellectual qualities. Now, I agree with you a thousand percent: what matters is the feeling of love, nothing else. If one is lucky, one loves a brother like you, a brother who deserves it. But I fear I would love you almost as much even if you weren't the way you are.

You must certainly have expected something more intelligent than my first letter. But I just can't force myself to say anything intelligent. Accept it as an initial, passionate embrace. I wish I could tell you all the time how much I love you. I spend half the day thinking of you. With Veza, I talk about nothing but you. Someday, when I see you again, I would like to show you what I wrote down during the war, when we lived in mortal fear for you. There are poems to you, incantations, prayers. You would be amazed. A year later, it still seems a miracle that you have survived, that you are there. You can thank God I didn't become a Catholic out of pure joy. It's all the more cruel that you cannot be with me now, or I with you. You will certaily recover, and *soon*. What weight can it have, compared to the things you have already escaped? Perhaps in the long run, it's not so bad after all that you are leading a quiet life there and not overexerting yourself. The hectic life in Paris would surely prove especially bad for you. The peacefulness and the slow pace of life are two of the things I like best about England.

I'm writing to you in German. You don't mind, do you? The other languages are all superimposed, and in reality, so is German. Most of all I'd like to write in Spanish, but in our own, old-fashioned Spanish. Isn't that a laugh? It's remarkable that we discovered Spanish literature independently of each other during the war. *I* had intended to *recommend* Gracian[291] to you, but also the Spanish satirist Quevedo,[292] who is almost as great as Swift.[293] Not a week goes by that I don't read a bit of Spanish. I especially love the old "romances" (ballads) that are much closer to our mother tongue. It's my ambition in the coming years—once I have completely mastered English and can write it as well as I do German—to write in Spanish. I have a very large favor to ask of you: in your next letters, can you go through all our relatives in order and report *exactly* what their fates were during the war? I don't plan to do anything with this information, I would just finally like to know. Has Poulou[294] returned? Please send both Jojo[295] and Poulou my address and tell them to write. Now, don't think you won't get another letter from me for a long time. If you're not averse to this lowly level of correspondence, I'd like to write more often now. Will you answer right away? Please don't punish me now! I embrace you with more love than ever.

Your brother Elias.

Are there any English books you'd like? I have a large library in English now and can send you anything.

VEZA TO GEORGES · *December 4, 1945*

Mrs. Canetti
7 Chestnut Close
Amersham—Bucks

Dec. 4th

Darling George,

You must have my long letter by now. The day after I wrote it, your brother fell ill and had a heavy influenza. He is still in bed, but the temperature is going down. I *sit up* with a flu now, for since the war I have never had a chance of remaining in bed with my grippe, which (like lots of people) I have every month in winter. It is hard and dull to describe, how miserable I felt, with all the worry about him (he has been coughing since half a year), he is still coughing, much worse of course and I am so tired.

My only consolation, relaxation, pride and warmth is the thought of you. It *keeps me alive*. I'll write a long letter to-morrow, a real letter, a love letter, a letter to you—

Did you get my message through Marcel? It does not smell lovely as yours, but has only a faint flavour, only a faint charm, only a faint capacity left, to stimulate and it is old and wrinkled, dark and dry—like me.

That's it. I *am* a handful of tea!

All my love,
Veza

Kindly write at once if you got a parcel from Daniels from Paris.

VEZA TO GEORGES · *December 15, 1945*

Canetti
7 Chestnut Close
Amersham Bucks

Dec. 15th

Georg!

Three letters and no answer! I did not cable because there was a letter on way which came before a wire could reach you from Amersham. We are terribly upset, write at once, wire, dont be so cruel!

Veza

VEZA TO GEORGES · *January 15, 1946*

Mrs. Canetti
7 Chestnut Close, Amersham, Bucks

January 15th 1946.

DARNLEY,

If a book for your birthday does not come in time, it's owing to your neglecting me. I proposed to be firm this time and you shall never get more than an answer to your letter, but this answer, helas, the very day I get it. So as to speed up your reply without injuring my pride too much. When I read the first page, I quickly put your scent on my hair, your scent, it is delicious and it never exhausts, and makes me feel a bit of *myself* again, and reminds me of your voice, which is the nicest thing in you, bewitching, unforgettable and which you can never lose. I promise you, you won't get any laments and telegrams, if you neglect me for your blasted vanities, you just won't get my delightful letters. —When I read the second page, I wanted to take off the scent again, and I don't sense it anymore for I am worried, though I cannot think the operation is serious, after all I was told about it, and you would tell me if it were, nobody can cheat *you*, fortunately, and you could not cheat me, I would die if it were, I very nearly died before your first news came from France, last year, there exists a letter, a last letter to you, which your brother has kept for you. I would die if you were in danger and if not by a natural death, I would help out. I cannot live without knowing you *exist*, and if I shall never see you again, I must know you *are*, and if a year or two after your operation you'd tell me you got married and are madly in love with your wife, I should not even be jealous, for there is something between us, that will not exhaust itself, it has never been consumated and will outlive the presence, my state of mind, my cynism, my hatred of myself, there'll always be that affinity between us, our life story, yours, which resembles mine, only yours is in a grander scale, everything with you is in a grander scale . . . and so is your greatness in writing about your operation, as though you explained things about one of your patients, and of consoling me about it.

No, not Smerdiacov.[296] But in his complicated life he has sometimes to take refuge to such a lot of lies, that he confuses me (to whom he lies of course, too) to a degree as to drive me mad. Hence my cynism, but which has been much aggravated through the facts of a century so hopeless, so devoid of beauty, poetry and noble thoughts, that you begin to praise the English, because they tolerate you, and even find an encouraging smile, nay, after six years of asserting yourself, in spite of your small bank account, detect that you are different, but somehow worthy of admiration. You *are* right. I admire their character, their dependability, each the result of their lack of passion. They are free of any passion, warmth of feeling (which they deride and call sentimentallity), enthusiasm, but they are dependable, and never could have happened here what happened in Germany, because it is not fair, it is not done, it is against the gospel, against the words of Christ. I *am for* religion, Benjamin, *for* religion, since the average mind wants to know why they are kind, decent and since they want a reward. We who have it in our blood despise it, you *are* right. I find it dull, oh how dull they are, and I could never speak to them as I speak to you, not when you meet them. After six years you may start being yourself, but always with a charming apoligy, with a »bonmot« that ameliorates your harshness—and that, maybe, is good for your character, too, for Belsen made me so hard, so cruel, so sarcastic, that I would not check myself, if they did not. Of course, *you* = France is my air. I shall not be able to go there for long, it depends all on you, if you do everything *to recover*, I'll come and help you one day. And cook a spinach pie for you. If you should get tired, I would not come. If I *were* to go, only if C. gets his English naturalisation[297] (which he will when his book comes out) but I could not stay long. He'll get me a »sineçure« at his publishers (reading books for the Publisher or well paid translations) something in my line and well paid. His translator, who is gone on him, takes advantage of his thoughts and in fact won't be able to write her new historical works without him, and since she has just become a partner of the publishers (a secret that we can only reveal to you) we are in a good position. And with these commercial facts I close my letter now, since there will be a birthday note in your book, and since I don't want to become too cynical, and since I am hungry, carrots boiling in my kitchen, which I'll have to serve you with every meal, when you come, come *you must*, we consider the invitation as our contribution to your treatment, and I'll feed you . . . not with the food that we have been starving with these six years, but with the parcels my relatives[298] send me from U.S. now. By the bye, I sent Kae a pound note for your parcel, and what about it? And how is your financial position? Let us know!!!

Your brother (I shan't read the first page of your letter to him, but the rest, and I get your letters here now, but still be careful) will he be delighted, we were worried, why can't you write one line? I would feel disappointed about one line, but not cruelly tormented.

All my love,
PEGGY

Yes, of course you'll get that book via Cape.
Darnley?[299] The lover who *ruined* Mary Stuart.

VEZA TO GEORGES · *1946*

P.O. Do *not* return this letter

Dear Georg*es* Kien,

You are French in the English version, and I think the true model of your picture. I think you walk about in the Etudiants,[300] just as your brother describes you in the »Madhouse«.[301] The Blendung, Autodafé is coming out at the end of March or even in April, and though the translation is good, it is not to be compared to the grand style in German, and that's why I am a little anxious. Not on account of success, on account of the effect on your brother, who does want encouragement badly or else he'll not go on working. I am nervous, to you I confess it.

I am more nervous still about you having to move and that tiresome spring before you. You *will* write to me darling, right before you go and as soon as you arrive and the date of the operation, because I want to worry a lot, it helps.

In Gower Street the medical department of the University library, has ordered fifty copies of Rich pato . . . etc.[302] They said, they ordered so many because the work is in demand, it seems to be an exceptional work. It has been ordered long ago, but did not yet come, or else we would have been informed. I am going to London expressly on Friday to inquire for it and pester them about it, and also to find my belated birthday present for you, which problem your brother could not solve, not that he was not very anxious to please, but because we can't get a darned thing, and I'll have just to get something that I was not very keen on sending you, only in order not to send a second hand book again. What concerns your brother, you could have two Rich-copies, because he wants to pay for it, and I insist on paying for it, but Peggy will win. By the way, I wrote »darling«, it is the first time in this country that I used this term, and never shall again, I only do so to flatter you beyond description, so that you should keep me informed. My tearing this sheet is a faulty action,[303] because this letter is strictly business and I feel ashamed about it.

No wonder your brother Nissim has no real friends but only parasites round him, the way he behaves, you can't expect more. And I can't blame your brother Elias, for resenting it, that I sent him the Comödie, since Nissim Canetti does not find it worth while to write to him and thank him for the privilege of being allowed to read it. We write this even to strangers who send us their Ms. And it may be, that your brother Nissim will feel uncomfortable about it one day. Not that we expected him to understand the value of the work. But we expected a letter of thanks. Well, there he is, rid of Edith, Canetti thinks it's better for him, and I hope he is right.

This is not meant to be a real letter and so I close, only telling you that I don't lack variety, concerning l.s (!) (hence no address on top of my letter). This one has better manners which even improved, since she saw the big advertism. in the Times, which will reflect some glory on her l. existence. Her hobby is sitting locked up in her room and conversing with all the deceased persons she knew. Which made me for a time frentic with fear, lest they should tell her, that they don't like me in the house. No such thing happened, though, and thus her hobby is not interfering with my life. It seems that English ghosts, spirits and guides, are in my favour, for at the other place, with my

Nissim Jacques Canetti, 1944

priest, their friend was called[304] to see if I am possessed by the devil or not (she being a clairvoyant), and it turned out, that she saw a light round my head, kind of a helo, signifying that there are great things ahead for me. Which prediction did not materialise up to now, but helped me to keep your brother off from London bombs, and anyhow I gave her a large tin of corned beef for it, which the clairvoyant gladly accepted, and probably had anticipated.

Dear beloved son, we speak only of you and . . . and did I call you Darnley, thinking it the name of the lover of Mary Stuart, who ruined her, because she loved him so? But was not Darnley her husband and Bothwell[305] was her lover? I keep thinking it since a long time now, and could ask my landlady, who is always ready to oblige, but I can't. I can't even look it up, since it is such a delicate subject. Darnley was the husband, dear, whom she poisoned, or killed, and I do hope you don't bear me a grudge. The name sounds so passionate, and anyhow she was in love with him, too, and only disappointed later on, and maybe I am wrong, and Darnley was Bothwell, after all, you see, I got them mixed up, because it is a childhood reminescence and at that time, I was in love with Darnley, Bothwell (not with Rizio,[306] he was only a singer and a commoner) *and* Mary Stuart, whereas now I tend to accept the English viewpoint, and think, Mary was a hussy and Elizabeth was grand, and really and truly, she did not want to have Mary Stuart beheaded, really she did not. I'll tell you why. She was a queen, and »uneasy lies the head that wears a crown.«[307] So she said: It is not possible to behead a queen and who would dare to venture it. Nobody must dare to! It was really done against her will.

With which interesting comment I end this epistle, asking you by the bye darling Darnley Bothwell and *Jack the Ripper* (whom at my age and with my present cruel constitution I like best): Do you know Elizabeth and Essex by Lytton Strechey?[308] If you don't, you'll have to start it, I can send *that* one.

All my Love,
Peggy

VEZA TO GEORGES · *February 3, 1946*

Mrs. Canetti
7 Chestnut Close
Amersham Bucks

Feb. 3. 1946.

Ah, your letter! In your last but one, the story about Sorel delighted your brother, who told it in London and Bucks, not without asserting, of course, that you had it from a secret source, and looking very important whilst telling it. Are *we* glad, that the question of your accomodations in Paris is settled in this magnificent way. The stage is very nice I know it, but, I am sorry to say, I don't fit in. I loved your little appartment upstairs too much, and like all criminals want to go back to the scene of crime. It has been demolished, and has no attraction for me, even if I could rent it again, going to Paris. I'll have to go to an hotel and must tell you a very disappointing thing: I love hotels. It's congruent with *my* pessimism. A house, or even flat would be too stabil for me. I have not yet promised myself that I can settle down for long. I sort of hesitate. I don't know where I am, yet. I *hate* too much. And I am too easily overwhelmed. I hate and despise and I *am* a pessimist and yet a word by a stranger passing, can knock me down. And another word can delight me, I own. This little place, is inhabited by lunatics. One came up to me yesterday, a former actress, deranged and still of rare beauty, though her eyes are dead, and said: »Plus il y a de merde, plus les fleurs sont belles.«[309] I repeated it to your brother, only regretting, that there is so little merde in me. And right I was. For I caught his thought. He thought at once of his blonde,[310] gratified and with silent triumph. —My *salon*, if I live, I'll have one, is going to be a detached hall in an hotel. I'm going to live in an hotel. It's transient. The last lodging, so to say. And there is variety.

What concerns your visitors, the femininum, I could kill them. I could kill all your visitors. Also the male ones. But being a pessimist, I'm afraid, you would kill *me*. And I'm not going to give you any advice. Once in Vienna in 1937 your brother went to a fancy ball. »There is an attractive blonde,« he told me, »and there are dark corners, she is devorced, you know, and very young and gay. What could I do« he asked me, »to give her sort of an impression, that I am a man of the world?« So with a very knowing smile, I told your brother how to tackle the blonde. I did it so well, that I have still got her on my shoulders, up in London. You want to know? I'm not going to help you, too. But that vicious creature thinks even to day, that your brother is an experienced »homme a femme«.[311] I wish I were a man. I knew the job. But I have not got the tool.

For God's sake, cross that last sentence out. For posterity's sake. No, burn the letter. This one, anyhow won't be historic. I am in a labil mood. Not up to the mark. Can letters really influence another remarkable letter writer? I learned his language by heart, Walpole's, I admit, but what I have to say is born in my womb. I could never write like him. Because I have not got the Lebensraum.[312] I shall have maybe, but . . . too late. I wrote to Broch after giving him a description of Anna's life: »An outrageous thing happened to *me*! . . . I grew *old*!« He answered back, that I can never be old, because I am sad. People with my pain in my heart cannot grow old. I think he wrote this to himself. He wants it this way, for he only recently moved in together with a young widow.[313] Will *she* be glad with pain being all that he has to offer her!

You are right, though, my last letter was inspired by the thought that you are going to have that operation. But in a different way. It gave me the courage to write it. I can never feel sorry for you, not for *you*! I admire you too much. And you'll sit in my salon, in the hotel hall when »Parker« will serve tea, and you'll be the piece de resistance and we shall vie in »ésprit«. Esprit is the only thing for which I long. My only sensual desire is ésprit. I long for ésprit. You may find them clever here. Witty. But they have no ésprit.

We are transformed somehow, since a few days, your brother and I. One grey veil lifted. If you see the enclosed announcement, you'll understand why and be glad with us. You belong to us. Without you, no veil could be lifted. There is not a day we don't talk about you in great length and heat. And argue and love and admire *you*. You'll see, that the publisher is fully aware of bringing forth a great novel. But if you could read the blurb that the translator wrote, and which I'll send you as soon as it appears in »The Times«—well you could have knocked me down with a feather when I read it. Yes, one veil, one grey veil is lifted. But we must always have you. Our only child.

»Murder will out and blood will talk.«[314] With that quotation of Macbeth my deranged actress dismissed me, and I did not quote that one to your brother, for he might have applied that one to me, and not without cause . . . We can't get the books, we would like, dear, and so your brother is going to haunt all libraries for a secondhand Retz for me, which I am dying to read. What concerns your book, my present, I mean, I did not post it. Your delay in writing me was one reason, I had missed the birthday and so I did not rush—my moody disposition is another. I hesitate, I do nothing else. I had three books, I still have them. One with the coulored pictures of old London. Your brother thought you would not like it. One with paintings by the people »Popular English art.« It is charming, but it was cheap. And of whatever books I thought, we fear you know them or we can't get them. I'll decide anyhow in two or three days, nothing but French books coming into my mind at the moment. I love Aubry, Napoleon,[315] and I love most of all Madame Bovary, the greatest novel to my taste, not as to the topic, but as to working it out. What language, what consequence![316] Kafka! Ours Canetti does not let me have and I get him only in English. And of course you know »*Light in August*« by Faulkner and do you know Forster? »Howards End«? This you must read at once, but this would not be a present, we can't get it new, it would have to be out of my library. There is one book I have in mind, which your brother is going to get for me to-morrow, he hopes he can. Have you any wishes? Write, for nothing to make him more happy than to send him to get books. And don't blame *me* for the delay of Rich, you'll get that alright. And if they don't stole your parcel, you should have it, the one from Kae, yes, Kae short for Kathleen, she is reliable like a clockwork. And you will get chocolate from U.S. I am worried, nothing there yet, but things take a long time. With which prosaic end I close my letter and might as well add, that your heart need not break about central Europe, »why! you are starved out« they said to me in hospital last year, not that they could help it, but we are dying here slowly, gradually, on bread potatoes and carrots. With a few oranges now this month, since the flu epidemic is serious and the flu of a serious kind.

I hate the things they are going to do *after* the operation, and do let me know beforehand, so that I can worry, for if I worry a lot, everything will turn out at its best, and do write at once and much love and your brother the scoundrel wants me to tell you, he is going to write you to night. Don't believe him, oh, don't.

All my love,
Veza

Veza to Georges · *March 16, 1946*

Mrs. Canetti
7 Chestnut Close
Amersham, Bucks England

March 16th

Darling Son, Dear Georges Canetti,
dite Le Beau, dite Le Savant, dite Le Grand
dite Phoebus, dite Romeo,[317] dear Benjamin,

Considering that my name is only Peggy, which in this country is the most humble and ugly name, in use only for antiquated housekeepers, old age pensioners and the like, I think the »distance« is large enough to allow me to write a love letter to you. And since the »distance« (French prononciation) is duly stressed, may I tell you that I love you in my dreams, even, where the distance is a little less stressed, but never quite overlooked being that of a prince to a commoner, but not more, a commoner in love, and once I dreamed, oh, it's six months ago, that we expected you here . . . did I tell you that dream, I'm afraid I did, so I'm not going to repeat myself, it's usually an »Angsttraum,«[318] fearing whether you will talk to me at all, when you see an old hag with wrinkles and so on, a sour look of disillusion in my eyes, and in the end I dream, that you most lordly kiss me and condescend to acknowledge me still as your sister in law, quandmême,[319] and you tell me so of course, with the mien of a beau of thirty four, handsome, tall, pale, with that exciting palor only happening in novels, or with the lovers of Queen Elizabeth the great, or with you, or Georges Kien, you keep telling me, you still like me and are not going to exclude me from your presence and even suck a toffee for me, a bonbon, and let me have the remainder. Which toffees I did not send you, my blasted sister in law[320] having changed her food store into a toy shop with leather goods, in a posh district more near London, and thus raising her social standard to three degrees, and we having eaten every scrap of our American food parcel, oh I could tear my hair out, it's grey anyhow. (Ten years ago I thought, well I'll dy it, when it's grey, and go to beauty parlours for wrinkles, and paint my cheeks and massage my embonpoint, and now I kind of relish in my destruction, I want it to correspond to my state of mind.) And will you please let me know next time somebody comes, a week before, so that I can »swap«* things for you, a new expression by the bye, which you won't find in dixies. Last night I had another Angsttraum about the operation with a happy ending, too, but always with you being very condescending, I won't tell you the dream, but tell you, why I know, that everything will turn out marvelous for you this time . . . I'll tell you what we did for your operation. We lost the bicycle. And we did not recover it. We could do lots of things to recover it but we shan't. We feel we must give it up. Do you see our point. Do you see that this time everything will turn out beautifully for us three? I said to your brother yesterday, »the balance weight of misfortune is the good fortune that *ends* it« quoting Saint Simon, whose work is as dear to me as are your letters. Yes, good fortunes for the three of us, I predict them. You'll see, so, pride of my old age, and heir of our glory fame and money (the latter will be there in due time), and three thousand books are there and two thousand unprinted pages of your elder brother, *you* are our heir, we made the will in the times long forgotten of the Blitz in London.

To be more exact and indiscreet, your brother was distressed, for now and then, that blonde you know, *that* girl, tries to blackmail him into divorcing and marrying her, under pretence that there is a great and rich nobleman, an M.P. and whatnot, who is mad after her and wants to make her her ladyship. Your brother, feeling he can't be in her way, tries to make sure that this grand personallity really does marry the treasure, to find out, that the titled Man does not dream of doing so, because he *is* married already and does not dream of divorcing his nice wife, the mother of his children, for that hussy. A reconciliation follows, because the great lord only wanted just an adventure and a short and cheap one, with a short and cheap one, which is exactly that one. In the end your brother lords it again, till two months later she finds another way to blackmail him into something and drive him to dispair, yes dispair, and the only thing I can do about it is to offer him a divorce, which I do with all my heart, not being ambitious. Not ambitious to cook meals, darn socks and write letters, letters of apology because he did not write letters. When I offer that divorce he gets a bit scared of having really then to marry one of the vamps and that settles it. But for a few days of misery, when I feel terribly worried about him which this time was aggravated by my feeling worried about you, everything runs smooth again, the dame feeling hurt so much, that the Lord did not mean business but only pleasure, that we have a truce. Would you have believed that, knowing the article in question? Darling George, you being my wiser, elder son, I confide all this to you, but do not mention a word and tear this letter, too. I won't have posterity know that the poet Canetti is a dupe of such a wooden idol.

Do you see now, that I must have news of you at once. Or will you add to my troubles, you who have always been so kind to me!

So generous, noble and protecting! —Edith wrote, about *her* divorce and all and she seems very satisfied with herself and her arrangements. I must say, I admire her initiative—I have none. About her letter next time. All my love . . . and do let me know everything. Did you get »Light in August«? The Rich did not yet come, but if by now you have no parcel from New Zealand, I begin to fear they have been tampered with. Shall think out another way.

All my Love,
~~Vez~~ Peggy

*meaning—exchange

VEZA TO GEORGES · *March 22, 1946*

Mrs. Canetti
7 Chestnut *Close*
Amersham, Bucks, England

March 22.

Darling Georges,

We feel, that there might be your operation any day now, and there is not a moment, when I don't think of it. Your letters about it, especially your last letter, was admirable, and I feel thoroughly ashamed before you, our baby son, who tackles hardships like a man, like a superman, whereas we, we break down, and but for you at the moment we would not see much sense in carrying on. You will let me know at once when it's over, and the jokes you cracked and how you feel, and the temperature . . . I know everything will be allright, in fact I see you getting the Noble-prize one day . . . I swear you'll get it. You'll get two, one for noblesse of mind.

We here are not very near the Noble prize, as you may gather from our last letters. I should not have joked about and ironised the affair, for it turned out to be a very grave, decisive point in your brother's life and all I can do at the moment is to hope and wish, that he should survive the shock. You'll see by his letter, what a hopeless romantic, selfless and naive brother you have, what a dreamer and poet. You have seen the person in question,[321] who spoiled my life and now spoiled his. It would be too long and also not fair, to tell you, what he has done for her, these years, and what he has *not* done for me. He'll tell you himself, that is, if I can get him over this critical period. You'll help me. You'll write him a love letter. Write it to his address. His letter was an appeal to you, answer it with all your kindness. He deserves your affection, believe me. If he does not get out of his mind, now, it is because we cling to *you*. Well, that girl thought it wise to do things thoroughly, and she, while calling your brother's attention to her entanglement with the M.P. plunged herself into a love affair with a Jew of the East end,[322] a proletarian, who falls for every silk stocking, but with the distinct tendency to get along in life and buy himself silk stockings. He is a writer of the worst description, and she is madly in love with him. In short: I have not seen her for five years, because I refused to meet her, on account of some defects in her character, which might land me in Scotland yard, where I did not want to land. For I have nothing left but my honour and pure record. What I feared most all these years was, that your brother, innocent to a fault, a spotless character, would land there and what I feared still more was, that she would plant a baby on him, a child of the butcher next doors, tell him it's his, and ruin his life with that bastard. It turned out, that there was that East end writer preventing that. For when she *feared* she was pregnant, she broke down, and confessed everything to your brother, not because she was fair, but because the writer *wanted* the child, to secure her the better for his purpose (and the money with her, that her parents would be forced to allow her in that case, when he married her, they are doing very well, they are in Sweden). The situation now is this. Your brother wants to put her before an alternative, either she loses him, or she gives up that man. And I, instead of wishing and praying that she would not give up her new lover, instead of remaining firm, I sent for her, invited her, opened a parcel before her, that I got that very day, containing all the delicacies of the New World, American delicacies, and Nylon silk stockings, I shared with her, pretended not to know about her new felony, pretended to like her, pretended to be keen on her company, and I shall meet her now and so to say mother her, and if she confesses everything to me, pretend to be sympathetic, I shall help her, genuinely help her, for your brother *thinks she* is distressed! And all that, son, because I want him to gain time to get over the shock, I hope his book will come out meanwhile, and that this event, at the moment not meaning a thing to him, yet will impress him, so that he can get over his despair. When you see me once, son, and when you find that my melancholy and bitterness is intolerable, when you find that I am a displaced person much placed below my station and talents, perhaps you'll now understand why. *She* was introduced in society, not I, *she* was placed on a piedestal and I was neglected, thrown into despair and nearly driven into a state of insanity. I am prepared to everything now and I have a cold contempt for everything. The life of you and your brother is all I care for, and shall try to save once again. I can do nothing for *you* but wish and pray, yes I pray to an unknown being. I try to do the absurd and impossible for that helpless, weak, innocent and half mad creature, your brother. I may once want to do something for *myself.* I shall do that, if I succeed in getting him safely over this abbyss. At the moment this is where I stand. —I shall keep you informed about everything, but beg you not to write about it. I usually get your letters before he comes to my place, but if once he gets a letter where you mention all this, he would believe himself betrayed by me, too, and that would be the end of it all. Mind you, if I get hold of her, it is also to be informed about everything and so to say watch your brother and protect him, you see that, don't you? You can mention in your letters, all that *he* wrote to you, (all that you think of her and)[323] all that I wrote about her except what I wrote in my last two letters. This you must not mention. And you must burn the letters, I ask that of you.

He worked *a lot* these years, but he can never *finish* his work which wants leisure and a composed mind, because of what he goes through with her. Every half year there is a catastrophe. He will tell you, through *my* fault he cannot finish his work, because I am always so depressed. I know you will see how things are, and I want you to see them. I have been reproaching myself lots of times, that I stand in his way and cost him money and don't make any, and yet, in my heart I knew, that I was wronged, that I had to step apart, that I had to take care of his merely physical well being and had to prevent that he does not lie under the table drunk, every other day, for that's the way of life she likes.

Is it not horrible, that I write all this to you? But somehow I want to clear myself before you. Somehow I have *one* thing left in my life that I insist on having left untouched by a flaw. It is my relation to you, and your opinion of me. And I shall never again have the courage to confess all that to you. To-morrow I might repent it. To-morrow I might feel I wish I had not told you everything. To-morrow I might have written how bright the sun shines in Denmark[324] and how inefficient I am and how grand everybody is. To-day I want you to see, what I stood up for. I am not a maniac, always seeing the dark sight of things, I am brave and clever, brave to a degree that nobody knows, except your brother, yes, I will say that for him, he would never leave me, never betray me, never belittle me. But of course, when he felt like sitting in pubs with her, drinking during the Blitz, wheras I forced him to shelter in a kitchen with me, he still thinks, *she is grand* and I am just an anxious woman. When I made scenes to save his life, he thinks I am hysterical. Or maybe he does not think so anymore, but that does not help me now.

Darling, do you see how we want you? Do you see how you are all we have left? For surely, all the success in the world neither mine nor his, all the money and glory shall never efface what I went through, and I have forgotten how it is, to laugh, to enjoy sunshine or to live.

Will you add to my despair and not write?

Peggy

GEORGES TO VEZA · *March 27, 1946*[325]

This letter is *my* property and I trust you'll *keep* it for me. Veza

C.[326] March 27, '46

My dearest,

I am beside myself at what you have written. Your grandeur and your goodness will not save him. He is *frightful* . . . His complete lack of clarity and self-control, his weakness in the face of resistance, his miserable obsession with something so foolish (compared with everything we've been through the last 6 years), his repulsive egocentricity, his alcoholic intoxication, his inability to deal with a situation that is not in the least unusual and only needs him to pull himself together—I find all this pitiful *trash* terrible, worse than I can tell you . . . And this is my brother? But this is not a man, it's a rag, a doormat you can treat any way you want! And this after all the years of terror in which even the biggest fool grasped what was really important, in which we learned to understand private adventures, blown up out of proportion by a corrupt and arrogant psychology, for what they are—namely, *silly trifles*. I know very well that they're unavoidable, but they are so paltry in comparison with other things that really count in life . . . Yes, I find him frightful, and please don't ask me to write him a friendly letter. I'm not in a position to do so at the moment. What I wrote to him is still the least hostile thing I could manage. Certainly, I love him, but this love has been so unremittingly crossed by disappointment—at how he treated my mother, at his laziness, at his weakness with regard to money, at his unproductivity (worst of all!), at his foolish adventures, at his arrogance, etc.—that it has become pale, lifeless, and weak, a love made of resignation and bitterness, without strength, without spark. I can do *nothing* for him. Perhaps it would be different if I were there with him. With pity to help me, my sympathy would perhaps revive . . . But from this distance I feel only disgust. My poor dear friend, now I understand what makes you so bitter, or rather, why you say you are so bitter—for the amazing thing is that you're not really bitter—why you have such a hard view of life. It isn't the bombs, or the privations, or exile, not Bergen-Belsen or anything of the sort. It is because for years, you have been witness to this harrowing spectacle of incapacity, cowardice, mendacity, *failure*, and because you yourself have been living under the power of these things, on board a galley that didn't belong to you and which you found terrible, except that on it was the thing you loved and could rescue by seeming to sympathize with the spectacle. What you have done and what you continue to do is *admirable*, and believe me, if anyone should ever be interested in what my brother was (which seems more and more doubtful), *I will do everything in my power* to see that people know *which one* of you two was truly great—great of character, assuming that he really is equally great in intelligence, which seems less and less likely to me. It would be too unjust if the truth about which of you is really important did not come to light.

There you have it. Don't be angry at my harshness. I cannot be otherwise—and anyway, if I were no longer harsh toward my brother, if I were capable at this moment of writing him a loving and indulgent letter, then he wouldn't really be my brother, but just some polite and indifferent acquaintance, which I will never be for him.

A heartfelt embrace from

Georges.

Continue to keep me informed.

VEZA TO GEORGES · *March 29, 1946*

Mrs. Canetti
7 Chestnut Close
Amersham, Bucks England

March 29th 1946

Darling Georges,

I just got your letter, id est, two hours ago, and after that I felt so ill and miserable, that I smoked a packet full of cigarettes, which poisoned me enough to enable me to write. Your brother has not seen your letters—I think he won't mind your insults, if only you write, I was going to cable to-morrow, it was the limit, I set to myself. Well I have your handwriting. I feel your depression, your fever, your impatience, I feel everything with you and I can imagine how you despise us, you, who are so brave and proud. Your letter to your brother is magnificent, it may mean a cure, and since I myself am going into all the details of his agony, there should well be one as wise as you to tell him the truth. He won't be cross, he never is, that's part of his helplessness. I shall write in a day or two all about him, now I can't, I am too upset about you, and how kindly you put everything to make it look not too unbearable. Going to the guillotine and consoling your friends . . . that's you. I know there is no real danger, there can't be, but every operation is like the gallows. I have had some, and I know. *I* used to crack a joke. And it's not even true, that the will to survive helps, for once I did *not* »will it« and I survived. There would be so much sense in my life if I could be near you now. This is quite an empty letter, all of them will be, as long as there is some more torture impending—you described it in gentle and precise terms—like in a novel—another two to three weeks till we can breathe freely—I wish I could put a hundred questions—I wish I were one of the nurses, the one that you prefer, of course, do write everything in detail again, the truth is so much easier to bear than uncertainty—and you have such a clever way to put things. I shall not go on now, but shall write another letter to-morrow, when I got over it a little. I wish you knew what you mean to me . . .

If only you write . . .

Veza
All my love

ELIAS TO GEORGES · *March 29, 1946*

March 29, 1946

My dear Georg,

Your letter did me a world of good. It wrenched me out of weeks of the dullest, stupidest despair. Even now, I can't explain why. I was an even bigger fool than usual to have borne you a grudge about it, and I really don't anymore. I am truly thankful for it. You are viewing the affair itself in a false light, very likely because you've been misled by a "witty" report from Veza. But there are things that are beyond joking. No one knows that better than you. I should not have written to you as I did, precisely because it was so serious. Nothing I said was made up, and you are very foolish if you continue to believe in hocus-pocus. I made a fool of myself with my letter, but such things happen. One is often attached to others precisely *because* one knows so well exactly what they are like, and there is no shame at all in wanting to do the impossible, namely, to find, completely within one's own self, a muddleheaded person. One can feel that one has utterly failed in a *work*, and that is a powerful and permissible feeling, but perhaps only a poet can understand that.

This would be the point for me to provide you with proof that they were not silly love affairs. At the moment, please exempt me from proving it. Perhaps I'll send you proof soon in another form. I know very well that there is no excuse for my failure to write you. With my unspeakably silly letter, I just wanted to tell you that *for the last few weeks*, my condition was literally on the brink of insanity, if not actually insanity, and that was precisely the time that it would have been a thousand times better to write. Your anger is justified, but blind. Your contempt is childish, since it concerns things totally foreign to you, and you are much too astute to believe that all people are necessarily the same. Concrete love sounds good, you're completely right. Still, only I know how much I love you. You can measure how badly one can go astray by the fact that, when I reread that laughable letter once more before mailing it, I then gave it to Veza to read, mentioning all my misgivings (I had already confided in her—something you will surely regard as contemptibly stupid). I told her I couldn't mail it; you wouldn't be able to understand it because you don't know all the circumstances. Veza has been a witness to the whole thing, and despite all the jokes she indulges in as a satirist, she knows it was deadly serious. She *insisted* that I mail the letter. Now, neither you nor I can deny that Veza is witty, wise, and possibly better disposed to you than she is to me, but she was obviously *mistaken*. Doesn't that make my own mistake a touch more excusable? *You will be magnanimous and return the letter to me because I am so terribly ashamed*. In your reply, there's only one passage I find unworthy of you, and that is your threat to break off "communication." I hope that is an utter impossibility. As far as the affair itself is concerned, you have been an incredible help to me, perhaps from the healthy instincts of a physician.

Of course, everything you write Veza about yourself is a million times more important. But you will understand that I *must* answer your letter to me. Isn't it actually a very good thing that we are getting at the unheeded seat of the infection? Couldn't it have caused damage and even become dangerous if we had continued to overlook it? I understand nothing in that regard, but I try to explain this side of things to Veza, who is in despair. Perhaps that is quite foolish. Let us know if you will perhaps have recovered enough by the summer to come visit us in England. We would treat you like an *emperor*. If it cannot be, one of us—maybe Veza—could visit you in France. They say it will soon be easier to get permission to travel. —I'm going to send this off now, as is. In the future, I will try to send you the kind of letter you want. But you will be disappointed. I'm not a letter writer like Veza. I am much too earnest and, as you can see, actually quite boring. But at least you will see that I'm trying.

In closing, I ask you once more to return that idiotic scrap of paper. Believe me that it was only *tasteless*, but *not* mendacious. Why should everything between us from now on be based on a *mistake*?

A most heartfelt embrace
from the brother you love,
Elias
I wish to God I could heal
you in the same way.

VEZA TO GEORGES · *April 1, 1946*

Mrs. Canetti
7 Chestnut Close
Amersham, Bucks

April 1st (night)

Darling Georg,

I got your letter this afternoon and managed to hide it and shall never let him see it. Your letter is cruel, because you don't tell me a word about yourself, and at the moment *your* life and welfare is certainly most important to me, more important than anything. Your handwriting is much better, healthier looking, but that's my only consolation and if you don't want to be importuned by telegrams, you better write at once and about yourself. At once. I dream of you think of you and have temperature and pains in my lung and shall not stop with all these »imitations« until you are well again. Pardon my previous notes, but of course your ordeal upset me a lot, and I only hope, I paid for you with all my sufferings, so that you should be well again, like a mother should pay, darling son. I cannot get over your magnanimity, your magnificence, oh where are more words of mighty meaning, that could do justice to your last letters, to your noble attitude, to that great noblesse of giving me consolation, when you are torn to pieces, body and soul. My landlady keeps telling me every day of cases, and that your case is a light one . . . and all I want to hear . . . and I was so very egotistic, writing you about us, when all that matters is *you*. It is true, I posted his letter, he did not want me to, but I had to. First, I did not see, how we would get over it, he was so miserable and I without much strength to bear it all and I wanted you to know *the truth* . . .[327]

You see, I want my picture to be in your eyes as I deserve it to be. And that's why I don't want you to ever see me again, but am much afraid I shall too much long to see you, to stick to my intention.

What concerns *him*, you are wrong, Benjamin. You must not judge others by your greatness, no you must not. Characters like you exist once in a century. And let me tell you, that the whole affair was my fault, really. I used to like her, and I sort of favoured the union. When I saw what a weakling the woman was, I of course turned against her, but he is no Jack in the box, there were his feelings to consider. And all the misery we went through and it did him good, that there was someone infatuated with him, admiring him, someone who brought the atmosphere of Grinzing into our gloomy boarding house rooms, into all that poverty fear and degredation. And there is another factor: he sincerely thinks that she is a gifted writer and that she can become a good writer. She published two books,[328] with his help, influence and actually with his losing much time on them. The books are no good, had very bad reviews,[329] but they are not without talent. It is far below what I have achieved meanwhile, and which was *not* published, at which he is very much ashamed now and which he will remedy now, this being in his power. I don't know if that can be remedied, because now you have seen my state of mind. When a woman of my passion, of my resources and possibilities, with my still existing power over others (when I chose to exercise this power)—has no children, no husband and no adequate Lebensraum, no sphere, then she must have success with her work, and he knows that. He is very sorry now, believe me. And if I don't succeed in reconciling you to seeing him like I see him, if you don't *love* him, if you don't come here to read his two thousand pages neatly written and locked up here in my library, if you don't love him and become lenient and help him to publish his work, order it, force him to end it, then I'll never have the courage to live on. Really I shan't. A deep understanding and a deep love between you two is essential to my frame of life. And you deserve it so much, yes and *he* deserves it, too. Believe me, he is a dreamer, he is not weak in an ordinary sense, he is full of fears, full of the horrors that we went through, and full of affection for those who were once attached to him—and also when they leave him. That is not weakness. I did a very dangerous thing, I wanted to show myself in the nicest light to you, that I can afford without exagerating, but at the same time I dragged him into something that I did not intend. You *must* love him. You don't know what he went through. And *because* he takes it too much to heart, all that happened, he got so attached to a creature, that has no feeling but for her welfare, no sympathy and no understanding of what went on these years. *I* felt it too much—*that* drove him mad—so he looked for comfort with a flighty creature. Goethe has had a much more simple woman, and he married her, and Rousseau lived with a housemaid. And he is wider, richer, much greater than Rousseau, and his work is here, exists.

In short the facts about the affair. He says, he can't leave her abruptly, because with his book coming out in May (not before) and with her being as I told you, she might do foolish things and cause scandals. I know, son, that this is only partly true and that he longs to see her and wants to rid himself of her *in* himself without suffering too much, slowly, gradually he wants it. And I help him, dearest. I have her here twice a week and if somebody can exercise a little good influence on her it's me. With that I have at the same time some hold on him, for if I would not act like that, he would see her in secret. Her attitude is, that she is madly in love with that East end journalist, that scribbler, but that she loves him, too, and *wants both*. (!)

Now there is one thing he would never do. He would not share. So to my opinion she is digging her own grave, for she is lost and definitely nobody without the good name, influence and noble background your brother offered her. This is, where we stand now, and I'll keep you informed about everything, but implore you not to mention any details as you did till now, you were reliable, as I knew you would be.

And another request. You *will* answer his second letter in a nice way and clever, and you don't know what *you* could do to make him finish his work and publish it (the publishers are waiting for it and I can't get him to finish it) *you* can. He is terribly afraid to lose you, he loves you more than anybody. You could help, son. You will do that to me, you have been that miraculous character in my life, that knight and »Ritter«[330] that took us out of the claws of the Nazis and helped us for years saving us from distress and saved our lives perhaps two days ago with a clever letter. The letter of a psychologist and psychiatrist. You will help me to make him work. Insult him, but tell him, that you love him. And do love him. Do see him, like you would have seen Kleist[331] and cannot quite see *him*, because he is your brother. He is incredibly kind to me . . . about this another time . . .

Benjamin. How are you. How is your temperature. How are the pains. When is that dreadful new blow . . . when. Do let me know all details, they hurt, but it hurts much more *not* to know.

All my love,
Peggy

Elias to Georges · *Probably April 25, 1946*

Thursday

My dear Georg,

You wrote such a beautiful letter I don't know whether I can really answer it so soon. But I must write, if only a few lines. Explanations would be ridiculous—your letter is much too serious—and you could only really understand me after a long conversation. But it is better that you don't completely understand me. It helps me a great deal that you see my affairs as simply as they really ought to be. The incidental reason for your animosity was something very important in my life. Perhaps you have not fully thought through the essence of a "work." Precisely for a person completely obsessed by his work, it is marvelous to make *something* from *nothing*. I thought I had succeeded. Now, of course, I know I did not succeed. But can you imagine, Brother whom I love more than anything else, that it failed only *by a hair*! If you ever get a look at the first hundred pages of the third novel,[332] which Friedl was working on up to the catastrophe, you will see I am right. It was the work of a real poet, something I can never say to Veza because it's too much of an affront; you must never tell her, either. That wild, chaotic, ridiculous creature had the makings of a poet. The first two books showed talent, too, even though they were still written completely under my influence. In the third, she was about to find her own voice. *The Monster*, by the way (the second novel), will appear in French.[333] The pen name under which Friedl writes (or wrote, for I scarcely think she will ever write anything usable again) is Anna Sebastian. Maybe in a while I'll send you the two published novels. I don't want you to think I'm completely crazy: it only failed *by a hair*. About this part of the affair—the public part, so to speak—you must be extremely tactful toward Veza. After many difficult years, Veza herself has developed incredibly as a writer. She goes her own way, hardly influenced by me at all. I now consider her *a born playwright*, and an important one at that. All she needs is more scope. In her hands, everything turns into a scene. She is loaded with dramatic ideas. Her comedies have a lightness and charm all their own. She has already finished three *good* plays.[334] To my misfortune and hers, I have no connections in the theater here at all. In time, especially after *Die Blendung* is published (on May 5), they will develop as well. I couldn't do anything with my own plays (which you very much underestimate) here either. And so Veza, who in her way is more talented and of course a thousand times more genuine, had to look on from the sidelines while that little female published two books. It was impossible to let her find out how successful they were. Veza is still completely convinced that Friedl got only bad reviews, but you can believe me when I say that I had trouble finding bad ones to console Veza with. I withheld all the good ones from her, some of which were glowing; and although she otherwise knows everything, there's one thing she doesn't know: that in "highbrow" literature, Friedl is regarded here as the most important young English novelist the war has produced. As soon as Veza has her first public success (and God knows, she deserves hundreds of them), I will be able to tell her about all that, but not before. I'm confiding this to you and you must believe me, since I can survey the matter better here, from close at hand. In Paris, you knew Friedl as an ugly, laughable, scatterbrained, silly little creature, a real paragon of muddleheadedness. So you could not imagine (nor could I in your place) how she had been transformed under my guidance. Not that she became an intellectual being, but she was obsessed with mythology and mythic figures and had a wealth of comic invention one doesn't find all too often these days. All of it had to do with me in some mysterious and delicate way; my words gave it life, my love gave her the steadiness without which nothing gets done. Now she is again just as she was in Paris. She looks exactly the same, except that she is perhaps a touch more confident as a woman because half the English literary set is running after her.

I had to write you this because otherwise, you could not know the facts. Veza is sure to be giving you only half the picture. She cannot possibly conceive what happiness it was for me to have made a poet out of nothing. She tells herself, plausibly enough, that since this poet is currently a nothing again, she can never really have been one. But there lies the fallacy; that is the miracle and the despair of what happened to me.

The other reason for your animosity is certainly the primary one. In no way have I broken faith with my twenty-five-year-old self.[335] In the last 5 years, I have worked more than in all my previous years put together. The work, which you know about, exists and is enormously rich. It is still not complete. There lies my worst malady: my dread of completing things. I can always work. I work every day, with strict discipline and regularity. Veza can confirm that literally several thousand manuscript pages exist. However, I must learn to finish things. That's what I will now try with all my might to do. Anything more about that would necessarily strike you as an idle phrase. I just must *do* it, that's all.

I hope what you wrote Veza about yourself is true. In case you don't want to upset her, couldn't you write exactly how you are to me *at my address*? 8 to 10 months doesn't sound very much like what you said at first. I think there is at least one good thing about my misstep: that it started a *natural* correspondence between us. I promise not to let it lapse again. Don't consider this a letter—it's only a hasty scribble. I couldn't stand to have you think that Friedl has been as you knew her for all these years. When you reply, please write to *my* address.

A most heartfelt embrace from Elias

Veza to Georges · *April 26, 1946*

P.O. Do not return letter to the sender.

April 26.th

Darling Georges,

How shall I thank you for your letter. I was dreaming during a whole day of going to Chateaubriant, and how I long to see you! How this alone is all I can wish for the moment. I have not yet decided *not* to go, but cannot at once start making the steps. Everything is still too unsafe here. I am still too unsafe. After yesterday, I don't know how I could face it. I feel like a soldier whose face has been torn into bits by shrapnells, I am not myself anymore, and how face you with that face. I must wait till we calm down. Also I shall make it dependent of your letters. If I get a lot and about yourself, not about other matters, I shall consider going. You did not even write properly about your state of health and the stage you are in. Yes, if you write properly, I may come. Of course I would not dream of being your guest. Why should I. I'll take with me whatever the government allows me to take, it won't be more than fifty pounds, I guess, but perhaps I may take more. This decision cannot be questioned. What a sweet letter you wrote . . .

I wish the Canettis, all of them (you excluded, for you are not the Canettis, you are *everything* to me) had not behaved so nice to me, I wish they would have behaved like the Ardittis, for I would gladly tell them—take him back, you can have him, I'd gladly return him, free of charge. For I am tired beyond description of so much honour and bliss.

He will tell you one day, he could not work properly, concentrate properly, because I—I am so moody, a melancholiac, I hope you will answer back.

I'll try to give you an outline of our life now. *She* went to the sea, with her Billy,[336] for Easter, and after five days she came back exhausted. If you saw her in that state, you would despise me for opening the door for her. Well, she came, and I pretended to be invited and left for an hour. In which she declared, she is going to disappear for some time, not telling him where she is, not giving any address, etc. She has to do this, you see, because she wants money all the time and it is the best way to get it. Also, she is very cross, that she has lost him, and avenges that on him. And maybe she wants to try how far she can go. She saw that she could go very far, for he, instead of coolly reacting, which would have puzzled her and put her in her place, he broke out into fits of despair, imploring her to let him have at least her address. Seeing the effect, she remained stern, of course, until *I* came. His face red up to the tips of his hair, he told me the sad tale before her, whereupon I calmly sat down and said, this is an excellent idea, and what more could a writer want than to go into solitude and work. This and a few other answers, caused her to take everything back and in half an hour she became a school girl and I have the honour of being very much in favour with her, »the only person who is sensible and benevolent and leaves her alone.« This, when *he* is torturing himself day and night, because he tells himself and me, that he is her *murderer*, he did not take enough care, he drove her into the arms of that other man, he is responsible for her maybe becoming worse and leading the life of a concubine (!), of throwing herself away every month to another man, of her talent going to pieces. (This about her talent, mind you, is a lie even to himself, to us to everybody. He is so ashamed of being a slave of his attachment to her.) Well, there she was with us, I served what I could muster, I was clever, lenient, even affectionate, and when she left, I offered to send her two books to an American agent,[337] a friend of mine with whom I have a say, since her publishers could not sell her great works to U.S., much as they tried. At which offer she was really disarmed for the moment, but this does not last, coarser feelings prevailing. There is one good thing, that though trying to win him back in some moments, there are her cruel moments, the ones I feared so much, and she cannot restrain herself.

You'll ask, why do I condescend to take part in all that. Why don't I walk out on them. I'll tell you why. Yesterday the day after she had been here, he had a complete breakdown, and cried for hours, and said it's all his fault and he had ruined her life, and his. And he loves her, and a work of seven years is destroyed, and he can't get over it. The reasons *he* gave me, the answers *I* gave back (this lasted five hours and I have this every other day and am completely exhausted, for my nights are sleepless) would seem *insane* to you. They *are* insane. And that is what I fear so much. That is why I don't save myself, why I don't escape—I fear for his mind. I cannot say more.

Better news. The date for Auto-Da-Fé is fixed at last and it is the fifth of May. We have a copy, it is very nice, of course War time paper but a good print and a neat black binding. The publishers are going to send you a copy, in a few days. This morning he got a letter from the publisher himself, telling him, to celebrate the event he and a few writers and his translater are going to have lunch . . . etc.

So, this cheered him up a little, and I can be quiet for today, but since he sees her tonight, I may have him in despair to-morrow. If you saw her! The way she looks! A tramp, not even washed properly, she was hitch-hiking with her Billy, five days, sleeping in bungalows, she came straight from there, dirty, course and vulgar. If you came in, you could perhaps—break the spell—no you could not. He has his enlightened moments and agrees in whatever I say and sees her vulgarity and her cheapness—but—still it is all *his* fault now. And he thanks me on his knees every day, because I have so much power over her, because I alone can manage her, because . . . I'll save these past seven years for him, prevent them from looking ugly, from having been spent in vain. Not in vain! When a genius spends his life winding up a screaming doll instead of unfolding his great qualities. To make him dictate to me sixty pages of his work I had to get so wild as seriously to want to throw my life away. This was last year. Sixty pages of the highest thoughts and new ideas, and there are fragments of two thousand pages, which he does not take the trouble to put together and to work them out. Ideas, which you will find in the works of his contemporaries, because he tells them to everybody, is highly praised and admired by them and robbed of the essential.

Pardon me—I am at my wits' end. I don't want any responsability, and of *course I tell him what I told you.* But—if I am not patient and sympathetic, there is the greatest danger of his going mad. You must believe me, I cannot tell more.

You could do a lot with your letters. *You must write to him.* He waits for your letters! You help *me* when you write to him!! Georg!

Expect a note from me in a day or two, when I shall give you a description of how happy I was with your sweet words to me. How I appreciate every hidden and open kindness. How I love you.

Don't worry about your work not yet published. We had to wait a year and a half *longer* than the contract stipulated it—paper shortage. I shall now soon get in contact with his translator, any day I feel composed enough to, and can I do something for you? She is now, as I told you Co-publisher of . . . She utterly dislikes and despises F. and *loves* Canetti.

Excuse rotten parcel of poor Mrs. Menczel, I asked for chocs for you. I can image what was in it, she sent me a similar one, all things, that we can get any amount of—here.

All my love,
Peggy

You won't give me away, darling, it would destroy my work, shatter his confidence and spoil it all.

VEZA TO GEORGES · *May 2, 1946*

Mrs. Canetti
7 Chestnut Close
Amersham, Bucks

May 2nd 1946

~~Darling~~ No. Ritter Georg,

When I feel as dejected as I was these days I have not the courage to make a decision. You see, the worst happened to me that could happen—I don't like myself anymore and in consequence cannot imagine that you would really like to see me. This may pass. It was about to pass when that new blow came a few weeks ago. I believe it may pass and even begin to collect cigarettes, for I am very much dependent on cigarettes and must have a few hundred, since I shan't get them in France. Your brother got your letter to-day, told me its contents and read the last lines to me. About yourself. Was I relieved! But even now, while I write I went out to make myself a few cups of tea, to strengthen my decision. I would start making the steps in a week or two, and intend to go by plane. Also, it may be August or September, though I want to come earlier, to be there without robbing you any of your precious time—I mean, while you are not strong enough yet to work all the time. You see, I may repent having come. For just as your brother in reallity is struggling, for that girl not to destroy what has been between them these seven years (or what he imagined *was* between them) so I made up my mind you should never see me again, for as you can see, I am not yet ripe to be fifty. I am still clinging to my nice life with you, the nicest memories of my life, and I don't want *that* destroyed. Just as your brother is struggling to rescue his dream. Nothing else matters with him now, he seems to be reconciled to the thought of having »lost« her. But he wants it to happen in a nice way. You'll understand that—you'll understand us both. Would August or September be too late? I would not like a lot of family to be there, for weak as my nerves are, they are not up to conversation. A sensible talk for half an hour, yes, but conversation, no. I can listen to a pretty woman flirting, I can watch her, but I cannot talk. So, your fans may be there, I love handsome women. Also, I could not come *every* day, every other day, maybe for a short spell, and sometimes I may have to phone, that I cannot come. And I would not stay in Paris. Paris without you means nothing to me, and there *is* another reason . . . no, there is no news of Alice[338] . . . and that makes me dislike Paris. I could not enjoy Paris . . . there is no news, her sisters are full of hope, but I am not.

My last meeting with F. was somewhat like a caricature. She herself looked like her own carricature, too. She was to come at one o'clock, and your brother stood at the station, fathfully waiting, while I sat at a nearby restaurant, waiting for them. He came alone and was so pale and destressed, that I dragged on the meal, so as to wait for the next train. At two o'clock we both waited, but she did not come. It was pathetic to watch him pacing the station up and down. At three she came. But like the Stuarts,[339] no unlike the Stuarts, I had much learned and forgotten nothing[340] in these two hours, and my reception was cool. And at the end, after a dull afternoon, which was fortunately shortened, because we went to a meeting and left her behind, and brought back my German friend—I told her, very politely, very dignified and condescendingly, that I only like guests, who appreciate the honour . . . which had a good effect. First, I need not have her here too much, and then, she said to your brother she does not really like to be with us, for she likes it too much . . . and she realizes, what she has lost, when she is with both of us. I don't know if there is a grain of truth in what she said, there may be, for she has lost so much, that the truth may dawn on her. But it did your brother good to hear it, and now everything is easier for him, with the book coming out on Monday. Your letter seems to have been very good, for he carries it about with him and said, he sees you love him and that is all that matters. Only *you* can help him now.

Will you be lying in the garden, when I come in summer? Or in bed? I am so lazy, I don't care a hang about sitting all the time, I'm just a fat lazy Spanish Jewess. And I understand your taste about books or rather your distaste. And agree about philosophical works, they are a bluff. And find History the only subject worth a little interest. Except the thoughts of your brother. He went so far as to tell me, that he wants to dictate to me a lot before I leave, in order to send you a great part of his work. You see how you helped me again. Will I ever pay you back?

We think I'll be able to take up to a hundred gineas, which I shall do. Can you answer trivial questions, then let me know. Is there a chance of my buying frocks without coupons in Chateaubriant? Can I buy underwear for your brother in Paris, he walks in rags. What else besides tea and cigarettes, do I want? We can get any amount of medical supplies, is there anything I should bring along? I shall not come without the Rich[341] preceding me, how could I. Not our fault the delay, believe me. And as to poor Regine having to surround my embonpoint with Paris chic, she could not make it, poor thing. A frock in Chateaubriant will do, any clean thing will do, we walk in rags and I get my stockings from U.S.

Canetti came back and will want to peep over my shoulder, the scoundrel. To prevent this, I must close. Without the usual assurances but you know them.

Peggy

Write about *the treatment*, still temperature?????

Veza to Georges · *May 11, 1946*

Mrs. Canetti
7 Chestnut Close
Amersham Bucks

Mai 11. 1946

Darling Son,

Before I give you all the details of my nice and nasty experiences in London yesterday, I'll first get rid of the business part: I took a taxi to Gower street, before launching out on what I did afterwards, in order to get the Rich. 136 Gower street, Medical library. The Gentleman was *still* polite, but I would *not* risk it another time! And he absolutely refused to accept an advance payment. »That won't make any difference« he said sternly, all the dignity of the firm, his learning and English blood in his face. So what else could I do than coaxingly tell him, would he not forget to inform us at once . . . etc. Which he »certainly« will not. I gave you the address, your brother's address is on the list there, so if you think it could hasten things if you write personally in your quality as a physician, referring of course to the fact, that your brother's name (Durris, Stubbs Wood) is on the list, by all means try. I cannot write to people in U.S. about it, the book being very expensive and I am not allowed to send any money there. Of course my relatives could do it, but I pester them so much with my food parcels, which they send generously, that I don't see how I can discourage them with book orders, not to speak of the fact that I cost them some money these years, you can believe me.

Now to the cheerful and sad event yesterday. You can't imagine how delighted I was, when I was snapped at in all the big libraries, where I asked for Autodafé: »It's impossible to get!« »Sold out, no, we can't order it!« »Unfortunately none left, madam!« I could have kissed them, especially a shop assistant at Selfridges, a thin haggard woman, with mad eyes, who was exhausted from telling people she can't get the book for them. So I went and bought a nice bag for my trip to France, took three lunches, two teas, four ice creams (which saves me eating to-day) and then met your brother to go to our dentist Dr. Hirschtritt,[342] I guess you know him, we brought him a book, since I never pay a penny to him for ruining my teeth completely. He is nice but has a nasty son, who turned Christian, calls himself captain, took an English name and does not speak to Jews. His poor father is very miserable about it, and about a few nasty things that sapling did to him, which I shall tell in another letter. We just were there, when in came the lad, to collect his mail, for his father has a posh address and he does not want his mail to be sent to Hampstead where he has the great misfortune to live. He came in and said: »I just read a review on your book in the Manchester Guardian.«—»Is it good,« asked poor Canetti, trembling inwardly. »No,« said the phylantropist lengthening the pleasure, by dragging every word, »it is very bad.«

Now you must know, that the publishers told us, there would be a bad review at the Mc G. the critic being 75 and against Kafka Joyce and all modern writers, his idol being Galsworthy. Still it depressed us, though we did not show it, you can be sure. And I only tell it to *you* and *don't* tell the family. There will be more good reviews and bad ones too (the review in the Tribune was very good). That can't be helped, and I would not mind in the least. For what I thought was, *good* reviews, and *bad* sale, and I having to scrub floors for the rest of my life, but the opposite is too amazing for me to be digested, and I don't know shall I cry or laugh. I would only laugh (the review in the G. being so that I as a reader would get interested in it, the book he calles »Insanity Fair« etc.) but poor Canetti is so distressed. Darling, when you write again, you will write nice and loving remarks about him. I don't show him *all* your letters (not the one I did not, the one I sent you back), but I want to show him your next one, with much love in it, he thinks you don't really love him. Which worries me more than anything else. The one good thing was, that Friedl came, we had ordered her to come, and she had such horrible reviews, and was so torn to pieces, except by two reviewers who were put on their job by the publishers, that when she came, she said the review is not at all bad, and so long, which made us laugh and cheered us up. That has always been her function in days of yore and in that, being unscrupulous and without feeling, she is excellent. She of course let your brother down abominably, for he introduced her to a lot of writers who would write good reviews if only she went and told them to, but she is so absorbed by absorbing her Billy, that she neglected doing it, and your brother, who has been invited by some important writers, who meant to write reviews, if only he once did them the honour of going to see them (it is exactly as I tell you) never went, because he was so heartbroken about her that he had not the strength of mind to be calm and make a good impression. If you ask him, however, he will tell you, *she* brought him luck. *Did not she get him out of* Nazi Vienna![343] Yes, *she* did that, you came because *she* did that . . .

I must close now, because I want to post Autodafé for you. I spent five guineas on the book yesterday, having to give it to all those we are indebted to, you being one of those characters. We cannot yet send it to the other Canettis, not before June, when we'll get copies from the second edition, so that we shall not have such high expences on it. You see, I begin to get into my usual train of sarcastic thought again, and if you want to write things, put a separate page to your usual letter, which must be so that poor dear old C. can read it, he longs for your letters. But never write, not even in a separate sheet, invectives against him, or that you don't love him. I won't have it.

All my love,
Peggy

Just posted book.

Veza to Georges · *May 24, 1946*

Mrs. Canetti
7 Chestnut Close
Amersham, Bucks

May 24.

Darling Georges,

At last a letter you skunk. Before I give you a description of the ordeal we went through two weeks ago, I'll begin with the end. It's not a clever way to describe events and goes against my dramatic abilities. I should put you on the pillory, as we were put on the pillory. And then gradually emerge with our grand news. But I have not got the heart to keep you in suspense and therefore you should know: your brother is the talk of London to-day, a craze, he has the best reviews imaginable, a broadcast that was so good (on the 22.—did you listen in?) that I, holding a pencil, could not go on writing, I really fell from my seat. »The Spectator« to-day brought a large review, comparing him to Swift and Joyce, I enclose the »Observer«, his translator is coming down here on Sunday to see me and to tell us more about all the favourable events, which are precipitating.

When I wrote you about the bad review in Mc Gard. that was nothing. Next day there was a review in the »Times literary supplement,«[344] the like of which has not been written since there existed reviews. The book and Canetti personally were torn to pieces in a way unheard of. We knew, that it came from a personal enemy, but this did not help. The public did not know that. The publishers in other countries did not. We feared the worst. We sat all alone for all of a sudden we had no friends. Nobody came. Our good friend Friedl had disappeared (!). When she came next day, it was only to tell us, that since there was that review in that paper, there would be *only* bad notices from now on. Because the critics here in this country are *one* clique, *one* imitates the other. It was all wrong. *Good* notices followed, as you see in the enclosure, and the crowning event was the broadcast on the 22. I sat in the room of my landlady, not knowing *how* that broadcast would be. The Man began by criticising Somerset Maugham. He continued by criticising »Cary«,[345] a writer of great renown, whom I love (I cannot get a copy of his book »A Horse's mouth«, else I would send it you, it's a charming book). When he had ended, and started . . . »Austrian writer . . . « my knees trembled. All A. listening in, half London listening in. I had written to lots of friends, to listen in. I thought I was a fool to sit with a stranger, my landlady, who would see the effect of every word on my face, much as I have learned in these long years to dissimulate. I quickly said: »If he is against a work like Cary's what will he say about Canetti« to forestall the bad effect. —This is how he began: »Autodafé . . . It's a magnificent book. It is hopeless for me to try and give you an idea of the richness« . . . and then I could not write on. I listened like in a dream. I thought of all the poverty, humiliation, misery of the last ten years. Of our agonies of despair two weeks ago. And I listened on. Everything that has ever been said in praise of a book was said, darling. I shall try and get a copy at the B.B.C. and send it you. And I shall send you the Spectator as soon as I can. And I don't write about it to anyone but you, having such an enormous mail to answer for your brother, since of course he does not do a thing, that I have not a minute to spare. With it my heart beating and in a cramp. I did not sleep since two weeks, first from fear, now from overjoy. You must know, the American contract was in danger, the two publishers could not agree on one point, namely the Americans want the right to sell the book on the continent, and Cape here very rightly said, *he* wants the rights, having gone through all the expenses of the translation. Well, Cape gave in, only that your brother should get the best publisher in Amerika, and as he wrote in a very flattering letter »have a big financial profit out of it.« When I say not to anyone but you—with a correction—I am sending a copy of this letter to the woman I love best after you two brothers, my cousin Veza Cansino.[346]

But certainly not a copy of this third page, that one is for you. Yes, your brother will easily manage now for me to get a re-enter permit, but before I get your formal letter I can't start. And don't forget to invite me for a few weeks only and *don't* write on your expenses or else they won't allow me any money. And I am coming, Benjamin. And shall tell you for weeks on end, chiefly about a personal enemy, and Austrian writer, and about all that happened. And the private life of Elias Canetti. Which is not so pleasant. For you see, the slime will fall in love with him again, when he is in the limelight. And I'll tell you about my ordeal walking through Amersham with a proud face. And how his friend here Marie Louse[347] had taken a flat in London, because she thought the book would be a failure and did *not* want the pillory. —Yes, we were alone. And only *you*, we know, would have been with us.

If ever you dare leave me without news for such a long time, mind, I shall not come. And let me know about the shortage there, I fear I shall be more hungry than here, without my parcels from N-Y and with your shortage. But I'll eat you.

No more to-day, expect foolish letters reviews, reports. And your brother *was* proud of your letter and does not want you to show the Observer to the family, he thinks they won't understand, and please *keep* all reviews for us, safely, the paper is scarce here. And take good care of yourself, what is life without you being well again.

All my love,
Peggy

Of course I crossed out all the darlings in the copy for Veza Cansino. You would like her, she is charming.

important: We must have the comedy back, for America, quickly please.

No joke *very important*. We want Comedy, for U.S.

Your brother was delighted about your letter. Georges Kien, was quoted in the broadcast.

Marie-Louise von Motesiczky, 1943

VEZA TO GEORGES · *JUNE 2, 1946*

Mrs. Canetti
7 Chestnut Close
Amersham, Bucks

June 2.nd

A KILLING LETTER

You beastly thing!

Writing me such a short note, and complaining, when I keep sending him the smartest reports, and doing nothing but writing to such an ungrateful, cold hearted Frenchman! By the way, do you stick my letters to the wall or do you just put them in a drawer. You don't lock them away, do you? I wish you would, though, because usually you are very careless about them and my husband knows all my love letters to you by heart and sometimes quotes them, much to my disadvantage. I would not like him to read my Amersham letters on his next trip to Paris, much as *he* would like to. He says, *he* has all the bother with me and you get the nice letters, and there is some truth in it.

There is not a word about yourself and what you do and how you feel and whether you are in bed all day, and what about the abcess. I had a bad bronchitis, I still have it, but when I could hardly move about I thought how you must feel, twenty years younger, and handsome, with so many temptations for a fine young scholar. With me, at least there are no temptations, definitely not. Are they coming into your room at five o'clock in the morning to change your bed sheets and make you look tidy for the first visit of the doctors? They do that in Vienna and I could kill them for it. Does everybody speak French in France? In the Clinique? I can't speak French anymore and hope nobody speaks to me. We laughed at your being anxious to know what dress I'd wear. I sent an old coat to the salvage for the displaced Jews on the continent, but they sent it back, saying it was too shabby for the concentration camp. A dressmaker changed it for me into a frock and it's my best attire. So that is my outfit. —I feel so weak from my bronchitis, that I don't know how I'll board a train or plane or anything and when I get to Chateaub. I may have my sixth Flu this year, why not, and not be able to see you for days, and is there a room for me at the hotel, and I'll ask the housekeeper nextdoors, will she lend me a nightgown, I have not got one, to pretend before the French chambermaid, that I am used to being dressed properly. I shall never wear it though, not having a change. When I wash one shirt of your brother he puts his second shirt on, not after we have dried it on the electric stove, because a third shirt he has not got, and that is the average equipment of the lower middle class. Of course I am the First Lady of Amersham now, but that does not make much difference as to our equipment, since we did not do what dear uncle Joe[348] did, who came to this country and bought himself a black-market tweed suit the very first day. We are respectable, but shabby.

Miss Wedg. as I told you was here and why should I be so modest. She was terrified of making my acquaintance, because Robert Neuman has told her about me: »she is shy, difficult, but extremely gifted, much more gifted than Canetti.« She had quite an hysterical look, when she stepped out of the station, and—what shall I tell you—she found me »enchanting«, which we heard first from a third person whom we sent out to investigate. To that one she told, what R.N. had said about me and how frightened she was. Gosh, I am tired, I was going to write you a five page description of that nice afternoon with Miss Wedg, who told me »call me Veronica« and how I won her heart, but here I am, exhausted and shall stop. We are progressing so wonderfully, that I don't know, did I send you the gorgeous review in the »Spectator«? And there is going to appear in a week or two a big essay on Canetti in the »Horizon« a leading monthly periodical, and in others, too, I forget where, and there was a third broadcast in German, to the blasted Austrians, and dear Canetti was interviewed in it, so that the Viennese should hear how he praised their town, and longs for Vienna, which made my flesh kreep, they should let *me* broadcast to them! Whenever I read how hungry they are, I go to the kitchen and eat an egg, sometimes I go to our posh restaurant, and think how hungry they are and eat roast chicken. Yes, it makes you shudder, but my dear auntie Olga was brought into the gas chamber together with her children and grandchildren, eight in all, they were killed before her eyes, so that settles it . . . by the bye, are there picture houses in Chateaubriant, because I must have a cinema every other day, or else I go mad.

Of course you want to know more about the private life of Mr Canetti, fortunately he is so famous and so enthusiasted about himself at the moment, that these things went a little into the background, or at least he pretends so to me. If it's only pretending, that is a progress, for there was a time when he could not pretend. He intends to write you these days and to send you the outrageous review, so that you should have fun, for it is fun now. I *shall* come to Chat. you scoundrel, and I'm only afraid you'll find, that I am more ill than you. And an ironic letter about your brother's private life next time, though not before I get a nice long clever letter again. Did you send the reviews to the family? Yes, I think there'll be a French transl. too. And I don't think so much of the Blendung, than I think of his two plays, which are really two great masterpieces, unique and immortal, they are both an »Ahnung«[349] of everything that really happened afterwords.

If you want to become a murderer for no apparent reason, then go and have tea with the upper middle class in Amersham. Bismark said: »Ich hab die ganze Nacht gehasst.«[350] —*I* keep »murdering« all night. By the bye, do you remember, Imgard von Wallpach, our nice Viennese Aryan friend? Her son was missing and I found him. I got into contact with the Red Cross, they found him for her and I wired the glad news to her to Vienna yesterday! Will she be glad! An only son, and he has a young wife. He is a prisoner of War in U.S.

All my love,
Veza

write at once!

Veza to Georges · *June 10, 1946*

Mrs. Canetti
7 Chestnut Close
Amersham, Bucks

June 10th

~~Darling Son~~, no,
Benjamin,

This is a quick letter full of love, which I want to be there before the 15th,[351] since I suffer from megalomania, I harbour the hope it will mean a little bit to you, this letter. And moreover, I am not going to write anymore, I'll come! With the excellent connections we have now, with »Autodafé« under my arm, everything will be arranged in 4–6 weeks I hope, and you'll have a foolish little fat Spanish Jewess who is eating the whole day, telling you seven years of a life of emigrants in this country. You'll have funny descriptions by the score, of landladies, my last the funniest, who, by the bye gave me four weeks notice (I have to quit here in four weeks, your brother not knowing it yet). She is a T.B. and has got to take a nurse now, wanting the room for it. This is the outward reason, the inner reason is, that the chief quality in this country with people here . . . I am very sorry to say so, for I love them . . . is envy . . . she can't bear our fame! All of it in detail, I don't feel like writing—I'll move to London as quickly as possible and secure a home there and then come. I just wrote a letter to Merkels, that I shall soon see them, they'll be beside themselves! For God's sake don't mention my having to move, this time I am elated, for it means going to London for good, poor C. loves this place unfortunately, so I'll break the news as late as possible. Was I glad to read that there is someone who comes and adores you, and whom you love . . . there is someone else coming and just now is the right time, when my son is still in bed and impatient, when you are well again, you'll have the world! This letter is so foolishly happy, on account of your being so much better and soon alright, your brother is happy with me! We are mad! Our son well again soon! Our only child and all we have got! I feel all that I went through was not in vain, if my two sons prosper! Wait, I am lucky, and just when I come there will be good news about your work coming out. Nissim's theatre is here on the 17th, does that mean he is coming! That would be fine! I shall only send you reviews and reports now, but no long letters! I'll come! They are asking fervently for my writings in Austria, so I'll have to write there in France not having anything in German now. —Your brother got a letter from an agent to day asking for the right for his book for the film![352] She writes »I just finished this great novel . . . « Of course you are right, the reviews are stupid, but oh how glad I am! Expect short news and be patient, time will pass quicker when I am there, how glad I am to come to Ch. Paris would not be the real thing, they would not leave you to me in Paris! Try to arrange it so, that your fans are not all there when I come, only one or two, though I like my sons to be admired.

Much love, expect lots of short notes
We are both with you on the 15th

Veza

Very urgent: Return enclosed broadcast, we have no copy. Please return at once.

Veza to Georges · *July 6, 1946*

Mrs. Canetti
7 Chestnut Close
Amersham, Bucks

July 6th

Darling Benjamin,

There were many reasons for not writing—one being that we swanked so much to everybody about your two books coming out[353]—

in fact we swanked so much, that in the end your brother lived under the impression, that *he* had written them himself and he got still lazier than he is, after such a strain. Yes, to look at him when he told about it, was really to doubt his common sense (which anyhow he has not). I don't think I can write to day on the subject, this is more a business letter. I am unsettled and before I settle down in London which will be the case in two weeks, I feel I can't write a proper letter to you. Busy looking at accomodations, busy writing letters for your brother's business is good, and busy revising my translation of »The Power and the Glory« by Graham Greene, which I translated seven years ago and which is coming out now, and of course I *would* get the proofs just before my removal. I had to translate this book seven years ago in eight weeks for the publisher wanted to bring it out at once. I translated eight weeks day and night, typing most of it myself, and when it was finished and I exhausted (we owed the rent and I lived on tea and bread) the war broke out. I would have had seven years' time to do the work. It is quite a good translation, compared to others, it is excellent, but I would have done better, if not so hard pressed concerning time. It's anyhow good that it comes out, because here translating a good writer (and he is famous now here) means something. A Viennese writer,[354] going to Vienna now, is taking a play of mine to the Josefstätter Theater, and your brother is beginning to stage me.

I do hope you will answer this letter at once, and not punish me for being all excitement and exhausted. Of course your brother never bothers to answer not even to his publishers and if I leave it like that I only punish myself. He got the offer now for Italy,[355] a professor there wants to translate the book, he translated Gerhardt Hauptman before. He will have to wait for months till he gets an answer from Canetti, for that I cannot answer, he has to contact his publishers first, and that I cannot do for him, so if you see me one day and find I am definitely insane, with »a mask, that I seldom lift« as a lady told me yesterday, you know part of the reasons. If you see me . . . there are great difficulties . . . I may have to wait till your brother is promised British nationality, which he will, I can't risk going, even if I get a re-enter permit, reasons next time. I hate all this business talk. I still hope to come but that may be autumn and whoever wants to see you should come, I am miserable enough, and that is the main reason why I did not write. I shall contact Daniels next week (in four or five days) and hand him out some tea and explain everything to him. He *is* blazing that your brother is so successful, why, I pray? He still repeats the things we told him about Ehrlich[356] because he wanted him to buy something of Ehrlich! When you are back in Paris, do you think with your great name and influence you know somebody who offers Merkel a flat without their paying a black-market sum for it?? That great painter can't go to Paris, not having the blackmarket sum, he can pay a decent price for the rooms, though. Where are your books? Send them to »Durris«, Stubbs Wood, Chesham-Bois Bucks, that being for the moment our safest address, but write an air-mail letter at once to this adress above, which is still valid two weeks. And where are the reviews? You'll have only good ones, I swear, but attacks are good for you, they stimulate the controversies, which are better for you than silent, harmless approval. We experienced that, we paid hard for that experience. Your brother wrote you a long letter, which I saw, which he read in part to me and which he is going to tear up. Why, God knows, he included his bad review, too, thinking that might cheer you up and just in case you have one. He is a good brother, believe me, but no man of action. No, that he is not. Future generations will admire that, I myself admire every postmaster-general.

Do write at once and about your state of health and the books and the family and your dreams and the weather, and your food and your joys and concerns and your little niece, where is she, and about your friends, and the sana, and the nurses, and everything—your letters are all I've got.

Love from your brother and still more from
Peggy

Your brother wanted to wire congratulations I prevented him—I thought perhaps you'd get excited . . .

VEZA TO ELIAS · *August 1946*[357]

Mrs. Canetti
35 Downshire Hill, London NW3

Beloved Canetti,

It's hard to resist beginning with "heavenly child"[358] and Bauscherl.[359] I avoided them for the sake of posterity, but on second thought, I won't deny myself the pleasure, because this letter isn't for posterity anyway. So, I'll only mention business matters in passing and start right off with what will interest you most, namely, Margarete[360] really likes me, and just think, I like her too, and last night she brought me a big jug of cider and said that just outside the door there was a huge barrel of it I could draw from, to which I replied, "Certainly not,' and I just now gave her matches (I mention this more for the cultural historians— the shortage of matches anno 1946—and she cordially invited me to lunch with Jan and Martin[361] and I thanked her most graciously).

And now, here goes: in the afternoon I was at Anna Sebastian's. (At this point, perhaps because I am a playwright and love creating an effect, I must interrupt myself, for to my joy I have noticed that I have the only copy of the comedy in my drawer, and I will certainly see to it that a copy is made.) The door was opened by Evelyn, who looked very attractive. On the landing stood the new husband, and with the dignified furrows and bona fide wrinkles in his face, he reminded me appealingly of someone—no, fortunately not of you. For a long time, I tried to think whom he reminded me of, the way he stood there, working on the restoration of a house he will have to leave eventually, and I finally realized he reminded me of *myself*. On the next landing, Angela was on the telephone, beaming and pretty as a picture. She pours out over the telephone all the adventures she hasn't dared to have, and, well, I liked that.

"But . . . the third one, ah the third one . . ." I'm singing it to Offenbach's music, "stood off to one side without a word." Sebastl[362] lay in bed and gazed silently into my eyes with soulful mendacity. Since I had just been to the post office to draft a telegr. "Sebastian all right" which I didn't send only because it was Saturday and the clerk was too tired, I'm well satisfied that she's not running a fever and that together we ate the Pathé de Fois gras that Canetti was unable to have for dinner the night before because he never has anything good, or anything at all, for he has divided up his life and put it at the service of three witches,[363] one old and flabby, one young and wicked, and the third gnawing and wormy. They suck his blood until he looks like a weary dwarf on the edge of imbecility instead of shaking it off—shaking off everything he has taken on his shoulders and already repaid a million times, that is, everything he never received. For each witch has long since extracted her payment.

So I sit down and unpack my gifts. Naturally, I had just secured some first-rate biscuits and excellent peaches in town. I bought four of the latter and intended to tell Sebastl that Canetti had told me to bring her twelve but they were too expensive; four are enough. But since I ate two of them on the bus, I decided it was better not to tell her that fairy tale and brought her just two, thinking how large they were and how small the ones that Bauscherl got.

So I told her that Canetti was worried about her and I wanted to send a telegram that she was OK but the clerk wasn't cooperative. Whereupon Sebastl sprang from the bed, revealing lovely plump extremities, and could not be dissuaded from dashing naked—no, in her dressing gown—downstairs to dictate the uneconomical telegram, not knowing that I would leave the money for it on the table in sterling. She came back with tea and then the feast began and I reported how a clever porter had spied you out, recognizing that here was a gentleman who always pays for everything, and that I hoped you had seats for your journey to Cornwall. I also told her—for it's true—how right Canetti is to love train stations so much. Because Paddington Station was intoxicating and I'm planning to go there more often from now on and just stand around. I also told her that I stayed much longer, long after the train was due to leave. However,

I didn't tell her I was still hoping to catch a glimpse of Bauscherl. Even though they were already queuing up for the next trains, I was still hoping, nor did I tell her how hard Bauscherl had looked to see if she would come after all, but she didn't come, and how he hated me because *I* was there and she wasn't. No, because she doesn't deserve to know.

Back home again, I sent off all the orders from Canetti and the reviews to the Italian and . . . oh . . . I forgot . . . I'm sitting with Friedl. Well, she was touched by my situation and rushed right out to find me an apartment for the middle of Sept., and we're going to go there this week (she told me this as news, forgetting that she had already told me about it). And then she railed against Posy, whom she's jealous of, because Posy is matter-of-fact and has already planned the number of children she will have. I was somewhat puzzled, remembering that Sebastian is wont to plan altogether different things, things somewhat more brazen than sweet children, but I didn't say so.

I left two hours later. We decided that she would soon call on Margarete and then on me, and if I have the flu, Margarete would return the favor and come too. A final, heartfelt, soulful gaze from the clown's face; the buffoon was already suppressing a laugh.

Back at home, I wrote to the woman from Hungary, using an uncertain address, for I can't find her letter. I also ordered oplatka.[364] The whole week is filled up because I'm going to Brighton on Thursday.

I'll close now, dear Bauscherl. That's enough for half an afternoon in which nothing happened, and I'm wondering if *I* won't write the comedy about Sebastl's jolly house—certainly more tempting than Amersham—and the weather is beautiful and I will wander around London all day, and just don't feel sorry for me that I'm not in Cornwall, for London is enchanting and completely new for me, and has some country too, and it's nice where I'm living and I don't have to polish anymore or admire old corpses. And as for going to see Georg, I won't go until two of my plays are on the stage and a novel is being published at the same time, for I want to keep Georg's image of me intact and not show up there as a decrepit (no, *not* a discarded)[365] Frau

Canetti, and so you shouldn't go around saying that you've submitted my play to the theater in the Josefstadt[366] etc., but for once in your life take my delicate side into account, for if I've become a washerwoman, it's through no fault of my own. And Georg will see me historically or not at all, but certainly not hysterically (that was too tempting to resist). Whereupon I close with the assurance of my love, because more extensive assurances from Sebastl are already on their way. When I arrived, she was just writing them so she can better enjoy life.

Veza Canetti[367]

VEZA TO GEORGES · *August 1946*

Mrs. Canetti
35 Downshire Hill, London N.W. 3

Darling George,

This is the first time that I am typewriting since I left Amersham, and I can only write a proper letter when typing. I had no strength whatever left to write to you, and since my letter to your brother contains my whole life story, I betray him to you, and send you a copy of this letter, anticipating your promise, that you will burn it after reading it (twice). It is a token of my love to you, for I never betray Canetti except to you. You'll also see, why I don't come yet, but your brother will hurry up things for me now, if only it were that I should go and see you. He has all the power in the world, and out of a nothing, namely that frequently mentioned Sebastl, who is no other than Friedl, he made a respected writer though there is a deadlock now. For since she has no time now to sit with him and *he* writing her books, there is no book coming forward, and your brother is in despair. So I gave him the alternative, either he becomes a genius again, or he remains a slave. In the latter case he'll get rid of *one* witch, I told him that very clearly. Whereupon he gave me another big cheque. To get rid of me? No. He fears liberty, it would mean much worse chains.

To complete the grotesque comic picture I tell you, that I live now in a very nice private house with the *cousin* of Friedl[368] (!) who however has about the same opinion of her than I have. Will you really not write to me? Will you really resent, that I want to keep you? To keep the image? *You* who wrote such poetical letters to me, such a lot of fiction, nearly all of them are fiction, but the last letter was so beautiful. And so kind. Do I have to lose this? You see, a duchess always remains a duchess, even when a grandmother, and I want to be a duchess, before I see you. One on the stage. For I am very gifted, as you will read in the papers one day.

Will you *not* send me your reviews and *not* report on the success of the book? Or will you, with the eye of a great physician and philosopher, that you are, see through my state of mind and help me again, as you helped me so often?

You are the principal character in a play that will wander to all countries and that will be performed on all stages, and you are the one, in the play, that smoothes everything, the other main character, drives everybody to destraction.

About the »Blendung«: There was a bad review in Horizon all through the fault of Miss Wedg. who wanted her friend to do it, whereas a book seller in Charing Cross wanted to send a gorgeous review and was prevented by us, since we thought Wedg. knows best. She is terribly upset about it, not that it matters much except that your brother of course felt it terribly. A grand review of Wedg. is coming out soon, I forget in which periodical. Moreover an Italian professor wrote and wants to translate the book, of course we answer only after two or three months or not at all, and each answer costs me ten years of my life to get your brother to do it. We lost probably Sweden and Danemark, because Canetti does not bother to write a letter and I have a very delicate position towards Miss Wedg. namely I can't talk business with her, it would spoil our relationship, which after all is more important to me than business. Did I tell you that the American publisher was in London and wrote to Canetti. Who went to see him in his Hotel to find him amazed, because he saw that young impressive and Christian poet, having been prepared to see an old lean and haggard looking, shabby scholar. »The Pyre« is going to be the title for the book in Amerika, a title *I* chose, since Autodafé as he says, is no good for U.S.

I shall not write to you to-day of your grandiose books. Even I can read and understand them, so marvelous and humane is the style, I want an extra letter for that. It's too precious to be mixed up with my nasty life story and personal matters. We should <give> them to the dau<ght>er of Lord Croft.[369] Uncle Joe wrot<e> that you are *well* is *that true*? This blot[370] is a kiss.

Peggy.

VEZA TO ELIAS · *August 28, 1946*

Mrs. Canetti
35 Downshire Hill
London NW3

Copy about Maud Arditti

August 28, 1946

Beloved Canetti,

(Please don't mention this letter to anyone.)

Oddly enough, I had asked Maudie Arditti[371] to meet me in front of the lost property office in Piccadilly, and as I approached the gate, I saw a woman walking past me. I thought, I must be a bit confused, for the woman looked like Maud, but it wasn't she. I, *Veza*, am beginning to forget faces. I was very relieved that this woman wasn't she, not our lovely Maud, but I was chagrined at the similarity. The woman came back. I stepped into her path on purpose, just to be sure that this unknown, appalling face was not Maud, whom we had seen only a year ago. She recognized me. "You must really be happy," she

said as if reciting a lesson, "that Elias has had such enormous success. You always believed in him and now it's really come true."
"Thank you," I said to the stranger. Even her speech was strange. We continued walking. "I've been gravely ill, very gravely ill. But now I'm three-fourths cured. Three-fourths. I'm only one-fourth still sick . . ."

She was insane.

She has recovered enough that she knows it. "I was mad," she assured me, and looked like Mathilde. "I didn't understand what people were saying to me. I couldn't speak myself." We went into a restaurant, and I chose a table far away from the others. I was so shocked that I thought I was mad myself. "The worst thing is the persecution complex. I have to leave soon, go to the chemist's, buy medicine. It started with my not being able to find my way home. And when I finally did get home, what I said was all mixed up. We went right to a gynecologist, because everything always begins in your belly. He said I was quite healthy, and he wasn't the right doctor for me. I had a psychosis. Then I was treated in a convent. After meals, they lowered the blinds. Then I walked through the fields by myself for hours. Now I'm in analysis. I have to buy my medicine in Wigmore Rd., because if men see me going into a chemist's, they'll think I'm sick. Such is the world."

Luckily, I had been very cautious in saying why I wanted to meet her, for I didn't want to let such a letter out of my hands, but she had understood and stuck to her guns. With her garish clown makeup and a thousand wrinkles in her face, she was planning to get married. "In four weeks I'll be cured. I'm improving rapidly. The doctor says I'm a big help to him because I'm so bright. I have two suitors, besides the one from you. One of them loves me a lot and wept because I rejected him. But he hasn't divorced his wife yet and has a family to support and he's poor and wants me to work and earn money." It turned out that her other suitor, with whom she was as good as engaged, visited her in the convent, "and probably because he saw me in a deck chair, wrapped in blankets, he changed his mind. That's heartless, isn't it? I told his aunt how things were; I'll be well soon. I seem quite well, don't I?" "Completely." We had to eat quickly because she wanted to get to the chemist's, and on the way there she got upset because a lady had "stared at" her legs, "because I'm wearing these elegant hose," the poor creature said. "I hope I won't jerk my legs around or say or do something improper when I meet your suitor." I said he wouldn't be in London until October. That was all right with her, because by then she'd be completely recovered. By the way, she doesn't have good control over her arms and legs and drops things all the time. Of course, she can't remember anything and what she said was quite confused and obscene. But on one point she was sly and completely normal: when I asked her age, she made herself younger.

Apropos of making oneself younger, a funny story occurs to me that's just too good not to tell in closing. Namely: when I was visiting Mrs. Somlo, who's utterly normal and comes from Hungary, she started in, "I have a rare quality, dear Mrs. Canetti, namely, I tell the truth. And so I won't keep from you the fact that I have a son who's 37. I know, you're not supposed to do that, betray your age, but what's the point? I've got bags under my eyes, you know, I've got wrinkles. In a word, I don't make a fool of myself like my friend Ilonka. We lived in the same building in Budapest. According to her, she was 37." (She seemed to be obsessed with this number.) "Just imagine, she didn't give in even when the Nazis came. She'd rather go to a concentration camp than admit she's over forty. There were always roll calls and we all had to assemble in the corridor and give our ages, and whoever was under forty had to go with them. She preferred the concentration camp to admitting she's over forty, and if she's not dead today, it's only because two young girls escaped and took her with them." "Isn't she 37?" I said. "I'd very much like to meet Mr. Canetti, because cars don't impress me, only intellect impresses me. I have lunch in Dorchester, but only because of my friends. He can be wearing sixty diamonds for all I care." (She meant Mr. Canetti.) "I'm not impressed. Intellect is everything. Somebody's got to have something to teach me; that's how I've always been." A gentleman and a paragon of good upbringing, with *elegant* manners is—Karl Hirsch . . .[372]

Veza to Georges · *August 28, 1946*[373]

Mrs. Canetti
35 Downshhire Hill
London NW3

August 28

Beloved child,

I'm sending you a copy of my strange letter to Bauscherl because it is about your cousin Maud. I wanted to marry her off to our dentist,[374] who is doing splendidly. He has a good practice and was looking for a wife. She begged me to introduce her last year, because I had also "married off Renée so well," and I promised I would. I'm always matchmaking. Sometimes I'm successful, sometimes my clients die in the gas chamber, but I keep at it, and as Thackeray says, every kind woman is a matchmaker. I do it, however, because I'm interested in how the story will come out. In Renée's case, two children came out, hopefully not redheads. I married a very sweet young Viennese Jewess to a cousin of mine in Belgrade, and how they thanked me. Her parents followed her to Belgrade. She was poor as a church mouse, my cousin rich, in short, they were all murdered and I'm frightfully tired of always having to think about it, and I don't like waking up in the night. Unless you write that you're doing much better. Wasn't your dizziness caused by weakness? And if someone is as famous as you, so magnificent and talented, it doesn't matter if they're sick, or not as much. Dear child, I was terribly ill, more or less like Maudie, but without the obscenity (I'm confiding this to you) and I'm in constant fear of madness, and in the bus I say the bus number instead of "Twopence" and I only playact, and how good that none proclaim, Rumpelstilzchen is my name,[375] and I felt so sick, oh so sick, but I couldn't stay in bed, because the landlady must not find out, and I didn't have a convent like Maudie or any elect. treatments, and no doctor . . . By the way, not everyone died in the gas chambers, Renée's husband's entire family emigrated to America on *her* money. They, too, were poor as church mice and they only got her money (I wish your brother and you had a little more Arditti in you) because she had it in Vienna and those poor people dared to risk their lives by going to the bank and withdrawing the money (that meant the death penalty for Jews) and they risked it. You've got to when you're poor, and they all left, even the sons' girlfriends, a total of twelve people, left to join Renée's husband. Renée's father, a certain awful Arditti, must have been not a little "pleased." But they were good, hardworking people. You see that I'm somewhat confused since I met Maudie, it was such a shock. Last year, I was seriously run down and she was jolly and looked quite youthful—what a pity that one can't do anything to help, for after all, after twenty years of service to Canetti, I get to live in a (charming) little room, as a favor and without paying any rent. I pay only my expenses, and since I don't accept hand-outs, I give the boy German lessons—this for a tiny room in London—which I wouldn't do for a guinea an hour.

Georg, Canetti is in despair because I wrote him about your dizzy spells. You know, I didn't want to come: I look like a cretin, but then when I talk, I'm very smart, but I was terribly sick and you can see it in my face. My friends are alarmed, and that's why I didn't want to come, but if you get dizzy and are still staying in Chateaub., since I've admitted everything to you anyway, may I come *after all*? Either I'll be amusing, or I'll call and cancel. "Not able to come today because I'm weary of life . . ." May I come?

Veza

How are you? Don't abandon us to our fears!

Elias to Georges · *August 31 (?), 1946*

Perranporth, Cornwall

My dear, dear Georg,

Veza writes that you have been suffering dizzy spells for a few weeks and were in Paris to consult a doctor. Please write and tell me exactly what it really is. Don't be afraid to use expressions that are somewhat too technical; I've gotten used to them by reading your books—you'll hardly believe me when I tell you I'm really fascinated by the method and clarity of your books. Tell me what these spells mean. Write in such a way that I can discuss it with a trained person here. Is it something that prevents you from driving, for instance? Is it something that recurs periodically and slowly gets weaker, or does it have to disappear completely before you are well again?

Sometime I must write you a long letter about Veza. I am personally convinced she will come. To get you to really comprehend her hesitation is a very difficult thing to do. I think she imagines that you still see her as she used to be. Your image of her is very, very important to her. I find her more beautiful than ever. Her head has become wise and mighty; she has a sort of emanation that very few people have. Her wit and her love combine to produce something new. Now the remarkable thing is that Veza, who is already so important, especially to you, wants to hold her own in public as well. Things have gone badly for her for too long. She needs a bit of success, perhaps only to tell herself that her luck is not always bad. Please, Georg, tell me clearly what sort of "theaters" these are that Nissim has. Please believe that I want nothing for myself from him. But if he really does have decent theaters, it would be literally idiotic not to get him *seriously* interested in Veza's things. She is a *born* dramatist of the first rank and he would certainly do well with her plays. Write me what you think and send it to my old address, where I'll be returning tomorrow: "Durris" Stubbs Wood Chesham Bois.

I've spent three weeks here in Cornwall, by the sea, at the foot of wonderful cliffs and old tin mines. It's one of the most interesting parts of England, tunneled through for millennia, the oldest mining country in Europe. There's a tunnel nearby that extends four miles out under the sea. Some tunnels are said to be three miles deep. Five minutes from where I'm staying, tin was already being mined by the Phoenicians. But they also found gold, silver, copper, lead, and today they mine tungsten. You will be surprised to hear me mentioning such things. For the first time in my life, I'm deeply impressed by a mining region. Many of the entrances are right by the sea. When you come to England, next year I hope, I must show you Cornwall. The old language has been lost but the people are enormously proud of their tradition, and since they have spread all over the world, they sometimes remind me of the Jews. You must replace the exodus through the desert with the mine as their central myth. They don't care where they dig for treasure, whether in ships or in rock, but dig they do. —I had to tell you at least this much about my three weeks here; they were a salvation for me. I've finally gotten rid of the last psychic traces of that old story. The sea has healed me. Now you must get well soon and completely, and write at once

to your brother,
Elias.

Veza to Georges · *September 4, 1946*

Mrs. Canetti
35 Downshire Hill
London NW3

Sept. 4. 1946

Darling Child,

What a letter! It came this moment and I wish now I were there! I wish I could see you and feel all these pains and nauseas and giddy spells with you! I shall live now. Do you know! You saved my life. I was sick and tired again (for a change). Nothing means a thing to me anymore, not even the fact, that I have to get Bauscherl out of the claws of that vamp, and that I am succeeding marvelously. Not even the fact the »Hochzeit« is going to be performed in Vienna![376] Nothing. *You* mean everything. I shall even bring that great sacrifice and let you see me. It's really such a great sacrifice because my way of becoming immortal was, to remain in your heart unpolluted. I wanted never to be seen by you again, to remain so. I don't care for immortality and all that atom bomb chimera, I care for being in your heart, what I always was. How can I, when you see me. But I shall sacrifice that, for I must see you. I want to see you now and talk to you. And cheer you up. Strange enough, I have some of my former vitality, and I am never dull. Except when I telephone, that I can't come on account of the balance of my mind being disturbed. (That is the formula in court after suicides. Suicide while the balance of her mind was disturbed. Fear nothing. I shall outlive everybody.) And don't fear, that I could come before you want me to. I know exactly how you feel about it, I feel too often that way myself not to respect it. I shall be able to reenter this country owing to good connections we have. I can come a few weeks after you write you want me to come. And dear child, you will help me. You'll write at once and let me know at once the change of your address in case you go to Paris. I have heaps of money to stay in posh hotels in Paris. I spend a pound a day here, and don't pay for my lodgings at the moment. I would never live a day longer than you, so take good care of yourself, son. This is no phrase. You can imagine how I feel about that new operation and my admiration and *adoration* for you to put it in such a nice, charming noble way for me to digest it! An operation is an operation and we two know that. Your operation makes me ashamed of myself. Of complaining. Of having wanted to give in. Of ever wanting to give in. Also I want your telephone number! As soon as you have got over it, I want to hear your sweet bewitching voice. I posted a letter to you from Canetti on Sunday. I don't know what he wrote, but believe me, your giddy spells and condition saved him, too. I think he is really out of the claws of that creature. I did not tell you the whole truth about her character, but shall when we meet. At the moment, she does nothing but getting out money from your brother, to have a happy life with the other, and she succeeds. He is going to finance her trip to Sweden now, to meet her parents there. I am glad of that, though, for we have some hope that she might remain there. Anyhow he is going to write to her, when she is there, that everything has to be over. In that he is quite serious. Cornwall helped. He fell in love a little there with quite a young girl, who kissed him a lot and it gave him back his self respect. Before, he sincerely believed, that nobody love<s> him and that he is not attractive to women anymore. He telephoned with that girl before me, moreover our friend, the Doktor,[377] told me, that this is true. I do everything here to make him meet other women, that was my chief reason to go to London. Don't mention darling, that I copied my letters to him for you, it would hurt him. Also make him think that you see a great change in him, after Cornwall, that helps, too. He wants you to believe in him and respect him. He was so upset about me, that's why he lost himself. —I had to interrupt now. I had an awful attack of giddyness myself—with me it's nerves, and sympathy with you. I shall feel all the trouble that you feel. That will help you. Your handwriting, by the way is very reassuring. I better close now. I shall write again in a few days. You don't know what it means to me to see your handwriting.

I got a letter from Edith yesterday, she seems very happy and still is much attached to the Canettis, especially to you. This is good, on account of the child. I am glad Nissim has a nice girl,[378] this is most important. Has he got those theatres you mentioned?[379] If not, I am not worried, he'll manage alright. Was I thrilled to read about your books being everywhere. They *read* so well. About that in my next letter. It's the style of a poet writing scientific prose. My machine is giddy, too.

All my love

Do Write!
I will—in a few days

VEZA TO GEORGES · *September 10, 1946*

Mrs. Canetti
35 Downshire Hill
London NW3

Sept. 10th

Dear Benjamin,

You do me a lot of wrong. For though I have not written, I have done the most important steps to go to France,[380] and spend Xmas with you. I won't feel so miserable, when you see me now, because anyhow since you are convalescing, you'll be much more comfortable with a good old mother than with your roués. You must pardon my pornographical enumerations, but I am in the habit of reading and re-reading the Duc de St. Simon, in order to escape from the less glamourous life at the court of the Duc Canetti and his courtisans, of which you shall get a glimpse right now. Let me only tell you, that I got a passport from this country to go to France, that I shall easily get the re-enter permit, but that I had to give up to the Home Office the precious letter, you worked out for me in May and that I cannot get a visé from the French consulate, unless you have another letter sent to me, by one of the doctors, attending you, by someone of Pasteur,[381] in short a credible letter that you are ill and want me badly. I am very sorry, but that's the only way with the French consul, considering that I am stateless. I don't grumble at being stateless, though, for it saved your brother from joining up during the War. I can only take 75 guineas with me, so that means that I can't stay too long (this to take away the shock, that you got when you read I'm coming). If I get that letter soon, I could be in Chateaubr. or any other sanatorium, about five weeks later. I am resolved to go, and since I am rather weak, I shall be very glad to be allowed to sit near you, without talking much, just sit near you. You need not fear that I shall collapse, and I don't think I shall feel very miserable and ill, having had a bad spell now, which is usually followed by a better period. I shall only stay in Paris for a night or two, and then stay with you all the time. I feel I shall get much better, when with you. I mean it, I could not write it otherwise. If you remember let me know if: I shall take with me soap, coffee, tea, and sugar. These things I have in large quantities here, and was told you have not got them in France. You must not write that I should wait a little, and come when you feel better, for if you were alright I would not come, I would want you to be in much more pleasant company. Even if you don't want me, fearing my moods, you must let me come, Canetti wants it, and he wants to come when I return. For one of us in the country, the other is always able to return in case of difficulties. We must be cautious, pardon us, but we built up an existence here, and how. With too much difficulties to dare running any risks.

The position in the affairs of your brother and St. Sebastian (that's Friedl) was the following the day before yesterday. This is strictly confidential. Your brother must never, never know that I told you all. But why should not you have a thrilling letter, when I have all the trouble. Not only trouble, I begin to be sarcastic about it, as you will see right now. Well, F. tried to commit suicide three days ago, but so (to quote Canetti) that she should be rescued in time. I had no idea of it, and saw her two nights ago, when I found her much depressed and she told me, with genuine feelings, that she was in despair because she had lost C. and does not love the other anymore, nay, that she had actually left Bill, broken every relation with him. *That* she told me at ten o'clock at night, and went on talking very charmingly, so that I was full of compassion, and had such a warm feeling for her, that I only did not go to the registrar, to marry her to Canetti, because Canetti *is* married already. I felt weakening a lot, though, and was about to say foolish things, forgetting how that vixen has deceived us before. But at twelve o'clock that same night the telephone rang, no, that was not Canetti, that was Bill. She spoke to him for half an hour in the room of her cousin, and came back radiant. Thus I knew, that there was a reconciliation, and that it is Bill again, and she could not quite deny it. The trouble with Bill is, that Canetti does not allow Friedl money enough for the two of them, and that, not getting enough money out of her he sulks sometimes. Well, Friedl, not without feeling for the situation and not without being ashamed, chatted on, but this time of the night, half past one, more cheerful. She left assuring me, that what she wants is a pure »friendship« not one of the flesh, just ideal friendship with Bill. This was so ideal, that she slept last night with him, and your brother caught her, not exactly in that act, but he rang up when it was not opportune and found out. To-night he is with her, your brother, because she must explain the situation to him, her having been with Bill all the night not meaning that she was in bed with him, no, they were probably on the sofa. Pardon the crude tale, but the events are crude. Your brother, up to his ears in love with her still, is sometimes in a very dangerous mood, and I have to watch him, and get in a dangerous mood myself. So this is why I did not write. For with it, being so ill, that I hope you'll get morphia for me to get over the worst agonies of pain (nerves) I don't know how to write, in which manner, in which whim, though I would always know *what* to write, as you see. I don't know if I am not going to marry him to her. Because I am so fed up with intervening, watching, warning and worrying, that I would find it best if he plunges still deeper into that cold water and gets a worse chill. Will you believe me now that I long to go away for a spell? She, it is agreed, goes to Sweden (your brother financing the trip and her stay there), and she is going to decide there, what she wants, sofas, beds, etc. Also Marie Louise is going for a month to Vienna, to secure her castle there, no, this time it is no St. Simon, it *is* a castle, one of the nicest in Austria and she gets it back. So Canetti might be alone for some time, which will do his work a lot of good. Did I tell you that Switzerland is interested in an edition? I looked into his Power Book[382] to day, it is marvellous, isn't it a shame that a genius should spend his time so unpleasantly. Byron at least had great fun, he has *only* worries and expenses.

Excuse this very unpoetical letter, but I had to tell you, I don't think anybody ever was in a worse position than I (now in London it's better, I see friends and have a bit of comfort) except those in Belsen. But then, to think of them makes you still more despair of everything and I am only hoping against hope for a few better years, since your operation, now. For if you got over that, you'll soon get over all other horrible difficulties. *But for you*, we would both not think it worth while to go on, in spite of your brother getting a great name now. All my love dear angel, what a great honour to know you, whose works are being distributed by the Institut Pasteur. *You will get the Nobel Preis!*

Poor Peggy
Nur Dich liebt[383]
Veza

VEZA TO GEORGES · *September 28, 1946*

Mrs. Canetti
35 Downshire Hill
London NW3

Sept. 28

Dear Imp,

You are just as bad as your brother . . . but I won't scold you, since you have been so brave, and so noble writing that letter *before* your operation, you *do* have to be a hero, and we much admired you. However I was so worried, that I felt incapable of writing to you, because you are more heroic than filial, no good son, I can tell you, your senior brother *never* leaves me without news, junior, and wrote *every* day from Cornwall, he, who never answered an offer for his book to be filmed. So don't do that again, it drives us mad. *Imp*. Yesterday after your telegr. came your letter, it seems that they did not bandage your arm to your right side, for how could you have written it. I suppose I won't get any details about your state and shall have to drop in at Chateaub. one day to see everything myself. I'll probably find a lot of »favourites« there, if not a few Roués, too, I don't mind women, especially young ones, but could you send your

Roués away for an hour twice a week while I am there? I don't like them. I suppose all the doctors take advantage of you, you being helpless in bed, handsome as you are, they would here, the trend amongst modern Englishmen being that way rather than the other. Oscar Wilde would have the Hell of a job here . . .

On the 15th of Sept. my brother found a four leaf clover in his garden in Kent, and knowing how we worry about you he sent it to me, I stuck it on your photo, where it is still working miracles. Will *he* be glad about the result. The trouble is, I could not just drop in without giving you a warning, since you would not know who that fat old lump is, that rolled into your room. It would be such a shock to you, that you would get ill again, which I have to prevent and I sincerely believe, I could hasten up your recovery, since I am lucky. Which does not mean that I am not having all the misfortune in the world myself, but I bring luck. In case your surgeon wants to prop a bit of flesh into your hips, I am at your disposal, they could take it from my hips, even my nose would do, there is enough for you on my nose, thick fat flesh, I'd be too glad to get rid of it.

We met a plastic surgeon the other day, a Jew from Vienna and he explained chest operations to us this way. »I slipped the mammilla, which was at the knees of the woman, through a crevice, on top, that I made, and used a stick to fix it, and there it was, sticking right under her chin now, and it even grew on, so that she could produce milk, if she liked . . . « That's how you surgeons talk. Not you, though, you in your book talk like a prince. Nobody has the feeling of being a carcass on *your* dissecting table. I shan't write in full length about your book today, because I am still exhausted from all that agony of fear about you, your brother not feeling a bit better, and incapable therefore of cheering me up. And this is the reason that I close my vitamin bottle, to day and hope to have more strength to write in a few days one of my scandal letters. Affairs (not the love affairs) of your brother are going on very well and we shall soon have not enough German versions for all the demands, lots of countries, not France, though, blasted people I don't know why they don't ask for that great book. You don't happen to know anybody in France who would exchange a German Blendung for Autodafé, we want it for Switzerland, where they intend reprinting it, in Germ.[384] Nissim might have one, but I suppose it would be waste of time to ask him that favour, Edith being out of reach now and too occupied with her new baby. In case you remember, send us the address of Joe and Elias,[385] we want to let them have Autod. when the third edition in November comes out. There'll be a few more splendid reviews and Horizon was flooded with insulting letters, the editor[386] himself told so to Canetti, apologizing, he had been in Brazil and knew nothing of that disgrace, he is reading the book now and enthusiasted. Also as I told you, they consider the Hochzeit for Vienna, we expect more news about it, post traffic still being very bad, they have so many zones there,[387] that what with quarrelling which zone and why and how, there is the greatest muddle in that country, with Nazis all on top, in leading positions, even among the police.

If you don't cause your »Favorite,« or your »Courtisans« or your »Roués« to write at once to me about yourself—no vitamin tablets. All our love, your brother got your wire only this morning, will he be glad, he'll kiss it.

Love,
Peggy, Pharao of Egypt

Elias to Georges · *October 10, 1946*

October 10, 1946

My dear Georg,

I just received a letter from Nissim (Veza had asked him for the comedy, which we have urgent need of) and he writes that you are doing a *little* better. If only it be so, if only it be so. In the meantime, we have both decided we must visit you this winter. I feel there have definitely been enough operations—hopefully not too many—and that you need to rest and recover for a good long while and *regain* some weight. We intend to visit you one after the other, first Veza for a month (or longer, of course, if it does you good) and then, perhaps a month after she returns, I would come. These are not idle promises this time. *Veza has her pass at last* (a so-called traveling paper that the English authorities issue to stateless persons), and even more important, she feels so psychologically restored by her stay in London that she has the courage to undertake a trip alone. So she really does intend to come, and now it all depends on your getting her a visa for France. The French, you see, are very chary of giving visas to stateless persons. A letter from you is not enough by itself. You'll have to get a prominent doctor (perhaps the director of the hospital[388] where you are currently staying, or Ameuille,[389] or the Institut Pasteur) to write a letter that will make clear who you are and above all, that a visit from your sister-in-law at this time is of cardinal importance for your health. I'm sure you can easily discuss this with one of your friends. If you think it will make a stronger impression, have them write that you need a visit now from your sister-in-law, and then from your brother; the latter not being able to come right away. "Brother," as a closer relative, may be more impressive. I think that the French will then give Veza permission. She can easily get a return visa to England.

Just give some thought to what plan would please you most. Veza can come as soon as she has the visa, as early as in two or three weeks, if you like. Don't worry about money; she'll bring some along. If you plan to leave Chateaubriand soon, she could meet you in Paris (where Nissim always keeps a room ready for her in a pension, but he writes that she could also stay with him. He is really very nice in his letters) and if you only remain in Paris a short time, she could travel on to St. Hilaire with you. You will surely have no trouble finding her a place to stay there. Her only thought (and mine as well) is to spend a lot of time with you. You don't know how distraught she was this summer about her disagreeable encounters with housewives, and how changed she is now since living among civilized people again. Moreover, there is now also a prospect of her getting her own small apartment, and that makes her proud and self-confident again. This summer, she was tortured by the thought that you must not be allowed to see her in her distraught state or you might not respect her as much as before. Everything about her is touching and poignant and human and I often wonder how it is possible that a being like her can exist at all in today's world. Don't think that she did not want to come; that would do her a grave injustice. In one respect of course, she's just like any other woman and wants to find out how much you love her. But I don't think she ever seriously doubted your feelings for her. It's always the reverse fear, that you could stop loving her because she has been through so much and has gotten eight years older. In reality, in her essence, she is not older by any means, just richer and wiser and better than ever. —In case you want to have me visit you first, I can come any time, or course. The only difficulty would be that I would have to submit my passport first, which would surely take another month. But if Veza comes first, I can get my papers in order in the meantime and be ready to come later. Besides, Veza (like me, not someone who reaches decisions easily) is now really eager to come. November in England has never been good for her. I fear that if she's still here in November, her spirits may flag again and she'll simply lose her courage.

Above all, be so dear as to procure us that important letter and think about the order you'd like us in. —

Friday

This letter has been lying about for another day and Veza just told me what's happening with your book. That *is* an honor, and at your age! I can't tell you how happy I am—with all my hundred hearts. I think I have that many, and even some you like. The Institut Pasteur may get somewhere again if it thinks so much of you. Georg, my tenderly loved *big* brother, you *will* get well again and the two of us will accomplish good and beautiful things. If only I could see you and embrace you right now. My yearning for you has grown so strong in the last few months that sometimes I just want to get on a plane and be with you in two hours.

I'll mail this letter now as is, although it's not the way I wanted it to be. But soon you'll receive another one with serious intellectual content. Today you'll have to make do with "just" feelings. And above all, think about what you would like. Of course, Veza can come first and I can join you in a few weeks if you'd like to have us both in France at the same time. We could take turns being in Paris and then a few weeks with you in St. Hilaire. Decide *how you want it* and that's exactly how it will be.

A thousand embraces and kisses, and love, and gratitude that you still love me.

Your brother,
Elias.

Veza to Georges · *October 24, 1946*

Mrs. Canetti
35 Downshire Hill NW3

Oct. 24

Darling son,

I just got your letter and am delighted from various reasons: first, your mood is better, second, your being able to go to Paris so soon, and then I never thought I would really get that letter from your Sana, because I thought you don't want me to come. Looking at the date, I *fear* it will have to be St. Hilaire of *course* not Paris, I don't want my nice eyes scrached out by the various women in love with you, and besides I would kill them all with my biting tongue. My plays go to Vienna, Salzburg etc,[390] so don't fear that you will have to read them, I shall have no copies left, they are keen on our productions now, there being not many writers left who write in German. I shall post a gillette blade to-morrow (best quality) in an empty envelope and you'll let me know, if this is the type you want. And mind. I come to see you, that you should remain quietly on your couch, to help you pass the time, while you are not too strong. What concerns stories, I'll bring them along, in my head, enough to go for a month. And of course I'll stay a month, if you don't get too tired of me. Unless the coat arrives in time, that my cousin[391] posted for me from New-York, I'll be dressed in rags, so please say, that I am an old governess who came to see you, or your nannie, or something. I can also tell you a »sale«[392] joke, right now, a French one, too. My cousin used to provide them for me, when I was younger. »A French lady . . . «—no, I'll keep them, as a pièce de resistance. Your cousin Elias Canetti wrote a charming letter to us, all about the Archiv, »Ihr habt einen verkalkten Vetter, der alles aufhebt . . . «[393] etc., we were tickled to death. Did you send him all the reviews for the Archiv? It would be a good thing if you did, for I am constantly moving, and thus lose everything dear to me. The idea that I could wear anything of Marianne,[394] I am about the size of auntie . . . I forget her name, the mother of Mathilde in Vienna.[395]

Your brother was impressed and thrilled reading about your book given to the congress members. He phones every day from Amersham to ask if there is a letter from you. To-morrow I'll show this one, will *he* be glad! The taste of your French people is *not* so good, for the publisher, that refused to translate his book (in account of paper shortage) took Sebastian's book, written by Canetti, and it just came out in France, every other country having refused it. For that muck they have the paper. I want to send it to you, just for fun, she promised me a copy, but your brother will not let me have one, for fear that I might send it you. He said, nobody in France of the family must read it, he is ashamed. So if you can get it somewhere, do, here it was called »The Monster«,[396] no reason to change the French title, Anna Sebastian, the author. I don't know the publisher, but wait a while I still hope to get it for you. Also I'll at last send you Macauley.[397] Why don't you grow a beard? I never knew that you are shaving already, I thought kids don't shave. I shall certainly not complain of your beard, I am not the kissing type anymore, I better bring a whip.

Since you want pornography: well, she is hand in glove with Bill again (I could find other metaphers, but you are maybe not strong enough to swallow them), and your brother pays the »Bills« which pun is not unintentionel. When I come back from France I intend to get married to a non-poet (your brother must not know). Not that I have a special preference for anybody, but I have offers from a few old gentleman, and I feel so tired of living in a muddle, I simply long for respectability, and if I can find one, who is a castrate, I'll plunge into the adventure. Your brother must not know, for glad as he would be, to get rid of me, when it comes to it, he starts whining like a cry-baby, and you have to console him. I will sell myself to the one, who has a flight of rooms, cut glass at table and a butler. Strange enough, you find them in this country, even at my age. If he has strict rules about Luncheons and Dinners, if he changes his suit for diné, if he goes to church regularly, he gets preference, I long for rules, regulations, strict thinking, and I don't mind whiskers. I don't mind anything, unless it is a muddle and from a distance I even don't mind minding your brother.

Nissim wrote me a nice letter, too, he knows an address where I could stay, unfortunately he thinks I shall stay in Paris and recommends a boarding house, very cheap indeed, I would not mind paying for a week, even if I stay only for two days. I told him I *do not* want to stay with relatives. Frankly, the prospect of having to go through all the relatives, before I reach you, is appalling, and if you know an hotel, where I could find a room without informing anybody, I should be most grateful. I cannot go through all that strain of telling them about their famous relative, who, at that moment may be revising the third novel of Anna Sebastian, sitting like an idiot and admiring her work, her beauty and her charm. Broken hearted, because she loves Bill and will go under (that she will) and land in gaol, and die as a street girl (not in Piccadilly though, there they would not pay her the usual rate, they are beautiful, in Piccadilly) or whining, because *she* is in Sweden, and I am in France, instead of being glad to be left alone, with so many fine women, who are after him, now, that he is a celebrity. He is so comic, that I only feel miserable, when I see him, with his very beautiful head, a noble smile, deep lines, which are like the lines in a new born little bearcub, not belonging in that face. With his voice as mild and fine as yours is. With his naiveté and ignorance of women, having described Therese,[398] and written the »Hochzeit«. With his incapacity to cope with reality, when it comes to *live* it, and not write it. Yes, I laugh, when I am alone, and fear to meet him, the »Don Quixote« who wrote Don Quixote. »And who is going to write my letters for me?« he said three days ago, when I talked of going to France. Yes, who is? »I'll forward them to you, to France« was his way out.

I enclose the empty envelop of a gillette, so that you should tell me, if it's the right one, there are three kinds, and I send the blade tomorrow in an empty letter, for you to decide.

Now, sweet son, my only pride and ~~the Jacob (that's the one who did not get the Linsen~~)[399] (I did not like the quotation and comparison, it was taken from the bible and does not fit into this letter) all my love, I'll write in a few days. I've seen a few old French films, »La Femme du Boulanger«, »L'Atalante«.[400] They *are* lovely. (Out of my passion for you I went to French films).

Peggy
Veza

VEZA TO GEORGES · *November 6, 1946*

Mrs. Venetia Canetti
35 Downshire Hill
London NW3

Nov. 6th 1946

My Love,

I have been to the French consulate today from 12 to 3 o'clock and I would be very hopeful, to get the visé soon, if a friend had not told me, that I have not a chance to get it soon, since I am a bloody foreigner, and the French are much worse about that than the British people. He said that lasts ten weeks or so, with only that letter of your sana. I have been told that about the British travelling papers and got them in five days with very much courtesy, so that I am not quite downhearted, but tell you the truth about it. I shall give them two weeks, and then go and pester them and try to get someone influencial here, to interfere. As it is, that gentleman who told it me, is the Viennese son in law of Lord Croft,[401] who is an MP and a millionaire but this fact does not count so much, than the *British* passport of, say a toilet cleaner, or charwoman, or even a crook (a crook is one of those men who are going to entice me to be deported in Marseille and rob me of my money etc). Will your brother laugh when I tell him that. Son, you must get used to the fact that I am fifty, but look ten years older and am so fat, that they call me granny in London (grandmother). Your letter made me blush, for if you talk like that to me, which you will not feel like, when you see me, but will want to, out of chivalry, the first week, maybe (not the second, you'll feel bored of me by then), I'll quit. I have the dignity of a matron, dear, and I don't want to blush. If I did not know, helas, that I am uncapable of falling in love, and cannot even be a prey to your very great charms, I would not come, for you are a great danger, with your voice, but chiefly on account of your noble attitude. For never to lament, no, to write in such a charming manner about all your ordeals, is beyond me and I am so ashamed of my letter, that I posted yesterday, that I only hope, this one reaches you before the other. And this one is more cheerful, because I have been to the consulate and see a chance of sitting near you and seeing you soon. I shall have my glasses on, to see you better, I wear glasses, have no theeth, not even false ones, and walk with a stick. So you'll find I am more ill than you, for beside my several complaints, old age is an illness.

What you write about having to stay in Ch. and the reason, oh what a hero you are! How admirable! You will recover completely, you'll see, with so much spirit and courage it's not possible otherwise, besides, *your* cases recover completely, as you may read in your book and as I have been told here by prominent physicians. And you will live longer than you would have lived, being healthy, because you have no chance to throw your life, youth, strength away, like your brother does.

Thank you for your very precious instructions, what concerns my having to walk half an hour to your sana, this is a point that I don't mind at all, even if it is an hour, and at night I shall use a torch (that electric lamp that you carry in your pocket) and shall not use the cars of your doctors, not wanting to make conversation with them. I am very easily tired out, son, nerves, and what I hate most, is conversation. Besides I shall never stay very long from reasons just mentioned, I would get tired, so would you, by the bye. I intend to travel by plane, thus not much chance for the crooks to deport me, only, there may be no berth, in that case I'll have to take the train, which is no affair. I shall follow your instructions concerning the taxy, but I never look in the glass, dear, I hate my sight and shall just deliver the lagguage and drive on. I shall certainly not speak French to anybody, having forgotten what little I knew, and sometimes have to hesitate when I speak German, to find the proper words. I suppose I can't stay long in France, for I am only allowed 75 pound sterlings from the Home Office and I was told everything is terribly expensive over there. But what I have, I'll spend staying in Ch. I don't care a hang for Paris. I come to see *you*, not Paris. You are more than Paris to us. Also I shall tell you all the nice things in the world, but you are not allowed to be nice to me, from reasons mentioned on page two. You'll have to be very respectful and say Küss die Hand,[402] when I come and go. My chief quality being *pride*.

I see your brother only the day after to-morrow, he *will* worry about you, that's why you must not leave us without news. And don't forget to write to *him* and tell *him* you want him badly there. He was so well, when he came back from Cornwall, that rotten wench destroyed his composure.

I think I told you, that I am going to have a flat this month, not nice, only for a year, but I have to take it, though I feel very well, where I am now, I shall tell you everything about it. I can't continue writing, I must leave my stories now for you, when I am there, I only think of seeing *you* soon now, I wish I could fly this moment. I *may* consider seeing the family, but can't bother anybody to take me to a train. I took a wrong train once in Paris, so why not repeat myself. Besides I don't think I will. You see, I am full of »preparatifs,« that's the French word I believe. Much love and expect a letter in a few days. No—*all* my love

Veza

Veza to Georges · *November 10, 1946*

Nov. 10th

Dear St. Georges,

The crown of your noblesse was, we think, when you refused to read the »monstrous« book, which refusal enchanted your brother, who is still in a sad mood, though with funny intervals, for instance, when the cousin of F. where I live (and whom I like) went with him at one o'clock at night to F. who lives half an hour away, and where one cousin reproached to the other, before him, the nasty things they have said about him, each to the other, whereas F. who saw her prey escape her anticipating very rightly, that the one here, whom I'm going to call Gill tries to entice C. away from her, which I favour secretely, because she is a much better character. Helas, she does not know that C. only likes her, and sees her, because she is the cousin of the other and because he wants to talk of the other and find out, about the Goldman of the Eastend. The cousin here, has probably more chance to have a better record in life—she is heiress to one million pounds and has now only the beggarly sum of about threehundred thousand in her bank book. Her house at the address which for obvious reasons I don't put on top to-day,[403] is one of the finest in London, I leave the description for our personal interview.

When I was about to move in, I was given the following characteristic of her: mean, stingy, cruel, hard hearted, jealous, tyrannic, self-willed and wicked. Maybe she is all that (though I doubt it very much) but the funny thing is—cruel as she is—she fell in love with me and I got to like her, maybe also, because her story is strange. She lost her fiancée at an early age, right before her marriage, he died, which drove her to distraction. She seems to have had a few lovers, mostly great names and then a constant one, a great physicist[404] in this country, who was married, had two step-sons, who bear his name and who did not want to divorce his wife, though she lived with another man. Gill wanted a child of that man and had it, being the exceptional case of a lady of society with a natural child. A very courageous thing to do, which I admire, though not too difficult, considering the pavement of gold which she is able to offer this child. That lad, nine years old, is a prodigy, he is more clever, educated, charming and artistic than any grown up person I know and I adore him.

The father of that child carried on a long time with her, but being a passionate man, had a lot of sweethearts at the same time, so that she pined away for him, he promising to come, but delaying with Fionna, or Diana, or whatever they were called, who were probably ten years younger and much more beautiful (she is attractive, slim and quite clever, highly cultured but not beautiful).

After ten years of suffering she got fed up and took a young lover. A handsome man who was with her here when I moved in. But since she is a matter of fact woman, she did not expect him to live ~~leisurly~~ leiseurly (I can't spell the word) on her money, but she wanted him to take a job, and got one for him. Which he took, but thought if he has to work, why live with a woman of fourty two, when he can have two of twenty one and he left her. It's heartbreak house now here, I am terribly sorry for her, when I see her walking, no, gliding through her big house, with all the finery, and only having that tiny son sitting in his nursery, where I spend much of my time, it being filled with all the Egyptian excavations (photos of course, thank goodness) that exist, since her father[405] is the greatest authority on the subject. This is the situation, for me pretty comfortable, but it may get too hot for me, and in that case I find it quite lucky, that I shall have a flat of my own, watching things from the distance.

Noble Lord of the gangway, you would do me more justice if you *did* read the book. Your brother said I should write a play about it all, and started suggesting some mysterious developments, causes and aims. I said: Not *me*. If I write it, this will be the subject: a woman, with sex appeal, coarse and vulgar, is the heroine. As a reward for having all bad qualities, living for her lust, double crossing, *stealing*, lying, deceiving and slandering, everybody bows to her. Since she has no parts, they are admired. Since she has no beauty, it is praised. In fact, she is one of those two impostors in the fable, who are weaving a material that does not exist, and whoever does not see the material, is a lyer and must die. Even the king pretends to see the material, and the two impostors get a lot of gold and silver threads to weave it, which they put aside and one day vanish with it. She is that impostor, and that's *my* play, I told him. Not that I am going to write it. Besides I told him, that I am writing everything about it to you, in a funny way, because, I said, I have to get rid of that burden somehow, and seeing it very tragic, I have to transform it, in order not to get mad myself. I added, I am going to take all these letters away from you, and burn them, since I don't want posterity to know what a fool he is. —This is my only way to tell him off, he is in such a dangerous mood, that real scolding would upset him and he is in a very bad state.

Being in no good state myself, I have to pluck myself together in a superhuman effort, and now my only pleasure is, to think of how I shall be with you and tell you everything.

Not that I am not glad to be in London. I must admit that. I adore the town, the people, the sea-gulls, Guy Fawks, the children, and the cats. I adore London. I like the good manners of the people, their decorum, I like to go to the exhibition now on, called »The King's own pictures,« I like to get official letters with »On his majestie's service« printed on them. There is more behind it all than just ceremonousness—there is history behind it all, in the Royal Academie's King's own paintings, in his majesty's service, in the Lord Mayor's Show, in Guy Fawks.

I do hope this letter erases a little the bad effect of my previous ones and I do hope you'll get it, and I shall not add any razor blades, though it would help erase, because I don't want it to get lost, but I shall send four blades in each letter from now on, starting in a few days.

Much love, and if you don't write at once what is the matter with the contretemps, describing everything in detail, no charming letters from your nasty sister in law

The Duchesse des Ursins.[406]
(dite) Peggy

I am terrified of that Clinique, all the dignity there, your great position, are you hauty? Will you be condescending?

VEZA TO GEORGES · *November 26, 1946*

Mrs. Canetti
35 Downshire Hill NW3

Nov. 26

Mon très mignon et charmant et très beau-frère,[407]

Helas you are a double crossing skunk. You went to Paris to enjoy yourself, and I don't believe a word about giddiness and if I can't find you *in bed* when I come to Ch. but sitting up, I shall do, what aunt Trottwood did, when David Copperfield was born, I shall turn my back to you and off I go to Strasbourg. Herr Hoe[408] is one of the old gentleman I have in mind about getting married to, he is a castrate alright, charming, adores me and is well capable of having a housekeeper waiting on me. But I don't know if that is enough. For a butler it is I want and cut glass at table.

On Friday we were so upset your brother and I, I having said a few cruel words to him, that we both thought life is not worth while, with all his success kreeping along. We were tired beyond description. On Saturday went to the castle of Sir J. Wedgwood,[409] of the famous Wedgwood family (china factories, patrons of Coleridge, Conrad and now of Canetti, to remain in the *C.* business), a nephew of Josia Wedg.[410] that Jew-Protector. We were received in a castle, such a great castle it was with grand paintings, a secret cell behind the wall where the monks used to hide, and everything belonging to a castle except the ghost. The ghost was mother W. whereas the father is charming. Veronica, was with us of course, taking us in her car, and I need not say she is your brother's translator. Well, we were there and your brother said the most wonderful things about »beauty«, »taste«, »truth« and whatnot*, and from our calm and aristocratic demeanour no one would have guessed that there are storms in our tea-cups.

It seems that Sir J. was delighted with your brother and we were begged to come again. But such is our corruption and so low have we sunk, that we prefer to be in London in a box-room to the halls and porches and woods and glasshouses of Seals Hill, yes, they liked us, and the old ghost told me confidentially (Veronica adores you and your husband) hush hush. Cheerfully we sat there eating from one to six, that reminds me, I shall have to write a letter of thanks, for this is done here. And in the end we were given a box with eggs. Have you got eggs in Ch.? Eggs is all I care for, not aspiring as high as marzipan. I could live on eggs, and hope to get them in France, here we get *one* a month. Yes *one*. Veronica, who »adores« your brother even took off her glasses at my request, for she is very shy, reticent, modest, dressed like a char, for being English and only 34 she is not yet enlightened as to the effects of frills, scent, and all the frivolities of life, and I wish she had more time for me to teach her, for I want her badly for your brother, *you* would like her, anybody does, she is plump, with red baby cheeks, and a nice dimple in her left cheek. Quite dark, looking like a Jewess of the time of Abraham. But she has no time. She is one of the five directors of Cape, she publishes one historical work after another, she is editor of Time and Tide[411] (but this is a secret). —Talking success, I told you, through much cabale and intrigue there was a bad review in Horizon on Aut. but for »the first time in the history of Horizon« to quote the editor (the famous critique Conolly), there is going to be another Essay, a sharp rebuke of Julia Strachey,[412] the snake who did a Hitler to Canetti, and by Tornb~~oy~~ee[413] or whatever his name is, a great critique. Horizon got such a lot of insulting letters from the various fans of Canetti, among them a book seller, that Conolly read the book and started apologysing personnally to Canetti for it, before a big party.

Son, it seems that even *your* name mentioned in a letter does not speed the French up, for when it is the question of a foreigner, they get stubborn like mules. We'll have to wait and I'll write amusing letters and not know what to tell you about when I come. I do hope you wrote to your brother, who is working hard on that third novel of Anna Sebastian,[414] but though he works hard, it's muck.

He brought Egon Friedell's[415] book yesterday and started reading to me the Life of Lichtenberg, who too, never finished anything because all questions are too great to put the finishing touch. That imp, your brother, was delighted about having a fellow genius like him, but in the end it turned out, that L. was professor of so and so university,[416] whereas your brother writes novels for a bitch.

All about her new turns when we meet. I don't like to say, when we see, for I wish you would never see me. It was my last fata morgana, I thought I could leave you in the belief that I am, what I was, instead of what I am, well . . . there they go, the dreams of my life, instead of a star, the atom bomb will burst into your pieceful cell. Is it a nasty little cell with oil walls and the table fixed to the floor, like lunatics have them? Or is it a nice hospital room which I like, for my dearest cousin used to spend ten years of her life in sanatorias and I kind of got to like sitting by her side. Much love, son, you are a vicious, luscious, Casanova, with all those men . . .

Peggy

All my bloody love Bloody PEGGY *WRITE*
Please return letter of Canetti

*having talked about brothels and bitches with me on Friday,

enclosed 4 *Razor Blades*
Please acknowl. Razor B.

Veza to Georges · *December 16, 1946*

Mrs. Canetti
35 Downshire Hill NW3

December 16th

Adorable Son,

I am touched beyond description, just having your letter about the »incision«[417]—I had a lot of misfortunes, but what a recompense to have a son like you! I cannot tell you how relieved I am! I am so psychic, that I was frightfully miserable since ten days, tired of life, and since ten minutes, since your letter came, a heavy load is lifted, I can breathe again. Sweet son, don't let me without news, don't you feel too weak? How about food? Write only about you and how you feel! How can you think that I don't want to see you, when I want nothing else! There is no trace of a visé, and that may last another month, just as it was predicted to me, though I did not believe it. I don't see a chance of coming before January, I just talked it over with your brother. Who left a minute before your letter came! To-morrow *he* will be exuberant, you know you are *everything* to us, no aim in life without you! We both seem to be ambitious only for your sake, »to tell Georg« and he even thought he'd soon be able together with Nissim to buy a cottage in a nice French village, so that we alternately can live there—with George, who will want to live much in the country, a cottage for George, that was his idea!

Now darling, I posted by the same mail a »Mappe«[418] with ten gorgeous couloured reproductions of georgeous Kings and Queens and a comment to know who's who. This is your brother's Xmas present, my Macaulay—I was in half London looking for it, your brother still has hope to find it, I bought a Swift, Gulliver's Travels, but he laughed at me and said, Georg has got that, so my Macaulay will arrive after Xmas, I fear, and maybe even a second hand version.

A queer thing happened to us . . . I have a cousin, called Veza, much younger, and very beautiful and attractive, terribly elegant, luxury being the essence of her life—she wrote from Amerika: My husband is ill in a sana in Northampton, would you be an angel and go to see him? He'll give you his clothing coupons, tell him . . . and a long list of things I should tell him. I love him, though he is only a cousin by marriage, and twenty years older than Veza. Off we went to Northampton, Canetti and I, with books, and I with flowers, and we were talking of the nice chicken and lovely lunch, that we'll get, he being a rich man and very generous and hospitable, a real grand seigneur!

When we went there, we were taken to a ward with a dozen beds, gloomy, nasty (a private ward mind you, very expensive). The orderly pushed the curtain aside, there lay, what *was* my cousin—*insane*! You can imagine my shock, the calmest most placid man in the world. His wife went to America with his two young, lovely daughters. She liked it so much there, that she forced him to sell his house in Mc and follow her, she not wanting to come back to England. He disliked America so much (being an old Spanish Jew, frequenting Synagogues, Zionists, old aunts and Jewish clubs) that he got deranged after his flight back to Manchester. His family put him into the asylum, and now he raves against my cousin, his wife, he *hates* her, does not want her to come and see him, the poor thing in New York is in despair for the doctors don't allow her to come near him. »If she comes, only with her parents,« is his condition, her parents are very old, can't make the trip in winter . . . such a mess, and I don't know what to tell her to do. For she has no place where to live, I not yet having my flat. It was the shock of my life! C. says it's a new method putting them all in one ward, the depressive cases. His arm was heavily bandaged, suicide attempt. C. thinks all in one ward, one prevents the other from overdoing their lamentations, they restrain a little, while watched by so many others. A nice lunch, after twenty minutes he turned us out, for twenty minutes he had used the most insulting language imaginable all against my poor cousin, who is so charming, and whom he had adored! Off we went and had tea and toast and jam and that's all we have in this darned country.

Yes, I am a reader of Hutchinson's,[419] but not from enthusiasm, you noble minded knight of the six heroic adventures. No. I only revise the books *they* send me. If I were to recommend a book, they would not pay for it. Still I am grateful for suggestions. The first good review, (you will be shocked) I wrote of Benjamin, L'enfant Tué.[420] But it is Hutchinson, you know, not Cape, for that publisher it is a good book and incidentally it is. What I fear is, that he really was a collaborat. but having lost his son in Africa, no, in Mulhouse, fighting the Nazis, is enough atonement. What do you think, let me know. I turned down a »Life of Tolstoi«, by a Swiss. There are enough ants who fed on that carcass.

I do hope this letter is a bit of fun to you, and if I don't see in the new year my ten reproductions decorating your cell, off I go again. All my love and for God's sake, write! »The Tower of Babel«[421] is coming out in February in New-York (Autodafé), I find T.O.B. a very good titel. All my love, my eternal love . . .

Veza

For God's sake don't tell any Spanish Jews about my cousin. He has two marriagable daughters!!!!

That was a »trap« of your brother about my letters! the scoundrel!

Dear son,

I forgot to ask you—are your publishers doing something towards the translation of your books? If not let me know which are the corresponding publ. in this country for scientific works, and we can contact them.

Don't forget to answer this.

A funny story. A Duchess here, who had been to France came back with a dozen eggs which cost her 5000 pounds. For in one hand she held her handback with 5000 pound jewels, but soon neglected that, keeping an eye all the time on her twelve eggs, so that they should not be stolen, and her handbag disappeared.

If the Rich is not sold out in U.S. you'll get it through my cousin now, direct from there. Please repeat correct title in next letter. Razor blades in next letter. Love

Veza to Georges · *January 1, 1947*

Mrs. Venetia Canetti
14 Crawford Street (near Baker Street)

London first of Jan. 1947.

A HAPPY YEAR!

Prince Handsome,

First let me tell you, how wicked I am and how sweet your brother is. When he saw your photo, he thought you look ill and thin and deep set eyes, and he got terribly worried and kept the photo, so that you'll have to send me another. I saw it first and all I thought was: oh how I envy him, he is so thin, and has that clever expression of one who knows more than everybody else and not my idiotic face of a melancholy maniac etc. So you see, it won't hurry up the visé, but when I get it, I'll send you the letter from the consulate, to demonstrate to you, how nasty the Fre<n>ch are, and you'll see at the dates, which have to be quoted, that I applied for it two months ago and might have to wait another month. I am sure to get it, though. I think it will just come when I feel stronger, I am usually very weak in winter and might arrive a corpse in Chateaub. I hope you noticed my new address as from Friday the third of January. I move there on Friday but have got it already. The lady where I stay now is broken hearted. Usually in blasted Amersham, they turned me out. Because I was so *sad* looking (!) and they wanted someone to buck them up. Being dead carcasses they wanted me to revive them, the plague on them.

Darling, my cousin Veza worked wonders when she met her husband. I was with her (oh I forget you don't know, she came by plane risking her life) that's the Veza type—by the bye—and when he saw her, the bloody fool, he turned King's evidence, and abused everybody else and stared at her in amazement (which he can, he is twenty years her senior) and praised her and admired her, having *cursed* her the week before, called God's vengeance on her, so that she is under the impression, we all were against her, sort of intriguing against her, since of course we did not tell her the truth.

Another news—F. left for Sweden, and tackles your brother with cunning letters now, making him terribly jealous about another man[422] that has turned up who used to love her in Vienna. He did, it's true, if only you could see him, he is a kind of Gogo Lancelot, a half wit, that never could find anybody to like him and when he found a wife she divorced him.

I'll tell you everything about it when I see you, I don't feel in the mood for jokes, since I am full of compassion for your brother, who seems more than ever on the verge of insanity to me and I am not joking. He has always been a border case, and now I am not anymore strong enough to cheer him up and help him. No. I am a border case myself. That's a letter about maniacs anyhow, and the only strong minded, strong bodied, sensible, adorable character in the letter is the man to whom it is addressed, prince handsome. I said, I should send you a photo, to prepare you for my idiotic physiognomy and your brother very seriously urged me to do so, thinking you'll get the shock of your life when you see me, but I don't want to spend twopence on a photo of myself, hating myself so much. I am a success though. As a reader to Hutchinson's, who pour books on poor me. I turned down a Cassou,[423] feeling like a Lord to do so, since he seems a craze in France. What a lot of noble ennui with nothing behind it but scenes of amour, »amour« not love, brrr! I gave a nice (!) report about him, sorry he can't see it. I must close this nasty letter, how charming yours are, I feel ashamed! But I am just getting over a horrible flu, and am moving out, and have to read a blasted manuscr. by a German Count,

I feel I'll tear him to pieces, and . . . I adore you, I may lose my job in going to see you in France, it's my only achievement in this country in nine years, but come I will, and as soon as I get the blasted visé, and by plane. It will be better for me when the days get longer. The nice things you wrote about the map, and about everything, how much ésprit, can't you write a novel? I'll praise it beyond description to H. In French! Write in F.

All our love . . .
Bloody me.

Veza to Georges · *February 11, 1947*

Mrs. Canetti
14 Crawford Street
London W1

Feb. 11. 1947.

Lieber Sohn,[424]

While you were having your seventh ordeal, I had the Flu of my life. It was an exceptionally heavy flu, and one where you cease to think altogether and are only miserable. But this is good in a way, for it means I shan't have one the coming six weeks and since I hope to get my visé *now*, the last time limit having elapsed, I'll be quite fit when in France. Also I shan't lose my job, I don't think so, I managed to have made myself kind of indispensable. This is important, son, I can't be a burden to a young poet, can I? And as to furniture, no, I could not yet afford to buy furniture, but I'll get a radio, which is twenty pounds and more than we can afford. Don't forget, your brother is a highbrow writer, a genius, not a Feuchtwanger.[425] You should have seen us sitting miserably together your brother and me, while he had a good second review in the Horizon, which you get by the same mail, and while we got the gorgeous announcement of the American publishers, both which items I beg you to send to Elias for the archiv. We were miserable, because F. had a . . .[426] in Sweden, and because she felt depressed, and because your brother thought she would die. Although I knew she would not die and that her letter was just blackmailing, there we were miserable beyond description, I only, because he seemed terrified, since he had killed her (in his thoughts, of course). He was the cause of her death, and we two guilty people sat there and were mourning. I with only tea and bread in my stomach, while she had chicken in Sweden and was quite alright, as we know now. But some people, especially artists, never worry, and have such a cheerful view of life! Yes, and then I had the bright idea and said: ring up her lover . . . perhaps *he* knows if she is dead. Well, Willie[427] was not worried. He was amazed that your bother was, he was just spending the night with another girl friend of his, but he was not cross, that your brother rang, no, he was even flattered, he would like to sell her to us, for a cigar, for a recommendation to a publisher, for a Linsengericht.[428] And your brother was suddenly changed and that is that.

I have a pain in my left lung, son, and it will not pass until you write you are better. And how can you write such a sweet letter in such a state? What kind of a being are you, anyhow? And why don't you insult me, for not having the visé yet? Why don't you tell me, to use our influencial friends? We can't. I'll tell you why. We are amongst Nazis again, dear. The terrorists[429] caused that, and we shall save them, to save our skins . . . It might easily be that I go to France and there is a law, that Jews who left may not return. For that purpose we must save our influencial friends. For I *shall* get permission to go and to re-enter.

We have not only the terrorrists, we have Shinwell, too.[430] Just our luck . . . he is a Jew . . . and he messed everything up, and God messed everything up, it is cold as it has never been before in this country, not since twenty years. And I feel so weak . . . tinned food since eight years . . .

I close now, I want you to have this letter soon, and the good news about America, and I shall write in a day or two, I adore you, and I have a bad lung, it hurts, only to remind me of the sweetest most beloved most venerated being on earth . . . don't get depressed, help us, we have only *you*, what would life be without having to think of you, and to love you . . .

The razor blades are alright, a better improved edition of the blue ones, if you don't want them, you can always have the blue ones.

Do write . . . don't leave me like that, we are anxiously waiting for your letters.

Peggy

ELIAS TO GEORGES · *February 22, 1947*

Saturday, February 22, 1947

My dear Georg,

Your letter hurt me a lot, but how small is my pain compared to yours. I would gladly accept more. Before I admit how right you are in general, and how wrong in the particulars, I want to give you a piece of good news. Veza has permitted me to be the first to write and say that her visa has finally arrived, *four* months after she applied for it. Now it's up to you when you want to see Veza. She thinks you would prefer it to be toward the end of March, when you're feeling stronger. Perhaps it won't be so cold anymore then, either. She suffers bitterly from the cold. But in any case, you know that whenever you want her visit, you have but to say so and she will be there in a few days.

I know that I write you far too little. I know that I depend on something that develops between me and other people, something enormously powerful and, as I believe, always alive. I know that behind this feeling is a mystical arrogance that is unforgivable, for the other person *needs* words and signs and direct communication, to say nothing of deeds, in which I'm quite a weakling. You can despise me for that, as you do now—I will never love you the less for it. However guilty I am, I love you anyway, *but* in this latest outrageous accusation you do me a *bitter injustice*: as soon as I received your letter, I got in touch with the appropriate people about the streptomycin.[431] Their *unanimous* opinion (two or three weeks ago, if I remember right) was that the results in England were rather worrisome. The government had not yet approved the drug because some patients being treated with it had gone mad. They were still working on using it in a different form or dosage, and until they had good results, they couldn't think of using it widely. Veza wanted to write you about it immediately, but I persuaded her not to. It was too difficult. I told her she should not crush your hope for such a certain cure right after your new operation. In the meantime, better treatment results might arrive from America. For the time being, it would be better not to say anything about it to you. I preferred you to think ill of me and suspect an unforgivable indifference than for you to suddenly have to give up a hope that could help you over the first critical weeks. Besides, if only we kept quiet for a while, we could *perhaps* soon give you really good news. So that's what happened. In the meantime, we *have* heard from America that the results are improving.

You may think as badly of me as you choose, but in this matter, you were wrong. I still think I did the right thing. At least you will have to admit that I was justified by the course of events. Daniels has promised to write you.

In the next few days I intend to send you the American edition of the *Blendung*. As you know, the title there is *The Tower of Babel*. I hope that you can still take some pleasure in something from me. I don't know quite what to write you. I have the feeling that with your letter, you wanted to establish a real *inner* distance between you and me. As far as I'm concerned, that is not possible. But maybe it was only a violent fit of temper on your part, the kind you've always had, and even if that's not the case, you could be fair and accept my explanation. There are as many witnesses at your disposal as you like, beginning with Veza.

You see my relationship with Fr. in a completely false light, namely, in Veza's. God knows it's not a question of *volupté*.[432] You must understand that my concern for her is exactly like concern for a *child* (for I don't have any myself). And if I don't simply condemn her lock, stock, and barrel as does Veza, who is justified in hating her, it's related to the fact that I clearly recognize my own mistakes. She has certainly suffered more under me than you have, and from the same character traits of mine. She took revenge in a very mean, female way, thereby hurting herself more than me. Now she's lying ill in Sweden with a nervous breakdown after being treated for weeks by a terrible quack who almost killed her. You can't expect me to gloat. I can only be sad about it. Her people bombard me with letters and beg me to come to Sweden because she wants to see me so badly, and then to take her back with me. That I certainly will not do, because it wouldn't be good for either of us. I think that we really don't belong together, but I don't intend to ascribe to myself any sort of arrogant superiority over her. She is a person very close to the edge of insanity. I was over that edge when I lost her. What makes you think you know everything about it just because Veza writes you witty letters? As if anything *real* were contained in them. Is that worthy of you? Can you pass any sort of judgment before hearing Friedl's side? You haven't even heard my side. You don't know the full extent of my indictment of her, and you know *nothing* about her defense. You would be astonished how familiar and true the things she says about me in her defense would sound to you (but never the word *carence*,[433] more likely its opposite). But perhaps this is boring you. I would be very grateful if you wrote to me. It would be nice if you would take back the things in your letter that were factually wrong. But it doesn't matter if you don't. Just write in any case, to show that you don't want to create a barrier between us from your side, a barrier which nothing in the world could create in me, not even if you were to turn against my work. An embrace from

Your brother Elias.

VEZA TO GEORGES · *February 22, 1947*

Mrs. Canetti
14 Crawford Street, London W1

Feb. 22. 1947.

Dear Son,

I pardon you the »chêre belle-sœur«[434] and whatever you wrote, but shall let you know the plain truth about the drug, however not before telling you, that the visé came this morning. First the drug. We kept reading and informing about it, that is, your brother did, and a month ago, they gave out, that the drug must not be used in this country, because in U.S. they found out, that it is not yet safe, having an excellent effect on T.B. but a bad effect, in some cases, on the *brain*. This I wanted to tell you (this week they gave out here, that the method has improved to such an extent, that there is no bad effect anymore). I wanted to tell you at once about it last month, but your wicked (!) brother shouted »I must not, for they will soon get better results, and it will discourage you and that is the reason, why Daniels, too, does not write about it, we must wait, I should simply ignore it, that would be better than a negative report«. In fact, he says, *now* they found another method to use it, and we shall send you printed information as soon as available, it seems to be wonderfully working *now*, but not yet applied in this country, they still wait for further U.S. results.

What concerns the visé, since I got it to-day you will believe me, when I tell you, they sent it last week and it got lost, and I had the hell of a bother to secure it. It was sent to Hampstead, and Margaret, who forwarded a few dozen letters quite reliably, put the number 8 instead of 14. Now No 8 in Crawford Street is the Montague Mansions, a block of houses reaching till 13 with threethousand offices. I travelled from one block to the other, finally a good tip to the postman did it, and I got it to-day. I will follow your instructions and ask the visé for the middle of March and leave here about the twentieth, not because of the inconveniences, but because of a bad collapse I had in the street the day before yesterday and which is maybe a consequence of the flu. All points to me to the heart, but since I am a neurotic, a maniac so to say, I must not say that. I *could* walk home, and after a few hours I felt better. Dare I travel by plane? I wonder?

Another thing is my melancholia, and whether you will not curse the day that I came. That can be repaired, though, for the sooner I return, the better for my work, for they can get a lot of readers, and I cannot get publishers. I was nominated reader by C.V. (this is Wedg.) but the dear girl left it at that and in two months I did not get *one* blooming book, whereas Hutchinson's are very consequent[435] and satisfied with me. But there is still worse to tell. The book in New York up to now is a complete failure, and your brother does not know to *what an extent*, for I managed up to now to hide the bad reviews from him, that pour in. Horrible, stupid, very American, very callous, biting, killing reviews, so no hope to get a dollar from U.S., *up to now*. That *can* get better, I do hope it will, but our situation is now, that with the book coming out here 3rd impression, we shall only have a year to look forward, a year of just a simple life without as much as a chair to buy, and it is a blessing, that I earn my rent. Up to now I don't earn more than that, a monthly rent here being a yearly rent on the continent. I have to tell you all that, for inspite of heart trouble and a depression I would leave at once, however since you think it better to come at the end of March, it is better for my position as a reader. The more I read, the better they are pleased with my reports and will take me back when I cease for a while.

What concerns my going—could not you send me the key of your flat, and could I not sleep there two nights and not see the family? I am a clinical case of melancholia, which you will realize the horrible moment when you see me, and I am quite incapable of smiling, being cheerful, and mostly too tired to say anything at all. I don't mind that so much with you, or better, I can't help it, and being a physician, you'll understand. But the family would not, and I had rather see them, when back from Chateaub. when I need not be fresh from all the glory and success and my happy life with your brother. As to the expensive hotel—I'd rather take the boarding house Nissim wrote of, he did not give the address, he did not know the exact address, so if you can find a means to get it for me, I'd be delighted. Also, I am not equipped for a good hotel, having the suit that I wear and one frock. What concerns baths, that you can't get in France, fortunately I have my hot bath everyday here now, lovely, and can manage a short time without a bath. And if you remember, let me know if I can buy cigarettes in France, they help me a little, when my head aches, and I had two hundred, collected here, but we used them, having a terrible shortage since weeks here (and conditions much worse than during the war) and I am writing with stiff, icy fingers. I'll have to get friends to start collecting them here for me, that is why I ask. Tea I collected a lot for Georg.

I shall ask them at the French consulate, to let me have back the slip where they inform me, that after three months my request is granted. Actually it is three months and two weeks, but five days the visé was floating about. I hope they let me have that slip for you.

Perhaps I can take you back with me, when I return . . .

Friedl———had her operation and your brother is overwhelmed with letters, from her, her mother and sister where in a nice way, all the blame of her escapades is put on *him*, he should *see* that, but she adores him, wants to give up Willie, and return to him, all this after they got the leaflet announcing the Tower of Babel. The enthusiasm may slow down, when they hear about no Dollars (the letter says also, that she is very short of money and her parents extremely poor). I don't know what your brother is going to do about it, for I don't quite believe his protestations, that he sees through it. He thinks she is marvellous and he is definitely »hörig«.[436] All I know is, that I shall not protect him any longer, when this goes on, but shall ask for a divorce. He'll have to give me what little he earns, poor chap (and I shall put it away for him, for a rainy day) and then he'll soon get rid of the Benedicts, but will have some obligations for her, for *that* is what she wants, a brat, to bind him to her, and to have to slave for her, or a marriage. I don't care anymore, I am through with it all.

I am sorry this is not a cheerful letter, but do you expect me to be bright, after the news I got about you? How can we look ahead, with you being ill? Please, stick to »belle-sœur« and don't even write *»dear«*, you won't find me dear, I am dull. I shall not get married though in case I divorce your brother, since I see that I can make my own living, or will be able soon (up to now your brother kept me, and this since seven years). I prefer my liberty, *if life is* liberty. ?? Pardon this frank letter—but if you understand us better, you will maybe not feel hurt at all . . .

Peggy Veza

Write *at once* about yourself, we are worrying!!! Don't you see!!!!

VEZA TO GEORGE · *February 25, 1947*

Mrs. V. Canetti
14 Crawford Str. W1

London Feb 25

Dear Son,

The news is a little better in so far as he had a short but very good review, this Sunday here in the Sunday Times (the second in that paper) also there is going to be a broadcast again *here*, by the editor of a magazine,[437] who wrote to the publishers about this »remarkable« book. The best news is, that Veronica (this is Wedg.) did not see me yet, because she had so many broken pipes, that she had no water since weeks and a flood in her house and this is the characteristic feature of London at the moment. But that she wants to see *me now* about the *job*. I'll let her know that I won't start before my return from France. The book continuing here a success is a consolation.

Your brother wrote to you himself, and you'll certainly gather by his letter, that he feels terribly glad about the accusations of her and her family, that it is all *his* fault and he is resolved to repair this.

But I am resolved, too.

Much love and I am looking forward to seeing you,[438] I think of it all the time and that cheers me up.

Peggy

It is not 3 months it is *4* months since I applied for the *visé*.

VEZA TO GEORGES · *April 9, 1947*[439]

Hotel Lutetia[440] Bld Raspaille

April 9th

Sweet Georg,

I would prefer to describe my journey to you once I'm back in London. For now, I'll only say that it's not true about the French. After I'd been sitting on my *sac*[441] in the corridor for three hours, a gentleman offered me his seat. Although he got off the train a half hour later, he was embarrassed to be getting off. The others lit cigarettes, lent me magazines, and I solved the problem of luggage with hundred-franc bills. Apart from the sadistic soldier who assured me with cruel fury that I would miss my connection in Rennes, I was quite touched, and I like the French. As for the Lutetia, it is exactly the kind of hotel I wanted, and this morning I woke up healthy, between clean bedsheets (the ones in the Hotel Central had been previously used by ten loving couples).

It was touching to see Regine standing at the station, waiting to hear news of you, and though I was sympathetic, I tortured her a bit and kept her waiting. But then I said with a knowing look that I had the impression you liked her very much. And what will the consequences be . . . ? *Tu l'as voulu, Georges Dandin.*[442] Then she began to explicate things and interrogate me, and I got her completely off track—it killed her—by suddenly saying, He's very handsome! She hadn't expected such a confession and my courage robbed her of hers. If Henry Miller could hear her, he would buy her. Unfortunately, she has chosen *me* to tell her life story to and I don't pay much.[443] I found her royally amusing, especially when she thought she had caught me out. And yesterday, I liked her very well. What she will do to me today I don't yet know. She wanted to enlighten me about different kinds of love; she's familiar with all of them, which is unfortunately also what waiters think when they catch sight of her. I didn't want to set you up completely, so I said that Canetti would be visiting you soon. For in Fougerays,[444] she would be a displaced person, completely explosive, and the manageress would be annoyed, whereas the manager would react more like the waiters. She greatly mistrusted the halvah and was suspicious of me, but at that point, I became coarse. I told her you were cutting yourself a thin slice every day and have gained weight since. As far as love and sin are concerned, she thought I was a country bumpkin.

Canetti wrote movingly that he thought we had quarreled and that's why I went to Chateub. and he thinks my "jealousy" could be playing a role. As for that, Adonis, I'm only jealous of the boys in St. Hilaire, although I can empathize with everything. His exaggeration of my change of location was pure Master of the tower.[445]

The manageress must have been reprimanded by her confessor, for she was as sweet as sugar and the entire clinic was so happy to see me leaving at last that some ten of them crowded around me and the manageress wanted to take me to the movies. Then she wouldn't let me pay for the car. Seven of us drove back and I sat where otherwise the *gentlemen* sit in France. Briant was disgusting and so I ate humble pie—an omelet at my patron's—whereupon he became very cordial again and charged a *hundred* and seven francs. For another hundred francs, his stableboy carried my *sac* to the train and was I ever happy that it was a *sac* that I could sit on later, in the corridor. Everything went smoothly with 100 fr. bills and the engineer who threw me and my *sac* into the train car shook my hand cordially.

At the hotel I was apprehensive on account of my outfit, but then I have English people on the same floor who are dressed just the same and are just as fat, because only the gluttons come to France in such weather. I told Mlle. Lucy that the weather could be traced back to the atomic bomb. It was very dear of her to come and even dearer of you to send her, and I'll send her something pretty from London.

Canetti, by the way, is quite eager to get a lot of work done in St. H.

I'll write about the feet another time. At any rate, they were very tempting and I wouldn't have gone further than the *pansement*.[446] But why would so much beauty allow itself to be kissed?

As for the *pansement*, it's worth everything the trip cost me! Because we won't have to groan anymore, "Every day a *pansement*!" instead of looking it up in the dictionary.

Please write me an equally charming letter to 14. Cr. St. You are capable of it, and I expect to find a letter waiting for me when I return. For I have all sorts of "French letters"[447] to write but you won't get any unless you report regularly on the following: *pansement*, temperature, weight gain, *vertige, regime*[448] (no, not Regine) and general state of health. And if your letters are not precisely like that, I won't answer. One must learn from Regine, and all 3 of you are poison. The word was amusing, because Nissim often says to her when he leaves her and Lucienne alone together, *ne lui donne pas trop de poison*[449] . . . A poisonous kiss,

Veza

Veza to Georges · *April 16, 1947*

Mrs. Canetti 14 Crawford Street London W1

April 16

Sweet Georg,

In the midst of lovely flowers, grapes, marvelous American reviews, unpaid, misplaced bills (elec., gas, teleph.), scattered luggage, and numerous obligations, I'm writing an immediate answer to your letter, which I call "Poetry and Untruth,"[450] interrupted by the young Merkel,[451] who left his gloves here last night. Yes, he's leaving today but still stopped by yesterday. I'm not writing to thank you for your impertinent, ironic letter, however, but rather only to get another one soon, because after all, I'm a sadist (which you will notice later in this letter). I'm forced to summarize, however, because to describe my precious days in Paris I need peace and quiet. I shall do it, and Regine was a hit. This time, she was sweet as sugar *almost* the entire time. Not only because I had suffered such a fiasco in Chateau. (she doesn't know that, personally, I'm already far beyond fiascoes), but also because there are all sorts of things she wants from me, for example, that I pay a bill for her. And she wants to come to London, and says that *she* will find lodgings here. Since she won't, I'm threatened with a great catastrophe that I will only be able to bear because before she comes, she will visit *you*. For I arranged it all in such an amiable way that after she had a frightful, embarrassing, and delicious scene in my hotel with Elias Canetti,[452] she decided to forgive *you*, because he's even worse, and all I could do was prevent her from coming between the 18th and the 22nd. Perhaps she's already sitting there with you, however, and if so, be careful she doesn't pinch this letter. When Elias ran off in horror (at first, I regarded your version as poetic license, but then I saw that every word was true, and he hasn't a clue. He's being punished for something that doesn't exist) and she cried out in despair, "je suis une femme incom*prise*!!!!"[453] I comprehended the grotesque situation, especially since Edith broke with her because she had said to her, "I could easily steal your husband from you, and the only reason I don't is because you're my friend." In a word, I'm telling you the truth, she will delight and amuse you for a few days, and you must just be on your guard, since she is a woman who already knows three times a week how things stand with her, and à la Elizabeth of England, she will never forgive you that she is old and withered. Poor Essex had to lose his head for it,[454] and her way of beheading you will be significantly less dainty. She will say terrible things about you to people who are important to *you*. But if you can keep her in check, she can be very amusing for a few days, because she makes it unnecessary to read Henry Miller. I laughed at her until I cried and we parted the best of friends, except that she refuses to believe that I still love you so passionately, although I failed so miserably and she says with enormous, frightening banality, "Your disappointment with Georg will bring you closer to your *husband*," which made me slightly nauseous. She had a way of insisting that I couldn't possibly travel by Metro or eat in bourgeois restaurants, which cost me a lot of money, then at the end of the day, after having quite enjoyed it, she told me, "You are a great spendthrift." Naturally nothing succeeded with H.,[455] who was indignant that C. wanted such small pictures. He makes only large-format prints. Then he condescended to make small photos, but it will take him seven weeks to develop them in Paris, so that Nissim will have to wait awhile. Meanwhile, he lent me just a few from his collection. Since *I'm* directing this business, everything will be in good order. The last straw was when Regine saw the lovely presents that Elias Canetti left with the porter for me after she had kept me from getting to the hotel in time to see him once more. He had an appointment. She cried, "I'm through with him. He's *un lâche*,[456] not a man," and then she began planning to go to Chateaubriant. I tried a little Lulu,[457] but it didn't work. I tried harder, but it only made her more determined. And I really think she will make you laugh a lot. But "de ton cousin gateux"[458] made her terribly irritated because she was sure that the parcels were for her, but they were for me and one for the "Maharaja." More in my next letter about excursions with this branch of the family. —Bauscherl gave me a festive welcome, and about twenty new reviews have come, most of them good, some—particularly from the best magazines and newspapers—outstanding!!!! I was beside myself with joy, but have only read the pompous and extremely flattering titles and five of the reviews, because I had to write you. What a brute you are!

And now I'll close, for I'm mailing this letter only to get an immediate reply from you, and for God's sake don't let Regine see it, or she'll send me poison marzipan. And if I don't get one from you right away, you won't get the Paris letter!

Lots of kitschy love and other kinds as well—all the kinds there are, from

Peggy.

Instead of Loire *inferieure*[459] I almost typed *infernal* just now.

All my Love,

P.

Write at once about *pansement*, dizziness—but without any flimflam.[460] Weight!?

VEZA TO GEORGES (*Copy to Nissim*) · *May 3, 1947*

Mrs. Canetti
14 Crawford Street
London W1

May 3rd

Dearest Georges,

They say that in the 47th year of every century, a disaster strikes this country, and it has occurred—Regine is here. I was having C. V. Wedgwood to tea, so the good Canetti went to pick her up. She sprang from the train with the words "Barreau[461] knows your book! A friend of his recommended it, and he is enthralled!" Canetti was overjoyed, because he *loves* Barreau, and by the time she reached me, Regine had pocketed thirty pounds she cadged from Canetti. As she walked into the room, the money already stowed away, she said, "You know, what I said about Barreau was just a joke. He's never heard of you." I got so furious that I said, "Regine looks like a Toulouse Lautrec!" To which she replied, "You know, your wife is a great spendthrift!" Canetti was delighted with this, because there's nothing he likes more than spendthrifts, but later, when he went to supper with her (I sent them off alone, I was so exhausted), he realized that it was really Regine who had been my spendthrift in Paris. She now began to assure him that I was very cagey. Your brother loves a spiteful remark, but only if it fits, and he got angry and began to praise me to the skies, which ruined poor Regine's supper. He then put her in a taxi and sent her to her hotel. For he had given a porter a large tip to secure her a hotel room for the night, and she ought to be clever enough to keep it, because she's staying for a few days. She could just as well have taken care of her business with the bank by letter, but she loves adventure. That's why I invited my doctor[462] for her. He heard her out, calmly and amicably, but after half an hour, he suggested going to the movies, and today he's driving a half hour out of London to Purley to buy himself a house there, just in case Regine ever comes again. Out of desperation and despite the cold, Canetti is going to Amersham and will stay there until Monday, for he's absolutely exhausted. He was amazed to hear a completely different report about the family, especially how ugly Marcel[463] is. She couldn't very well say that about Lucienne. He is infatuated with her photo, which stands on our mantel, and so Regine said, "Well, you can't see her figure on the photo and you men always think big is beautiful!" She couldn't say enough bad things about my apartment, and yet we would be glad if I didn't have to move in January, and Canetti, who likes it[464] (the apartment, I mean), assured her that she couldn't live here anyway. We've averted that up to now. I prefer to read my letters in private. It will be a big nuisance for me to remain on good terms with her, and if Nissim blabs what I've written about her, she will poison the little bit of tea I send him (unfortunately, tea is rationed here and I saved a year for yours), and I don't know how I'll break it to her that I want her to bring a little chocolate (also a very small ration) to Lucienne. I'm already frightened at the prospect. Thank God she can't poison the sardines for you, and she's promised to take them along. Ah, it's going to be hard to keep her in a good mood. The third printing of *Die Blendung* appeared this week and there will be a review in the *Statesman* (an important magazine here) and in a new magazine that has just appeared and according to Miss Wedgwood is the best in the country as far as intellectual level is concerned. I hope Canetti's trip to Switzerland will work out. Unfortunately, he took his time getting his papers. I'll send a copy of this letter up to this point to Nissim so I don't have to repeat myself. And if you, you skunk, tattle on me again, *I'll* send the poison. As you can see, I'll score a hit, too! Lucienne should please write about you. And how is Georg? Does he need another operation?????

Veza to Georges · *June 4, 1947*

Mrs. Canetti
14 Crawford Street
London W1

June 4th 1947.

Machiavelli,

I wasn't worried, because I'm always worried even before I'm worried, and I have four people who write me—*four*. Regine is not one of them. I'll tell you right off: I have read the Sartre,[465] and that's why I'm writing you again, namely, because you're a Jew and I have as much sympathy for you Jews as I otherwise have only for myself. It would be a pleasure to recommend and push the book, but I'm sure it has already found a publisher. It's child's play to get it published here and as a reader, I can only offer things I have the rights to. If you want to write Sartre about it, do so, and make an inquiry; only then would I be able to throw my weight around. But his works, the rights for them, must have already expired. I found the book brilliant. I was deeply moved and grateful. What a noble soul, and the way he illuminates the touchy issues from all sides . . . I hope he hasn't harmed himself much, and I hope the Jews will thank him for it. I expect you to write a masterful response or supplement to it, and then we can do something with it here once the book is published in England. Regina[466] sent your brother the book but will never get an answer, neither from him nor from me either, so it's better if *you* write her.

You're right about the diabetes, but it's another matter entirely to get that somnambulist to give up some of his nectar again, and I have nothing but catastrophes on my hands. But first off, a happy bit of news that is important, and you will find it in this issue of the *Partisan Review*.[467] Please confirm receipt of it at once. It is not easy to understand, but it's the deepest, most intelligent review he's ever had, and we needed it badly and are optimistic again. The magazine is *very influential* in the literary world.

Your brother, the holy fool, wrote you because he really thinks my letters are important to you, and I hope you won't follow his advice to write and ask me to send Walpole's letters, etc. He doesn't know how you treat me—that I'm only good enough for the hills, but in the metropolis you won't even so much as say hello to me. I'll continue writing you because otherwise you won't know when he's coming and because I want to maintain good relations with the Capulets. I want him to have brothers. Because the hostile family here in England hates me so much they didn't even allow me into the funeral when the old Arditti[468] died. That was yesterday, and they made me wait outside in the tropical heat because the Sephardim don't allow any women at a funeral. So I walked around among the gravestones and spat on all the men's graves—no, I didn't spook, I spat[469]—and I only made an exception for beautiful names like Spinosa and Aphtalion. As a child, I was in love with a Frau Aphtalion, literally lovesick. She was criminally beautiful, and I hung on her smile. She smiled a lot; she was happy because she was so beautiful, and I waited and she smiled and I dreamed of her, and even today, she's one of the most beautiful things from my childhood. Another one was called—no, she wasn't called. I'm not going to say her name, but she was even more beautiful. She was oh so pale, so wan. Her brother—everyone was mad for him, but I loved only her and then she went and threw herself from the sixth floor because she was infatuated with an idiot who simply couldn't understand how such a pale woman could be in love. *She* was the Asra.[470] I hated that man, if you only knew how stupid he was, how he could have saved her with a *single sentence*. She was twenty-eight. I never shook his hand again, and he never knew why. I was just a child. You can see the love I'm capable of—for forty years I've loved those two women—and you've frittered away my love for you.

So I was standing in the graveyard, watching the boring procession of men, none of whom was mourning: it was too hot, Henry Arditti was too old and too poor, and his son is glad he doesn't have to pay for him anymore and can go back to his farm. He looks like a sex murderer who robs his victims after killing them and cuts off their hair for his mattresses in the country. No one was mourning and Canetti mislaid his feelings. He wasn't a bit emotional, and I began to smoke in the graveyard which is even worse than smoking in your corridor in Chateaubriant, where only the patients are allowed to, but not the *accompagnes*,[471] or whatever it was they called me.

On second thought, I'll send the *P. Review* in the same mail, but separately, so you will confirm receipt right away. Your brother is even buying the German Kafka-Brod[472] for you since it's supposed to be better and besides, it costs much more, and that's the decisive thing for him. He will definitely send you the Hitler, even if he has to conjure it out of thin air, but Elias C.[473] will send it as well. I will have to give the *Trials*[474] some thought, for your brother, who still has your interests at heart, thinks they are horrifying and in dulcet tones declares that Georg must not read them.

Well, after the funeral, we drove to the Arditti s. They were impertinent to me because no suitors want them, and Harry Arditti was the only nice one. The last time I saw him was thirty years ago, but he didn't make me feel uncomfortable about that, and so I told him I hoped I would see him again at my funeral, which startled him enormously. He was astonished I would say such a thing, these people fear death so much. And the whole thing was very ugly, because the mourning son was bargaining with a deaf Jew in the lobby, yelling into his ear in French, "combien *escequ'*on donne au Rabbiner?"[475] He pronounced it just like that, and I told Canetti, "in *my* family you didn't ask such things. You gave a big bill." And Canetti replied, "What can you do? They're Ardittis!" Have you ever seen such a sweet-tempered person? He's so charming and boyish, your brother, that he really is much more beautiful than you. The first time I saw him after Paris, I thought, poor fellow, what did I tell them about him? How beautiful he is, and they'll all think he's somewhat burly, but even the old doctor who examined him and certainly knows nothing about diabetes said to him, "*How young* you are! How young!" You all share a familial beauty. Nissim looks eighteen. Poor Canetti is so fearful of Chateaubriant because I told him how I had praised his beauty to everyone, and so *you* were infatuated with him again, which you would soon get over once you got to know him better. I said I would write Georg-letters to France and tell you about his devilries and you would respond like Noble, the lion.[476] I expect he won't come before August or Sept.; he doesn't have his papers yet, he missed the chance to go to Switzerland, and oh, how I had looked forward to his being there. Please answer his letter and tell him how serious it is with his sugar.[477] He continues to lose a lot of weight and eats bread ravenously. I really can't stand it. —The landlord of the man I rent from was just here to ask when he's coming back. Not that it really matters, but it can only hasten his return, and I had hoped to stay here another year. I have to add that we have good English friends who will put me up comfortably, but if only Sartre knew how often *I* have had to move. Your brother was reviewed in the same *Partisan Review* as Sartre. Don't send that *P.R.* to Elias Canetti; I can't spend so much money on you. See how frugal I've become! With this last cut and a foretaste and aftertaste of letters from me, I am your

Veza Canetti.

Your brother says you have become very smart.

VEZA TO GEORGES · *July 2, 1947*

Mrs. Canetti
14 Crawford Street
London W1

July 2nd

Dear Beau,

Your friend Marcel was just here. This week he wrote to say he wanted to see me. The moment Canetti entered the room, he turned somewhat frosty. The fellow is consistent. But then, he gave him a ride in his car. "Can I give you a lift?" they say here. Both of us were invited to a garden party, but I sent your brother alone because he's still young.

Daniels said the same thing that Canetti suspected, namely, that your episodes of vertigo come from the treatment of your wound. But since we are laymen, I'll maintain a respectful silence. He talked very nicely about his experiences on the continent, but unfortunately, he becomes somewhat stiff in Canetti's presence. He said he found you in splendid shape (but you should not have gone to Paris). Your brother, on the other hand, thinks that the experience will only hasten your recovery. —Many thanks for the telegram and the intervention on Canetti's behalf. It pleased us, of course, but here's how things stand: your acquaintance is only a reader. The best he can do is recommend the novel, which is already dubious. A reader can't do any more than that, and it can take weeks for everyone at the publisher's to read it and make a decision. But over here, he can't defer the definite offer[478] for that long. He's been hesitating for weeks as it is. It's a splendid offer for France, and Scotland Yard had nothing on this new Paris publisher. Can you find out if they're the ones publishing *Children of Vienna*[479] by Robert Neumann? That publisher is supposed to be ready to make an offer as well. Strictly confidential: the Fr. publishers offer at most a thirty-pound advance, but this one is offering a hundred pounds and 12 percent. Cape is astonished and continues to make inquiries. Your friend would have to make an offer within eight days, the matter can't be dragged out any longer.

For the past week, your brother has been reading the magnificent Kafka he bought for you, in German. This edition is more complete. He declares he must read it to see if there's anything in it "that could offend Georg." I said that luckily, Georg knew himself very well. Luckily, because he has no reason to be worried. But it is nice of him, all the same. Mlle. Langlois—you should have kept the poor woman from wasting time on a letter. She has enough to do. Daniels, by the way, found Chateaubriant charming. Of course, he doesn't have as interesting a social life in London as the Canettis. —You ask curious questions in your clever letters, son, but I cannot answer them. I'm a melancholic and everything makes me despair. If everything in the world were wonderful, including my life and both of yours, I would still despair, because as your brother says, "death exists." That it will come eventually—doesn't it drive you to despair that Goethe died? I'm without hope, as you can see. Hence my quiet amazement and emotion at your civility and gallantry. You have a page's ability to make me forget about myself. Unfortunately, it's not important to me that my hair is gray. If it were important, it would be black. But I'm rather satisfied with the consistency of my melancholy <*Half a line crossed out and illegible. Handwritten above it:*> That was an unsuccessful joke . . . But France was very therapeutic for me and I've gotten even better since my return, for it's beautiful here. And my sense of humor, which was still missing when you saw me, is slowly returning.

I had very little work when I got back, and Wedg. left for Italy and doesn't seem to be such a big influence at Cape any more. It was sad, because I don't want to cost Canetti so much (very clever, said Regine, who didn't believe me; very depressing, said Canetti, who believed me all too readily), and yet it's my most normal reaction. Canetti has a wonderful explanation for why there are melancholy people: because we eat meat. We kill animals, and they get their revenge from some of us who become melancholy about it. Deep, no?

My cousin Veza, whom I dubbed Peggy, went back to N.Y. with her husband (completely cured). Peggy is a good name. I've assumed it for good and since then have much more work to do and almost can't keep up with it this week. My cat Kien is a character. When I punish her by locking her in the closet, she doesn't want to come out again, and when I hit her, she's overjoyed. (Like the two Canettis.)

Tomorrow, I'll mail the Kafka at last. Your brother read me moving passages from Kafka's letter to his father; we were both crying. Friedl wrote two love letters, then one asking for money. She's entered into a pro forma marriage[480] and today there was another money letter. I'm not saying anything about it because his heart still beats for her.

Two days ago, on impulse, I almost wrote you a love letter, but now I'm a bit exhausted from reading Swiss authors writing about the Rothorn, the climbing accidents there, the conscientious hero with a bad conscience, the poacher, the blond beast—it made my hair turn white. French novels are so smug again, more intelligent but usually autobiographical and who's interested, anyway? Now I've got to read some more of this Gaston Baissett. Why don't *you* write novels!????

When Klemperer[481] met Canetti, he asked him if he knew a Canetti in Paris, with whom he was in the process of making a record. He said to tell Nissim he was giving a concert here on July 2 and that he should come over to hear it. I think you will be in St. Hilaire when your brother sets off, which is surely the best thing. He likes mountains and is there a normal hotel there? Because your brother is still in awe that I lived in a tavern (me too), he said he would never be able to: he would be *afraid*! Please write immediately and I promise to be funny again.

Once again, many thanks. Canetti was deeply moved that you went to so much trouble for his book. I'd like to live with the blacks in Africa for a while. Maybe then the sun would burn its way into me. HOW ARE YOU? All Our Love,

Peggy
Love,
Peggy

You're a real dear.

Veza to Georges · *July 10, 1947*

Mrs. Canetti
14 Crawford Street
London W1
Tel. WEL beck 9334

July 10th

Dear Jumping Jack,

Recently, the two of us attended a private party. The dancer, who was auditioning at the BBC to be on television, chose only a select audience, and considers me to be in that category (too). She promised us Herlie,[482] the greatest actress in England, who for the past year has been playing to great acclaim the leading role in *The Eagle with Two Heads*, a bad play by Jean Cocteau. She is so outstanding that your brother attended the bad play three times—and for her sake, we put up with an evening of dancing. Herlie was sitting in front of me, beautiful, proud, and with a cold eye, the hysterical eye of a great actress, I said to myself. I felt sorry for poor Canetti, for I saw that she would say two cool English sentences to him and that would be it. So I turned around. Behind me was a young girl, pretty as a picture, with a soft smile and such skin! I couln't take my eyes off her, which she noticed with delight, and I decided to speak to her. At the buffet following the gala performance, I was standing with Canetti, Anna, and Fistl[483] and I couldn't stop looking at her.

"Herlie!" Canetti yammered at me, but Herlie had taken off. The gorgeous girl consoled me, offering me a beer. I refused, but said—like a matchmaker—*he* drinks beer, and Canetti, spellbound by her beauty, took a glass of beer. Thereafter, she brought me sandwiches, coffee, and kept waiting on me with a heavenly smile. "Isn't she wonderful!" says Canetti. "Too bad Herlie has left, you poor chap," I say to console him. He stares at me as if I were crazy.

My pretty girl was Herlie.

Of course, I didn't let her loose and we had a jolly evening.

The next day, the doctor[484] got front row center tickets, aisle seats, and naturally, she smiled at us.

But he returned dejected from the garden party (it was earlier). Everyone had asked him about Friedl, and that night, he was so tormented and unhappy he came to my place. This affair will never end because she won't let go of him; he's too useful to her. I told him that *you* now see her and their love affair with completely different eyes since I was in Chateub., first, because I want to give you a chance to judge for yourself, and then I want him to be open with you and I want you to have an overview. And perhaps you'll really judge the situation differently than I. I've had enough and now just want to be an outsider. I told him straight out that he won't get any more resistance from me. I've left him and am ready at any time to have that confirmed by a solicitor. I'm through with this never-ending story.

The secretary of *Horizon* wrote from France to say that it's an unknown publisher and that a big publisher—I forget which, it starts with *G* and is your biggest one[485]—will ask for his book. So we'll delay a decision. The publisher that wants to read his book also publishes Kafka.[486] The question is, whether they'll take the book. It's doing well here again, including the new printing. We don't know anything about the U.S. yet.

Canetti met a publisher and right away wanted to get him interested in your work. He's got the biggest medical publishing house in England, but unfortunately, they're not translating any medical books at the moment. This man is crazy about Canetti and that's useful to me, because he also works with a publisher who will have some work for me.

I hope you have the Kafka already. I'll close for today. This is an undeserved letter, a bonus, since you haven't answered yet. But I think about you all the time and my only hope is that you're in good health. Write about that *at once*. Love

Write at once how you are doing!

Love,
Peggy

VEZA TO GEORGES · *August 27, 1947*

Mrs. V. Canetti
14 Crawford Street
London W1

August 27

Charming Georg,

I am beside myself about you—and terribly ashamed of myself for bothering you with my trivialities, in ignorance of your condition. For as you will know by now, we only just got your letter. Well, that was another big operation, and how can you be so angelic and not even complain! It beats me. And me with my stupid break-in! I'm so glad that you're leaving Chat. You will surely not be bored for a minute in St. Hilaire, because by God, your brother is fascinating. I would like so terribly much to be an invisible listener and hear everything you will have to talk about: the great problems he says he can only discuss with Georg, the only *really* intelligent man he knows. Please tell me at once how you are or I shall lose all restraint and start wiring you. Your brother will be beside himself, poor fellow—one blow after another. We don't take your operations as lightly as you do. It seems that your attacks of dizziness came from this complication and now will finally stop after all. *Please* send news right away!

Claudine[487] is here. We'll see her tomorrow; I hope she has more news of you.

Please send me the address of Arth.,[488] because Kutusov[489] won't give it to me—and let me know which language I should use in my answer. Not French for sure; I don't know the verb endings any more, and how come he can't speak English if he's read the book? Or does he know German? If only I had known he was coming, I certainly would not have gone away and would have been spared a great deal of annoyance, for example, at Hutch. they are furious with me because they sent me a book marked "urgent," but it was returned to them because of their own office's carelessness. I had informed them I was going away. But their office is in a frightful mess and they simply won't admit their own mistakes, and had already blamed me for something else. I'm curious to see how it will end up. There's an eminent Englishwoman (the slim one) who's having me translate one of my plays into English at her expense, because her mother is a great actress and definitely wants to perform me. Don't tell anyone about this. Once burned, twice shy, and you're the only one I put complete trust in, because you're the only one who wishes me well.

The break-in did surprisingly little damage, not much more than thirty pounds' worth. Of course, one can't put a number on the psychological damage. They stole a whole year of clothing coupons and sweet ration coupons, and since I didn't report the loss right away because I didn't know the burglary had taken place, I'm met with the greatest suspicion, not to mention the open hostility in government offices these days. As for food—I receive parcels from New Zealand and America on a regular basis, so no worries on that score. I'm going to send you honey with Claudine. Write me immediately if that is all right with you, or if there is anything else you want. At the moment we have no sardines, but do you want dried prunes? Raisins? I will see what the child can bring you from me. Razor blades to follow in every letter. Aren't the blue Gillettes better? Answer, you fool! — Our post office savings book was not stolen, but saving certificates, golden spoons, and trinkets were. Can you explain why the thief took only six spoons and left six others? Canetti says he was a philanthropist and felt so sorry for me because I own nothing that he divided my possessions with me. He left me all my food tins and a dozen bars of heavenly toilet soap that a fan of Canetti's had sent me from New Zeal. There's already a Xmas pudding on its way to us from the same dear Clare who isn't rich herself, but keeps heaping parcels on us. You can see that I'm sober again.

Before I went away, I got a terrible rash. As Canetti had said, it was from the cat, and the cat was gotten rid of. I suffered unspeakably because I got it from the cat, and I wished it was tuberculosis, only so that I wouldn't have been infected by an animal. (I'm telling you this foolishness for psychological reasons.) I was so horrified at myself for having been infected by an animal that I hoped the whole time it was T.B. One day the very sweet secretary from the Tate Gallery[490] called up. They are publishing a volume of reproductions in which the picture on each page is compared to a great novel, and one page in it has *Autodafé*. And since she lives just round the corner, she asked, "How many hundred fleas have you got?" And I learn that this whole neighborhood gets invaded by fleas in the summer because all the buildings are so dilapidated. I looked at my stockings. My legs were swollen, and there they sat and are sitting still. I have not a dozen fleas, or twenty, but hundreds, and they spray every day, and whoever tells you that DDT is good against fleas—they *love* it, my nephew says. They sell it because the fleas like it so much. To console me, Miss Frost sent me a picture from the Tate Gallery: *Ghost of the Flea*.[491] A man, like a ghost, covered with fleas! Now I'm horrified at myself again. Everything having to do with animals is so horrifying, one begins to believe that we really are higher beings. Unless one is familiar with the marvelous fable of the two lions in your National Gallery.

What pains me so much, so bitterly, disappoints me, prostrates me, is that secretly, quietly, happily I was hoping you would come soon. As far as housing here for *you* is concerned, your brother has half the highbrows in the city at his beck and call. Thank God everything is working out in this respect, and if he gets published in France, that's really a big step forward. I hope you can help me keep everything from falling through, because he's Kutusov, after all. Except that in the end, Kutusov did intervene,[492] but he will hesitate and hesitate. No human being has ever impressed me more and nothing has ever tortured me so much.

Please write immediately what I should send back with Cl. Cigarettes, of course. I have no tea, but as much coffee as she's able to take along.

As for beauty—it will always love you, for half of all women are not like Therese,[493] however much your brother, the great "expert on women," maintains the opposite. The objective ones pursue him because he is a dreamer; the dreamy ones do not pursue, and he himself is always on the defensive, a little God of Love. You will be delighted with him, his otherworldliness in this obtrusive world!

I wish you well from the bottom of my heart. Ah, the little fellow was right to be worried when he saw your photo . . . he was quite distraught, I mocked him . . .

Write immediately, at once . . .

Peggy

I'll thank God if he's in Paris in 5 weeks.

Veza to Georges · *September 20, 1947*

Mrs. V. Canetti
14 Crawford Street
London W1

Sept. 20

Dearest Benjamin,

C. is in the Cotswolds with the Glocks.[494] He is a distinguished English musician. I already wrote you about her (the boy for you). I feel freer, writing you a letter you will destroy. He's in a terrible mood and it's because of F. In two letters she writes of her glowing love for him, in a third—because he hasn't come—of sitting by the sea and dreaming—she insinuates—that someone else is there. She has entered into a sham marriage and I'm starting to think that she only writes him so that he will finish her novel[495] about the sham, because she just sent it to him and of course, he'll be working on it for months. As terrible as it is, I wish she would pretend to love him instead, because another of her letters arrived yesterday together with the novel (Cape will only take it on his say-so) and he was instantly transformed, and previously he'd had such attacks of despair that he not only . . .[496] this time provoked scenes with Marie Louise about something that didn't matter to him at all, as he later admitted to me. He confessed that he'd invented a pretext to torture her (only because he himself is so tortured). So I've realized, in his case, that everyone must be unhappy after his own *façon*,[497] and if he prefers to be unhappy with F., then let him be. It is certainly better than this situation, in which he gets no work done, and what is so alarming (I read this about Kleist,[498] who was always planning something), now he's planning a novel, before that it was a play; nothing gets finished. Naturally, we can't count on the *Blendung* forever, and need other sources of income. Since my unlucky trip, I've been put on ice by H.[499] This was already the case after France, but they were so enthusiastic about my reports that they started sending me things regularly again. Now they're furious that I'm always going off somewhere, and of course there are enough readers who thank them for work on bended knee. Things may get sorted out, but I'm on the point of selling myself, and that's no joke. At my age, it's not very tragic, it's rather flattering, but I imagined it to be more dignified and I'll only do it if all else fails. For in America, the matter of sales seems not to be going well. We haven't received a statement yet. Don't mention the bartered bride (!!), or he'll feel betrayed by everyone.

We haven't reached an agreement with Arthaud yet, because Contou[500] promised us everything and then the memorandum arrived with various promises deleted. So yesterday, I had to protest, and we will see if they give in, for your brother will not. They have conceded the hundred pounds. But Cape warned us that the French don't keep their promises, so we're cautious. In addition, after careful consideration, I turned the negotiations over to Cape, for which he unfortunately takes ten percent. Then C. returned from Wales and didn't want Cape, so I had to write him. But now that he has seen how they would treat him without an agent, he wants Cape again and I had to change course again, which won't make the best impression on Contou. A lifetime too late, I know that I never should have given in to him. He has always destroyed everything for me and driven me to distraction. You must *tear up* this letter at once.

The sad part about it is his own frame of mind. I hope it's neurosis and nothing worse. I've read too much about Nietzsche, Kleist, etc. not to be worried.[501] I am currently in quite good health and provide him with a lot of support, but I would like you to help me, too. It's too much of a burden for me. Besides me, you're the only one who really loves him, so give him some attention!!

For example, he lost his chance for a trip to Switzerland because he was so morose, so desperately unhappy on account of F., that he didn't want to go, though he'll give you a hundred stupid excuses why. And he would have been a completely made man financially, because a theater director who has admired his work since our days in Vienna is waiting for his plays, the *Weltwoche*[502] was intending to publish a big feature about him—everything had been paid for by PEN—but he didn't go. He will go to France, because you are the only person he wishes to see, but the delay has to do with F. writing that she wants to go to France too, but when he asked if she was coming, she suddenly didn't answer. He will go even if she doesn't come, but it's so hard for him. And how touching his loyalty! He's wanted to get rid of me a hundred times. I'm a great burden, and he knows what he will always mean to me in any event, but when it comes to the point of doing it, he thwarts everything, just as he always has. Of course, I tell myself that his peace of mind is more important than my comfort, and I give in.

This all plays out without being explicitly talked about, so don't say anything about it. If he gets a love letter, then he doesn't begrudge me what he thinks is my "pleasure." When he is despairing, then he destroys any possibility I have of protecting my back, which I only want to do on his account, because I want him to have a large bank account so he won't have any more excuses. He has a long life ahead of him, but I want him to indulge himself a bit more; for example, he should buy an apartment, which would cost him a thousand pounds. Now he has to get out of his studio, and that has also upset him. He's had a terribly unhappy life. He doesn't want M. L. as a wife. She, on the other hand, makes all sorts of demands, especially on his time. It torments him, but he feels indebted to her, and he's become so fearful, that the fact that she would always be on hand if he ever got in trouble again (which will never happen) induces him to remain chained to her.

This is a very naked letter, but perhaps you can help him out of this confusion. I am no longer able to. His prison is himself, especially his fear, which neither of us will ever be rid of, since Hitler.

You must not make any of this known or talk to anyone about it. He will tell you all about it himself, but you will be *in favor of* F. It's better that way.

I wanted to give Claudine money, but she's been brought up so frugally she prefers to be dependent on strangers, so I don't know exactly how he will do it. When he goes to France and signs the contract with A., the government will perhaps allow him to be paid something there, but he is incapable of saving money and it won't be very much.

I'm not going to write anything about you in this letter, except that we anxiously await your bulletins. And you have already received a nice letter, and I'll write you daily love letters, but I do it not for psychological reasons, like you, but instead, out of love.

Peggy

Of course you could not read the fourth volume of the *War Trials*. Please take good care of it for me. I have all the volumes, ten so far, and C. needs them for his work. I myself read every line and am overjoyed to see those vermin being fried. None of them knew anything about concentration camps! But they had to deal with Chief Justice Jackson.[503] He's an American.

Please tear up at once!!
A letter like this must not be allowed to survive please write me that you have torn it up.

VEZA TO GEORGES · *September 27, 1947*

Mrs. V. Canetti
14 Crawford Street
London W1

Sept. 27

Dearest Georg,

I haven't been sold yet, because everything is starting to get better again (for me as well). Canetti has two passionately enthusiastic offers. Arthaud has agreed to everything (but only 8,000 copies) and Labastie[504] came to London especially to visit Cape and offer a higher advance, *any* translator we want, and everything else your brother asks for. He says he *loves* the book. Nevertheless, Canetti has just decided in favor of Arthaud,[505] because your friendship is the best guarantee for him, as I emphasized to your friend. Your brother was in Bath and was approached by a policeman, asking if he would do him a favor and participate in a lineup. They were trying to identify a child molester. Trembling with fear, Canetti went to the lineup, where he stood with seven other men with mustaches while children were led past. He looked at the children beseechingly (the real perpetrator, a dapper gentleman who was the last to arrive, got into the middle of the lineup and acted very defiant) and expected any moment to be identified as the child molester. He gave an innocent smile, felt completely exposed, and was mortally glad that the children didn't identify anyone, not even the criminal. Then he had lunch at the house of a doctor who had a stomach in a glass jar on his dresser. He gestured to the stomach during lunch, saying he had just removed it from a probable cancer victim who had only a tenth of his stomach left. Canetti then had to go to his lab with him, where he threw the stomach onto the table like a cutlet, and two doctors now began to palpate it, and in 4 days they'll know whether it's cancer. It was an exciting day for your brother. That's all for today. Write at once how you are. *At once*!

All my love,
Peggy

VEZA TO GEORGES · *October 15, 1947*

Mrs. V. Canetti
14 Crawford Street
London W1

Oct. 15

Dearest Georg,

I don't know if this letter will reach you, since I have only a vague notion of the address and don't have your previous letters here. They're locked up in A. It's not a tragedy, because this is only a business letter. Namely, this Arthaud is not being fair. More than two weeks ago, we agreed to the draft contract, but the contract has still not arrived and the other publisher, Droin, keeps writing urgent letters. He's been writing them since May, and as they told me at Cape, he doesn't have a lot of paper and will end up taking some other books, and although he would still take *Autodafé*, he would have to postpone publishing it until he got more paper. So they advised me to write an urgent letter to Arthaud. Nevertheless, I waited half a week more and wrote yesterday with your brother's concurrence. But instead of dictating the letter to me, he sat here at my place for hours, correcting F's manuscript (that went on for four hours) and couldn't spare even five minutes for his own affairs. So I wrote what they had recommended at Cape, namely, that if the contract does not arrive this week, or at least a cable that it is on its way, Mr. C. will be compelled to give preference to another publisher. "You will understand, that Mr. C. cannot afford to miss his other opportunities,"[506] I added politely. The letter was proper and as it should be. The contract has not arrived today, either, but I am certain that my letter will have an effect. Your brother, however, is in despair because he thinks I wrote too harshly. If you agree, I would like to ask you to smooth things out with a personal letter saying that I have just written you that over here, Cape urged me to write and so I felt compelled to do so. After all, Droin has been writing since *May* and another passionate letter arrived yesterday. He writes charmingly and offers an even greater advance and plans to budget 250 pounds just for advertising. But if you don't think it's a good idea, then don't do anything.

As for F, a letter from her now arrives every other day. She hates Sweden, can't stand it there, and wants to come back here and of course, loves your brother passionately, loves *only* him, and forever. This means that all her speculations have gone to the devil over there, or that she wants to come back to her Bill over here, and since he can't even pay for her trip and only your brother would finance everything, including her stay here, she's taking this way out. That's why he's so confused and also suspicious, and he's lost his head so that, as I said, he can't devote even five minutes to his own affairs. He hopes to persuade her to stay in Sweden and then she can come to France as a reward. How he expects to pay for that I don't know, because she's expensive and doesn't live as I do, on packages and hand-me-downs from relatives in America.

I implore you to write at once about how you are, and forgive me for closing this now. We're both recovering from the flu and are feeling quite dismal, and I'll write you a funny letter in a few days, once I've got your correct address. Nissm sent the invitation we asked for right away, really sweet of him. Did Claudine tell you about us? Aren't you feeling too weak after Paris? Do you like it in St. H.?

If possible, please intervene with A. and in general, let me know what you think. He was already extremely unfair before, until we defended ourselves. How will it be once he has to start paying royalties!? The Fr. publishers, unfortunately, have a miserable reputation.

Peggy

VEZA TO GEORGES · *October 27, 1947*

Mrs. V. Canetti
14 Crawford Street
London W1

Oct. 27

Sweet Georg,

I'm writing you immediately and sending it airmail to help you pass the time. It's really a shame that your boys have been replaced, poor Duke of Orleans,[507] but I imagine you must already have all the students at your feet. The thought of your eyes makes me immediately spellbound and I think of your eyes when I read your letter, which is again delightful. I can't imagine how I ever thought that *I* wrote good letters. Naturally, you made me wait a long time, but I wrote to my satellites at once and so was not concerned. In this one point you are worse than your brother, who had another fabulous review in a new journal that is very good and critical. It's difficult to get hold of with the current paper shortage, but you will get a copy soon. In addition, you will receive—but *not* so soon—an extremely interesting book, a proof copy of *To the Bitter End*,[508] written by a high official in the Nazi regime, which makes absolutely clear that the generals had been planning a putsch, and if the blockhead with the umbrella[509] had not gone to Munich (which finally convinced the German people and the police that Hitler was right and would accomplish everything through blackmail and without a war), the terrible war and the misery of millions of people would have been avoided.

I am delighted to hear about your trip to Switzerland. It means you'll soon come here, and I swear you won't be disappointed. He— needs approximately the same letter you had them write for me. You commission him, etc. Say *nothing* about money, because this letter is for the French consulate. Quickly, please, since he really wants to leave soon, certainly before the end of November. Arthaud answered immediately by cable and *with* the contract, but since Cape wanted to act important—because *you* did everything but *they* get the percentage for a fait accompli—they sent it back because they found out that Arthaud had swindled them out of a thousand copies he won't pay any royalties on. As if he couldn't sell those thousand copies anyway. That's what every publisher does, and it just makes more unnecessary headaches for me, because of course I thought Contou was having difficulties. At least this time it's not *my* fault. I was against more bargaining over such a trifle. But I won't trouble you with this anymore. Cape must now pay the price himself.

Now I'm going to tell you why they threw me out of Fougerays.[510] I didn't dare to before, but surely you will never go back there again, so I can risk it.

Here's how it was: that nice, haggard saint, the cleaning lady, scrubbed my floor every day. One day, I said, "Mais vous travaillez beaucoup!"[511] and the poor thing stared aghast at a door. But behind that door, and thus deceitfully *just outside* mine, there lived the manageress who had heard every word, which I only then found out. And that's why she threw me out, not without having told me in conversation how much trouble she had with the staff because none of them wanted to stay. I did not say to her, however, that the hygiene in her sanatorium was limited to the polished corridor, and that the same charwoman who carried out the basins (and that's a polite word for them) also, with the same fingers—naked fingers—counted the butter rings on the plates that were lying in an open chest, setting the full basin down on the floor to do so. I didn't eat breakfast at all after that, but I didn't tell *that* to the saintly woman. You will still be agonizing over the door and the manageress, but *I'm* rather happy. But that ascetic creature will continue to let herself be exploited, because it's part of her religion. And the manageress will leave soon. She's the hysterical type who can't hold out for long.

Your brother will entertain you well in St. Hilaire, and he's letting F. come along too and is very reassured since I told him you already know about that. I promise it will be exquisitely enjoyable. She won't start flirting with the patients. She thinks too much of herself for that. And with the doctors, it can't do you any harm at all, and for the rest, she's very amusing for a half hour. She has a coarse way of telling a story that we people with fine nerves can appreciate because it tears us out of our usual ruts. She makes an enormously healthy impression, hasn't a care in the world. For her own well-being, she lets cares roll off her back onto others, usually onto your brother, and she doesn't lose any sleep over others, because she doesn't love anyone. And people like her are the happiest of human beings. It's just wise to put the best face on things, and you can see through her maneuvers better that way. By the way, there is something forgivable about her relationship with C. It's a touchy subject. Expressed in the most delicate possible way: he never has put her into the situation Lucienne is in, nor has he often led her to fear it, and she is a young woman, and perhaps the evasions were not as pleasant as she made them out to be. That only makes you happy if you are in love. You will tear up this letter. Dear me, what a Freudian slip. I've just torn it. I only wrote this—not to be tactless, but because I just found out about it recently, and thus there are extenuating circumstances, and it is my artistic nature to see all sides (as you once stated in much more beautiful words).

You will be receiving a pile of blades, not soon but for *sure*. I cannot send them by letter any more because of the censor, but your brother is bringing you enough for half a year, or as many as he can bring with him. Tell me what else you need. Once again: do you want honey? I'm already collecting tea. Jam? Marmalade? Please answer. The madman is going to bring you so many books that we've been arguing about it the whole time, because he doesn't even want to take along the tea to leave room for more books. In addition, there are eighty books he intends to reclaim from friends in Paris. If I know that lot, they'll say the Germans stole them.

Can't he stay with Nissim the first three or four days? He's coming to you then anyway, and it will be more cozy and also cheaper for him. Although I doubt the latter, because one returns the favor and that costs *more*. Or should he stay in a hotel? Please tell me honestly. Write it on a separate slip of paper and I will then influence his decision. Nissim invited him so cordially on the telephone that he doesn't really believe me when I say he doesn't have enough room. Please let me know.

You have never written anything about the Nuremberg trials. I continue to read them feverishly. *Before* Gisevius, a minister of *justice* (I am sending you his book), had his hearing at the tribunal, they tried to intimidate him with threats. Göring had the brazen impudence to try it, but Gisevius promptly testified to the threats at his hearing, which had a brilliant effect. Gisevius saved Schacht,[512] who had actually been involved in the Hitler putsch (the one in 1939) from the very first.

Thank you very much for your intervention with Contou. It was really charming. The blockhead was torturing me to death. He didn't think much of the way everything was finally arranged. That's how he is. Please say explicitly "Bring tea!" so that he brings it. Nissim wants tea too; I'll scrape some together. With the help of the lovely boys on the second floor, much love, you most beautiful boy, and it seems to me you must be in wonderful shape because taking a plane to Switzerland is quite something. Isn't your beautiful cousin beautiful anymore? The one in Switzerland, in Lausanne?[513]

I've thought about it so long that I'm afraid no one will buy me anymore, but actually there are all kinds of good prospects again. And it's so much more beautiful and sad and difficult to live in dreams if you have it in you. When you have it in you, you imagine that *La Porte Etroite*[514] is your own story . . . Do you think me very ridiculous? But most of the time I'm keen and you will have brilliant fun at my parties and your brother, the great Canetti II, will assure you, "She's wised up, she really has, believe me."

All my love,
Peggy

Is the address right??

VEZA TO GEORGES · *November 11, 1947*

Mrs. V. Canetti
14 Crawford Street
London W1

Nov. 11

Dear Orleans,

Many thanks, but I didn't read your letter for the Home Office. It would have upset me even though everything is "fake." I think it's bad enough that an intellect like you—and what's more, a handsome young man of extraordinary beauty and great charm—has to be lying in St. Hilaire with all that mercury in his blood, and it pains me greatly. I'm just glad that you have already seduced all the youths, and that the thing with your boys is in good working order.

Some business matters: poor Menczel writes all the time asking for money and it's driving me to distraction. The few pounds I can spare cannot be of any help in Dollarland, and so I wrote her a somewhat distraught letter, because of course it grieves me not to be able to help such a worthy person. Since I feared she would approach you, I hinted that we annoy you constantly with demands. There was no other way to keep her from writing you. She sent quite a desperate letter, and then after seriously upsetting me, she wrote to say that it wasn't so bad after all and things were already much better. She thinks we have an enormous income in dollars, which we do not. This as a guideline for you, because you can afford to help her even less than we can. Our currencies aren't worth anything in the U.S. However, I think that she took my hint, sensitive as she is, and won't upset you too. She's done this frequently, and every time I desperately scrape some money together comes the news, "Not necessary, things are going better." It's just that since the Nazis, she's as deranged as the rest of us.

I don't know what Nissim was thinking, but he had a swing musician who was visiting England write to Canetti. C. thought we should perhaps give him something and invited him to lunch in a restaurant. First he cheerfully accepted, but then he called up and said Canetti should come visit him because he had a hangover. At that we were convinced that he wanted to speak to him alone and Canetti went to see him. He was greeted by an old hag, a former diseuse, all made up and utterly grotesque. She complained loudly about the people in Edinburgh because the chorus girls there have to wear stockings, yet all Englishwomen walk the streets with bare legs (with dirty bare legs, she said, and that's a slander). The swing man didn't want anything at all and didn't even know that Canetti was an author. He thought he was in the swing business. Now, Canetti has no time to waste on such acquaintances, and please tell Nissim so in a gentle way. He can drink alcohol on his own, and it's not necessary for him to drink. The man had nothing to tell him and went back to Paris.

The contract with Arthaud isn't here yet and I'm nervous, but it's not my business anymore.

Atlee's[515] secretary paid us a visit recently. Ten Downing Street called to make the appointment, right after the call from the swing man. He is charming. You will like him a lot and he you. He ate nine sandwiches I had made. As Attlee's lieutenant, he had just picked up De Valera[516] from the airport. He arrived at five and at seven-thirty your brother had the quaint idea of suddenly leaving him sitting at my place in order to go to a party. He (Francis) is so blinded by the *Blendung*[517] and its author that he wasn't the least bit angry and stayed at my place until eleven, and I'm enclosing the clipping as historical documentation and the only reason he didn't mention visiting the Canettis was because he didn't know that I would send you the clipping, otherwise it would be in there. Graham Laurison[518] is his name. I'm also enclosing it because I want to know if this letter gets censored. Our letters are now being x-rayed. Don't forget to write and tell me. And perhaps you'll really come this summer since we have friends like him. He is so modest that he's always apologizing for being alive.

Naphthalene! That reminded me of happy bygone times, when my mother's servants would put up my beautiful clothes in naphthalene. I haven't smelled it since then, but maybe my bag was next to one with naphthalene at the airport. Now the whole apartment smells like n. because my dear old aunt sent me a beautiful brown fur coat and I can throw out my caftan. It was packed in naphthalene and—*am I glad that it is a lovely brown fur*.[519] I thought—because unfortunately, the Jews have no taste—that it would be seal or even astrakhan, genuine East End of the worst sort. I would have exchanged it, but thank God, it's very beautiful, longhaired with amber stripes, and it helps me get over my depression after another bout of flu. Poor Bauscherl has it too and his cough would move a stone to tears. He's so sweet and naive and yesterday, there was a letter from F. saying if she didn't see him soon she would throw herself out the window. Such are the joys of his life. From another quarter, Marie Luise is pestering him; she wants to go to St. H. too, because you're so handsome and she thinks you will love her as much as you do me. She doesn't know that a relationship like the one among the three of us needs long years of love, pain and irony, fear, charm to be sat through, and a magic power so strong that nothing can burst it apart and no one can force his way in. —Thank God you made a list of the things. I have *too many* tins with jam and marmalade, etc. and now the fool is taking them along because you said to, also honey. My relatives are inundating me with parcels and in these parts, that's the most important thing.

No, I'm not thinking about making the trip, Sunny. You must come here. Travel in France and the coldness of the surroundings in a French hospice hold no attraction for me. How charming the English are in this respect. And Paris is very beautiful, but without gnomes and . . . Of course, I like Lucienne and Nissim really very much. The children too.

All my love,
Peggy

Write at once about drafts, wounds, weather, food, frame of mind! Otherwise, no letter for you!

VEZA TO GEORGES · *November 23, 1947*

Mrs. Canetti
14 Crawford Str. W1

London, Nov. 23

Dearest Child,

Canetti has sent you a telegram. I am unable to write an amusing letter, but I'm not worried about you. The only thing that tortures me is your ordeal . . . and the long time in St. Hilaire. And all three of us are no sinners. Your brother is a saint. Unfortunately. He will do everything possible to be there for the operation and won't bring any of his girlfriends along. Even before, he wasn't very eager to, and now even less so. I wonder if it's catching. For the past two weeks, I've been suffering intense depression—a sort of cardiac neurosis, for I'm often quite nauseous. Caught from you?

Of course I'll come in June, but you must promise to introduce me properly. Say your Nannie is coming so people don't burst out laughing again.

Everyone will be entranced with your brother, and I only hope he won't be in the midst of one of his "periods." He claims he has "periods" just like women do. I think I told you about it. Henry Miller also writes about this. I gave him the same book you have,* but he didn't read it; things like that bore him. He only reads scientific works.

The Arthaud contract has been *signed*. It's going well. I don't know whether I told you that he had another fantastic review here. He's bringing it along to show you. It appeared in a very critical journal called *Critic*. Sales in America are not good, but CAPE says that when it appears in Paris that will influence the U.S. and it will do very well. I continue to read for Hutchinson, but since it doesn't pay much, I'm going to translate a Robert Neumann play into German. Your brother thinks it's degrading that *his* wife is translating such a dilettante. What do you think?

Apropos, a delectable anecdote about Bernard Shaw's translator—his name is Trebitsch[520] and he made a real hash of it. But the work made him rich and famous. He tells everyone he meets (and it's in circulation as a bon mot), "Shaw undermined my whole career. I sacrificed my own works to translate his!!" For years, Shaw refused to hear how bad the German translations were. But now he says he's going to take revenge and translate Trebitsch into English.

I wouldn't worry about the time after you've recovered. We would be great bumblers indeed if we didn't have a solution by then.

We've had a wedding[521] over here and at the same time, a rumor was circulating that the queen was pregnant again and this time, it would be a boy and the whole "fuss" was a waste of time. I turned on the radio so I could make fun of the wedding, and instead it was so beautiful I sat in my room and wept. Even the extremely vapid princess had a tender voice. Philip is handsome and of course, people are happy he's a foreigner.[522] As my cousin's chauffeur in America said indignantly, "She could *not* have married an *English* duke!!" Why did I cry? Because I was once a princess, too. That was during the monarchy and every summer, I sat in our villa in Ischl[523] and the Kaiser was always riding by and waving and I waved back and my mother was convinced he was waving at *me*. That happened every morning, and I was seven years old. Miss Wedgwood cried too, by the way (we were celebrating the day together at my place). She felt the same way, but she wasn't crying for her childhood. She cried because she had never been a princess. I like her too much to think so, but it seems she is ugly. And what's more, she cried out of reverence. She's a historian, a Conservative, from a famous family—tradition and all that. She followed my advice and read St. Simon, and she's overwhelmed.

I'm very sorry to inflict this handwriting on you, but I'm too weak to type. I don't need to tell you—we're waiting for a line from you, and telegrams will only disappoint you. You'll think Canetti is already on his way. Please write at once, immediately.

I'll order the book.

Who will operate in St. Hilarie? Isn't it always done by that fat cook in Chateubr.???? An answer right away, please.

Peggy

*I couldn't get hold of *Capricorn*.[524]

Veza to Georges · *December 21, 1947*

Mrs. Canetti
14 Crawford Street
London W1

Dec. 21

Dearest Child,

I will never forget how you wrote in spite of your condition. In the meantime, you will have received Swift for Xmas (he'll prove grimly refreshing for you, especially now), and two jars of honey, I hope. I told Jacqueline[525] she could keep one jar for taking so many things for me, but she said you needed it more, and I'm eager to know if she's kept her word and given you both. After all, I only deprived myself of it for you, and we did enough for Jacqueline. I like her, although your characterization of her was unfortunately right, as usual. However, I think she's kindhearted and for me that's always a great asset. Mandarin oranges are dirt cheap here at the moment, rotting in the fruitstands. She'll bring you some. Please don't swallow the peel; you'll get bloated and think it's another bedsore. I had to tell you that, since you're a doctor and have no way of knowing it for yourself. Twenty-four razor blades, since girls are afraid to take more than that. I would have sent a hundred more things, but I couldn't ask her to carry them, since this time I had to send something to Elias Canetti and his wife: condensed milk and cigarettes. I'll send tea with your brother. I'm still saving it up. So he'll come in January and now he's really bringing his work together and talks of being done in six months. If he can read it to you, it will work wonders, and please see to it that he doesn't make it too long and tell him he can publish a second volume in two years. In other respects, business matters are looking up. I shall only report results, but everything is going well since I decided to forge his signature on business documents too, and when he gets offers, he's enormously grateful, even though he threatens me beforehand and says I'd better not dare. We certainly will have to buy you that cottage in Austria or Germany.

It doesn't make me cheerful to write that your brother is going on lecture tours this year and getting 25 guineas per lecture about art. Of course, Jacqueline raves about you like everyone else. She will tell you all about us, but of course she didn't have the chance to meet all the interesting bigwigs. It can't be done in three weeks and I can't marry her off in that short a time either. I don't know anyone who's ordinary enough. (Elias C. asked me to find her a husband, and I could, of course.) She tired me out. Your brother was furious; she cost him time. In the end, I gave her some instructions about how to act and then he liked her well enough because she was a little more "respectful."

Forgive me, but would you appreciate it if I were cheerful in *your* condition? I can only sleep with the help of pills and then only from six in the morning.

Every possible good wish
from us both
dear Child,
Peggy

Veza to Georges · *December 31, 1947*

Mrs. Canetti
14 Crawford Str. W1

London, Dec. 31

Sweet Georg,

Of course I'm only writing because I want an answer, and what's more, you have so much credit with me you can scold me as much as you like . . . for example, the fact that you wrote me after your operation. Your brother and I, we're constantly sick. Every winter it's an epidemic; we get one flu after another, bad coughs, and I don't believe in medicine if it can't deliver us from this plague. And some idiots believe you're immune for a few weeks after having one—I get one after the other with hardly five calm days in between. You can't just go to bed in this age of slavery, because you have to do everything for yourself. Not even to mention depression.

Your brother is going to be published again in Germany and Austria. Even his plays will be in print.[526] Other positive developments are still up in the air. I won't write about them until I know something for certain. The plays had to be in book form, otherwise he wouldn't give them the novel. Everything's in order with Arthaud except for the advance. It hasn't arrived yet, and of course your brother will not remind them about it. The contract has been legally signed. I get very little to read. I just destroyed Emil Ludwig's autobiography.[527] Strangely enough, he praises the Russians to the skies—"The Americans have replaced thinking with statistics—but the Russians despise money"—and that's why he loves them and their regime, even though he's not a Communist. Curious for someone who's such a nincompoop and an admirer of Bismarck.

Fritz Jerusalem[528] is here from China. He is practically your equal in courage. He fought in Spain and then in China and is now on his way to Austria to take up an important post (he's a doctor). He brought his Chinese wife with him. She is said to have performed great heroic deeds that didn't quite make sense to me when they talked about them. I haven't liked the few Chinese I've met, but *all* of the many Indians.

I wasn't exaggerating about the cottage in Central Europe for July. Not in France, unfortunately, but perhaps next year, if Arthaud gets a good translator. It doesn't matter so much to me anymore how much money I cost your brother, because since I've been initiating all the foreign deals—despite his strict prohibition—everything is succeeding. I even forge his signature. Why was I so respectable and respectful for 20 years? I earn him everything I cost him and many honors besides. I'm telling you this to forgive myself, so to speak. I know how noble your thoughts are, but actually, this money ought to go to you, and we live with that thought in the back of our minds.

Forgive my miserable handwriting I'm feeling too weak to use the typewriter.

Jacqueline herself wrote how happy her Mama was with the honey, and she sent me sugar that I don't need. If only she'd sent it to you. I have plenty of everything for you here and hope that Fritz will bring you something from me. Very likely, he's such a decent man. He's traveling by way of Paris and will mail it the rest of the way. If you or Nissim know anyone willing to carry parcels from me to you, they're all welcome to come. Everyone in America is heartbroken to think I'm starving, but I have about 10 pounds of jam I haven't even touched, to say nothing of all the rest. I'm forwarding some on to Austria. I'm writing these idiotic things so that Nissim will send people to me who are willing to take things back with them. I hope you received the little package on the 24th. Jacqueline promised me you would.

I'm delighted that everything is healing, not to mention your *innocent* brother. He was very upset by your scolding. When we are desperately worried about you, you mustn't scold us in addition. I think it's your allure and not your books that makes people admire you so much. The truth is, everyone's madly in love with you. I was so depressed at Xmas time that I wrote *fröhliche Weinachten* to Veronica Wedg. I was thinking it must come from *weinen*.[529] It beats me why

Jacqueline isn't married yet. She has so little spirit that she'd take any man with a fixed income who pretends to be educated. You described her very well. I imagine she looks like your father and is good-hearted like him. That's just my imagination, of course, for I didn't know your father. It's me taking sides for the Canettis. I even like Nissim, who's said to be so miserly (is that true?). With me he wasn't miserly at all, but perhaps he sighed and complained afterward. Not my fault. I absolutely didn't even want him to pay for the theater for me.

Your brother is going to go on lecture tours here. It will pay well, provided he can get the lectures written, he's so pathological.

Please be a dear and write me at once. Of course you belong to us. Everyone we want belongs to us. You forget how fascinating people find us. You would be very impressed to see us among our English friends and see how we've made a conquest of them. We even force them to like Chaplin's film *Monsieur Verdoux*![530]

A letter right away, if you please. Next time, I'll even send you a Walpole letter! A healthy New Year, my Child, from your brother and

Peggy.

Good luck!

❦

VEZA TO GEORGES · *January 17 and 22, 1948*

Mrs. V. Canetti
14 Crawford Street
London W1

Jan. 17, 1948

Dear Candide,

I can't think of a more lovable figure to insult you with, and Candide[531] is sure to annoy you. No letter. You alone have the privilege of clemency. I see red with anger and the typewriter writes red with anger. It's on strike. I'm writing only because it's your birthday and I hope the book your brother sent you will arrive right on the day.[532] You know what our wishes are for you. And we know what you wish on us, but at the moment, I can't let your brother go. He's not in good health, in very bad shape, has to get better by himself. And the second point of equal importance: he has to get his affairs in order. We are receiving very favorable replies to the "business deals" I have set in motion, and I will certainly not let him leave until he is financially secured here and in France, which he is gradually getting to be. In addition, it will soon be legal here to take money out of the country, and by God, that's important. I heard Jacqueline's lament that they'll have to pay 20 pounds for Regine. What indignation I have brought down upon my head. I should have prevented it. Frankly, I wouldn't have been capable of doing it even to Regine. Bauscherl has no idea how unfriendly the family will be about this matter and I'm not going to tell him. Your anger on my head, but *I* won't let him go, and the third reason is this: he will want to sit with you for hours and I'd rather have you get much stronger before he does. And there's nothing more to be said: I'm the mama, and the two of you have always had strict mothers.

I've been through a bad time, unfortunately, and that's why I forgot that you had ordered a book from me. I can't find the passage even though I have all the letters, so I'm asking you to repeat it for me in legible handwriting on a separate piece of paper. You've seen me, so why are you angry with me that I'm "a mental case"?[533]

January 22

Bauscherl wrote you that this is the reason he hasn't left yet (at least, I think he did). As far as *he's* concerned it's the only reason. But without all the other considerations, I wouldn't have made him wait. Please confirm receipt of the book right away. I *didn't* send it *recom.*[534] so it would arrive quickly and now I'm worried about it. All our love and good luck!

Your Peggy

Elias to Georges · *January 18, 1948*

January 18, 1948

My beloved brother,

Your angry words have been passed on to me, as you wished. I don't hold them against you. You have every appearance of justification on your side. However, I also have no intention of doing what you fear the most: beating my breast and breaking into wild avowals of remorse. It is not possible for me to do so, since I have nothing to regret. You simply do not know the facts. During the months of November and December, Veza had another of her severe bouts of depression. It was the worst attack of that kind in three years, although not quite as bad as back then. This time, she did everything she could to conceal it from everyone except me. She didn't see many people, and when she had to, she kept such control of herself that really only quite close friends were able to notice anything. At such times, she sleeps hardly at all and eats even less. Every bite she can be induced to swallow costs lengthy persuasion. She explicitly *forbade* me to tell you the truth about her condition; your opinion is so important to her that even in the midst of depression, she fears you could despise her or suddenly like her less. I had to respect her wishes. If I had tried to write you behind her back, it would have come out sometime, since the two of you have no secrets from each other, and she would have lost all trust in me. Her trust, however, is very important precisely during these bouts of depression, since it leaves me a modicum of influence over her, so that I can keep her alive until the attack has passed. Besides, it didn't seem to me especially wise to inform you of her condition. Now that she's so much better, she's permitted me to write you—if not in every detail, at least in general—about her depression, which is in abeyance. That was the reason *she* wrote you so much less often.

The news of your operation arrived during her worst spell. You cannot imagine the effect it had on us. I was ready to come to you immediately. I assumed Nissim would wire me if and when the trip became urgent. I was deathly afraid to leave Veza alone. Even today, I'm convinced that it would not have ended well. That's what caused the fight; for an eternity we had no news of how your operation had gone. You must believe me that this one time, we were in no better condition than you.

"I acknowledge all of that," you will reply. "But why didn't you *write* me?" Try to imagine: what should I have written? In a letter, I could have notified you of my arrival or said that I wasn't coming. Both would have been uncertain, and thus untrue. Not a single sentence in any sort of letter would have been accurate. However, there are situations that are so critical (and this will amuse you) that even I cannot tell a lie. Such a situation exists when the two human beings nearest and dearest to me in the whole world are actually both in such grave danger that neither must learn of the other's condition. —It also seemed better to me that you had something to look forward to—an arrival, a letter, anything—than having all of that cut short by a letter. You can still reply that at a moment like that, you would have felt compelled to leave whatever you were doing and come here immediately. However, you have never seen Veza in that condition. When she's like that, she refuses to consult a doctor, closes herself off from everyone, doesn't eat, and there is *absolutely no doubt* that without me, she would simply perish. Even now, she invents all sorts of excuses for why I should postpone my trip to France until March: you will be feeling much better by then and we would be able to discuss more things with each other, I might harm you with my cough, and all sorts of similar reasons. In reality—and she is certainly not conscious of this—she is still afraid to be left alone, and she feels that her condition will be so much improved in a few weeks—toward spring—that she'll be able to get along without me. She has an unutterably deep and tender love for you. She surely loves you much more than me, but for the guerrilla war against her melancholy, she needs someone she doesn't stand in awe of, someone to whom she can show herself to be ugly or despairing or nasty. She really feels no reserve toward me, because I have already seen her like that and nevertheless respect her even more, if possible. She thinks that you, however, must never see her like that. Otherwise, you could suddenly decide that she's not in the least lovable. It's easy to see from this whom she loves most, but God knows, I wish that everyone in the world would love you more than me or anyone else. You deserve it.

I would like you to accept my explanation. I can't make it any plainer and more straightforward than I have. I've spared you grandiose emotions; you're right to mistrust them.

Write me exactly how you are feeling. The proximity of your birthday after all the frightful things you have experienced fills me with a curious happiness, as if now, at least, the worst is past. I don't know if you will really like the book I'm sending you. In any case, Gide was very impressed by it and I know you think a lot of him. I have so much to tell you that I often see us already sitting together and having long, intimate conversations. It would really be nice if there are times I could sit with you for an hour or two, or do you think that will be too much? I'd like to read a little to you sometimes, too, if it won't tire you. Be *completely honest* and tell me if you think it's not good for me to wait until March to come. I will of course act according to your wishes. Veza and I are going to have a quiet birthday celebration for you here, to which you are cordially invited. Although you're far away, we'll treat you like a visitor. Apropos of visiting: of course Veza will come see you this summer. She's already looking forward to it. I don't know if she's accepted your invitation yet. If not, it's only because right now, she doesn't feel up to any traveling. But that will soon pass and she will love to come.

It will be a pleasure to find a "Couver" <?>[535] at your place. Are you doctors always more cruel than the rest of us? There's a marvelous exhibit on India here that I wish you could see. I would love to give you a guided tour and explain it all to you. I've become such an expert on Indian mythology that all the English writers have me show them around. It's hard to believe how much one learns oneself on such occasions.

This summer, I'm supposed to give three lectures on Proust, Joyce, and Kafka,[536] speaking in English and without notes, at a large summer school for professional musicians out in the country in Dorset. It won't be easy, but I'm looking forward to it nevertheless. I'll be in very good company: the other speakers on literature are Eliot,[537] Forster, and Father d'Arcy (the famous English Jesuit).[538] Moreover, I get an honorarium of 50 guineas for the lectures. We need it desperately. My dear, dearest Georg, a hug on this and all future birthdays and write me a long letter about yourself.

Your brother Elias.

VEZA TO GEORGES · *February 18, 1948*

Mrs. V. Canetti
14 Crawford Street
London W1

Feb. 18

Dearest Georg,

Your brother was terribly happy to get your letter and he will certainly be there before Easter, shortly before Easter. "Veza doesn't write" Why? Because she doesn't get a reply from you and she will continue to send one letter for each one she receives. Thank God Canetti is somewhat stronger, or at least somewhat fatter, and I don't know what to say about the cause. I'm afraid it has to do with him now receiving ardent love letters expressing the best intentions and even quite beautifully written. He had to leave his studio apartment near Victoria Station and is living with a refugee[539] who serves him rich breakfasts and charges a lot for them. I cook for him myself three times a week and he looks better now and I'm glad he has a round little face again. He was looking like a shrunken

Elias Canetti and Clement Glock, Bryanston, 1948

head—terrifying. But I must stress that he's gotten better since the love letters. You'll be able to see and judge the sender for yourself and in any case, you'll find her delightfully amusing and must tell me what you think. Your opinion will surely be smarter than mine. As for her chemical makeup, she reminds me frightfully much of Lucienne. I say frightfully because this seems like an omen. She has the same coloring. Her flesh makes that same somewhat languid impression. I can't express it except through chemistry. All this is only a sketch. He'll tell you more himself and I'll tell him you know she's coming. You will also respect him as he deserves, not only because he's great but also because he's good. You know yourself that he loves you more and is kinder to you than I am (because he's kinder to everyone). Please see to it that he eats properly. This is necessary because his only concern will be that the carrot pixie eats enough. That's my nickname for her, and she'll see to the eating herself because she thinks only about herself, all day long.

By the way, it makes no sense to write Canetti in Amersham. He's never there and his mail gets forwarded. How am I ever going to persuade him to go to the Bulgar. consulate? He's almost as afraid of it as he is of the police, and I always tell him poor Aunt Ernestine[540] will starve to death if he doesn't go, and over time, I hope to convince him to. Such are the small sufferings of a great man and the great ones of yours truly.

As for me, I have nothing to do (nothing lucrative, I mean) and plan to go to America in the near future. (There's a slump here, *also* in book sales, thus my lack of work.) A childhood friend of mine has a house there and a car and shower baths and whatnot, and since she knows how I was raised, I'll have a good time. She also has contacts in publishing and believes in me. Of course, I must get much stronger and it will take a while for me to decide.

Your Aunt Arditti[541] went to visit her son on his farm. She couldn't put up with the fights between her daughters at home anymore. The King's Farmer[542] was visiting her son and sampled her baked goods and asked her to cook for the king when he comes to hunt at Sandringham.[543] So she went to cook for the king, and curtsied for the queens, and found the younger one[544] charming and the older one[545] enormously clever because she asked her advice about buttons. She thought Princess Marguerite[546] unprepossessing (because she squinted at her) but Princess Elizabeth[547] made an impression. The King's Farmer is very courteous and with his own hands turns the turkey roasting in the oven before he goes to church, in case it's too heavy for her. Cissi[548] went to visit her, but when she was having a look at the kitchen, the police phoned that "there's a strange woman around the church" and were assured "it's all right" by the King's Farmer. So the king is well guarded. Poor old Aunt Arditti has to curtsey a lot and her daughters can pester me all they want, but I'm not going to pay the apprenticeship fee for the three of them. I'm expecting another visit from Jacqueline, and she, at least, is harmless.

Your brother is to give three lectures in Dorset in August and get 50 pounds for them. He can repeat them in other parts of England and it can be a nice source of income. If—if he finishes them in time, about which I'm already having nightmares, because they are all famous men on the program with him and I remember him dictating his lecture in Vienna a half hour before it was to begin, and we got there twenty minutes too late. Perhaps you can stir him up a bit. Whether he gives the lecture and can repeat it elsewhere unfortunately depends on F's letters, or on her behavior when she is here. So I'm on anxious lookout for her letters and breathe a sigh of relief when they're like they are now. Because unfortunately, my mood depends on the shape he is in, and he is such a big, everlasting *Wunderkind*, but so pure and trusting, that he never sees through anyone except when he's writing a book. In his imagination he knows the world; in the world he's pure imagination. With this lovely syllogism I will close, and I haven't written anything about you because I'm so happy you're doing well that this is the first time I've been able to write a decent letter again, and what more proof do you need?

All our love and since I get a letter from your satellites in Paris every five days, Jaqu. Ed. etc.,[549] we're not worried if you don't write. You just won't hear anything from us either.

Your
disgustedly[550]
Peggy

ELIAS TO GEORGES · *March 5, 1948*

Friday

My dear Georg,

I still can't quite believe I shall see you in just a few weeks. I think about it so often that sometimes I believe I'm there already. But I have to write you anyway because there are so many arrangements still to be made.

I would like to spend the entire month of April up there with you, except for perhaps a few days with friends[551] who have invited me to Vaucluse. Friedl will come with me. I hope you don't mind, but I must explain it to you in any case. First of all, you should know that Veza, who has a comprehensive view of this entire affair, not only condones it but is very much in favor of it. I punished Friedl for her crazy behavior with 1¼ years of banishment. She is very much changed, to the extent possible for her, and bitterly regrets what she has done. Meanwhile, she has worked hard and has completed a really talented and remarkable novel (500 pages!).[552] I had promised her she could spend three weeks with me when the book was finished, and I have to keep my promise. She knows that after that, she must return to her people and has sworn not to become unpleasant and troublesome as she did before. She's 32 now, after all, has remarried in Sweden, dresses better, behaves like a human being; you will definitely not need to be embarrassed about her. I have to discuss her finished book with her. Her scribbling is the only thing she really takes seriously; she's learned a lot from me, so despite everything she's done to me, I can't leave her in the lurch as far as her writing is concerned.

I promise that you won't have to see her if you don't want to. She knows I want to be alone with you for a while at first and she will not bother us. Later, if she doesn't irritate you, she can of course come with me sometimes. If it's all right with you, I'd like to arrive in Paris the week before Easter, see Nissim and the other relatives, wait for Friedl there, and leave for Grenoble with her on the Tuesday *after* Easter (March 30th). She and I would stay there overnight and arrive in St. Hilaire on Wednesday, the 31st. I'd like you to reserve two nice sunny rooms for us starting on that day, next to each other, for several weeks. Please tell me exactly how much rooms with breakfast will cost. I know that the family will pay for *me* because I cannot bring any money from England, but Friedl is coming from Sweden, where she's allowed to take money out of the country, and of course she intends to pay for herself. So please write and tell me exactly what it costs. In case no rooms are available two days after Easter, you'll have to rent them beginning one or two days later, or include Easter. Please see to all this right away and write *at once* how things stand. It's important that the rooms be nice and livable. I also intend to work, and she too should get right back to work so that her restlessness doesn't take hold again.

The time is probably a little too tight for Easter itself. For many reasons, I don't think I can get away from here until Wednesday or Thursday, so I would be coming to you right in the middle of the Easter holidays when things will surely be very hectic. But if it's really important to you, I'll come for Easter itself. Would you mind terribly if Friedl came with me right away? You know, I don't think it's a good idea to leave her alone in Paris. For the time being, she's very serious and composed, but Paris agitates her. You know from experience how she gets when she's there. It's better for her to come to the mountains right away, when she's at her most human. Again, I promise you won't hear or see her any more than you want to. I'll have my mail forwarded to you at the sanatorium. I've been telling my friends in London that I'm staying with you in the sanatorium. For many reasons, above all from pride, I don't want people to know that she'll be up there with me.

Now, there is something else I have to discuss with you. A few days ago, two chapters of the French translation of the *Blendung* finally arrived. To my surprise, I found myself completely unable to judge the quality of the translation. My French has become totally rusty, and it's time I refreshed it again. So yesterday, Veza sent you a copy of *Die Blendung* in German and the two chapters in French. Please take the time to read them first, *all the way through*, to get an impression of their style, then compare them with the German for accuracy. You're the only person I have whose French I can trust. So it's up to you whether I can say I'm satisfied with the translator. Of course, one always has to make corrections and I hope you will do that for me later, but I *can't judge* the skill of the translator himself *at all*. Please do it *right away* and tell me what you think. Because they're waiting for my decision. Perhaps you will have more detailed things to say about it. I need the translation back; please keep the German copy there. I send the most cordial embrace. Ah, if only I were already there with you, my dearest, dearest, dearest brother,

Elias.

Veza to Georges · *March 6, 1948*

Mrs. Canetti
14 Crawford Street
London W1

March 6

Dearest Georg,

I'm writing this time on account of Canetti, who read me the letter he wrote you yesterday. I would like to *implore* you to give him a friendly response and say it doesn't matter to you if F. comes along. The touching fellow would prefer to see you without her, believe me, but what he can't admit to you in his amorous affliction is that he's afraid to leave her alone in Paris because she'll immediately "be up to some mischief." There's no sense fooling ourselves. Since receiving her love letters, he's done more work than he has for years and he'll read you marvelous chapters of it. He's also planning to complete it this year, and if he's on good terms with her, that is, if she allows him think he is, he will finish it. The price to be paid—that he will work on her novel in France (this is what *she's* looking for from *him*)—is not too high, in my opinion. They sent it back to her; the end was awful. Perhaps it will really be good and I'll even be happy if it is. Then her ambition will be satisfied and she won't behave in such a mean way. Please be very friendly to her so that if she torments him, he'll tell you all about it. If he cannot talk about it, it can have the worst consequences, and I won't be there. You will find her simply amusing.

As for his work, it's full of magnificent new ideas. Perhaps it may not always seem so to you, since you're not as trained in following it as I am. If you have any real objections to it, that can only be of use to him, but be cautious. The weight of a snowflake could make him incapable of finishing it. And *I* know it is an original work. You're more attuned to art. Proust is an artist, but not a very original one. I'm reading him currently because your brother is going to give a lecture on him as well.

As for the translation of *Autodafé*, I am "miserable." It is so literal but so contrary to the spirit of the book, so uninspired, that I wish it weren't being published in French at all. It's a heavy blow. I didn't really tell him how bad I think the translation is. It's boring. And "gouvernante" for "Haushälterin" or "excusez" for "aber ich bitt Sie"[553]—not to mention the stylistic mediocrity . . .

Jacqueline is coming back in a week and will bring you a bit of tea and maybe some honey, too. Canetti plans to bring only books, even though I told him how disappointed the relatives will be. You don't need to worry about his clothes: his black overcoat is well tailored, the best-quality cashmere, his best dark blue suit—cashmere, two quite serviceable gray suits. He can't take more than that on the plane. God knows, he looks more presentable than Nissim or Elias Canetti. Just mentioning him makes me laugh. We are famous here *quoique*, not *parceque*,[554] I almost want to say because of and not despite.

I have to go see Jacqueline now. Your brother doesn't want to introduce her to his friends because of the really terribly banal comments she makes, especially in public, and here in England we're as snooty about intellect as you are about clothes in France. She's a bit insulted, but a friend of Canetti's,[555] a repulsively ugly and disgusting Jew but a talented poet, is taking her to a club this week, and my nephew took her out and is going to go dancing with her, and I go out with her. It's martyrdom to think that Claudine will be coming soon, and there's also a prospect of Regine coming to visit . . . Is your room as beautiful as in Chateaub.? Request any books that occur to you, he's happy to bring them all. Once more, please behave in a way that will gain his trust! He's in such good form now and was so miserable before. I want him to remain himself. He will bring you much joy.

Love Peggy

You could easily write like Proust!

VEZA TO GEORGES · *March 8, 1948*

Mrs. V. Canetti
14 Crawford Street
London W1

Dearest Phoebus,

Could you please describe this radiography in more detail? Again, it is torture not to know what it means—not another operation, I hope? And what was making you depressed was the foehn wind. It's hard on people with delicate nerves and even some Englishmen *are just going to pieces*,[556] the ones who are at all capable of escaping their phlegmatic nature. Most of this half of the population is now largely anti-Semitic and that is beginning to manifest itself in whispered comments in the movies whenever Palestine is shown, since a few Tommies have bit the dust. Five million victims of the gas chambers have disappeared into oblivion. And the rest who are not anti-Semitic are panicky because of what they imagine to be the threat of Communism. It would be easier for it to triumph on Mars than in England, but they fear it anyway. Not even Freud knew anything about panic, about what it really is, i.e., why it occurs *and what* it is. But your brother will read you a brilliant explanation.[557] He has a green pass, which is extremely valuable, because it allows him to leave England any time without needing permission, and he can always return without a visa. He'll get a French visa tomorrow and is eager to get going.

How can you write such charming letters when you've just gotten over the flu (all by itself the flu can make you too tired even to die) and the x-rays . . . I don't know the Bester woman, but if she's beautiful, I like her. I would tell Schles you have to work hard for the next two weeks because your brother is coming and you need to finish an essay. Your brother won't be able to get rid of her either, but give Friedl an SOS and she'll take care of it promptly. In the meantime you will have read the catastrophe from Arthaud. I now pin all my hopes on the German-speaking countries, where everything is off to a good start, with the plays as well. Thank God not everyone there is as namby-pamby as you and your brother Nissim, and they know how to appreciate immortal works (the plays are more brilliant than the novel). I use as many parentheses as Proust. I always skip over his. I'm having a miserable time finding work, but that can change for the better from one day to the next. It was a wise thing *dass Du gesauft hast*.[558] I think *gesoffen* is correct. Both of us are losing some German, even the poet. It feels good to know that your head physician is named Cohen—the sounds of home.

Jacqueline was quite touching yesterday. She suddenly asked me to tell her my life story. She said we were always talking about Canetti and never about me. Then I just kept on telling her about Canetti. My doctor,[559] the same one who didn't buy me, had a gorgeous girlfriend for six weeks, 20 years old. He's 60. I breathed a sigh of relief, because he used to come and sit with me 4 times a week and every time he did, it was torture to hear about everything in the editorial of the *Chronicle*. However, she wanted to hop in bed with him all the time and he couldn't keep up. Besides, he doesn't like spending all night with a woman because he likes to take out his false teeth and then his mouth collapses. It came to differences of opinion and now I'll have the devil of a time reconciling the two of them and even more work protecting Canetti, because Jackie (that's her name) is definitely after him too, now more than ever, and he doesn't like having women in bed too often either. I'm sorry about it, because she's very pretty and a nurse, a job she loves passionately, so I'm already thinking about the worst case, if the doctor doesn't function, and how I could send her to St. Hilaire. You always have the excuse of your wound, and that's certainly why you *have* it. The doctor's also excusing himself with his lumbago. That's all for today. I would love to be with you and it will do me good to hear about everything from Canetti, and to hear everything about Canetti from you, and I have very few passionate wishes, but I do have this one: that the two of you love each other as deeply as I love you both, and that he bring you luck, i.e., good health. I brought you none, but he is "lucky." Please reply at once, my child, and as I asked you to, and don't hold it against us that we're bothering you about the translation. Paris is important because of America and the plays. Are you writing your autobiography yet? *A la Recherche du temps gagné*[560] by you, you swot.

All my love.

Love Peggy[561]

Veza to Georges · *March 17 and 19, 1948*

Mrs. V. Canetti
14 Crawford Street
London W1

March 17.

Beloved child,

I am very moved that you have done this boring job for Canetti even though it cannot have been what you wanted to do. The precision of your characterization of the translator (I think it is a woman)[562] is Proustian and we will follow your advice completely. I'm quite serious when I compare you to Proust. You write like him, and better to the extent that you have the harshness of the times in your style and you would cross out much that Proust should have crossed out. He's a master at describing relationships, not of people with each other but of a single person to others, and I am more impressed by the death of the grandmother—that is, everything that preceded it—than by the characterization of Swann (although brilliant, it's not new). I like reading him and do so with the greatest admiration for his ability and his art, but what's missing is the passionate excitement I feel for Saint Simon, because Proust comes from St. Simon. He's his disciple. I'm passionately excited by *your* artistic abilities and I wish you would finally admit to having begun your autobiography. I also implore you to tell me how the x-rays were. Don't leave us to worry!!!

Unfortunately, Jacqueline didn't take any honey for you because she was shlepping so many other things along for herself. She does it mostly because she's so terribly practical and that's certainly better for her future, although I would have done more for her if she weren't. But even so, I did enough and she was very enthusiastic and threatened to come again. Even worse, Claudine is coming to visit now, and the family gives no thought to how tedious it is for me. I was able to unload her sister onto my nephew, who took her dancing, onto Canetti's friend Steiner, who is happy if a girl even talks to him, and as I explained to your brother, she is so lacking in spirit that she's not choosy in her sexual partners, and since she leaves men cold, she's happy with Steiner. Of course, she expected to be introduced to our "posh" friends, but as I said, Canetti had no intention of doing so. She would undoubtedly have expressed her superiority in front of Atlee's secretary by saying to Canetti, "Today, at last, you're better dressed," thereby demonstrating the preeminence of Paris. Besides such inherent banality, I must say that I share the taste of the English, who laugh at French fashion, so her remark would have fallen flat. But she's bringing you some tea. The day before her departure, I received half a pound from America, hermetically sealed. And she has no perfume. She doesn't use any and is proud of it, and probably she doesn't use it because she has no fragrance—no inner fragrance—and because too much money would evaporate. (And so the tea won't smell.)

I'm still having problems getting work. Today, for example, they sent me an Italian book, but I don't know enough Italian.

March 19.

I got interrupted at this point, but now I'll tell you first about Canetti's trip, and then about the amusing contretemps—amusing for *you*. Well, Friedl has an infection and can't come for another month, so please tell the beautiful landlady you love so much—while Regine loves the boy more (I said I thought it was the other way around)—that you're not *canceling* one room but *postponing* it, but I don't know exactly for how long. If Canetti tires you out too much, he can go to Strasbourg and come back to your place later. He's also been invited to stay in a tower somewhere in lovely France. He should be in St. Hilaire by the 31st, but even that isn't *completely* certain, because he's not getting his visa until tomorrow and then needs a new letter from Nissim, hopefully already on its way.

Regine stormed in here yesterday and slobbered all over your brother, although it was directed at *me*. But then I left the room to give him a chance to intervene generously in her financial affairs, and when I returned from the kitchen, all he was hearing was "Je t'adore," accompanied by the unpleasant physical manifestations he fears from her. He told her she looked like Barrault. *I* told her that you had written to say how beautiful she looked at the wedding—extremely elegant and young—and so we dispensed compliments and the only one to suffer was me, for your brother fled after an hour while I put up with her for three more, and this morning, Claudine woke me up after *three* hours of sleep to say that she's coming today. It's enough to wring tears from a stone, but no one weeps for me. For your brother is goodness itself and in his kindheartedness, it doesn't matter to him at all that people pester me. He would let them sleep in my bed, that's how kind he is. But Regine will bring you some honey, and that reconciles me, and if she doesn't annoy me again, I'll have a better impression of her this time. She seems more resigned, somehow refined, but perhaps that was only because of Canetti's gallant gesture. With her, you never know how long it will last. She was very attractive, and even though I didn't listen to her views on the world, marriage, politics, and nylon stockings, I liked her face. By the way, she's in love with all the Canetti males, even with Jo, which is touching. I called the doctor up right away. He wasn't keen, but I will try to bring the two of them closer together, since the young nymphomaniac has left him and I can't put up with him. I'll send razor blades with Canetti. I forgot to send them with Jacquel*ine*; perhaps Reg*ine* will bring some too. As you can see, I have a case of "ine"itis.

Write and tell me how you are!

Veza to Georges · *March 21, 1948*

Mrs. Canetti
14 Crawford Street
London W1

March 21

Dear Playboy,

The French connection didn't work and the French won't release the file number, so it's better if you postpone Canetti's room as well, which won't matter to the blond landlady, because he'll stay the same length of time. He doesn't want to give a date but will send a telegram. Of course, it's still possible that he will come on time, but even then he will send a telegram. And after Easter, he'll surely be able to get rooms. He'll probably already have one in the train compartment, complete with *putaine*.[563] He's still expecting the visa any day now, or in three days at the latest.

Friedl has an "infection."[564] If that means a certain operation (my guess), I will thank God. I hope it's not V.D. Last year at this time I spent lovely hours in France and what luck that Chat. was so ugly and the matrons so vitriolic and carbolic-smelling, or I would be very sad that Bauscherl is traveling *alone*. Regine is furious again because we have no time for her but I had the slobberer call up at a time when Bauscherl was here and so she shrieked into the phone at *him*. Jacqueline is more content and since I have no time to write, I'm sending the illustration. The family is quite dissatisfied with my appearance, but green velvet corduroy by itself isn't enough. Everyone looks from the velvet to the face.

Peggy

Please don't be angry it's really not *his* fault this time!!!

Elias to Georges · *March 22, 1948*

Monday

My beloved Georg,

The visa, which ought to be here any day now (I applied on February 12th), hasn't arrived yet, so that I will hardly be able to get a ticket before Easter. There is absolutely no doubt that I'll get it in the next few days, but it does make me terribly angry. I'm so boundlessly happy now, looking forward to seeing you, that every day of delay is annoying. I'm writing only *to fervently implore you* not to be insulted or angry with me. It will be only a few more days. Friedl is very ill and will not be able to come for another two weeks. So you'll have to cancel her room for now (but of course, she will need one later on). As for me, it's best to tell them right away that I won't be able to be there by Wednesday. As soon as I have the visa and can buy a ticket, I'll wire you when I will be in St. Hilaire. Then I'll count on spending only three days in Paris on my way to you. But it could be that by then, I'll only be able to get a ticket to leave England on the Tuesday or Wednesday after Easter. Don't be impatient, my dear, dear Georg. I say that although I'm impatient myself. I'm so afraid the delay will cast a shadow over our reunion. I'm bringing lots of things to read to you.

I've received the letter from Nissim[565] inviting me for the entire time. If it's no trouble, I'd be glad if you could *quickly* write me a letter in English as well, stressing how much you would like to see me again on account of your illness, after nine years apart, and that of course I would be your guest for 2 or 3 months in Paris and St. Hilaire. Please write *legibly*, and state explicitly that you are my brother, because in Nissim's letter, one can't read *anything* and his name is not even in there. It's better for the English officials if I have it *clearly* written down. Please use sanatorium stationery. Your answer can easily be here by Saturday. Exit permissions for the general public are not valid until May 1st.

Farewell. I feel as though I'm there with you already, and I'm happy we'll be by ourselves at first.

Your brother Elias

Veza to Georges · *March 28, 1948*

Mrs. V. Canetti
14 Crawford Street
London W1

March 28. Sunday

Dearest Georg,

God willing, Canetti will leave here at 9:20 a.m. on Thursday and will be at the Gare du Nord by 6:10. I'm glad he's taking the train. (April 1) He'll stay in Paris until Monday morning and then come to you. He will be by himself. F certainly won't come for at least two more weeks. Since she got an "infection," his verve and enthusiasm for his work are gone. He's also suspicious, and I try to allay his suspicions, but he asks other women too, and they don't.

I have a great favor to ask: he has to have three big lectures ready by the beginning of August. He's read a *bit* of Kafka, less Joyce, and no Proust at all. He has to give the lectures *by heart*, each one an hour long. If he does what he did in Vienna, where his last lecture was canceled—no, postponed—on account of "illness" (!), it will be the end of him here and he will lose his best friends. But if you value my life, I ask you to urge him to complete the lectures. He's not so young anymore, and learning a lecture in a foreign language by heart will take some time. My nerves can't take having to admonish him continually from this distance. I'll die of shame if he doesn't do it. Ask him to *read them aloud* to you; of course he'll tell you every day that he's still working them.

I would like him to stay at least three months, in St. Hilaire as much as possible. Here, his parasites keep him from working, his "admirers" from Prague,[566] a pack of miserable snoops. Ask him about them. He's put all his connections at their disposal. They are predictably irritating and have made him predictably unpopular.

I'm writing to Contou that the translator should call him *before* Monday, because of course he wants to postpone this as much as possible. It will be so wonderful not to have to be a slave driver for a few weeks! In Paris, he should have his 80 books shipped to you. They're still there, assuming his good friend returns them to him.

Please forgive this letter, but I'm having a hard time of it. He's his own worst enemy; I could murder all the others.

Regine was here again and I invited the doctor over (he was leaving for the Isle of Wight). Canetti was much amused when she burst out that she would like to go away for two days as well, and the doctor recommended Bournemouth. He said the island was too far. Of course, one feels awfully sorry for her at such moments, but I'm already Claudine's *gouvernante*, by which I don't mean housekeeper, which is definitely not a good translation. Because housekeeper is an historic word and she ought to look up in Don Quixote how h. is translated, certainly not as *gouvernante*. Jacqueline has already said she's coming in April, and then I'll be a procuress.[567] I'm afraid I'll have run out of zest by then.

Please see to it that Canetti doesn't discover any patients there whose lives he feels compelled to save and then doesn't do his own work. He's always happy to find touching pretexts and sometimes he outright convinces the dying to play along with him so he doesn't have to do anything. That sounds harsh, but you'll see what I mean. This isn't a letter for you; one for you will follow shortly, but I'm constantly in France now in any event and don't know why I should have to write you. He's not bringing anything with him *at all*, and it's even a battle with the razor blades, but Claudine will help.

Best wishes and I wrote to Nissim, but if you see him, you'll tell him when C. is arriving anyway.

All my love,
Peggy

Your letter just arrived and Canetti is very happy. He's going to be with Nissim only until Monday and on the way back, he'll stay in a hotel and there will certainly be no reason for Nissim to get annoyed. It's more likely he can help him and he won't need anything from him.[568] He also knows that Lucienne must not catch sight of F.

Elias to Georges · *April 4, 1948*

Sunday

My dear Georg,

I'm ashamed that I've left you without a letter up to now. But you can hardly imagine the bustle I live in. On my very first day here, I ran into Honor Frost. She was delighted, and that night, we went to Nissim's theater[569] together. I think she found it quite entertaining. I haven't had a minute to myself. I had just arrived when Nissim promised to wire you about the condition of the little one,[570] but I haven't been able to find out if he actually did. She's very much improved, the nurse is excellent, and the fever has passed. She cries lustily; the whole house revolves around her. Lucienne looks very good. —It wasn't possible to live at your place. There's not even a gas stove there.

I succeeded in hiding from the relatives until Friday evening. I'll tell you a funny story about how I finally betrayed my presence. —On Wednesday at 2:30, Honor left by plane for London. The night before, we went for a five-hour walk—until 4 a.m.—through the darkened streets of Montmartre. It was wonderful: the buildings, the solitary trees, the stillness, and that terribly unhappy girl (a very lovely creature with a death mask) to whom I never can get any closer. When I'm with her, it always feels like I'm walking beside a drowned woman.

Friedl arrived two hours after Honor's departure, plump as a dumpling, a moonface of a woman. She and I have quite a small room in an old hotel with a lot of atmophere, the Hôtel des Saints Pères, and during these few days, I've been happier than ever before. Her parents have really spoiled her. She has beautiful clothes and no longer looks so bedraggled. She's quite childlike and playful again. She has shed her intellectual image as if I had never made it into one of her attributes. She speaks German and English with a Viennese accent as if I had never known her to speak otherwise. She is still very exhausted from her illness and must lie down for many hours a day. I sit next to her as if at the bedside of a sick child and answer her silly questions by the millions. She knows that all this will last only a few more days, and perhaps it is her remarkable lightness and insouciance, which I have never experienced before, that make me so happy. You know, for the first time in my life, I feel like a normal human being, as if we were both in a Renoir painting in Provence. Oh Georg, grant me, grant me these few days. Don't write alarmed or worried letters to anyone about them. Don't spoil them for me by thinking badly of me. I have such an intense relationship with you that a critical look, a disapproving thought could smash everything to bits.

William Glock is coming to Paris on Tuesday and I need to see him. So I won't reach you in the sana. until Wednesday or Thursday at the latest.

I had another meeting with my translator. She made an excellent impression on me. She's overjoyed to be able to continue the work and has accepted most of your suggested revisions. She has a deep, passionate love for the book and I now think it couldn't have fallen into better hands. I'll see Contou tomorrow. Yesterday I had lunch with Elias. We talked about nothing but you—justifiably so.

Au revoir until Wednesday or Thursday; an embrace from

ELIAS

VEZA TO GEORGES · *April 1948*

Georg,

Please, dear child, write me at once if the curriculum was not sent off on the 15th. Because the readers and the publisher assume that he looks like Kien, with a crooked nose, and that won't help him. I'm expecting great things from Germany. Even before, he had the most fabulous reviews there. I forgive you everything since receiving your charming letter. If only he weren't his own prison. Always get him to tell you everything about F. Do *not* show him this letter. Unfortunately, he's the most distinguished character alive, too good for the times. Will write soon, must take the negative[571] to the post office. Have written the publisher[572] about you and your work. Perhaps they also translate scientific works.

Much love. Your letter was a Proust. For your benefit, he has already lived in St. Hilaire, except that it was Combray.

Peggy
is my Lucky Name

Elias to Georges · *April 17, 1948*

Saturday

My beloved Georg,

This is the most beautiful place[573] I've ever seen in my life, an old castle town on a rock with views in all directions out over the parceled fields of Provence. I'm staying in a huge room way up in a castle tower. One feels free and peaceful and detached from world events. The inhabitants are remarkable as well, their faces most impressive and sometimes unbelieveably beautiful. I will have much to tell you. Mail is not collected frequently here, on Saturday and Sunday not at all. So this letter won't be picked up until Monday and will reach you by Tuesday at the earliest.

On Monday, my friends[574] are taking me to a big market in Cavaillon; on Tuesday we drive to Les Baux, Arles, and Tarascon. Avignon was wonderful, but nothing, really nothing can compare to this place. I will have to come back here again. I think there can be no better place to work. I'll send you a postcard from Gordes. We were there yesterday, but Ménerbes is much more beautiful.

I shall arrange to travel on Thursday and arrive on the late evening bus. But if I don't show up by shortly after 7:00, you'll know that I had to stay overnight somewhere, and I won't arrive until Friday.

I've been thinking a lot about our conversations, and it's quite remarkable: your essay on the Jews[575] made a particularly strong impression on me. Out of fear for the safety of you and the others, I perhaps developed too much in the opposite direction during the war. My resistance to the *tenor* of your essay (not to its contents or form) was very strong while you were reading it; you must have sensed that. Now, in retrospect, I am *personally* thankful to you. Your approach is freer than mine; on this point you have kept yourself *broader* than I. I wouldn't say I have completely rid myself of an almost subconscious Jewish "chauvinism" yet, but at least the boil is lanced—and high time, too. I like being there with you so much, even though I often get on your nerves, and I'm already looking forward to visiting you in France again. —Maybe Friedl will come to St. Hilaire for two weeks in early May after all. I think you will simply find her amusing. —I always see you in my mind's eye as you were the last time, at the "Concours."[576] I'm so pleased by how fair you are in weighing everything up—oh, devil take it all, I'd like to say a thousand sweet things to you. You'll just have to wait until I can do so in person. I can hear the voices from the sana., how they call out your name with so much hope, and I'm happy for you.

Elias

VEZA TO ELIAS · *April 18, 19, and 20, 1948*

Mrs. V. Canetti
14 Crawford Street
London W1

April 18, Sunday

Dearest Bauscherl,

When I asked Kae during her German lesson to explain what a *faulty action* was,[577] she said, "Well I suppose, if I forget my bag here, it means, that I'd love to come again."[578] And then she left and forgot her hat. She's completely under my spell, for she's madly in love with you. She came back today with Bruce to get her hat. If Bruce was once the ugly Communist, he must have changed a great deal. He's nice and smart and overawed. I told him that Canetti is a nobody in France because he's with his brother, who's a celebrity in France where they know only the Docteur. *It's my way of rubbing it in to them and it worked.*[579] Say that as succinctly in German. On the other hand, some English expressions make me quite nervous, for example, *disembark*, such a negation of an affirmation. The word annoyed me to death in the report on Musso.[580] Kae will come again tomorrow. She looks so sweet that I will go for a walk in the sun with her, which is a pleonasm because Kae herself is so golden. Can't you find a publisher for Georg's essay on the Jews? What about Droin (who's going to call you up in Paris), or with Arthaud? At the moment, the English are interested only in anti-Jewish books, but luckily they're forbidden by the censor. I wish I could read it. I've witnessed the same thing myself: Georg enthroned before his disciples. I think that's why he's sick.

I urge you to read Proust right away. By the time you've read to page 350, all his characteristic elements are there and most of the figures have been introduced. To say nothing of the pleasure: the first volume is flawless. The same paradox is repeated again and again, for example in the first volume, when Swann is extremely clever in conversation with a duchess, but struggles greatly "when the fair is in humble circumstances. Just as it is not by other intelligent men, that an intelligent man is thought a fool, so it is not by the great gentlemen but by boors and 'bounders' that a man of fashion is afraid of finding his social value underrated."[581] This Swann, by the way, prefers to sleep with "her grace's maid."[582] Which I wouldn't have thought, having begun with volume 2.

Bauscherl, even though I'm a fervid fan of Georg's, he wrote me that letter only at your request—I'm thinking of the gripping passages about me—and I won't correspond with him again—properly and as always, à la Walpole (who wasn't as crass as I am)—until you are back home and I have material for him, because who provides better material than you? There's no one here now for me to pick on, because Georg isn't familiar with the characters here. If you don't have those essays drafted by the time you get back, I have an exit strategy ready. I'll go to Vienna, Honey, I've still got it in me. I won't stick around to watch you dash it off at the last minute and go to D. trembling with fear.[583] You didn't mention the curriculum and you're not in a very good mood, Bauscherl. Maybe it will be better when you're with Georg. How was the brains trust? Did Georg giggle and not know anything? The sana. seems to be wonderful. Everyone admires it. It's just like him to get another new suit already. Put it on and let it get covered with snow.

I'm going to the Doc's for tea today with the Kaplans, "a pleasure," as you are wont to remark. Since I can't think of anything impertinent to say, I'll tell you that Adler's works[584] are "sterile" and any poem of yours is better, stranger, and greater than his about the lotus blossom in the pig's bladder. I'll mail this letter tomorrow so it will get to St. Hilaire just when you do. Georg definitely writes like Proust and is probably a poet. Although he's always staring at microbes, they stand for the sea. He actually would like to explore the sea, "but they didn't recognize him" and gave him a goldfish bowl.

April 19, Monday

So, the tea party yesterday was even more boring. The topic: the Jews.[585] Mrs. Kapi said the terrorists[586] were to blame for everything and I said, "Shooting hostages is the worst and most abominable crime by far."[587] I thought nothing of it, but it's one of Back's set phrases and I just pinned it on. Mr. Kaplan said, "We owe the terrorists such a debt of gratitude we ought to send them . . ." and then he thought better of it. It seemed safer just to owe them thanks. "We are indebted to them," he corrected himself. And the Doc picked up the *Statesman*[588] and began to read three columns aloud, and they deserved it. "Za vef of hetraid . . ."[589] I didn't mind, because I wasn't listening anyway, and I said, "Ja, der *Statesman*."

Even though you believe only a hundredth of what was in your last letter, be careful, Bauscherl. Regine would believe anything you wrote. I have to say, by the way, that despite her degenerate state there's still a trace of yearning, nobility, and love that never forces itself on you. In all fairness, she loves Georg, and I don't think she will ever show it, but she is there for him. As for you—you write life, but your own life is a slip of the pen—and everything in your letter is phony. By the way, be on your guard: the old man is coming to Paris on the 13th and will be there for four days. Don't show your face at Merkel's beforehand, and try to not be in Paris at all. He sent the young Merkel to Daniels who was supposed to give him advice, but Daniels is so miserly that he advised him *against* it. (He wanted to take a position in a hospital *here*, a stupid idea, for his English is nonexistent and he makes a very bad impression. He should go to Vienna.) I had him ask Daniels why he doesn't write to Georg. He claims he just wrote him. Dr. Kaplan was terribly disappointed that you were in France. Try to be more cheerful, Bauscherl. I hope you had a good time in Provence. I'll close now so the letter can reach St. H. by the 22nd.

The most beautiful wishes to both of you,
Donna Venetia.

Tuesday

Kae had a glazed look in her eye today and was dull and shrunken. Bruce is no miserable snoop and they say he's never spoken so much in his entire life as he has here. The only funny thing at the Boston Tea Party was a discussion of cured ham, but I ran off after that. The old man claimed that the only properly smoked ham was from Poland and Dr. Kaplan declared that smoking hams was like giving anesthetic. *We* give an injection *here*, an injection *there*, until it's well-done—but here in England, they don't smoke the ham all the way through. Whereupon I opted to have my supper in a Baker Street restaurant that you don't like, although Georg would. Across from me sat a hussy with large eyes but the piercing glance of a bird. Since such eyes are rare here, I was fascinated and noticed to my astonishment that the weak creature was hypnotizing me. It was strange, for she was quite unconscious of it and couldn't have imposed her will even on a cat. The effect was like that of a dynamo. Proust, too, has me enthralled. Another important point is the way he expresses everyday things so exquisitely that you're willing to accept them. For instance, the way Swann sees a beautiful bouquet or a brooch in a shop window and immediately sends it to Odette because he thinks she will like it, too, and then she'll always be reminded of him when she looks at it. He's not afraid to do this often, and the effect is quite novel. To Swann, by the way, Odette looks like Zipporah, Jethro's daughter in one of the Sistine frescoes.[590]

All my love. I'm mailing this letter now so it arrives in St. on the 22nd. Jacqueline is here . . . the baby is still alive and has pains in its ears. Most 3-pound babies in England are quite normal after 4 months.

Veza

Please: 4 Nuremb. Trials![591]

❦

VEZA TO GEORGES · *April 21, 1948*

Mrs. V. Canetti
14 Crawford Street
London W1

April 21

Dearest Georg,

I'm not writing you proper letters right now because for once, I'd like to dream just for myself. I can't do that when Bauscherl is here; then I have to *think* all the time so that *he* can dream—and think about what? "Did he send the curriculum?" for example. Which, unfortunately, you won't do for me. You are Proust and I will leave you; what I long for is a tax official, or for all I care a chick sexer or a tea taster. I would like his picture to appear in the catalogue so people won't think he's a hook-nosed Hebrew. That would influence the critics and bookstore owners, especially in Germany. And how is the lecture coming? I've been copying half of Proust to make it palatable for him. And what about the analysis (for this is a business letter)? Did you finish it already? Don't lie to me about it, because he'll lie to you about it. The apothecary had no reason to find sugar. Please find out yourself if people are interested in the aphorisms and help me get him to allow them to be published in Germany, for then he will at least have salvaged his reputation here in England. Please be a little nice to me. I'm determined to go to Vienna so that I can dream. All I really want now is a barrel,[592] but for *me* as I am, not distorted, as I am not. Don't be angry, just help me. I think you would have become a Swann, except you were lucky (as Broch believes) to get sick and become a Proust instead. Moreover, it doesn't matter if you free the world from a plague, for "the Lord looks after his own."[593] He'll look after both of you, but only you deserve your great gifts.

All my love, and if you don't write, I won't write either, not even business letters.

Your Peggy

Odette is very much like F.

VEZA TO GEORGES · *April 26, 1948*

April 26

Dearest Georges,

I'm writing in great haste, for I must go to the silver wedding,[594] not the wedding, that's over, but the king will drive by here. You understand that it's important. After all I've read in volume 7 of Proust, I assume it will be a pleasure for you to listen to the heartbeat of the beautiful Canetti lad, and it will be a great relief for me. Please take it seriously. Perhaps my worries are exaggerated, but I don't see how, what with your *father*[595] and your brother's fainting spells every three months, which he will deny. Can you overcome your disdain for other cases, which you regard as little critters crawling around, and examine his heart despite the analysis? I'll never be able to get him anywhere near a doctor again, and he does *not* look well. But believe me, he's *lively*. I admire you enormously on account of Proust; somehow it's *you* who wrote it. In the second half, it becomes even more powerful. Please, I'll never ask for anything again, but examine the scalawag and take a look at his feet. The latter purely for aesthetic reasons, because they have a classical beauty. And don't be so indignant that Canetti is handsome, too. It's not so clearly visible in him; he doesn't stretch out lengthwise as much as you. The chapter about inverts[596] is so masterfully written that you think the Greek statues in the British Museum are in love with each other, and yet it's not at all aesthetic.

I do much more for *your* family, Jacqueline is here with me . . .

All my inverted[597] Love,

Peggy

Elias to Veza · *May 3, 1948*

Monday

My Türmchen, most beloved creature,

Your two letters just arrived and I'm terribly ashamed. Your arguments are as loving and tender as ever. I don't know what gave me the foolish suspicion that everything had to do with Steiner. I formally beg your forgiveness. You can see that I have given in to you on essentials of the curriculum vitae, which now ends with the aphorisms. I hope you can still use the curriculum. It would be a shame to have done it for nothing. It's quite good, don't you agree? I assume the people at the publisher's won't slip me in behind Jahnn[598] in the new catalogue. In the old catalogue, I got shoved in at the last minute and I think it turned out quite well, considering. My dear, quiet little Türmchen, you have to understand that I was a bit annoyed at those people. I suddenly had the feeling that Weismann wanted to get out of *Hochzeit*.[599] Upon calmer consideration, I agree with you that he will print it with my own afterword. I couldn't have asked for anything better than such an opportunity. Once and for all, I shall explain my dramatic principles, and you can count on me to do it *well*.

If you only knew how much letters mean to me in this backwater! A letter from you is like getting the whole wide world. When all is said and done, London is marvelous and there's nowhere else I would rather live, *nowhere*, and you won't budge from London, either. You can't scare me with Vienna: *you won't go there under any circumstances*. Everything will work out wonderfully. With you, nothing can fail for me. I'm not really sad, but I am somewhat dazed and in a strange way spellbound by Georg and by the atmosphere in this sanatorium. What I would like most is to sit down and write a book about him. Sometimes I think I really do love him as much as I love you—but that isn't entirely possible. Oh, if only he gets better, if only he gets better! Everyone here lives from his ideas. All the younger doctors ask him for suggestions for their research projects. And in the midst of all that, he is so totally unassuming, treats everyone like a human being, is so wise and broad-minded. He's superior to me in a hundred ways, and perhaps I'm only more of a poet than he because he's free of these terrible fears I have. If the three of us could live together, it would be my dream come true, my greatest hope, my yearning, my commitment, and our *good fortune*. The idea of a shared house in the South of France where Georg could always come to convalesce, where you could escape the English winter, where I could work, where you would also work on your own things again (there, one is forced to do so)—he was very pleased with the idea. I have the feeling that it will be realized, perhaps in the not-too-distant future. —Dearest Türmchen, for God's sake please keep writing *de-*

tailed letters. With Friedl coming soon, I need your letters more than ever, long letters, with your best wishes and astute observations. I can't understand why, but I'm not looking forward to her visit anymore. If she had come last month, it would have been fun. Now I'm so preoccupied with Georg that everything else is actually a distraction.

In half an hour, my bus leaves for Grenoble and from there I'll take the night train to Paris. I'll mail this letter in Paris so it reaches you sooner.

O Türmchen, Türmchen, how I love this Proust! I'm more than grateful to you for reading him so closely. He's so dense that I can't possibly read more than two volumes completely, and I would be lost without your helpful *precision*. You'll see, I will write *wonderful* lectures and I'll get many, many more engagements, and we shall have a nice income. Don't worry: I intend to *work* as never before. Georg has saved himself by work, and he's right to keep telling me that the only salvation from my anxiety is work.

Farewell, my sweetest Veza, my girl. Your words have something so noble about them. *I repeat*, I envy Georg every letter he's ever had from you and I love him so much that I wish him a *thousand*! more letters from you.

Your yearning, thankful
Gog,[600] who asks your
forgiveness.

Beginning on Saturday, mail your letters to me in St. Hilaire again.

Elias to Georges · *May 3, 1948*

Grenoble, May 3, 1948

My dear Georg,

You will think me quite ridiculous for already writing you from Grenoble, but I'm very ashamed of the scene I made this noon. It's really your bad luck that I get my mail before you do and then read it. You need to know that I pick up every unopened letter in mortal fear—to say nothing of two or three at a time from people who mean so much to me!

My first impulse after reading Veza's letter was to return to London immediately. Of course one calms down after a few hours. But it seemed so important to you that I not stay in France too long that I'm a bit frightened. Maybe I did tire you out a lot after all, or working on the translation is getting on your nerves. Please write me in Paris and tell me candidly if that's the case. If it is, I will of course never mention the translation again. You must not think that I've been going through it with you merely for convenience's sake. In the *car*,[601] I was thinking about why working with you like this makes me so happy—happier than anything else since I got to France. I think it's because you're *teaching* me things in my own domain of language. There have been years of my life—the ones of my greatest influence on you—when I dreamed of nothing but a *genuine* collaboration between the two of us. That it has now become possible, and precisely because of the two different linguistic cultures we live in, seems like my wish is beginning to come true. Besides, I'm happy about anything in which you're my superior. I have no "theory" about that. Find one yourself.

Mme. Cohen[602] was standing outside the exit of the funicular and greeted me like an old friend. She has a childlike intimacy which I like very much. For a moment, I was sorry she wasn't coming to Grenoble with me.

Dear, dear Georg, recuperate well from my visit. May I also tell you that you're completely right about the name-dropping. I do it all the time; Veza encourages it, but Marie-Louise is embarrassed when I start doing it in company. I only protested because it's so true, and I'm going to stop doing it. Farewell, and write soon.

Your brother Elias

VEZA TO GEORGES · *May 7, 1948*

Mrs. V. Canetti
14 Crawford Street
London W1

May 7, 1948

Dearest child,

All I can say is: you're telling *me*! Your assessment of him is completely correct, but you passed it in anger, just as I did when I wrote that letter, which I regretted in retrospect because he is so vulnerable. He's just as you picture him, but without the contemptible motives. Believe me, he's immature, an enchanting, brilliant child. That's why I was forced to turn into a Fury and I can assure you I'm absolutely right about the "aphorisms." Kierkegaard was starving[603] until he produced something that was a "seller." That has an ugly sound to you up there on your heights, but since he needs peace and quiet to write his marvelous works, I'm not asking him to write the "Diary of a Seducer" like Kierkegaard, just to *print* what he's already written. Germany pays him in sterling. Of course, it would be easier for him if he didn't have to take care of me as well. On the other hand, he has to, because he had me so run-down I couldn't take care of myself, and it's only since he's left that I've been doing everything for myself. I didn't have the courage until *now*. I didn't even answer requests for my own works because it was so terribly hard to take care of all his correspondence and business. There's a *germ* of truth in what I wrote him about Amersham, and yet it's not his fault—that's how a real poet is. Goethe was forever breaking down, and he was rich. So it's no wonder that *he* is the same; he was born into such frightful times and has had to struggle so hard. Just read what he has to say about you, how noble, how insightful, how *fair* it is. He wants always to be fair and that's why he never defends *himself* and he's a saint, believe me. Unfortunately, he's behaved the same way toward that barnyard trollop. But you will see . . . what you will see. He won't read Proust anymore; he'll work on *her* novel instead. And as for the other two authors, he's read perhaps ten pages of Kafka and twenty of Joyce. Nevertheless, his lecture will be brilliant—for the audience. The only thing I fear is their questions. You can't answer questions about Proust; the sentences and allusions are not simple. Do you know what? He gave me Proust to read, starting with the second volume. The first was missing. He said it didn't matter, and of course I didn't understand that marvelous work. Now I'm making a point of always telling him about it so that he finds it appealing. Scenes like the one at the Guermantes' get him excited. Please be *kind* to him again and do *not* yell at him. If you do it just once, I'll be grateful to you, because it will give him pause. And how right you are with your plan! It's just the thing! It could be his salvation if he follows it! I pestered him here for months: Work on the lectures! It's not just 50 pounds but thousands of pounds! He can repeat them ten times here in England, including on the BBC. Meanwhile, I'll translate them. He can take them on tour to the continent. He can have them printed. In England, *one* essay earns him a fortune. He will produce nothing and then I shall collapse. I'm certainly a melancholic but I have very manic times too, like now, when I've initiated a hundred different things. And several of them will succeed, like the deal with Germany, which I've done behind his back. He said the publisher was too unknown! I yelled at him: Make them famous! The famous publisher Knopf did nothing for him because it didn't need to champion his book. If something doesn't sell, they have a hundred other things that will. This *unknown* publisher will *have* to champion him because they don't have any other famous authors yet. What a struggle, what disputes—then he was overjoyed that the plays will finally appear in book form. I had to write the German publisher that *you* had sent the author's biography. I couldn't expose him. I followed your advice and sent only the dates. I should have remembered that he likes to make a big scene at first, get up on his high horse, and then is very happy to have his bio appear and ends up writing it after all. And now, on account of that wench, he won't want to see the charming Mr. Glock in Paris, although he's been such a help and arranged the lectures for him and will do even more. *Eminent* Englishmen envy him this association. But I'm serious, my child, that if he fails to write the lecture, I'm leaving for Vienna. I swear to you. You know how I worship him. I'm happy he's away. I breathe a sigh of relief. I become myself again. I was a bundle of fears, worries, helplessness, like him. After twenty years of drudgery, it's contagious. I have no one to talk to about him, for of course, I'd never expose him to a soul, and so he's the angel and I'm the devil, which doesn't bother me at all, but my soul has become devilish by now. That Steiner fellow sat here with him for two days out of every week. Canetti basically loathes him, but out of pity sits with him from noon to eleven p.m., gets nothing done, Steiner leaves with some good ideas he's written down for himself, and Canetti is left with a breakdown. The following day, he sees him again because he "pities" him. I can't go on like this, believe me. *I* have certainly been a misfortune for him, but he has been one for me, too, and I never would have fallen so low if I hadn't had to threaten suicide in A. each time so that he would at least dictate some of his work (first of all, so I know that it really exists, and second, because he writes everything in a kind of shorthand only he can read and no secretary could ever decipher).[604] Please forgive me and destroy this letter immediately. You've always been our salvation. Save him now and keep an eye on his Dulcinea[605] as well. See if she isn't with him just so that he'll write her novel. Put her to the test, please. He's the unluckiest person I've ever seen, and all on account of his childlike, touching weakness. I'm sorry if I influenced you by my angry outburst. It was undeserved; he does without everything himself so he can provide a good life for me. I would like him to go to Strasbourg. It can only help. And then he should return to you in St. Hilaire by June 15th and write the lectures there. Ah Georg, if you only knew! I have these scenes every month and I'm petrified because I tell myself how sick your father was.[606] He himself has *hypotension*, which was already diagnosed in Vienna, and in addition he won't *listen* to me anymore and I can't go on. Don't let him leave without a plan. Don't let him leave without having read at least some of Proust. Quiz him every day in St. H. Speak with Dulcinea in private, flirt with her, anything to get him to work. When he gets back here, there will be a hundred friends lying in wait for him, first and foremost that emetic Steiner. He'll get nothing done here with Marie-Louise hanging around his neck. She really thought I was threatening suicide "so that he wouldn't get a divorce!" And she herself gives him exactly the same "medicine." Because that's what she calls it when I do it. I often long for postal workers, bookkeepers, people who work with numbers, pedantry, order, just because everything in him is so chaotic and it's made me the same way. Without you, he'll call off the lectures because F. will write that she doesn't love him, or she'll come here and be up to her old tricks again, start having affairs, then he'll lose his zest for life and won't care a thing for reputation, money, fame. I've experienced it all, and *how*. I've pleaded for the goodwill of that harlot so she would come and not leave him to die in his own bed before my very eyes, to die on the telephone, calling her up when she isn't there. Swann is a boxer compared to what Canetti has done for that selfsame wench. Please don't say a word to him about this letter. I know you and I assume I have your word of honor. Help us, save us as in Vienna!!! We know what you mean to us. Read his letter and send it back to me. Such a dear sweet letter! And how sweetly he writes me and of course, I was unfair. What can one do with someone who's *afraid*, terribly afraid, to go to a consulate, to say nothing of the police? M-L, for example, knows about this fear and knows she only needs to threaten him with a scandal. He doesn't really like her but can't get free. All his parasites know about his fear and exploit it. The night before he left, I was up until 1:00 a.m. writing letters for other people. Our own business didn't get done.

If it weren't a question of money, I would put up with it. His motives are benevolent, nothing but benevolent. If the reason he's already going to return in May is because he needs English tobacco for his pipe, write at once and I'll send him tobacco with Jacqueline—just as long as he stays there. You know how much I love him, but I'd be overjoyed if he were to stay there for half a year. People here think I must have a lover because I'm so rejuvenated, refreshed, and cheerful since he's been gone. That's a terrible thing to say about the best and most charming person who's ever lived. You must read his letter from Paris before *she* arrives. The poor fellow is in heaven. He's worshipping a stone!

I won't write you again until he's back in England. It just won't work, you understand. Thank God Charlus is back at his machinations, because Albertine is just too tedious. I live more in Proust than in real life. Bless you—health, happiness—you have much more happiness to come.

All my love,
Peggy

Veza to Georges · *May (?) 1948*

Dearest Georg,

So, there's been another operation you've elided as if it were just snowflakes. Those are obviously the "few tenths more" about which you are sure to leave me in suspense again. But I'm going to slip away to Vindobona.[607] I'm determined to, since my only ally[608] has already fallen for that nebulous baloney. I'm not reproaching you. You were weak before the operation, and in his presence, everyone turns weak. It's his allure, and I wish I could write my memoirs and entitle them "Xantippe." Readers would shed tears over Xantippe's fate.

When I read Proust, I think I'm reading you and that's why I prefer music even to Proust, because it's already a fulfillment, but Proust makes me so sick with longing—for myself, for what I *used to be*, for beauty, luxury, paintings, duchesses, aperçus, and that Attic salt totally absent from conversation here. However clever the English may be, they're never dreamy. You're a very great personage, for you have within you all those things I just enumerated. Just get better soon, and love yourself as much as you love others. You didn't inherit quite enough self-preservation instinct *either*. Your brother has absolutely none. Perhaps because he is going to be immortal after all—a word that makes me *tremble* with painful emotion about this dream. When will the next war be and who will survive it? Today, I'm worried about Palestine[609] and I have the faint hope that it will be as it was in Russia[610] and the Jews will suddenly march forth. The *faint* hope. You know my views. The result—you've discovered it for yourself, just like me—disappearance, annihilation. Please have a heart and tell me how you are, my faithful subject. With destructive, wicked, proud imperiousness,

Veza.

Elias to Georges · *May 27, 1948*

Thursday

My dearest Georg,

Seeing Strasbourg again has been a terrible disappointment. The people I once knew so well are nothing but tedious, smug burghers. I wish I hadn't come here. One should never revisit any place or person—*except you*. Everything else should remain a memory.

I'm writing you today only to ask you to put a stamp on the enclosed letter—an *airmail* stamp (24 francs)—and mail it on Saturday at 2:00. It's my last letter to Marie-Louise from St. Hilaire, so to speak.

I'll write you a real letter in a few days. On Monday I shall be in Paris, for three days, I think.

Strasbourg cathedral is still standing, but many other things have been destroyed. The terrible thing is that I'm not really even sorry

Georges Canetti

because I find the people so unbearably common and low. Madeleine Cohn is the only one I still like. Be well and forgive this hasty letter. Hoepffner is waiting for me downstairs.

A hug from your brother
Elias.

Veza to Georges · *June 10, 1948*

Mrs. V. Canetti
14 Crawford Street
London W1

June 10

Dearest Benjamin,

I don't think a few germs showing up again is so bad. If you weren't a doctor, you'd know that everybody has some germs at one time or another. But write how you feel anyway; I don't need to tell you it's important to us because it weighs you down. Wouldn't it be possible for you to come visit us? I'm keeping this apartment until at least January 1949 and I would cook for you. Although after France, your brother finds everything here awful, all the things I cook taste delicious to me, that's how bad everything I don't cook is. At least it will be a change and nourishing. Three times a week, I cook for the scalawag, and until Oct. it's not so bad because we can still get fruits and vegetables.

His trip to Strasbourg was not what he expected, but it was nice for me because Herr Hoe. sent me the most delightful thing (completely forgetting that I'm *fair, fat, and fifty*[611]), namely seven enchanting tiny little Chinese figures, each one delicately carved and painted and a centim. tall. And in addition, he's given me an assignment to send him a "Letter from London" once a month. "Then you can accumulate some francs for yourself," he had Canetti tell me. That's all, but I'm happy he was there. We owed it to the dear old gentleman. Your brother came to me on Sunday aftern., dead tired, a sleepless night—he expressed himself more drastically. He complained about F. for two days. On the third, he took some of it back. Yesterday he was in despair because he had no news, and today, overjoyed when a letter arrived in which she loves him passionately and unfortunately plans to come tomorrow or Tuesday. Maybe on Tuesday, in which case she'll come with his rival. That will be a great relief for me, because then he may write his lectures after all. So far he's *only* been tired and exhausted and fearful. He was already afraid when he arrived at my place, for example, because they stamped some official phrase on his passport which they stamp on everybody's passport and which doesn't mean a thing. Then he was afraid that F. would come, then that she wouldn't come, and now, that she's coming. And he was on the telephone all day for several days, but no one wants to rent her a room, no matter how much money she has, because of something he didn't discuss with you and would never admit to you. It's what you find repellent in her face, namely, that it doesn't bother her to see her cousin fire the charwoman for stealing, even though it wasn't the char. who stole the purse. He'll discuss this quite openly with me and her cousin, but otherwise he protects her and would sooner call me "nuts." But that's understandable. I hope she doesn't bring with her the child she had with Nemetz,[612] but we could even pay for that. The legally mandated support payment is not too large and your brother can add a voluntary payment, but only when he has the money. It was easy to see that she would have "thrown herself"[613] at you, too, as you put it, but she always had a weakness for you and you have a weakness for her, but weaknesses are your *strength*. Your brother also realized that it's better to leave you alone with your roués in the evening. I didn't like the ones in Chat. Charlus had a better time of it, despite his gray thatch. He was more in love with criminals and was able to pay them well. Do you remember the lavatory attendant's monologue? The only other person who could have written that is Canetti.

I'm not going to write you a long letter because you're so mean and I'm not about to cast pearls before inverts. I've perfumed it with your Chanel Numero 5, which Bauscherl actually purchased for me along with egg liqueur bonbons and dried bananas, which was very sweet of him. Your perfume is especially delightful. I don't dare touch it; I can smell it even when the bottle is closed. I sent you honey with Jacqueline, who complained that you didn't acknowledge the tea I had sent earlier. But despite the perfume, no "London letter." I get five calls a day from all sorts of Helgas (Helga[614] was here last week and is enchantingly beautiful). I'm going to turn them away today because the scalawag isn't officially back yet.

Now I send you many kisses. I wouldn't dare really kiss you, but in a letter it's considered a nice compliment. You inv's. need these feminine frills. I'll love and bless you forever, in the first place just because, second because you're Proust, third because you're so smart and handsome—yes, handsome too!—fourth because you have that voice that's gotten huskier in Bauscherl (what with all his disappointments)—and last but not least, because he's made this plan he finds very satisfactory and perhaps I'll send you yet *another* letter, one from him about you that you don't deserve. But only if you write back at once. F. confessed to having two lovers in Sweden. That's worth something and he doesn't need to have such "feelings of guilt toward her." I'll end this now—unwillingly—but out of Albertinian defiance. Wonderful, that misunderstood telegram. Wonderful, the second half of Proust, beginning with the grandmother's death.[615]

Your last letter contained passages of Proustian grandeur as well, but it's not profligacy that disgusts you. Anna would continue to please you although she is much cheaper in this respect, absolutely indiscriminate, but it hasn't completely demoralized her. —I like you because you are *wise*.

Every possible fond wish
Peggy

Can you smell the 5?
Wonderful!
Some of the comedy text (proofsheets) was already here waiting for Bauscherl.

ELIAS TO GEORGES · *June 15, 1948*

June 15, 1948

My dear Georg,

It's been three weeks since we parted; it seems to me like both the blinking of an eye and an eternity. You won't count my short note from Strasbourg, so it *is* an eternity since I last wrote.

Strasbourg was awful. Paris was awful. I don't even care to write about it. "Nagel" insulted me and my plays in the most shameless manner. He has no plans to get them translated. For the time being your color theory seems to be correct. By the time my plays have been produced all over the world (and you will live to see that day), your color theory will explode, but meanwhile, why shouldn't you compare me to Goethe? Unfortunately, it's the first and only time someone has dared to make the comparison, and it will also be the last time and I'll be demoted to just an ordinary successful dramatist, ugh.

I'm feeling better now that I'm back in London. I'm happy to be seriously at work on my lectures. Not only have I worked my way through the entire *Ulysses* again, I'm also back in the midst of Proust. At the risk of even more contempt from you, I'm going to read right through the whole of Proust in the next three weeks. It's possible, even though you don't think so. I clearly recall the only really ugly moment between us: you thought me capable of talking about Proust without knowing his entire work. Well, I *could* do it, but I never would; I have too much respect for him.

My dear, dear Georg, isn't it curious how many thorns still remain in one's flesh? It stings me that you don't think much of my plays. It stings me that I broke down so badly in your presence over those letters (I'm always that way with letters. You didn't read Proust well enough to understand what really happens at times like that). It stings me that I didn't get any work done there. It stings me that you saw that appalling Friedl with me (she just returned to London and is living with Veza, who will chew her up and spit her out in 24 hours). It stings me that I wasn't *alone* with you to the end. There are so many things you *didn't* tell me! It stings me—this is the only one that really hurts—that my presence alone was not enough to make you fit as a fiddle again.

I saw Jojo[616] with the family. His pictures (I saw only three of them) certainly show a lot of talent. Precision and honesty, concentrated austerity of form, together with a fondness for large format that is rare nowadays. It's all a bit dry; his colors come from classical Italian painting. They're beautiful colors, and he owes the most to Braque. It was a pleasant surprise. To tell you the truth, from my memories of his early works, I wasn't expecting *anything*. *How much* is really there it's impossible to say after seeing only three pictures. But don't write him anything except that I was impressed. The family is terrific; I could have invented them myself. Compared to that lukewarm, fatuous, passionless Canetti brood these people are wonderful (the old lady! Aunt Esther! The uncle who's so very *proud*—you should have seen them). I won't be able even to think of the Canettis any more for a couple of years. We ought to change our names. If only I had done so in time. At any rate, I won't allow Veza to call me "Canetti" anymore. My only consolation is that you have the same name. It's easier for you: at least there's no other Georg in the family. Most of all, I'm annoyed by the one whose name is exactly the same as mine, devil take him.

Ever since I left, I've been envying you your peace and quiet. There are many things about you I envy. I wish I had your good sense, your freedom from fear, and not this crazy mixture of softness and generosity that my life has managed to hold together so far. Not that you are less soft, but your softness is fused with loyalty rather than generosity. Don't take this letter too seriously. It's not really a letter yet, just part of a monologue about you and me I've been reciting since I left, a continuous monologue. Next time I'll interrupt it and write a proper letter. In the meantime, write me if you can, but in concrete terms about yourself and everyone there—every person I met, even the most boring.

Farewell. A hug and kiss from your
Elias.

Nissim and Lucienne were in Belgium. I only saw the little one. She's getting on quite well. In retrospect, I hate Paris, just as I always have.

Veza to Georges · *June 24, 1948*

Mrs. Canetti
14 Crawford Str. W1

June 24
twelve o'clock at night

Dearest Benjamin,

You letter was so scintillating and enchanting that I have to write at once, even though it would be better to wait because it's nighttime and I'm not allowed to type (on account of a curious old woman on the second floor). Well, here's what happened: for nine days, your brother was on the telephone looking for rooms, breaking all our agreements to keep his arrival secret. For nine days, he went *begging* to F's *good* friends (!). Nobody wanted her. But since he had loftily told me that in *no* case would she move in with me, I felt sorry for him because he had no one to turn to but me. She stayed with me for a week, drooping lower and lower from her heights. The funny stories and her plans will have to wait for the typewriter to make it easier for me. Mostly, Bauscherl hangs around with her and doesn't get much work done because he has to throw up a smokescreen for M-L and has alerted all our friends, only some of whom I can fend off, and all because F. needs a room. (over)

<on the verso:>
He found an expensive room for rent through friends of *ours* who don't know *her*.

This letter gives an inaccurate, unfair picture of him, except to you. Destroy it right away! Please!

I didn't read all of Proust for him, but I did work through it all, with notes and ideas, etc. And I always told him that I understood everything, had sympathy for the situation, could empathize. *Now*, after I've smoothed the path for him and the shiksa has lived with me, eaten with me, taken baths and slept with him here, I understand *nothing*. If the lectures don't get finished, I'll go to my solicitor and apply for a divorce. This may not seem to you like a serious threat, but it is. M-L. would demand marriage at once, so would F., both with threats. I told him why divorce would be a blessing—for *me* it would be. I'll continue to help him and push him. But *I* shall be the winner only if he doesn't give the lectures—I'll say no more, because it makes me tired. On the second day of her stay here, someone picked her wallet which contained a check for 33 pounds, 3 pounds cash, and documents. She's an indescribably messy person and *I'm* the only one who could get her to finish typing her novel, for which she expects an advance, God willing. Both of them are effusively grateful and emotional. He has two splendid offers—I'll send you the letters—to deliver lectures here in London, all because it's in all the papers that he's going to lecture in B.[617] A cycle, here in London, with *Forster* and the greatest Eng. authors. If he doesn't lecture in B., that's all down the drain. He's already saying he won't be able to finish the other lectures; he has only 2 months for the one with Forster. All he really wants to do is hang around with F. because the painter[618] is coming, and *you* fell for that just as *I* always used to. He's *afraid* of the painter and we've already talked—he and I—about how we will *not* help launch him here. That's *her* main idea. In addition, she told me she definitely wants a child, right now!! He's a bit suspicious, but that may be just an act. I'm ashamed to be answering your witty letter like this, but you're the only person who will feel sorry for him and help save him when I resign my office.

I very much approve of your plan to return to Paris. If you don't overwork yourself, the few germs will soon disappear. The psyche is so important: if it is happy, then the body is happy too and works toward health. Just don't work *a lot*. I think that's something you've added at last to your store of wisdom. That's why I never get terribly worried about you; you're such a magnificent work of art. He talks about you all the time and is even really going to write you every month—he hangs onto you as though you were what is missing in his character. Please destroy this letter. He says that he found all my letters complaining about him at your place and read them. Can that be true? Please answer this question. And now, I want to thank you a million times for Proust; he's my favorite modern author. He is my element, my consolation, my air, my yearning, my fulfillment, my justification, my pride, my salvation. All the exact same things you are too!!! More to come—

Edith wants to move here with husband and child. It wouldn't bother me and the child should make us happy.

I'll get hold of that book you wanted and you can lend it back to me sometime. I'm so crazy about Proust I'm reading him a second time. I no longer want to read anything else but everything he wrote and biographies of him. One just arrived from Paris and seems to be very good.[619]

All my love. Should I send razor blades? Write at once!!!

With love,
Peggy

I would be grateful if you tell him how proud you are that he's going to give a lecture with Forster here in London *as well*. And not a word about my BETRAYAL!

ELIAS TO GEORGES · *Probably June 28, 1948*

Monday

My beloved Georg, one hand is still holding your letter while the other is already compelled to begin an answer. As far as writing is concerned, our roles have been reversed. I awaited your answer in great agitation; my frequent letters are probably beginning to annoy you. You know there's no one else in the whole world I *could* write to without feeling that it's pointless and dishonest. You're the only person who *knows* me and yet perhaps still likes me a little (the women don't count, and besides, one always writes *down* to them).

I'm very concerned that you are suddenly taking a fatalistic attitude toward your illness. For heaven's sake, don't commit yourself to Paris yet. It is a great step forward that you are finally becoming skeptical toward further specific medical interventions. But it's simply criminal to connect your own person with your work and your theories. You are not your own best piece of evidence, nor should you almost always interpret everything as a catastophe (forgive this abbreviated version of your thoughts. You will know what I'm referring to). For God's sake, keep yourself and your whole future life *open*; leave *yourself* out of your theories. Oh, what I wouldn't give for your illness to have no connection to your own work. How can a system like that, with one's self in the middle, be correct? In your own way, you are doing what Nietzsche did, except that your system isn't a process of becoming God—instead, you're turning into a tuberculosis with all its ramifications and possibilities. If you could see that clearly for once, the way I saw it when I was with you—with love, but from the *outside*—perhaps you would resolve to sever the connection between yourself and this dreadful system and then, but only then, would your will to live be strong enough to overcome the illness. Don't think that I say this facilely or heartlessly. It takes courage, but much more courage from you, to acknowledge it, and strangely enough, I'm convinced that you and only you could muster enough courage to do so.

I won't say anything more about it, because it's so deadly serious and important. You could only see it *precisely*, in all its details, if I were to write a story about it, but of course, I can't bring myself to do that. But when you're healthy again, I will do it once, for you alone, and then you will destroy it as the last remnant of your illness.

I have a curious conviction about you. I believe that you will get well because I love you so much, and I'll thank you not to make a face at such an apparently—but only apparently—naive sentence.—

—For two weeks, I've been preparing my lectures, reading nothing but Proust. How could you have said it's impossible to read the novels straight through, one after another? I've finished the first six volumes (*Swann*, *A l'ombre* etc., *Du Côté de Guermantes*) and in addition *Le Temps Retrouvé*. I haven't been this impressed by anything for years. You're right, of course, that the last volume is especially wonderful. The theoretical passages in it are the deepest and most convincing things any artist has ever written about his own method. There's nothing left to interpret. I'll be on my guard against adding too much of my own thoughts. I'm still insulted that you could have assumed even for a moment I would give a lecture on Proust without being familiar with every *syllable* of his work. In the end, the whole point of writing the lecture may be really to absorb the work. My diffidence and hesitation in the face of works like this—in the end, the only thing that counts in the world—is religious in nature. It's the diffidence humans used to have toward God. I don't like to joke around about this. One always prepares for great encounters in the same way: by evading and circling around them. And the enormous, inevitable leap you make when the moment arrives is, I believe, the most legitimate form of veneration.

You really did me an injustice, and did it to me in an area where I am at my most blameless. I can't resist imposing a penance on you. I expect you to make me a present of *the complete Proust in French*. If you want, you can send him two volumes at a time, but I'd prefer having him entire for my birthday, *from you*.

I already have Pierre-Quint's biography.[620] There are exciting things in it about Proust himself.

Perhaps you're right about Paris. But consider the makeup of the family who ruin it for you. Your own name walks its streets every single day, looking like . . .[621] (You know that old story, don't you? About another mix-up and being mistaken for the leader of a jazz band?) I think family is something like a mortal sin. There's nothing more lovely than a mother, a brother, a father, a sister, but each one *singly*. All together in one spot, they're deadly. Their breath stales the air and they suffocate each other. Such a monstrous phenomenon ought to have only *one* representative in every city in the world: *a single* brother, *a single* son, even a single aunt—but *separated by great distances* and never all together. One should have to *seek them out* in their various towns, with effort, and gatherings of the entire clan ought to be prosecuted as conspiracies and punished with incarceration.

You can measure the truth of this by the fact that as rich and undeniably beautiful a city as Paris is, a family can still make it poisonous and gloomy. The next time I come, I only want to see you. For me, you replace all the relatives in the world except for Jojo.

Will you continue to write me about the sanatorium? I would like to know exactly what *everyone* I met there is doing, not just Cohen. I ran into . . .[622] (is that how you spell it?) on the street in Paris. It was pitiful to see how impoverished and sad he was. The sanatorium had enlarged him from a human being into a person. I cannot understand how a fellow like that can stand to go on living afterward. There's something wrong with the whole system of hospitals and sanatoriums. They cure people and then send them back out into the desert. How can you expect them not to die of thirst?

Farewell, my dear, dear Georg. Don't allow your ocean of affection to evaporate too quickly. I'll be satisfied just with the salt that remains, as long as you send some frequently, packed into letters.

Your brother Elias (who still can't contain
himself at the beauty of that word, "brother")

❦

VEZA TO GEORGES · *July 1, 1948*

Mrs. V. Canetti
14 Crawford Street
London W1
Telephone: WELbeck 9334, in case you come

July 1

Dearest Benjamin,

Your brother was thrilled to bits by your charming letter and immediately sent you an equally delightful answer. He's in such a good mood since the *putana*[623] is staying with us that nothing else matters to me. Because in a good mood, he can do anything, and although the lectures aren't any further along than they were in my last, desperate letter, I still hold out hope that he'll write three of them, because now he's really reading Proust, with great enthusiasm, and loves him more than Joyce and Kafka, which proves how talented you are. He just arrived at my place after a jolly night. He's quite fresh, in a splendid mood, and is meeting with Francis,[624] Atlee's secretary, who's quite terrified because from here, it looks like war.[625] I don't believe it for a minute. All the English would be dead in the first week, we're so starved, and the Russians don't want a war either. But there is great fear of one here. You and Proust, however, know it takes more than a skirmish. It takes aggression in the populations themselves, or the time must be ripe, or something else that you could explain better. At any rate, I don't believe it will happen, for biological reasons. I think Bauscherl secretly hopes it will, so that he doesn't have to give his lectures. He's the laziest person the world has ever seen. Please write a lot about his lectures so he'll be afraid of you. If you want to say anything extra, you can do it on a separate piece of paper. I get the mail first, but I want to be able to show him your letters since he's always very worried about you. No one loves you as he does. He says it's good when you scold him about F. because it helps him act with more firmness toward her. I'm all friendship and goodwill. Unfortunately, I've got the latter in my blood and it's getting much worse. The former is pure diplomacy to keep my sway over her when she lashes out. She's somewhat submissive to me. That's how we mothers are.

Otherwise, we're having a jolly time here. The doctor[626] has received a letter threatening that Jackie's husband will sue him for 5,000 pounds' damages for alienating his wife's affections. We've had long discussions about it and your brother lives in mortal fear because Jackie was also chasing him while having an affair with the old man and the latter wants Canetti to save him by testifying to that in court. Don't mention "court" in your letter. The mere word makes him sick with fear and if the husband really sues, it will mean a break with the doc, since Bauscherl would rather die than appear in court. F. has turned his head so thoroughly that Steiner is completely sidelined. That's a triumph for me, because she's preferable to that tapeworm. You're sure to think I arranged it all out of Machiavellian instincts. I'm quite honored that you see me in such a diabolical light and call me a sadist. Yet for the two of you, I'm the greatest of mother cows. I've always told the dreadful Regine how much you like her, etc., and God knows it wasn't easy, since she then goes overboard and gets such a swelled head the room almost explodes. I'm glad to be rid of this family. I couldn't take it anymore. They always want to be introduced to everyone—such irritating pretensions with no inner justification. Since you've certainly gotten to know all our friends: Kae had her baby, a girl. You're going to have to come see us at last and marry Helga (she's enchantingly lovely). It's very nice of me to be writing you again, and I won't send this airmail because that takes just as long to reach your paradisiacal spot as regular mail. I cook for the scalawag every day. Since France, he hasn't been able to get used to the English diet again. That's how things stand, and our only fear is M-L. She mustn't find out. F., however, puts great stock in compromising herself with your brother. I'm enclosing one of the letters; send it back right away. I answered it myself, in the affirmative. I tell myself we can always turn them down later. I definitely want him to lecture in London, and you should definitely mention the letter and how impressed you are. Thank God he wants to impress you, for you're the only person who has any power over him. He's such a sweetheart you can't lay a hand on him. As you said, he always slips out of your grasp. I'd like him to go to Paris again this fall to see to the translation. If you don't help with that, we're lost. If it's bad, the book will of course not succeed. I know it's an enormous imposition, but you've always helped us, always.

Farewell and write about yourself, yourself, yourself!!!!!!!

All my love, fervently,[627]

Your Peggy,

sadist and sapphist.

Veza to Georges · *July 26, 1948*

Mrs. V. Canetti
4 Crawford Street
London W1

July 26

Dearest Lindore,[628]

I know you've waited in vain for my letter, but since I'm a sadist, I'm glad. And you like it. To make up, I'm perfuming this with your perfume. Sadly, a tenth of it is gone already, even though I keep it well hidden. Up to now, I've been a slave driver, and now the Proust lecture is finished. It's very good and two hours long. Luckily, Canetti has been moved to the third week, so that the Kafka will be finished too, but there's not going to be a Joyce. But then he hasn't read Joyce anyway. He's read all of Proust, not for the lecture, but out of pure passion for him. But he's going to tell you flat out that your idol Gide wrote an essay on Proust and added, "although I've read only half a volume"! I hope it won't be too hot for you, and since you have a noble character, I hope you won't take revenge. I'm no masochist and we're very impatient to hear from you. Your brother is quite worried. He doesn't believe that I haven't written and fears you're not well. Please reassure him or I'll have to write Edith and Jacqueline. Friedl is a comical whirlwind, and now her sister is here and hopes to borrow some of Canetti's limelight to catch a man with the following characteristics: complicated, clever but not too much so, well educated but not too much so, very well dressed, rich, handsome, young, English aristocrat if possible, capricious so she doesn't get bored, and snobbish. None of these movie-star qualities figure much in our circle of friends, and she'll come up empty-handed. Bauscherl did a good job editing Friedl's novel and it will probably be accepted. Bauscherl ordered the book for you. It wouldn't have worked via my relatives; they would have been too horrified.

Your last letter was scintillating again and everyone here is looking forward to your visit. Six days of Lulu is too much; I hope you survived them. I'll send you the Proust lecture, but C. says you're too clever and you'll think it inadequate. Nevertheless, Bauscherl has found new things in Proust that are not mentioned in other commentaries and essays. For example, the large influence of the *Thousand and One Nights*, not just of Saint Simon, and that's why there's never an end, never a chapter break, because the *Thousand and One Nights* never ends either. He has a lot of things to say about the nonexistence of money, i.e., about all the money that exists like the riches in the *Thousand and One Nights*, and the introductory lecture[629] is divided into Proust, the Poet of the Past; Kafka, of the Future; and J., of the Present. Everything in Kafka is vague, unfinished, there is no end. He expresses this much more richly and precisely. He's enchanted by Proust and has read all of him. Charlus is a figure from Dostoyevsky and P's characters unmask themselves later on, as in the *1,000 and One Nights*, thus Rachel, Charlus—it's all thoroughly and beautifully explained. When William[630] told me on the telephone that Canetti won't be lecturing until the third week, I asked him not to tell C., because then he would make his lectures too rich, too original, filled with too many new ideas. He would have too much to say (!). I asked him to say only that it's *possible* he'll be in the third week. That's what the good William did, but he blushed and stuttered at the indignity, even though he's very fond of me, and Canetti told him straight out that I had coached him. So now he knows the truth and you can imagine what his tempo is like. But I'm ecstatic that P. is almost finished and just needs to be dictated. Of course, he's far from satisfied and he won't let it be printed. F. has him wrapped around her little finger again and is up to her old antics, but since I'm on such good terms with her now, I speak my mind openly and that perplexes him.

He's happier with her here, and I find that reassuring. It won't last. She needs him for his "influential friends"[631] and for Cape the publisher, so she makes an effort, and I'm reminded of Swann and tell myself that the illusion is probably the important thing. Within myself, I've destroyed so many things I used to believe in that now I'm helping him maintain a relationship that's nothing but tinsel. O. begins to bore Swann, too. I myself have become sufficiently hard and distant to find her amusing, and now she really flatters me because this year, the whole town has switched to my side with flying colors, and they have to ask me how to behave.

Please don't be cruel. Send news of yourself. Bauscherl so eagerly awaits your answer to his letter. The most cordial, passionate embrace from your everlasting, faithless friend.

All my love,
Peggy

VEZA TO GEORGES · *AUGUST 20, 1948*

Mrs. V. Canetti
14 Crawford Street
London W1

August 20

Dearest brother-in-law,

I shall write you *one* more letter only because you are completely right about the Spanish edition, but you won't get another from me until next year on your birthday. We were so happy about the Sp. edition, especially your brother. In my case, there was a bit of envy mixed in, so that I forgot to write about it just because we were talking about it so much, also from envy. With your Proustian sensitivity, you are also absolutely right to think that my last letter was not completely *up to the mark*,[632] even if you didn't say so. But I was so angry at your brother because nothing had been written and I had to hound him continuously, that I also became angry at you since you're his brother. Now I'm reconciled (with the lectures), because they're almost finished and Bauscherl is going to Bryanston tomorrow, God willing. That is, if Friedl doesn't have a headache. I'm expecting him any moment now so he can pack. There's just a little passage about Kafka still to be written, and he'll probably get it done tonight. Anyhow, Kafka isn't until the third day. The introductory lecture is marvelous. Even Francis thinks so, and he doesn't care for Sebastian's[633] works, although he likes her and the two of them have already gone on excursions, because his wife is off on a trip.

Happy news about the end of Sept. in Paris. I already knew it since I correspond with Jacqueline, who of course told me about the great event with the refugee and also enclosed his letter. It says that his aunt and uncle think she's all right, except that her voice is harsh (heartlessness? he jokes) and she carries herself like an old maid. She asked me if his letter is a love letter. I didn't reply; it seems a smooth business transaction to me. But you can't judge from a letter. I've never seen a girl so pretty who's so lacking in charm at the same time. A corpse would make you feel warmer.

That's why I advised her to give it a trial period. She can't be very choosy about noses, for I don't know anyone as repulsive as Steiner, and she liked him. —My nephew will be in Paris at the beginning of Sept. and will call up Claudine, but he's a bit fearful, so it's not a sure thing. I'm sorry you won't see him; he's an attractive boy and has recovered appreciably. He just won a prize for the best caricature in a magazine. Your letter and the description of the Joes was delicious.

I don't remember who the Bourdon woman is—not the nurse who looks like a ventriloquist's dummy, I hope? Please tell me what aspect of you I imitate? Is it my dreamworld? Then I want to hold on to it always and I'll do it, too, for I don't like my life. I would not come to Paris, not even if Lord Nuffield[634] gave me an airplane, for you would surely have no time for me and Paris is lovely, yes indeed, but I wouldn't see it. I would see only E.C. and all his women, and you would be *gené en public avec moi*,[635] for I'm really "not fit to be seen" (Robert Neumann's favorite expression). This letter has become too long even from a woman who's been insulted, so I'll close. I continue to read for Hutchinson, but they won't print a single good book, and I'm writing short stories for young people for an Eng. magazine.[636] Clement is illustrating them and says they'll earn us a lot of money. *Wait and see*.[637] Bauscherl will write you about himself and it's a mystery to me why *he* got no answer to his delightful letter and had to worry on that account. Please just tell us how the latest x-ray turned out. I wrote you again as well. Stay handsome, smart, not *too* good, not *too* soft, and keep a diary. Write in it every day. Because you're a brilliant writer.

Alles Liebe,
Peggy.
All my love
Peggy[638]

Veza Canetti in Regent's Park, London, about 1952

Elias Canetti after finishing *Crowds and Power*, London, 1959

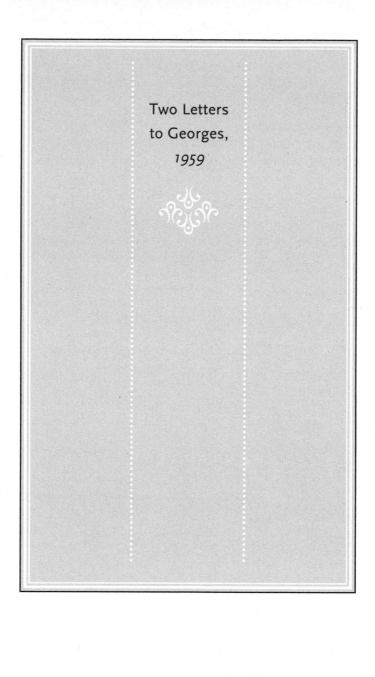

Two Letters to Georges, *1959*

Veza to Georges · *June 24, 1959*

Mrs. V.J. Canetti
8 Thurlow road[639]
London N.W.3

June 24, 1959

Dear Chevalier Suprême,[640]

I broke a glass this morning and thought, that's good luck, and then Canetti came in with your letter. He was overjoyed and excited, especially because the ceremony will take place in that most sacred place and your mother will be watching (I sometimes have such wistful yearnings too. I understand very well why, and what can we know about that, after all?).

As you can imagine, your brother was determined to come. But then I had to ungently remind him that July 7 is the deadline for him to send off his work,[641] and my opposition made him very downcast. He thought about it and promised to stay just one day. It's not that—such an intense occasion, such joyful excitement would interrupt the flow of his thoughts and he still has two weeks of hard work ahead of him. I cannot come myself, because I'm in mourning again. This time (please don't laugh) it's for my Milli, whom I killed: I sent her to the vet and he extinguished the light in her clever eyes. Cleanliness is coldness, dirt is warmth—I had her destroyed because she was ailing and making a mess. Now our flat is clean, but how I miss her. Only your wonderful news today allowed me to forget.

We console ourselves with the thought that you will be surrounded by lots of people. Afterward, too, you will be busy getting ready for your wonderful trip and so it's better for Canetti to visit you and Jacques when you get back from Brazil. But please don't leave us without news, especially about when you're leaving on your vacation. Perhaps Canetti can slip in a few days to spend alone with you with a clear head and freed of the burden of intense, concentrated work. As a sign of his joy (and his pride in you), he's sending the little section about "Survivors."[642] I'd take it to the post office for him, but he'll want to do it himself and make a ceremony out of it.

Your two bouts of flu were terrible because they surely made you very anxious without any cause. You know as well as I do that you'll catch the flu eighty more times, twice a year, and it will never put you in any danger. But of course, we were very sorry about it—because you were suffering and as always, you said nothing about it, like the great, brave man you are.

We wish you much happiness and a jolly celebration, Chevalier. Will the two of you address each other only with "Sir" from now on? Canetti is very glad that Jacques is feeling well. That was "the chance of life"[643] and won't be repeated.

Canetti will write himself, and better.

Veza Canetti
"the sister-in-law of the two Chevaliers"

Elias to Georges · *July 3, 1959*

Friday, July 3, 1959

My dear Georg,

Now the great event has taken place and my congratulations come too late, as always. There are so many reasons I would have loved to be there. But I simply didn't dare to because of Veza. The manuscript is supposed to be sent off on July 7, in final form, and I'm working—well, the way you probably always work—literally day and night. Veza has had a really miserable year of it and for months has been living in such tense anticipation of this moment that any interruption would have the gravest consequences for her. It is splendid how she has worked her way so completely into my book and gone over every sentence with me. The suggestions she made have been invaluable. She sensed wherever something was unclear and didn't spare me, and her feeling for the German language has a delicacy and depth that astonished me *every day*. But while . . .[644] me intellectually, she was living in a sort of psychic night. I remained with her every single day. As she helped me, I watched over her. The worst is over. The work, i.e., the first volume of over 1,000 pages, is complete. You wouldn't recognize it now after that miserable garbage you saw 10 years ago. I used about 300 of the old pages that you read, but with extensive revisions, and only the three psychiatric chapters you didn't like have remained by and large as they were. "The Case of Schreber"[645] now seems to me more important than ever. It contains most of the discoveries I have made, collected together in a strange, delusional system which thus provides invaluable evidence.

I'm thoroughly satisfied. I know that with this book, I've achieved a kind of immortality and if I should die tomorrow, I won't have lived in vain. A year ago, I would not have been able to say that. I deserve the Nobel Prize for this work, either for literature or for peace, but of course I won't get it.[646] But that doesn't matter: I *know* for myself that no one else has penetrated so deeply into the confusion of our century. I could not have done it in less time. I say that although I'm very well aware of my indolence. But I'm beginning to think that this indolence was nothing but a defense against overhaste and "logical conclusions" that could only block true insight.

My dear Georg, I know very well how terrible what happened between us a year ago was. I have thought about it a lot. You delivered a very heavy blow to me, and the way I love you and the way I am, I could not have reacted with any less ferocity. For a long time, it felt as if I had cut the last bond between myself and my past. I was determined to finish my work and then take my own life. To my astonishment, I held firm to this resolution right up through the spring. Then I began to feel that all sorts of things that had seemed destroyed for good had secretly begun to grow back. It was a good thing I was so heavily preoccupied with my work and with Veza. That didn't allow me to surrender to my inner debate with you very often. Today, I feel vindicated in my own eyes. Whatever you think of me, your doubts about me (and in the end, that's what the whole thing felt like to me) have proved to be unfounded. My work, which no one could honestly have believed in anymore, has now been completed. I've been saved and intend to keep on living. In the future, there are many different things I want to write. I shall not be dependent on anyone again. Perhaps I will never again completely *trust* anyone, either, but that only means that I've grown up. It was high time. My vehement joy at your news made me realize again how much I love you. I wish you a beneficial journey and embrace you as your old brother,

Elias.

Please don't tell Veza a word of what I said in this letter. She is *always* imperiled.

You write life, but your own life is a slip of the pen.

VEZA TO ELIAS, *April 19, 1948*

London–Paris–Zurich

VEZA CANETTI died in London on May 1, 1963, at the age of sixty-five, without ever seeing her own works in print. In 1980 Elias Canetti dedicated *The Torch in My Ear*, the second volume of his memoirs, to her memory.

GEORGES CANETTI, renowned tuberculosis researcher and vice president of the Institut Pasteur in Paris, died in Vence on August 27, 1971, at the age of sixty. The executors of his estate were the children of his brother Nissim (Jacques) in Paris. In 1977 Elias Canetti dedicated *The Tongue Set Free*, the first volume of his memoirs, to his memory.

ELIAS CANETTI married the art conservator Hera Buschor in 1971. Their daughter Johanna was born in 1972. He lived with his wife in London and Zurich. In 1981 he was awarded the Nobel Prize for Literature. Hera Canetti died in 1988. In 1990 Elias began to champion the publication of Veza Canetti's works. He died in Zurich on August 14, 1994, at the age of eighty-nine.

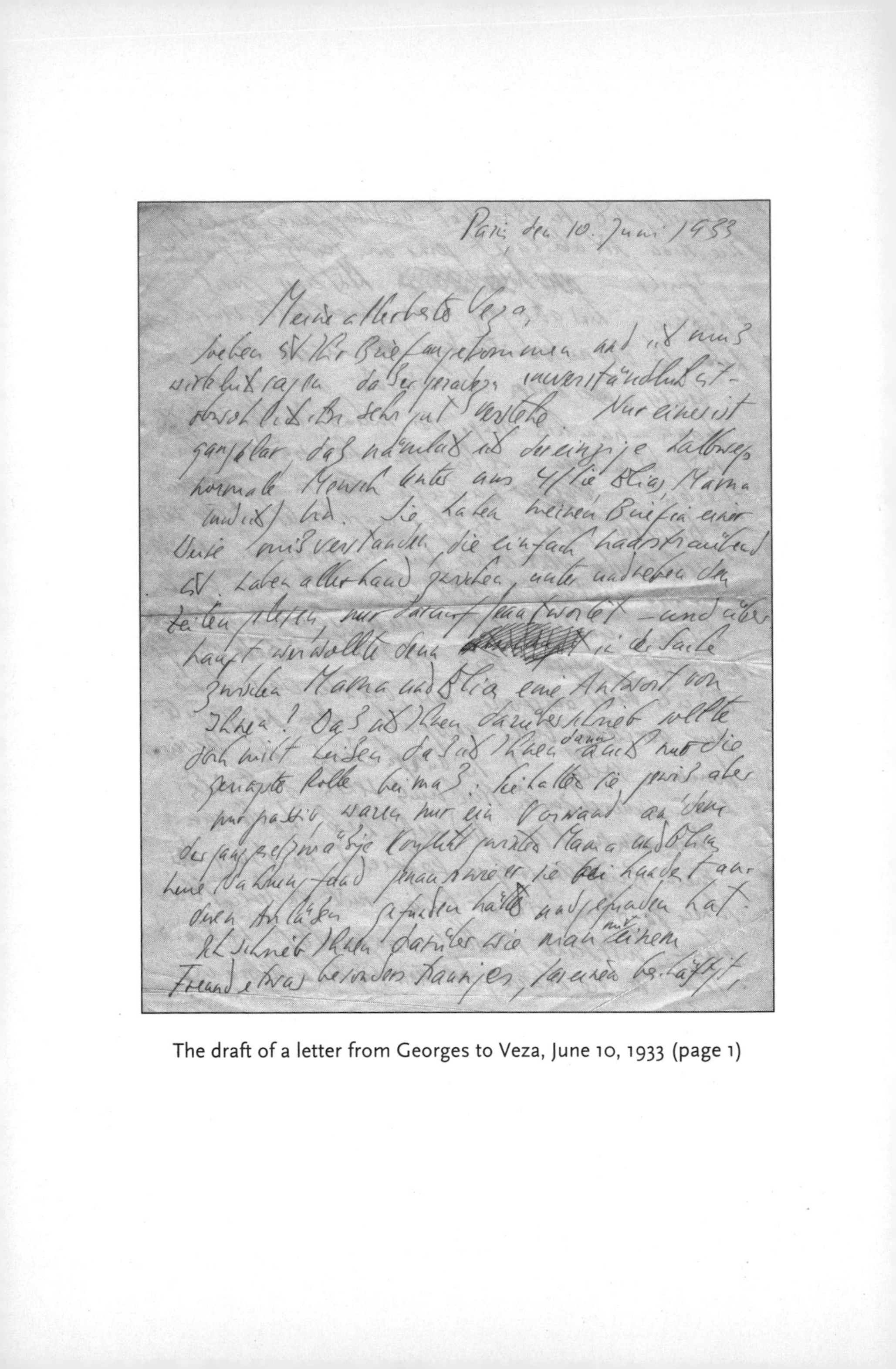

Paris, den 10. Juni 1933

Meine allerliebste Veza,

The draft of a letter from Georges to Veza, June 10, 1933 (page 1)

Zürich, den 22. Januar 1935

Elias's letter to Georges, January 22, 1935 (page 1)

29. Nov.

Süsser Georg!

Jetzt machen Sie auch noch eine Entdeckung! Wenn Sie nicht so schön wären! Und diese Stimme allein würde genügen! Ich hab so Angst vor Ihnen, das heisst, vor mir, dass ich zu meinem Schutz die Baronesse Birgitte Eleonore von Klenau für Sie nach Wien bestellt habe, lesen Sie selbst. Sie ist so schlank als ich dick bin und so jung als ich alt und bildschön und elegant. Es gehört viel Selbstverleugnung dazu, dass ich sie kommen lasse. 20 Jahre alt und um 20 Kilo schlanker als ich. Aber

Veza's letter to Georges, November 29, 1937 (page 1)

Mrs Canetti c/o Mrs Fistoulari

21 Campden Hill Court ,Campden Hill rd , London W8

September 21. 1945.

Dearest Georges,

no,this is not my address,its Annas,Anna Mahlers,I put it on top,because we are supposed to give our address and I dont want th this letter to come back,for reasons you'll soon understand.In this country they are so courtious as to open your letter at the P.O. and returning it without reading it,to the address on top.In an anvelop "on your majesty's service."

I just got your telegramm and this inspires me to write you a long letter - up to now I could not,and you can imagine how downcast we were,when the op. was postponed.So now,I can enjoy the magnificent letter that came in the morning,and that we read twice.Your brother w i l l be happy to see the telegr. to-night when back from London. We knew it is a slight operation,but what operation i s light.And above all,your magnanimity in writing and even cheering us up and being brave as y o u are brave. Write at once how you feel. Paris??

How long do you think you'll have to stay in the sana? Dont forget to thank Regine for the wire.And answer sober questions,not only the great ones.How longz Because for your physic it may be good but for your psychic Paris is surely the better place.Also send me a list of the things you cant get in Paris,food ,I mean.Dont forget,a whole list,+) we dont know here,we live in the lap of luxury concerning food,compared to Belsen ,of course ,for everything can only be taken relatively. +) We get plenty to eat,as much as we like,but always the same monotonous things - I am sick and tired of bacon,cheese,roast lamb,biscuits and dried eggs. Owing to good connections of yours brother to a baroness, we get shell eggs now and then,but a lady here said the other day to me: this is my shell egg of 1945.She gets one a year.

+) I'll do my best to find a way, legal of course!

Veza's letter to Georges, September 21, 1945 (page 1)

-2-

1911 (there it is and I was so careful it should not come forth,
I seem to be a spiritualistic medium, things coming forth against my
will, ectoplasm forming 9 9 9 ,no 1911. It just shows. Even though
nearly dead, very nearly, I manifest my affection for G.C. which I tell
you, because my old age, decay and despair, I am a clinic case for despair,
a melancholy maniac, shall not destroy our ties, by which word I dont
mean cravats. Nothing shall destroy the afinity between us three,
E.C. included. Not even I shall destroy it.) I'll - w a s I careful-
tell you now, why I'm going to move to a boarding house soon from here,
not a London one, but here, near your brother, who remains the usual,
dry address that I usually give you...Durris...brr . the whole address
is stingy, miserly, mean, filthy, as the owners are. I suffered two years
during the Blitz, not wanting your brother to go back to London.
Oh, how we had to fight to get the exorbitant rent. When I washed a pair
of stockings all in secret, they w o u l d find it out, for they are reli
gious people, the man being a retired country parson .His wife was
58, when they met, he at that time being 68. They lived in all innocence
together in their bed, if that disturbs you. For they are pious people
and, kind of saintly. So saintly, that they drove me out of my wits,
telling us every week we would have to leave, because the Germans may
invade and then they would get killed for harbouring Jews. Only when t
there was a bomb on Amersham, they grew mild for a while, because they
feared the wrath of the Lord even more then the Germans. Oh how I
prayed for bombs! For when they stopped they did fear God much,
but the Germans more. At last I was half mad and moved into the house
of a proletarian, a woman who could neither read nor write.- "I go to
the dance every night" - she told me apologetically, and I felt this

Veza's letter to Georges, September 21, 1945 (page 2)

ACKNOWLEDGMENTS

Thanks to Françoise Canetti, Suresnes; Johanna Canetti, Zurich; Julia Breimeier, Ravensburg; Hanna Burger, Vienna; Iso Camartin, Zurich; Ingrid and Marcel Canetti, Paris; Daniel Demellier, Paris; Christoph Eggenberger, Zurich; Ariane Fasquelle, Paris; Bernd-Jürgen Fischer, Berlin; Ingrid Grüninger, Stuttgart; Sven Hanuschek, Munich; Veronika Hoffmann, Munich; Jochen Meyer, Marbach; Marc Rassat, Paris; Ines Schlenker, London; Gerhard Schuster, Munich; Yves Sobel, Suresnes; Raphaël Sorin, Paris; Elizabeth Winter, London.

The translator owes a huge debt of gratitude to Karen Lauer and Kristian Wachinger, the editors of the German edition, for their patience in answering questions and clarifying obscurities.

NOTES TO THE LETTERS

The notes refer to the works listed in the Bibliography, pp. 419–421, in abbreviated form, first to the English translation if one exists, then to the German original. [DD] following an annotation indicates that it has been added by the translator.

1. In their prewar letters to each other, Georges and Veza use the formal second person pronouns (*Sie*, *Ihnen*, *Ihr*). [DD]
2. Georges's draft breaks off here. [DD]
3. The conductor Hermann Scherchen (1891–1966) had invited Elias to the Workshop for Modern Music, of which Scherchen was the organizer. It was held in Strasbourg on August 7–16, 1933. Elias Canetti devoted two separate chapters of *The Play of the Eyes* to Scherchen (*Memoirs* 618–624; IX 44–51)—whom he describes as power-hungry—and to the workshop (*Memoirs* 628–636; IX 56–66).
4. Edith Vanburger, the first wife of the middle brother Nissim Canetti. Nissim, born in Rustschuk in 1909, was a record producer and concert impresario. He settled in Paris in 1926, became a naturalized French citizen in 1931, officially changed his name to Jacques Canetti after his escape to Algeria in 1940, and died in Paris in 1997. Cf. Jacques Canetti's memoir, *On cherche jeune homme aimant la musique* (Paris: Calmann-Lévy, 1978), p. 68.
5. London: Jonathan Cape, and New York: Simon & Schuster, 1929. German translation by Richard Hoffmann (Berlin: Zsolnay, 1930).
6. Veza Canetti's cycle of stories *Die Gelbe Straße* (*Yellow Street*) was published for the first time posthumously, in 1990, as a "novel," with a foreword by Elias.
7. Mathilde Arditti, daughter of Bellina, the eldest sister of Elias and Georges's mother. Mathilde married her cousin, Josef Arditti. Elias wrote in 1971 that he had loved her very much and regretted not having mentioned her in his autobiography (Hanuschek, pp. 188 and 624).
8. In the original: "Canetti wird bald laute Erfolge haben," an untranslatable play on the words *laute* (loud) and *lauter* (nothing but). [DD]

9. Probably the Ardittis. Both the siblings and the cousins of Georges and Elias's mother Mathilde Canetti, née Arditti, lived in Paris. The Canetti brothers were close friends of their cousin, the painter Georges Arditti.
10. Georges studied medicine in Vienna from 1929 to 1931 and in Paris from 1931 to 1936.
11. The Powys brothers were John Cowper (1872–1963); Theodore Francis (1875–1953), author of novels and numerous short stories influenced by his Christian faith; and Llewelyn (1884–1939), who lived in the United States, Switzerland, and Kenya, and published a total of twenty-six books, including a novel, a biography, essays, and autobiographical works.
12. John Cowper Powys had already written his first novel by 1915, although he also wrote several philosophical works.
13. Elias and Georges's cousin Renée Arditti, sister of Mathilde Arditti.
14. In *The Play of the Eyes* (*Memoirs* 753–754; IX 208), Elias writes that his mother did not learn of the marriage until *Die Blendung* was published in October 1935. It is only in this context and at this point in his autobiography that he mentions his wedding.
15. The *Arbeiter-Zeitung* (*AZ*: Workers' Newspaper), main organ of the Austrian Social Democratic Party. In his foreword to *Yellow Street*, Elias praises it as "Vienna's best-written paper" (p. x; *Die Gelbe Straße*, p. 8). Under various pseudonyms, ten of Veza's stories appeared in the *AZ* in 1932–1933, including "The Canal," which later formed part of *Yellow Street*. In 1932 Engelbert Dollfuss became the Austrian chancellor in a conservative coalition and dissolved parliament in March 1933, declaring it deadlocked. Thereafter, he governed by means of the wartime economic emergency law of 1917, harshly using its powers against the left. On January 21, 1934, he banned the sale of the *AZ*.
16. Even after 1938, there were advantages to being stateless: Veza was no longer threatened with deportation, since after Austria's Anschluss (annexation) by the German Reich, stateless persons, unlike Austrian Jews, were not subject to the Nuremberg Laws of 1935, which severely limited the rights of Jewish citizens. Emigration was also easier: Veza and Elias did not have to submit a statement of their assets and thus did not have to pay the *Reichsfluchtsteuer* (the penalty fee for "fleeing" the Reich) but only to produce an *Unbedenklichkeitserklärung* (certificate of nonobjection). See Hanna Burger, "Staatenlos. Die Verrätselung einer Biographie," in John Pattillo-Hess and Mario R. Smole, eds., *Elias Canetti—Chronist der Massen, Enthüller der Macht* (Vienna: Löcker, 2006).
17. After the violent suppression of the insurrection of Social Democratic workers on February 12–14, 1934, both the Social Democratic Party and the unions were banned.

18. *Die Blendung* (The Blinding, published in English as *Auto-da-Fé*), written between fall 1930 and September 1931.
19. *Komödie der Eitelkeit* (Comedy of Vanity), written between late 1933 and February 1934 (Hanuschek, p. 303), first published by Hanser Verlag in Munich in 1964, first performed in Braunschweig in 1965.
20. In addition to the Deutsches Theater in Berlin, Max Reinhardt also directed the Viennese Theater in the Josefstadt from 1924 to 1937.
21. In a letter to Georges on December 10, 1934, Renée Arditti mentions that Elias has written "two film manuscripts." She adds, "Unfortunately, there aren't many opportunities here, since the émigrés are strong competition, and Elias lacks the right connections to the film industry. Don't you think it would make sense to send the manuscripts to Nissim?" Veza mentions the second film manuscript in her letter of December 20, 1934; see p. 25 above.
22. The violinist Anna Amadea Leonie (Dea) Gombrich (1905–1994) was the sister of the art historian Ernst Gombrich. She was born in Vienna, where Gustav Mahler and Arnold Schoenberg were friends of the family. She emigrated to England in 1936 and married Sir John Forsdyke, the director of the British Museum. See *Memoirs* 647–648; IX 80.
23. Scherchen introduced Elias to Alban Berg. A chapter in *The Play of the Eyes* (*Memoirs* 760–763; IX 215–219) records the deep personal impression Berg made on him. Elias remained in contact with Berg until the composer's death on December 24, 1935.
24. Nissim Canetti began working at the Polydor company, the French subsidiary of Deutsche Grammophon Gesellschaft, in 1930. He discovered Edith Piaf, among others.
25. In July 1934, Scherchen held another workshop like the one in August 1933 (see note 3 above).
26. Receipt for the fee for a residence permit.
27. The *Strassburger Chronik* by Jakob Twinger von Königshofen (c. 1400). For what follows, cf. *Memoirs* 635 f.; IX 65 f.
28. In Austria, the growing threat of war had been palpable in the recent putsch attempt by the National Socialists and the assassination of the federal chancellor Dollfuss on July 25, 1934, although the rebellion was defeated. Mussolini, who was still allied with Austria, had deployed troops at the Brenner Pass, causing Hitler to distance himself from the attempted putsch.
29. Karl Kraus (1874–1936), founder, editor, and from 1911 on, sole writer of the periodical *Die Fackel* (The Torch), was a fierce critic of the corruption of language, contemporary journalism, and the First World War. He was also a riveting public performer of his own and others' texts and a powerful

early influence on both Elias and Veza. [DD] The July 1934 issue of *Die Fackel* referred to here was entitled "Why *Die Fackel* is not appearing." Since the Nazi accession to power, Kraus had published nothing but a brief eulogy for Adolf Loos in October 1933 and a poem which contained the lines "Ich bleibe stumm; / und sage nicht, warum" (I'm staying mute; I won't say why). This was harshly criticized in the Austrian press. Now, in the 315 pages of the *Fackel* in question, he explained his silence as follows: "In my life as a polemicist, many intellectual currents have flowed together: the Great War and everything that went before and came after . . . but I don't feel equal to the phenomenon of Hitler" (p. 249). At the same time, he criticized the Social Democratic uprising of February 1934, violently suppressed by the Dollfuss regime, as "a wretched troop intoxicated by the false slogans of editorial writers. They did terrible things and suffered even more terrible things in return." Kraus defended Dollfuss against the Social Democrats, calling him perhaps "a more serious friend of the working man . . . than the office boys of the revolution" (pp. 256f.).

30. On January 30, 1927, during a conflict between members of the Social Democratic paramilitary organization Republikanischer Schutzbund (Republican Defense League) and a nationalistic veterans' organization, a disabled socialist veteran and an eight-year-old boy were shot and killed by the rightists. When the three men who had confessed to the crime were acquitted on July 15, workers in Vienna rioted. The Viennese police chief Johann Schober ordered his men to use deadly force to quell the riot, and ninety people were killed. Karl Kraus had posters put up saying, "I call on you to resign." Cf. *Memoirs* 491f.; VIII 239.
31. Antihero in the *Iliad*: ugly, ill-born, and ignoble. He berates Agamemnon and demands they be allowed to return home, whereupon Odysseus gives him a thrashing.
32. Theo van Gogh (1857–1891) worked at a gallery in Paris. He supported his brother Vincent (1853–1890) financially and also tried to sell his works. Their deep and heartfelt relationship is documented in their extensive correspondence. It was published in 1914; a German translation appeared the same year.
33. Jules (1830–1870) and Edmond (1822–1896) de Goncourt had an intense correspondence, marked by mutual sympathy and extensive knowledge of literature. Beginning in 1851, they kept a joint diary, the *Journal des Goncourt*, with "reminiscences of literary life." After Jules's death, it was continued by Edmond until shortly before his own.
34. Nissim Canetti's wife, née Vanburger.
35. Rachel Calderon died on October 13, 1934.

36. Wladimir Vogel (1896–1984), Swiss composer of German-Russian descent. He was a participant in Scherchen's workshop in August 1933 (see note 3 above).
37. Wladimir Rosenbaum (1894–1984) was a well-known Swiss lawyer of Russian descent. He and his wife, the pianist Aline Valangin, played hosts to the avant-garde in their house in Zurich and offered refuge to the persecuted. Rosenbaum was arrested in 1937 for having provided an airplane to the Spanish Republic in its fight against Franco in 1936. According to the account in *The Play of the Eyes* (*Memoirs* 717; IX 164), the plan for an opera foundered on the failure to give composer and librettist equal rights. Among Canetti's literary remains is the typescript of a libretto entitled *Affenoper* (Opera of the Apes), but it may not have been written until the 1950s (Hanuschek, p. 224).
38. Elias met the sculptor Anna Mahler, daughter of Gustav and Alma Mahler, in May 1933 (cf. *Memoirs* 639–642; IX 69–72), and developed a "violent passion" (*Memoirs* 631; IX 59) for her. At the time, she was married to the publisher Paul Zsolnay. By August 1933, when Elias was in Strasbourg, Anna had already sent him a letter ending their affair. On her importance for his life, cf. his note of February 21, 1979: "I think . . . that my love for Anna changed me so decisively that nothing was ever the same again" (ZB 59, quoted by Hanuschek, p. 272. Cf. *Memoirs* 675; IX 114).
39. The "comedy" *Der Tiger* (The Tiger), published posthumously in *Der Fund*; and *Der Oger* (The Ogre), published posthumously in 1991 and first performed in 1992 at the Schauspielhaus in Zurich.
40. See note 19 above.
41. Alma Mahler was married, in succession, to Gustav Mahler, Franz Werfel, and Walter Gropius. She was the mother of Anna Mahler and Manon Gropius (*Memoirs* 625 ff.; cf. IX 52 ff.).
42. Probably the Austrian actor Rudolf Forster (1884–1968). After beginning his career in silent films, he appeared in Georg Wilhelm Pabst's *Dreigroschenoper* (*Three Penny Opera*) of 1931.
43. The oldest sister of the Canetti brothers' mother (cf. *Memoirs* 105 ff.; VII 122 ff.).
44. A conjectural reading of the original: *einen Hendelbrief. Hendel* is a roasting chicken in Austrian dialect. The German equivalent of "having a bone to pick with someone" is "having a chicken to pluck with someone."
45. A condition in which air is present in the pleural cavity, causing a lung to collapse. In earlier years, a pneumothorax was artificially induced as a treatment for tuberculosis.
46. In the Sanatorium des Étudiants de France in St. Hilaire du Touvet above Grenoble, where Georges would be treated repeatedly in the coming years and later would work as a doctor himself.

47. See note 37 above.
48. According to *The Play of the Eyes*, he read the first part of the *Komödie der Eitelkeit* (*Memoirs* 717–722; IX 165–170).
49. This must be the manuscript of *Der Oger*.
50. During his years in Vienna, Elias had a close relationship with Mathilde Camhi, who was the same age as he and related to him on his mother's side. According to her son Raphaël Sorin, she was the first person to believe in Elias's talent.
51. Parisian avant-garde theater in the Symbolist tradition, founded in 1893. In 1896 it premiered Alfred Jarry's absurdist satire *Ubu roi*, igniting one of the greatest scandals in the history of the theater.
52. Joseph Canetti (1886–1977), younger brother of Canetti's father, lived in Paris. Cf. the family photograph from 1938 on pp. 110–111.
53. That is, passing his examination to become a physician. Georges didn't submit a doctoral dissertation until 1939.
54. The cavity in the lung where tuberculosis caused necrosis.
55. Underwritten financially by the Strasbourg newspaper publisher Jean Hoepffner, the novel *Die Blendung* (The Blinding) was published by the Herbert Reichner Verlag (Vienna, Leipzig, Zurich) in October 1935, dated 1936. On Stefan Zweig (1881–1942), cf. *The Play of the Eyes* (*Memoirs* 726 f.; IX 176 f.). Elias was contemptuous of Zweig for being a representative of "popular literature" (*Memoirs* 714; IX 161) who "owed his reputation to sheer bustle" (*Memoirs* 790; IX 252).
56. Madeleine Cohn.
57. Here behold . . . war's final resting place.
58. On March 16, 1935, Hitler had reintroduced universal conscription in violation of the Versailles Treaty. He justified his intention to increase the size of the German Army to 580,000 men as a defense against the Soviet Union. In response, the Soviet Union signed mutual aid pacts with France and Czechoslovakia. In the Stresa Pact of April, Great Britain, France, and Italy agreed to oppose any further German violations of the treaty. Great Britain, however, concluded a naval agreement with Germany on June 18, which set the relative sizes of the German and British fleets at a ratio of 35:100. The British considered this evidence of the success of their policy of appeasement. (Late in 1935, however, Germany rejected an agreement on its air force. On April 28, 1939, it simultaneously withdrew from the naval agreement and from the German-Polish nonaggression pact.)
59. This refers to past arguments with his mother. Cf. *Memoirs* 374 ff.; VIII 103 ff.
60. The American edition of *Auto-da-Fé* did not appear until 1947, published under the title *The Tower of Babel* by Alfred A. Knopf in New York.

61. Once Stefan Zweig became one of its authors in 1935, the Herbert Reichner Verlag was considered a "Jewish" publisher. While the sale of its books was not forbidden in Germany since it was a foreign (i.e., Austrian) publisher, the contents of its warehouse in Leipzig were confiscated in 1936, and it took a diplomatic intervention to get them returned. The firm was liquidated after the Anschluss in March 1938.
62. See note 19 above.
63. On September 2, 1935, Veza and Elias moved to an apartment at Himmelstrasse 30.
64. The apartment at Ferdinandstrasse 29 in the second district (Leopoldstadt), where Veza had lived first with her mother and stepfather, then from November 1933 until August 1935 with Elias.
65. Hagenberggasse 47 in the thirteenth district (Hacking), where Elias lived from May 1927 to November 1933.
66. In a letter of November 14, 1935, Thomas Mann congratulated Elias on the publication of *Die Blendung*. In Elias's reply of April 25, 1936, he thanked Mann "for the lively feeling of confidence which I imbibed from your approval as from a sweet spring, I who had been dying of thirst for years. I was often in desperate need of such reassurance, because there have been more than a few attacks on *Die Blendung*." Thomas Mann, *Briefe*, volume I (Frankfurt a. M.: S. Fischer, 1962), p. 118.
67. In *The Play of the Eyes* Elias pays tribute to Mann's novel for its "reflections on death," to which it gives "scrupulous treatment" (*Memoirs* 788; IX 250).
68. The French state examination, which results in a ranking of all examinees.
69. Following "most daring," the word "novel" is crossed out and replaced by "book." For several years, Elias pursued the project of a novel entitled *Todfeind* ("Mortal Enemy" or "Enemy of Death"), whose central figure was to be a paranoid. In February 1942 he set the project aside and began to write aphorisms (Hanuschek, p. 647), but continued to collect notes for his *Totenbuch* ("Book of the Dead" or "Death Book") for the rest of his life.
70. Elias had sent Thomas Mann a manuscript copy of *Die Blendung* in October 1931, but Mann returned it unread, pleading "lack of sufficient time and strength"—"a hard blow" to Elias (*Memoirs* 788; IX 250).
71. At the time, Austria's leading liberal daily newspaper.
72. Abraham Sonne (1883–1950) published poems in Hebrew under the pen name Avraham ben Yizhak. Elias encountered him regularly in the Café Museum in 1933–1934, and describes his admiration for him in *The Play of the Eyes* (*Memoirs* 686ff.; IX 127ff.). Theodor Sapper (1905–1982) wrote

for numerous newspapers and magazines, translated works from Spanish and French, and was later a university lecturer and editor of the anthology *Alle Glocken der Erde. Expressionistische Dichtung aus dem Donauraum* (All the Bells on Earth: Expressionist Poetry from the Danube Region). Elias especially admired the novel Sapper was working on, entitled *Kettenreaktion Kontra* (Chain Reaction Contra).

73. Thomas Mann's letter of November 14, 1934, mentions Heinrich Mann's *Henri IV* in addition to *Die Blendung*.
74. In English in Veza's letter. A paraphrase of what Byron wrote in his notebooks about the public reaction to cantos 1 and 2 of *Childe Harold's Pilgrimage* (1812), according to Thomas Moore's biography of the poet.
75. This is the first of several letters written on letterhead imprinted "Dr. Elias Canetti / Wien-Grinzing / Am Himmel 30."
76. The British edition (London: Jonathan Cape) was not published until 1946, the American (New York: Alfred A. Knopf) in 1947.
77. Partly illegible.
78. Elias was awarded a doctorate in chemistry by the University of Vienna in 1929.
79. On Elias's "twin brotherhood" with Fritz Wotruba (1907–1975), cf. *Memoirs* 656 ff.; IX 90 ff. and X 51–60, as well as Kurt Bartsch and Gerhard Melzer, eds., *Zwillingsbrüder. Elias Canetti und Fritz Wotruba* (Vienna: Sonderzahl Verlag, 2005).
80. Both as a person and as an author, Franz Werfel (1890–1945), with his "'O Man!' rubbish" (*Memoirs* 628; IX 56), was among the Austrian writers Elias hated the most (cf. *Memoirs* 675–679 and 701–703; IX 114–119 and 146–148).
81. See note 29 above.
82. The review appeared in the literary supplement of the *Neue Zürcher Zeitung* on Sunday, January 12, 1936:

NARRATIVE PROSE

Die Blendung by Elias Canetti

When the fantastic is portrayed with fiercely realistic methods, it usually makes a powerful impression. And so this remarkable novel by a very talented young writer is not just utterly enthralling, but also thoroughly accomplished, even masterful. The question remains, however, whether it really deserves the title of literature, or is it simply a brilliantly written thriller, a snazzy virtuoso performance?

In the course of 550 pages, it recounts how the life of a dreamy scholar and pathologic bibliomaniac is destroyed by allowing a woman into that unworldly, uninhabited, loveless life. He marries his housekeeper and from that moment he is lost, done for. Piece by piece, his lonely but by no means empty life is dislocated, spoiled, wrecked, utterly ruined. This process, in all its complex stages, is told with great skill, but with a certain harried breathlessness. Here, one senses a contradiction: what would lend power and spice to a short story becomes torturous in the course of such a long book. There is an interesting but discomforting tension between the tempo of the book and its dimensions. And perhaps it is not just this tension that endangers the narrative, calling it into question. Perhaps it is also the discrepancy between the actual, pathological content of the novel and the extensive breadth with which it is narrated.

The narration is a technical masterpiece. The novel's three sections—"A Head without a World," "Headless World," "A World in the Head"—grow organically one from the other, and the fabric of descriptive detail is consistently dense. The psychology of the characters is logical, if somewhat exaggerated. Many a novelist whom I rank much higher as a poet could learn a lot from this author—to the extent that writing can be taught at all. One admires this new novelist for never being out of breath. But it is precisely the perfect, seamless functioning of his prose that is uncomfortable. The rhythm of the book often sounds less like breathing than like a motor. (published by H. Reichner, Vienna)

HERMANN HESSE

83. The Italian edition of *Die Blendung* was not published until thirty years later: *Auto-da-fé*, translated by Luciano and Bianca Zagari (Milan: Garzanti, 1967).
84. In *Der Sonntag*, the Sunday supplement of *Der Wiener Tag*, February 2, 1936. Elias is quoted as follows:

"Lately, there's been a lot of talk again about sunny literature. People want novels that make them feel good, like being on a ski vacation. The writer should flash them a smile with a mouthful of ski instructor's teeth; his soul should be a white, unwritten field of snow, as should the soul of the reader. As for me, I have a different—perhaps old-fashioned—notion about the writer's calling. I would be ashamed to leap out of the world I live in, no matter how beautiful the mountains I landed on. Even though I'm well aware that those mountains are the only refuge from the gas chamber that awaits me. The poet is the conscience of his time (please forgive me that pathetic and overused phrase), and if that means he has become the conscience of hell, then that's the fault of the times we live in. Our world is, for the most part, the realization of old and even ancient images of hell, with the addition of a few newly invented levels. Hell has made progress; everything makes progress. As far as I know, it didn't use to be the custom to deprive our sins of a voice in such a comprehensive and radical way. So it's not my fault that reading this book makes you feel like you're suffocating.

"This novel is planned as the first of a series that will be what might best be described as a *comédie humaine* based on psychotics. It stands in conscious opposition to the sociological novel which takes as its object ordinary, average individuals. In order to portray life, one must look to the extremes. I want to make comprehensible for my readers the seemingly incomprehensible daily lives of these outsiders. The moment they have comprehended them, they become complicit in their folly. We can only empathize with what is also present in ourselves . . .

"In my opinion, the fate of the individual human being is sealed. There is no escape except one that seems to me to have an almost biological character. I believe in a deep and authentic drive in all individuals to be subsumed into a higher species, the mass, and to lose themselves therein as completely as if there had never been one *single* human being."

85. Paul Fischauer (1898–1977), Austrian writer and journalist, emigrated to England in 1934.
86. The hope of an edition published in France by Grasset was not realized. A French edition of *Die Blendung* did not appear until 1949, published by Arthaud as *La Tour de Babel*, translated by Paule Arhex.
87. Possibly Henry Muller (1902–1980).
88. Nickname for Elias, a regional expression for a small child or a small, ungainly adult.
89. Elias's friend from his schooldays, Hans Asriel, had committed suicide. His sister was Nuni Asriel and "that small, heroic woman" was his mother, Alice Asriel. Veza had lived in her house and Alice had been a friend of Elias's mother since the First World War (cf. *Memoirs* 119–124; VII 138–144). Hans Asriel had introduced Veza to Elias (cf. *Memoirs* 343 ff.; VIII 68 ff.). On Elias's retrospective analysis of his relationship to Hans Asriel, cf. *Memoirs* 122 f. and 402–406; VII 141 f. and VIII 136–141.
90. Bucky Calderon owned a small sweet shop in Lightwater near Bagshot in southeastern England. Veza had visited him there as a girl.
91. The Polish violinist Bronislaw Hubermann (1882–1947) was considered one of the leading virtuosos of the time.
92. *Sic*; the postmark is November 10. [DD]
93. *Napoléon et son temps* (Paris: Flammarion, 1936), by the French historian Octave Aubry (1881–1947).
94. The International PEN Congress was held in Paris in June 1937.

95. Either Elias's cousin Mathilde Arditti or Mathilde Camhi.
96. A German-language adult education center founded in Prague in 1917.
97. In the spring of 1937, Mazáč in Prague published *Die Blendung* as *Zaslepení*, translated by Zdenka Münzrová.
98. On the Strasbourg newspaper publisher Hoepffner cf. *The Play of the Eyes* (*Memoirs* 722–725; IX 171–174) and note 55 above.
99. Mathilde Canetti died in Paris on June 15, 1937.
100. On paper with a black border.
101. That is, Elias's paternal aunt or uncle.
102. Probably Jacques Vergnet, a patient at the sanatorium who died at the end of the 1930s.
103. On paper with a black border.
104. See note 46 above.
105. Probably one of Veza's last three publications under the pen name Veza Magd: either "Hellseher" ("Clairvoyants") in *Der Wiener Tag* (Vienna, March 14, 1937), later in *Viennese Short Stories* and *Der Fund*; or "Das Schweigegeld. Eine Geschichte aus einem Luxussanatorium" ("Hushmoney: A Story from a Luxury Sanatorium") in *Die Stunde* (Vienna, April 11, 1937), later in *Viennese Short Stories* and *Veza Canetti*; or "Geld—Geld—Geld. Das Leben eines reichen Mannes" ("Money—Money—Money: The Life of a Rich Man") in *Die Stunde* (Vienna, May 1, 1937), later in *Viennese Short Stories* and *Veza Canetti*.
106. Paul Valéry, *Rhumbs (notes et autres)* (Paris: Le Divan, 1926).
107. In *Crowds and Power* (479; III 570), Elias refers to the "important book" *La mythologie primitive* (Paris: Alcan, 1935), by the French philosopher and sociologist Lucien Lévy-Bruhl (1857–1939).
108. Probably the *Histoire poétique de quinzième siècle*, 2 volumes (Paris: Champion, 1923) by the French historian Pierre Champion (1880–1942).
109. Sergei Metalnikov, *La lutte contre la mort* (Paris: Gallimard, 1937). Metalnikov (1870–1946) was a Russian immunologist who investigated the psychic conditioning of the immune system.
110. In 1936–1937 Georges attended lectures on microbiology and had an internship at the Institut Pasteur in Paris.
111. On paper with a black border.
112. In 1937 Georges became the director of the laboratory of anatomic pathology at the Hôpital Cochin in Paris under Pierre Ameuille, where he worked until 1944.
113. Renée Arditti had married the conductor Josef Blatt (see note 134 below).
114. In late winter 1916, amid food shortages in wartime Vienna, Mathilde Canetti suffered a breakdown. She was in a sanatorium and then took Elias with her

for a few weeks' convalescence in Reichenhall (*Memoirs* 134f.; VII 154f.). Four years earlier, while visiting the same spa, she had been courted by a doctor. She later told her husband about this man and the lively conversations she had had with him. Elias later came to regard this as the reason for his father's sudden death (*Memoirs* 63–66 and 753–758; VII 74–78 and IX 209–213).

115. In *The Tongue Set Free*, Elias writes about his daily walk with his mother to Nonn and its churchyard: "That was where she would like to be buried, she said. She was thirty-one . . . nothing was so intimate and personal as Nonn, that was her place." *Memoirs* 134; VII 155.

116. After their stay in Reichenhall, Elias and his mother traveled via Munich to Switzerland and took up residence in Zurich.

117. The physician and university lecturer Julius Weiss, director of the sanatorium where he and Mathilde had met and where he courted her. Elias describes his jealousy of this man in *The Tongue Set Free* (*Memoirs* 127–132; VII 147–153). According to that account, however, Elias's outbursts against him were purely imaginary, and they didn't meet up with him again until Munich, where he helped them obtain travel documents (*Memoirs* 134–137; VII 156–161).

118. Cf. p. 59 above.

119. The poet Friedrich Hölderlin (1770–1843) spent the second half of his life in incurable madness.

120. Marie-Madeleine Comtesse de La Fayette (1634–1693). *La princesse de Clèves* (1678) was the first psychological novel in French. It portrays a woman unhappy in love.

121. The popular version of Thomas Carlyle's definition of genius. In Book 4, Chapter 3, of *The History of Friedrich II of Prussia, called Frederick the Great* (London, 1858–1865), Carlyle defines genius as a "transcendent capacity of taking trouble, first of all."

122. An illegible line.

123. The *Strassburger Neueste Nachrichten*.

124. In a 1936 journal entry, Elias defines a paranoiac as someone "for whom everything always means murder: stepping into his field, picking a cherry from his tree, touching his fingernail" (ZB 5a, quoted by Hanuschek, p. 646).

125. The visit paid by the Paris psychiatrist Georges Kien to his brother, the Viennese sinologist Peter Kien, at the end of *Auto-da-Fé* (423–456; I 463–501).

126. Cf. the description of Veza's stepfather Menachem Alkaley (died 1929) in *The Torch in My Ear* (*Memoirs* 392–398; VIII 124–131).

127. Presumably abortions. Cf. Elias's note of January 1935: "The second time that nothing came of a life. To think that Veza was killed six times and I only twice!" (notepad 28, ZB 3, quoted in Hanuschek, p. 723, note 22).

128. Hermann Broch's novel *Die Verzauberung* (The Enchantment), written in 1934–1935, was published in 1953 as *Der Versucher* (The Tempter). Elias had met Broch (1886–1951) in 1932, and the older writer was the first to proclaim Elias, in January 1933, a young colleague with talent.
129. Regine Béhar-Ova (1897–1993), the daugher of Aunt Sophie and sister of cousin Laurica, is mentioned in *The Tongue Set Free* (*Memoirs* 31 ff.; VII 39 ff.).
130. On paper with a black border.
131. Possible reference to the Japanese invasion of China in July 1937.
132. A work of cultural criticism published in Paris in 1935. The German translation appeared in 1936. The French surgeon Alexis Carrel (1873–1944), 1912 Nobel laureate in medicine, called for a melding of science and humanities in a general "science of man" (but also contemplated eugenic measures such as the gassing of the mentally ill).
133. The most famous of the wine villages surrounding Vienna. [DD]
134. Josef Blatt (1906–1999): conductor; student of Clemens Krauss; director of the opera in Reichenberg, Teplitz, and Brünn; director of the opera school at the Vienna Conservatory (1933–1934). He emigrated to the United States in 1937.
135. In 1937 Georges published an article on "The Etiology of Non-Tubercular Scarring of the Lungs."
136. Perhaps the wife or daughter of the composer Paul von Klenau (c. 1885–1946), until 1930 director of the Vienna Singakademie.
137. See note 15 above.
138. On paper with a black border.
139. From 1919 to 1921, Elias lived in the pension Villa Yalta in Zürich-Tiefenbrunnen (*Memoirs* 191 et passim; VII 221 et passim) while his mother and brothers were living in Arosa.
140. See note 60 above.
141. See note 69 above.
142. An expression for an exceptional person.
143. On paper with a black border.
144. Georges turned twenty-seven on January 23, 1938.
145. Georges did research at the Institut Pasteur during 1938 and 1939 with a stipend from the Fondation Roux. His dissertation was on "Latent Reinfection in Pulmonary Tuberculosis."
146. In Canetti's literary remains there are extensive notes for two lectures entitled "On Theater" and "The Death or Apparent Death of Theater" (cf. Hanuschek, pp. 306–308).
147. Elias first met Kokoschka (1886–1980) in Prague in May 1937 and encountered

him again while in exile in England. Cf. the portrait of Kokoschka in *Party in the Blitz*, pp. 154–160; *Party im Blitz*, pp. 165–172.

148. Hans Tietze (1880–1954) was born in Prague, taught at the University of Vienna, and emigrated to the United States in 1938.

149. Austrian historian and cultural philosopher (1885–1970), friend of Friedrich Gundolf, Hermann Broch, and Thomas Mann.

150. *Mass und Wert* (Measure and Value), a journal published in exile by Thomas Mann and Konrad Falke from 1937 to 1940, the organ of the conservative branch of German literature in exile. According to Lieselotte Maas, *Handbuch der deutschen Exilpresse 1933–1945*, volume 2 (Munich: Hanser, 1978), pp. 365 ff., nothing by Canetti ever appeared in the journal.

151. Some of the notes for the Werkbund lectures have to do with film as a new realm of shadows. Elias had already used this phrase to describe film in an interview in a supplement to the *Wiener Tag* of April 19, 1937 (cf. Hanuschek, pp. 307 f., and X 136 f.).

152. In the chapter entitled "Rhythmus" in *Crowds and Power*, Elias advances the thesis, "Rhythm is originally the rhythm of the feet" (31; III 32).

153. Joseph Canetti.

154. Aunt Rachel (1888–1978), the younger sister of Elias's father, was living in Palestine.

155. There is an untranslatable play on words here. Veza calls herself his *Feindin* (female enemy), which is (especially in Austrian pronunciation) very close to *Freundin* (female friend). [DD]

156. Kurt von Schuschnigg (1897–1977) became the federal chancellor of Austria after Dollfuss was murdered by the National Socialists in 1934. From 1936, Schuschnigg was also the national chairman of his party, the Vaterländische Front (Fatherland Front), and continued Dollfuss's authoritarian governing style. He was attempting to ensure Austria's independence from Germany, most recently by means of the Berchtesgaden Accord with Hitler on February 12, 1938. On March 9, he fixed March 13 as the date for a referendum on retaining Austrian sovereignity, but Hitler forced him to resign on March 11 by threatening to invade Austria with German troops.

157. On Canetti's enthusiasm for the physicist and aphorist Georg Christoph Lichtenberg (1742–1799) and the journals he called his *Sudelbücher* (waste-books), cf. a 1968 journal entry: "He is not dissatisfied with himself because he has too many ideas . . . The fact that he won't round anything off, that he finishes nothing is his and our good fortune: he thereby wrote the richest book in world literature" (*Human Province* 240; IV 314).

158. Arthur Neville Chamberlain (1869–1940), Conservative prime minister

from 1937 to 1940, maintained a policy of appeasement toward Germany until March 1939.

159. *Scheiss* = shit. [DD] Arthur Seyss-Inquart (1892–1946), Austrian National Socialist, was named Austrian interior minister on February 16, 1938, in accordance with the Berchtesgaden Accord. When German troops invaded Austria on March 12, he was named federal chancellor and implemented Austria's Anschluss (annexation) by the German Reich.

160. This is the first letter written after the German invasion of Austria on March 11, 1938.

161. *Am Himmel* = in heaven *or* in the sky. [DD] The letters of January 21, February 20, March 4, and March 23, 1936, however, are written on stationery with a letterhead that gives the address as "Am Himmel 30."

162. Carl Moll (1861–1945), Alma Mahler's stepfather and cofounder of the Viennese Secession.

163. See note 90 above.

164. Apparently a nickname for Elias. [DD]

165. Jean Hoepffner.

166. There is also mention of an "Aunt Bucka" in the encoded letter of April 11, 1938.

167. At the time, none of Elias and Georges's aunts was living in Vienna.

168. Colors traditionally symbolizing the Communists or socialists (red), the Catholics or conservatives (black), and the National Socialists (brown). [DD]

169. Jeremiah 8:22.

170. The familiar second-person singular pronoun. Perhaps Georges had suggested switching to it in a letter to her. See note 1 above and 261 below. [DD]

171. A dessert made from canned fruit.

172. *Türmchen* = little tower: Elias's nickname for Veza, who was a bit stout. [DD]

173. "Would you be so kind as to deliver this letter to the doctor as soon as possible? Many thanks." The entire letter that follows is an encoded fiction to fool the censor. "Uncle Bodo" addresses his "nephew" with the familiar *du*. [DD]

174. Cf. pp. 108–109. The "anthology" and the "photograph" possibly refer to a visa that Georges was supposed to obtain for Elias and Veza.

175. In the original, "nur immer einen reinen Tisch." Possibly a play on the German idiom *reinen Tisch machen* (to make a clean table) = to clear a matter up. [DD]

176. A palace in Vienna housing a famous art museum. [DD]

177. Conjectural for the original *Mädchenpass*. A *Mädchen* can be a girl or a housemaid. [DD]

178. The article "Das deutsche Ja!" (The German Yes), by Hermann Graedener, from a Viennese newspaper of April 9, 1938. The article speaks of "the true inwardness of the Germanic soul" and a "historically necessary new age of Germanness."
179. Like master, like servant.
180. Graf Bobby, the proverbially inept stock figure in Viennese jokes with frequently obscene content.
181. In this handwritten date, Veza wrote the Roman numeral V over a III, so that it is unclear whether she meant it to be a IV, a V, or a VI. The content suggests April.
182. Possibly a coded reference to a visa. [DD]
183. The classicist painter Georg Merkel (1881–1976). *The Play of the Eyes* describes him as "passionate" and a "good human being," "incapable of a vulgar action or word" (*Memoirs* 683; IX 123–124). Cf. also the "Laudatio auf Georg Merkel" of 1976 (X 95–100).
184. The Canettis left Austria sometime in October or November 1938, stayed a few weeks with Elias's relatives in Paris, and were in London by early 1939 (cf. Hanuschek, pp. 291–292 and 309). [DD]
185. Veza now addresses Georg with the familiar second-person pronoun *du*. [DD]
186. Sophie, Elias's paternal aunt, and her daughter Regine.
187. Probably the mother of Nissim's wife Edith Vanburger.
188. From this date until February 25, 1947, Veza wrote all her letters to Georges in English. With the few exceptions noted on pages vii–viii, her often idiosyncratic diction, spelling, and punctuation have not been altered. [DD]
189. Of Graham Greene's *The Power and the Glory* (1940): *Die Kraft und die Herrlichkeit*, translated by Veza Magd (London: Zsolnay & Heinemann, 1947), republished by Zsolnay in Vienna in 1993, revised by Käthe Springer. Cf. pp. 209–211. An undated letter, in English, from Friedl Benedikt to Georges refers to Veza's work on this translation:

8 St. Agnes Court
Porchester Terrace
London W2

Dear Georg,

I am sorry that I always bother you. But you will perhaps understand, when I explain. I don't know, whether you know that Veza is doing a translation. She works about 10 hours every day. For a book of 300 pages she gets *20 £*. She wants to finish the book in 4 weeks. From the 20 £, Veza has taken an advance of 5 and yesterday two people, whom they owe money came, and threatened to sell Elias' books, if he does not pay his debts, which amount to £ 12. So all the money for the translation is gone, even before it's finished. I don't think, that I must tell you in what state Elias and especially Veza is, who works so hard.

Georg, if you possibly can, send them money. But try to send them £ 10, so that they can pay their rent and still have money left for food. I have tried as much as I could, to find them a hospitality. But it is difficult, I have not succeeded yet.

If you send them 500 francs it's nothing, because they immediately pay the rent, they owe to the landlady and remain without a penny. Perhaps, if you have not got it, you could borrow the money. Because, you see, they *must* get out of this trouble, at least for a few weeks. I would like to hear from you very much.

Friedl

190. Veza and Elias had met Frieda Benedikt (1916–1953), the daughter of the newspaper publisher and independent scholar Ernst Benedikt, during their final years in Vienna, where the Benedikt family also lived on Himmelstrasse, kitty-corner from the Canettis (cf. *Memoirs* 749 ff.and 763 ff.; IX 203 ff. and 220 ff.). Friedl can be recognized in the figure of Hilde in Veza's novel *Die Schildkröten*. She followed Elias, who liked to call her his "pupil," into exile and published three novels in English under the pen name Anna Sebastian.
191. The New Zealander Kae Hursthouse, who took German lessons from Elias in 1940 and was engaged to Franz Steiner until 1938.
192. One of the panels of the altarpiece in the cathedral of Sint Baafs in Ghent. According to its inscription, it was begun by Hubert van Eyck (c. 1370–1426) and finished by his brother Jan (c. 1390–1441).
193. In the 1884 story "La Parure" ("The Necklace"), by Guy de Maupassant, the official Loisel and his wife become paupers because they lose a necklace. Madame Loisel borrows it to wear to a dinner so that for once in her life, she can appear to be a well-to-do, desirable woman.
194. A village in Buckinghamshire ("Bucks"), 110 miles northwest of London, near Amersham. Veza and Elias had moved to the area in 1940–1941, when residency permits for foreigners in London were increasingly restricted. At the same time, many Londoners were fleeing the bombing by moving to the country.
195. In Durris House, where Veza and Elias at first lived together, and where Veza returned alone several times.
196. Now lost.

197. Now lost.
198. Alice Asriel and her children Walter and Nuni were deported and gassed (cf. Elias's note of September 14, 1973, in Hanuschek, p. 57).
199. Beginning in June 1944, Germany deployed its newly developed secret weapons against England, called *V-Waffen* (short for *Vergeltungswaffen*—retaliation weapons): first the V1, an unmanned, explosives-loaded airplane, and then from September 1944 to March 1945 the long-distance rocket V2, the prototype for all modern rockets. Some 1,100 of these rockets reached London and southern England. The plan to produce a V3 was never carried out.
200. Friedl Benedikt.
201. Mathilde Arditti.
202. Elias did not have a German publisher at this time, but the translation of *Die Blendung* was being completed for the London publisher Jonathan Cape.
203. *Sic* in the original, "on" being probably a mistyping for "of." [DD] *Masse und Macht* (Crowds and Power) did not appear until 1960, published by the Claassen Verlag in Hamburg.
204. The historian Cicely Veronica Wedgwood (1910–1997), from the family of famous porcelain manufacturers. She worked as an editor at Cape and had recommended Friedl Benedikt's first novel to them. Cf. *Party in the Blitz*, pp. 16–19, 109–110; *Party im Blitz*, pp. 22–25, 121–123.
205. Elias had studied chemistry in Vienna.
206. Because of British censorship, Veza wrote her letters in English between 1940 and 1947. Kae Hursthouse facilitated the continuation of their correspondence via New Zealand in the first postwar months (cf. Hanuschek, p. 338), which may be the reason why Elias was able to write his letters in German.
207. This is the end of the letter returned by the censor, mentioned above.
208. In his *Mémoirs*, the Duc de Saint-Simon (1675–1755) describes life at the court of Louis XIV and during the regency of Philippe II, Duc d'Orléans, in the years 1692–1723. In his notebooks of 1992, Elias includes him among the great discoveries to be made in any national literature (V 388).
209. Nissim's wife.
210. The German invasion of France began in May 1940. Paris was occupied on June 14.
211. Since 1934, Georges had been in a romantic relationship with the doctor Marcel Daniels, whose mother and sisters lived in Manchester. Daniels treated Mathilde Canetti. Elias later regretted having destroyed letters from Georges to Daniels (Hanuschek, p. 287).
212. In a note of April 19, 1951, Elias calls the Viennese native Neumann (1897–1975) one of the "idols of his hatred" (quoted from Hanuschek, p. 375).

213. Marc (Marcel) Daniels was one of the coauthors of *Tuberculosis in Young Adults: Report on the Prophit Tuberculosis Survey 1935–1944* (London, 1948).
214. In the 1930s, the Communist Ernst Fischer (1899–1972) was the editor of the Viennese *Arbeiter-Zeitung* (see note 15 above). During the workers' uprising in February 1934, Veza and Elias sheltered Fischer and his wife Ruth von Mayenburg in their apartment. Fischer emigrated via Prague to Moscow. On April 10, 1945, he returned to Vienna just before the Soviets captured it. Cf. Ernst Fischer, *Erinnerungen und Reflexionen* (Frankfurt am Main: Sendler Verlag, 1987), pp. 268 ff. and 469 f.
215. *Toogoods oder das Licht* (Toogoods or the Light) was first published posthumously in *Der Fund*, 2001. Elias's description of the Milburn couple is in *Party in the Blitz*, pp. 32–47; *Party im Blitz*, pp. 43–60.
216. Popular nickname for the V1 rockets (see note 199 above).
217. The anniversary of Mathilde Canetti's death.
218. Father of the heroine of Honoré de Balzac's novel *Eugénie Grandet* and a tyrannical miser.
219. *Er giftet sich* (Austrian slang) = He's annoyed. "He poisoned himself" would be *Er vergiftete sich*. [DD]
220. Dea Gombrich.
221. Anna Mahler married the Russian conductor Anatole Fistoulari (1907–1995) in March 1943.
222. The brother of the protagonist in *Die Blendung*. See notes 125 above and 301 below.
223. Ernst Fischer.
224. Obviously a slip of the pen or a misreading. There is no such word in French.
225. Although discovered in 1928, penicillin was not mass-produced until 1944. It proved ineffectual against tuberculosis.
226. Nissim and Edith's daughter, born in 1937.
227. Friedl Benedikt and the painter Marie-Louise von Motesiczky (1906–1996), a pupil of Max Beckmann. She lived with her mother in Amersham, painted several portraits of Elias, and was a friend of Olda and Oskar Kokoschka, among others. Elias made her a present of one of his notebooks in 1942. It was published posthumously as *Aufzeichnungen für Marie-Louise* (Notebooks for Marie-Louise) (Munich: Hanser, 2005).
228. Now lost.
229. Nicolas Chamfort (1741–1794), French writer known for his *Pensées, maximes, et anecdotes* (1795).
230. Historic name for the kidney disease nephritis.
231. Full of spirit.

232. Results of the British parliamentary elections of July 5, 1945, were announced on July 26. The Labour Party won 48 percent of the vote and captured the majority of seats in the House of Commons. See also note 515 below.
233. On August 10, 1945, the Japanese government declared itself willing to capitulate to the United States, which accepted the surrender on August 11. On August 16, the Japanese emperor ordered his troops to cease fighting.
234. Kae Hursthouse had returned to New Zealand in 1942.
235. The Americans dropped atomic bombs on Hiroshima on August 6 and Nagasaki on August 9. This event preoccupied Elias for weeks in his journal. Some of his notes appeared in the 1978 volume *The Human Province*, where he writes under the heading "August 1945": "Matter is smashed, the dream of immortality is shattered . . . All certitude came from eternity. Without it, without this wonderful feeling of some permanence, albeit not one's own, everything is insipid and futile . . . We are so guilty, that we almost don't matter anymore" (pp. 66–67; IV 93f.). In the epilogue to *Crowds and Power* (465–470; III 553–559) and in the 1971 essay "Dr. Hachiya's Diary of Hiroshima" (*Conscience of Words*, 184–191; VI 303–310), this theme is taken up again.
236. The *Komödie der Eitelkeit.*
237. Elias Canetti, the cousin of Georges and Elias.
238. *Crowds and Power.*
239. There is no trace of censorship in the surviving letters.
240. Mathilde and Cissy Arditti.
241. *Dichter* = poet. [DD]
242. Roy Calderon, son of Bucky Calderon.
243. Veza's typewriter must have had the apostrophe on the same key as the numeral 9. When she fails to shift, "I'll" becomes "I9ll," the year of Georges's birth.
244. Henrik Ibsen's drama of ideas *Brand* (1866) concerns a pastor who holds uncompromisingly to his religious convictions.
245. Veza used various pen names in the 1930s; here she probably has "Veza Magd" (*Magd* = maid, maiden) in mind, the name she also used as translator of Graham Greene's *The Power and the Glory.*
246. Ernst Fischer was minister of education in the first administration of the Austrian Second Republic.
247. This tributary of the Rhône flows through Le Trouvet near Grenoble, the main town in the valley where St. Hilaire is located.
248. Spirit. [DD]
249. Anna Mahler's married name.

250. Correctly: "on His Majesty's Service," i.e., returned to sender without additional postage due.
251. The Nazi concentration camp Bergen-Belsen.
252. Marie-Louise von Motesiczky, from the Austrian family of von Lieben.
253. See note 215 above. On Mr. Milburn's miserliness cf. also *Party in the Blitz*, pp. 39 f.; *Party im Blitz*, pp. 51 f.
254. Now lost.
255. A London department store.
256. See note 202 above.
257. Elias wrote *Die Hochzeit* (The Wedding) in 1931–1932. It was first published by Hanser (Munich) in 1964 and premiered in Braunschweig in 1965.
258. Literally "young seamstresses" = cocottes, loose women.
259. Kae Hursthouse.
260. This proved not to be true. See note 198 above.
261. Except for the P.S., this short letter was written in German. In this and all subsequent letters written in German, Veza addresses Georges with the familiar second-person pronoun *du* instead of the formal *Sie* of her prewar letters. [DD]
262. A cousin of Elias and Georges.
263. The British periodical *Time and Tide* published contributions by many well-known writers of the time, including D. H. Lawrence, George Orwell, and Virginia Woolf
264. German *genial* = brilliant. [DD]
265. Cf. *Hochzeit*, II 53 ff. Changed by Veza.
266. Senior building official (a government post). [DD]
267. A figure in Heinrich Heine's poem "Es war ein alter König" (number 29 in the collection *Neuer Frühling*).
268. His heart was heavy, his hair was gray, the poor old king, he took a young wife. [DD]
269. Like Germany, Austria was divided into British, French, American, and Soviet zones of occupation.
270. (Russian) peasant.
271. See note 214 above.
272. Has a criminal record.
273. See note 198 above.
274. Maudy in Manchester. See p. 141.
275. Cf. pp. 130 and 134–135.
276. Cf. p. 116.
277. Cf. John 18: 38–40.
278. Cavern in the lung.

279. Probably streptomycin (see note 431 below).
280. Never published. No such manuscript has been found among Georges's papers.
281. Horace Walpole (1717–1797), whose *The Castle of Ortranto* (1764) is considered the first gothic novel in English, conducted an extensive correspondence with the cultural and political figures of his day, among them Thomas Gray and Voltaire.
282. See note 193 above.
283. On the Milburns, cf. notes 215 and 253 above.
284. In the first elections of the Second Republic on November 25, 1945, the conservative Österreichisches Volkspartei (ÖVP: Austrian People's Party) won an absolute majority in the National Council with slightly over 50 percent of the vote.
285. In fact, Ernst Fischer was replaced as minister of education by a member of the ÖVP on December 20.
286. During the war, the textile industry in Great Britain was strictly controlled. The materials used were regulated (silk, for example, was needed for parachutes), as were the amounts allowed for individual garments (for example, the length and width of skirts were prescribed).
287. In 1946, Flammarion in Paris published *Le bacille de Koch dans la lésion tuberculeuse du poumon* and *L'allergie tuberculeuse chez l'homme*.
288. Otto von Habsburg (born 1912) fled Austria after the Anschluss in 1938. After living in exile in the United States and France, he returned to Austria in June 1945, but was expelled by the Austrian government in January 1946.
289. Rudolf Hess (1894–1987), German Nazi leader, made a solo flight to Scotland in May 1941, hoping to negotiate peace with the Duke of Hamilton, whom he considered the leader of the British peace movement. He was imprisoned and sent to Nuremberg after the war, where he was sentenced to life in prison in October 1946.
290. Like all of Elias's letters, this and the following one are in German. [DD]
291. Baltasar Gracián y Morales (1601–1658), Spanish writer and philosopher known especially for his *Oráculo manual*, a collection of maxims.
292. In *The Play of the Eyes*, Elias wrote of Francisco Gómez de Quevedo y Villegas (circa 1580–1654): "He became, after Swift and Aristophanes, one of my ancestors" (*Memoirs* 819; IX 275). Cf. *Secret Heart of the Clock* 12; IV 382 and X 173.
293. Elias regarded *Gulliver's Travels* as one of his most important early reading experiences (*The Agony of Flies* 153; V 77 and *Memoirs* 44; VII 52). In 1967 he noted, "In Aristophanes, in Quevedo, in Swift he understands his own hatred" (*Notes from Hampstead* 143; V 212).

294. Nickname for Paul.
295. The painter Georges Arditti (born 1914).
296. In Dostoyevsky's *The Brothers Karamazov*, three brothers return to the house of their father, whom they all wish dead. But it is Smerdyakov, an illegitimate son of the old man and an epileptic, who murders him, acting upon the maxim of his intellectual half-brother Ivan that "anything is permitted." The eldest brother is found guilty of the crime and Smerdyakov remains undiscovered until he admits the deed to Ivan and then commits suicide.
297. Elias did not apply for British citizenship until 1952 (Hanuschek, p. 377).
298. Her cousin Veza Cansino (see note 346 below).
299. Henry Stewart, Lord Darnley (1545–1567), second husband of Mary Stuart, Queen of Scots.
300. The Sanatorium des Étudiants in St. Hilaire du Touvet.
301. In this chapter of *Auto-da-Fé*, the psychiatrist Georges Kien is described as a young professor "whom they loved because he was beautiful and kind" (395; I 432) and "treated the patients as if they were human beings" (396; I 434).
302. Arnold R. Rich, *The Pathogenesis of Tuberculosis* (Springfield, Ill.: Thomas, 1944).
303. Literal translation of German *Fehlleistung*, a "Freudian slip." [DD]
304. Cf. *Toogoods* in *Der Fund*, pp. 201–203, and *Party in the Blitz*, pp. 36–38; *Party im Blitz*, pp. 48–50.
305. The Protestant James Hepburn, Earl of Bothwell (c. 1536–1578), was thought to be the lover of Mary Stuart and the murderer of her husband Darnley. He married her in 1567, possibly after abducting and raping her.
306. David Riccio, Mary Stuart's secretary, who had originally come to court as a singer. Her husband Darnley murdered him in 1566 out of jealousy.
307. *Henry IV* Part II, Act III.
308. Lytton Strachey, *Elizabeth and Essex: A Tragic History* (1928).
309. The more shit there is, the more beautiful the flowers.
310. Friedl Benedikt.
311. Ladies' man.
312. Living space. [DD]
313. The Austrian novelist Hermann Broch married Annemarie Meier-Graefe, the widow of the art historian Julius Meier-Graefe, in 1949.
314. These exact words do not occur in *Macbeth*.
315. See note 93 above.
316. German *Konsequenz* = consistency. [DD]
317. Alias the Beautiful, the Wise, the Great, Phoebus, Romeo.
318. Anxiety dream. [DD]

319. Nevertheless.
320. Bucky Calderon's wife.
321. Friedl Benedikt.
322. The writer William "Billy" Goldman. Several of his books appeared in London in the 1940s, among them *East End My Cradle* (London: Faber & Faber, 1940).
323. Parentheses were added by hand and "better not" was written above this passage.
324. Perhaps a reference to *Hamlet*, Act I, Scene 4.
325. Veza's note at the top is in English, but Georges's original letter is in French. He addresses Veza with the familiar second-person pronoun *tu*.
326. Châteaubriant.
327. Four or five lines have been cut off at the bottom of this page.
328. In 1944, Cape in London published two novels by Friedl Benedikt writing under the pen name Anna Sebastian: *Let Thy Moon Arise* and *The Monster*.
329. Friedl's novels actually received quite positive reviews (cf. Hanuschek, p. 40).
330. German *Ritter* = knight.
331. Heinrich von Kleist (1777–1811), author of stories and plays, shot himself in a suicide pact with a woman friend.
332. Anna Sebastian, *The Dreams* (London: Jonathan Cape, 1950).
333. Anna Sebastian, *Le Monstre*, translated by Marguerite Lichtenberger (Paris, 1946).
334. The plays he refers to here are possibly *Der Oger* and *Der Tiger* (see note 39 above) and one or both of the lost plays in English (see notes 197 and 228 above).
335. Elias was twenty-five when he wrote *Die Blendung*.
336. William Goldman.
337. Possibly Graham Greene's sister Helga Greene.
338. See note 198 above.
339. Because of repeated political upheavals, the Scottish dynasty of the Stuarts lost the English crown and had to go into exile twice in the course of the seventeenth century, first in 1649, when Charles I was executed after his attempt to introduce Anglicanism into Scotland ignited the Civil War; and again in 1688, when James II fled after his policy of re-Catholicization encountered parliamentary opposition.
340. In 1815, Talleyrand is supposed to have said about the French nobility returning from exile, "They have learned nothing and forgotten nothing."
341. See note 302 above. [DD]
342. Their friendship with Emanuel Hirschtritt began in Vienna, where they went on joint Sunday excursions and Hirschtritt supported the Canettis financially, according to an April 5, 2003 interview with Hirschtritt's son Stephen Hearst.

343. In Veza's autobiographical novel *Die Schildkröten* (*The Tortoises*), Hilde (in whom one can discern traces of Friedl) fails in her naive attempt to arrange for an airplane on which the writer Kain and his wife can escape Nazi Vienna.
344. In the issue of May 11, 1946, the reviewer R. D. Charques wrote that the novel:

> leaves an impression of mere Central-European portentousness, a portentousness at once heavy and trivial. Mr. Canetti, it is plain, is a writer of formidable ambition, persevering, much impressed by an ideal of learning and scholarship and the pursuit of truth, and beset by a worrying and nervous solemnity of mind. As a novelist, however, he makes little contact with life. He has, indeed, only a leaning towards a monotonous, prefabricated and slightly grotesque fancy to take the place of the imagination which he lacks and only a fidgety recognition of the commonplace to substitute for the common touch. In making as he does a terrific and inconsequent to-do about trifles, and in thus inflating them to absurdly unlifelike proportions, he robs even the element of intellectual fantasy in the novel of the significance it might otherwise possess. Neither Peter Kien nor Therese "take on the semblance of a human being."

345. Joyce Cary (1888–1957).
346. Known as "Little Veza." Elias writes in *Party in the Blitz*, "The two Vezas had a sort of crush on one another" (p. 157; *Party im Blitz*, p. 169).
347. Marie-Louise von Motesiczky. It is possible that Veza's misspelling is not accidental. In the letter of September 10, 1946, she types the name with the *u* above the *L* (see p. 228).
348. Joseph Canetti.
349. German *Ahnung* = anticipation, foreboding, presentiment. [DD]
350. I was hating all night long.
351. The anniversary of Mathilde Canetti's death.
352. A film version of *Auto-da-Fé* was never made.
353. See note 287 above.
354. Possibly Robert Neumann.
355. See note 83 above.
356. The Viennese sculptor Georg Ehrlich (1879–1966) emigrated to England in 1938.
357. All Veza's letters to Elias are in German. [DD]
358. Perhaps a reference to the Grimm brothers' fairy tale "Hänsel und Gretel," in which the witch asks who is nibbling at her house and the children answer, "Der Wind, der Wind, das himmlische Kind" (The wind, the wind, that heavenly child). [DD]

359. One of Veza's nicknames for Elias. [DD]
360. Margaret Gardiner (1904–2005), Friedl Benedikt's cousin. In *Party in the Blitz*, Elias calls her house at 35 Downshire Hill a "citadel of modernism" because she collected abstract art and provided accommodations for many "transient residents and visitors" from the worlds of art and science (pp. 124 and 125; *Party im Blitz*, pp.137 and 138).
361. Martin Bernal, son of Margaret Gardiner and J. Desmond Bernal.
362. A diminutive form of Sebastian, Friedl Benedikt's pen name. Veza prefaces the name with the masculine article: *der Sebastl.* [DD]
363. Veza, Friedl Benedikt, and Marie-Louise von Motesiczky, with allusion to the three witches in *Macbeth.*
364. Czech *oblátka* = wafers.
365. There is an untranslatable pun here: *abgelebt* = decrepit, *abgelegt* = discarded. Between parentheses, Veza writes literally, "no, it *is* a *b*, not a *g*."
366. Cf. note 20 above. [DD]
367. Below Veza's signature, a handwritten line has been cut off. The body of the letter is typed.
368. Margaret Gardiner.
369. Diana Croft, daughter of Sir Henry Page Croft and wife of Fred Uhlman (see note 401 below; cf. *Party in the Blitz*, pp. 133f.; *Party im Blitz*, p. 147).
370. An inkblot and a hole in the paper appear at the words "daughter" and "wrote." The verb "give," on the other hand, was left out by accident and is a conjecture: Veza may have meant to write "send."
371. The cousin Mathilde Arditti.
372. Veza's cousin Charlie Hirsch, with whom the three Canetti brothers and their mother had shared the apartment of Hirsch's mother Olga Hirsch in the Radetzkystrasse in Vienna from September 1924 to October 1925. Elias describes Hirsch, who at the time was working as a lounge pianist under the name Johnnie Ring, as fat but handsome and possibly homosexual, a "flatterer" (*Memoirs* 368–371; VIII 96–99).
373. This letter is in German. [DD]
374. Emanuel Hirschtritt.
375. In the original, "niemand weiss, dass ich Rumpelstilzchen heiss," a quote from the rhyming chant of the title figure in the Grimms' fairy tale.
376. This performance never came to pass.
377. Perhaps Emanuel Hirschtritt.
378. Lucienne Torrès (in her career as a singer, Lucienne Vernay). Nissim had met her in Algiers in 1943 and she joined him in Paris in 1946. After his divorce from his first wife Edith, he married Lucienne on September 15, 1947.

379. During the war, Nissim had run a cabaret in Algiers called "Les trois ânes." In 1947, he opened the cabaret "Les trois baudets" in Montmartre, where Juliette Gréco, Jacques Brel, Georges Brassens, and other well-known artists performed.

380. On September 15, 1946, Veza wrote to Nissim:

> We've had two quite unsettling letters from Georg, and Edith also wrote me that he looks very bad. So I would be very much obliged if you would write us all the details about Georg, and if he is strong enough to survive this new operation. Today I also began all the [necessary] steps at the Home Office to travel to France, although at the moment, Georg does not wish me to come. However, it's reassuring to Canetti, and since it will take many weeks for my request to be granted, I would like to be ready. Canetti himself wants to defer a bit. He's built himself a livelihood here and it isn't easy for stateless persons to return to England. Actually, it's quite impossible, and only possible for us because he has very good connections. Please do not let Georg know I wrote you. Otherwise, he may fear that we know more about his case than he does himself, which isn't true. We only know what he told us himself, and that is bad enough. I would also like to know if you can have a room in a decent hotel reserved for me, because I don't want to live with relatives. The Home Office will let me bring along about seventy pounds sterling, which ought to be plenty.

381. I.e., from the Institut Pasteur; cf. note 110 above.

382. That is, the manuscript of *Crowds and Power*. [DD]

383. Loves only you.

384. The second German-language edition of *Die Blendung* did not appear until 1948, published in Munich by Verlag Willi Weismann.

385. Their uncle Joseph and their cousin Elias Canetti, both in Paris.

386. The author and journalist Cyril Connolly (1903–1974), one of the best-known critics of his generation, was the editor of the literary journal *Horizon* from 1939 to 1950.

387. From 1945 to 1955 Vienna, like Berlin, was occupied jointly by France, Great Britain, the Soviet Union, and the United States, and except for the inner city was divided into separately administered sectors.

388. The Hôpital des Fougerays in Châteaubriant.

389. Georges's former superior Pierre Ameuille (1880–1948). Cf. note 112 above.

390. None of Veza's plays was produced during her lifetime.

391. Veza Cansino.

392. French *sale* = dirty. [DD]

393. You have a senile cousin who saves everything. [DD]
394. The wife of cousin Elias Canetti.
395. Either Mathilde Arditti's mother Bellina or Mathilde Camhi's mother Sophie.
396. See notes 328 and 333 above.
397. The unfinished *History of England* by Thomas Macaulay (1800–1859).
398. The main female character in *Die Blendung*.
399. German *Linsen* = lentils. Cf. Genesis 25:29–34.
400. The first directed by Marcel Pagnol (1938), the second by Jean Vigo (1934).
401. The German native Fred Uhlman (1901–1985) was a judge, painter, and writer. He founded the Freier Deutscher Kulturbund (Free German Cultural Alliance) at his house at 47 Downshire Hill. Among its members were John Heartfield and Oskar Kokoschka. Cf. *Party in the Blitz*, pp. 133–137; *Party im Blitz*, pp. 147–151.
402. German *Küss die Hand* = (literally) Kiss the hand. An Austrian greeting and farewell, usually said by a man to a woman. [DD]
403. 35 Downshire Hill. Cf. note 360 above.
404. J. Desmond Bernal (1901–1971), an active Communist. In *Party in the Blitz*, Elias praises him for his "openness and curiosity about everything" and his "lack of arrogance" (p. 126; *Party im Blitz*, p. 140).
405. Elias, too, calls Alan Gardiner "the most important Egyptologist of the time" (*Party in the Blitz*, p. 124; *Party im Blitz*, p. 137).
406. A powerful noblewoman at the court of Louis XIV. Saint-Simon writes at length about her in his memoirs. Her name is associated with the saying, "She dominated, but did not rule."
407. My dearest and charming and very handsome brother-in-law. The phrase *très beau-frère* is a play on words, since *beau-frère* (brother-in-law) means literally "handsome-brother."
408. According to an unpublished note by Elias (ZB 60), Herr Hoe is Jean Hoepffner. Herr Hoe is also the eponymous hero of a story by Veza (in *Der Fund*, pp. 33–37).
409. Veza means Veronica's father, Sir Ralph Wedgwood. In *Party in the Blitz*, Elias writes that he had "the face of a Celtic magician" (p. 18; *Party im Blitz*, p. 24).
410. Josiah Wedgwood, the first Baron Wedgwood (1872–1943), great-great-grandson of the porcelain firm's founder of the same name. As Labour MP, he criticized the policy of appeasement and the restrictions on Jewish immigration (cf. *Party in the Blitz*, p. 18; *Party im Blitz*, pp. 24 f.).
411. See note 263 above.
412. English writer (1901–1979) and the niece of Lytton Strachey.
413. Philip Toynbee (1916–1981).

414. See note 332 above.
415. Egon Friedell (1878–1938) edited many of Lichtenberg's writings but never published a biography of him. In 1946, Eddy C. Bertin's English translation of his science-fiction novel *Die Reise mit der Zeitmaschine* was published as *The Return of the Time Machine*. In 1944, Otto Deneke published *Lichtenbergs Leben* (Lichtenberg's Life), the first volume of a projected two-volume biography.
416. Lichtenberg was professor of physics at Göttingen.
417. Georges had apparently undergone another operation.
418. German *Mappe* = portfolio. [DD]
419. A London publisher.
420. René Benjamin (1885–1948), *L'enfant tué* (The Slain Child) (Paris: Éditions nouvelles, 1946).
421. Published by Alfred A. Knopf in 1947.
422. Likely the Hungarian painter Endre Nemes (1908–1985), with whom Friedl lived in Sweden.
423. The resistance fighter Jean Cassou (1897–1986) published the novel *Le centre du monde* (The Center of the Earth) in Paris in 1945.
424. Dear Son. [DD]
425. Lion Feuchtwanger (1884–1958), author of popular historical novels such as *Jud Süss* (Jew Süss, 1925). He went into exile from the Nazis and lived in France and the United States. His works continued to be published by exile publishers and in English translation. [DD]
426. An abortion.
427. William "Billy" Goldman.
428. German *Linsengericht* = pottage of lentils (Genesis 25:34).
429. The increase in Zionist terror against the British in Palestine led to evacuations in February 1947 and to the gathering of the remaining Britons into security zones. On February 18, the British government declared the British mandate in Palestine to be "impracticable" and asked the United Nations to assume responsibility for a solution to the Palestine question. Already on November 15, 1946, Veza had written to Nissim, "The Palestine terrorists make it difficult for us to maintain our dignity, and God knows, the people here are noble."
430. Emanuel "Manny" Shinwell (1884–1986), Jewish Labour politician. As energy minister under Attlee, he was responsible for nationalizing the mining industry and was heavily criticized for his inability to prevent the coal crisis that crippled much of British industry in February 1947.
431. This antibiotic, discovered in America in 1943, was the first specific medication available against tuberculosis. Early testing showed that it had to be

used in combination with other drugs to prevent harmful side effects. For its discovery, the American Selman A. Waksman was awarded the Nobel Prize for Medicine in 1952.

432. Lust.
433. Shortcomings, inadequacy.
434. Dear Sister-in-Law.
435. German *konsequent* = consistent. [DD]
436. In thrall sexually. [DD]
437. Identity not established.
438. After Veza had finally left for France, Elias wrote Nissim:

Dear Nissim,

I am writing you in a rush. Our cousin Harry [Arditti] is going to Paris in a few weeks. He just arrived recently and I could not reach him until today. I hope Veza is already in Paris. It's possible that she's a bit short on money after all. Please be a dear and *press* 10,000 francs on her. So that she will accept it (you know how proud she is), tell her that Harry gave you the money for her, even though it's not true. You will see to it that she doesn't leave by herself and that everything is in order with her.

Many thanks and see you soon,
Your brother Elias.

After her return to London, Veza wrote (in English) to Nissim on April 15, 1947: "Dear Jack, excuse all the trouble that you and dear Lucienne had with me. Thanks for your intervention, I took only 4000 fr. (four thousand) from Regine, since it was too late to buy anything. Hope you are keeping fine and wish you all the best. Love to both, Veza."

439. This and all subsequent letters from Veza to Georges are written in German, although they contain frequent English words and phrases, especially in the salutations and closings. [DD]
440. In the 1930s, the Hotel Lutetia on Boulevard Raspail was a famous gathering place for émigré intellectuals. In 1940–1944 it was the headquarters of the National Socialist counterespionage office. After the war it was a meeting place for survivors of German concentration camps.
441. French *sac* = bag.
442. "That's what you wanted, Georges Dandin." A famous line from Molière's comedy *George Dandin ou Le Mari confondu* (premiered 1668), spoken by the cuckolded husband at the end of Act I.
443. . . . *und ich zahl nicht viel*: a double entendre in German: I don't pay (or) count much. [DD]

444. The Hôpital des Fougerays in Châteaubriant.
445. *Master of the tower*: in English in the original. An unclear allusion, perhaps to Canetti's nickname for Veza: *Türmchen* (little tower), perhaps to the end of *Die Blendung*, which was entitled *The Tower of Babel* in Wedgwood's translation.
446. Bandage.
447. Probably a play on "French letter," English slang for a condom. [DD]
448. *Vertige, regime* = dizziness, diet.
449. Don't give her too much poison.
450. "Dichtung und Unwahrheit," a play on the title of Goethe's autobiography *Dichtung und Wahrheit*. [DD]
451. The son of Georg Merkel.
452. The cousin of Georges and Elias.
453. I am a misunderstood woman.
454. Cf. note 308 above. After falling into disfavor with the queen, Robert Devereux, Earl of Essex, attempted a coup d'état to retain control of London and was executed.
455. Harry Arditti.
456. A coward.
457. Possibly an allusion to the eponymous heroine of Alban Berg's unfinished opera based on two plays by Frank Wedekind.
458. Your senile cousin.
459. The lower Loire Valley.
460. *Schwindel aber ohne Schwindel*: double entendre in German. *Schwindel* = vertigo and swindle. [DD]
461. Possibly the French actor and director Jean-Louis Barrault (1910–1994), best known for his role as the lovesick mime in Marcel Carné's film *Les enfants du paradis* (1945).
462. Perhaps Emanuel Hirschtritt.
463. Cousin Elias Canetti's son, born 1927.
464. The German pronoun is ambiguous: *Canetti, der sie gern hat* could also mean "Canetti, who likes her," hence the jokey explanatory parenthesis. [DD]
465. Jean-Paul Sartre, *Réflexions sur la question juive* (Reflections on the Jewish Question), published as a book in 1946.
466. The *a* is underlined to differentiate her from Regine. [DD]
467. Leslie Fiedler, "The World As Inferno," *Partisan Review* 14 (1947): 316–320.
468. Henry Abraham Arditti, one of the three cousins of Georges and Elias's mother already living in Manchester when the Canettis moved there in 1911 (cf. *Memoirs* 56; VII 66).

469. A pun in German: "nein, nicht spukte, ich spuckte."
470. In Heinrich Heine's 1846 poem "Der Asra," a slave pines for the "fair and beautiful Sultan's daughter" and becomes daily "pale and paler." He tells her he belongs to the tribe of Asra, "who die when they are in love."
471. Companions.
472. In 1946, Marx Brod's *Franz Kafka. Eine Biographie* (Prague, 1937) was reissued, in German, in New York.
473. Their cousin.
474. Either *Law Reports of Trials of War Criminals*, 15 volumes (London: H.M.S.O., 1947–1949), or *Trials of Major Criminals before the International Military Tribunal*, 42 volumes (Nuremberg, 1947–1949).
475. How much should I give the rabbi?
476. The kingly figure in *Le roman de Renard*, a collection of old French animal fables by various authors of the twelfth and thirteenth centuries.
477. Elias suffered from a mild form of diabetes.
478. *Die Blendung* was published in France by Arthaud in 1949 under the title *La Tour de Babel*.
479. The French translation of Neumann's novel was published as *Enfants de Vienne* (Paris: Éditions Atlas, 1947).
480. In June 1947, Friedl married a Mr. Widholm so that she could remain in Sweden.
481. The conductor and composer Otto Klemperer (1885–1973). After working in Prague, Strasbourg, and Berlin, he emigrated to the United States in 1933 and returned to Europe in 1947.
482. Eileen Herlie (born 1920) made her London debut in Jean Cocteau's *L'aigle à deux têtes*. Her screen career began with the role of Gertrude in Laurence Olivier's 1948 film version of *Hamlet*.
483. Anna Mahler's husband Anatole Fistoulari.
484. Perhaps Emanuel Hirschtritt.
485. Gallimard.
486. Gallimard published *Le procès* and *Le château* before the war and *La métamorphose* in 1946.
487. Claudine Canetti (born 1929), the younger daughter of Uncle Joseph.
488. The French publisher Benjamin Arthaud.
489. Veza here is referring to Elias. Mikhail Ilarionovich Kutuzov (1745–1813) was a Russian field marshal and national hero, commander in the "great patriotic war" against Napoleon. In *War and Peace*, Tolstoy portrays him as Napoleon's polar opposite who knows that as an individual, he cannot control the forces of history. In his command decisions, he relies on time and patience.

490. Honor Frost, art historian, friend of the Canettis, and later a maritime archaeologist.
491. *Ghost of a Flea* (c. 1819), by William Blake.
492. After Russian troops had long avoided decisive engagements, they stood and fought Napoleon's Grande Armée near Borodino on the Moskva on September 7, 1812. Although the French won the battle, they suffered huge losses. Napoleon was able to occupy Moscow on September 14, but after the great fire in the city, he had to begin a retreat in October, during which his army was almost completely wiped out.
493. The main female character in *Die Blendung*.
494. Sir William Glock and his wife Clement, a painter belonging to the Hampstead Group. Canetti writes in *Party in the Blitz* (p. 192; *Party im Blitz*, p. 207) that she looked "like Apollo." They lived in Marshfield in the Cotswold Hills.
495. See note 332 above.
496. Approximately twenty keystrokes here are illegible because of an ink blot in the fold of the paper.
497. A play on Frederick the Great's remark in support of religious tolerance, "Everyone should achieve salvation [or bliss] *nach seiner Façon*"—in his own way. [DD]
498. The dramatist and novella writer Heinrich von Kleist (1777–1811).
499. Hutchinson.
500. Jean Contou, an editor at Arthaud.
501. Nietzsche developed syphilitic insanity in 1889 and died in 1900. Heinrich von Kleist committed suicide in 1811.
502. A Zurich newspaper.
503. Robert H. Jackson, chief prosecutor at the first Nuremberg trial.
504. The owner of the publishing company Droin-Labastie.
505. The French edition of *Die Blendung*, translated by Paule Arhex as *La Tour de Babel*, was published by B. Arthaud (Grenoble and Paris, 1949).
506. Text between quotation marks is in English in the original. [DD]
507. Philippe I, Duc d'Orléans (1640–1701), known as "Monsieur" at court and married to Liselotte von der Pfalz, was kept out of politics by his brother, Louis XIV. Philippe was a homosexual and maintained a coterie of favorites in the Palais Royal.
508. Hans Bernd Gisevius (1904–1974) published a report on his participation in the German resistance, entitled *Bis zum bittern Ende* (Zurich: Fretz & Wasmuth, 1946). In 1948, Cape published the English translation, *To the Bitter End: An Insider's Account of the Plot to Kill Hitler, 1933–1944*. Gisevius was a member of the high command of the Wehrmacht and had connections

to the Western Allies. He was able to escape the notice of the Gestapo after the attempt on Hitler's life on July 20, 1944, and he testified at the Nuremberg tribunal in 1947.

509. Chamberlain.
510. The Hôpital des Fougerays in Châteaubriant.
511. My, but you work a lot!
512. Hjalmar Schacht (1877–1970), finance minister in the Third Reich, resigned in 1937 after criticizing Göring. In 1939, he stepped down as president of the Reichsbank in protest against wartime economic measures. After the unsuccessful attempt on Hitler's life on July 20, 1944, he was arrested as a coconspirator.
513. In *The Tongue Set Free*, Elias mentions an Aunt Linda, a widowed sister-in-law of his mother, and her two children in Lausanne (77f.; VII 90f.).
514. André Gide's 1909 novelistic "report" about the renunciation of love and earthly happiness.
515. Clement Richard Attlee (1883–1967), leader of the Labour Party from 1935 to 1955, member of Churchill's coalition cabinet from 1940 to 1945. He succeeded Churchill as prime minister in July 1945 after the Labour victory. His government instituted radical reforms, nationalized the railroads, natural gas, and electricity, and established the welfare state. He also withdrew the British from India and Palestine. He was succeeded by Churchill in 1951.
516. Eamon de Valera (1892–1975), Irish politician and founder of the republican party Fianna Fáil. Prime minister in 1932–1948, 1951–1954, and 1957–1959; president of Ireland from 1959 to 1973.
517. *Die Blendung* (The Blinding), the original German title of *Auto-da-Fé*. [DD]
518. Francis Graham-Harrison (1914–2001) became a good friend of Canetti's (cf. *Party in the Blitz*, pp. 19f.; *Party im Blitz*, pp. 25f.).
519. In English in the original. [DD]
520. Siegfried Trebitsch (1869–1956).
521. Princess Elizabeth married Philip Mountbatten, Duke of Edinburgh, on November 20, 1947.
522. Prince Philip was born a prince of Denmark and Greece on the island of Corfu and did not become a British citizen until the spring of 1947.
523. Bad Ischl, a popular summer resort for the Austro-Hungarian monarchy. Kaiser Franz Joseph (1830–1916) and Kaiserin Elisabeth ("Sisi," 1837–1898) had gotten engaged there.
524. Henry Miller, *Tropic of Capricorn* (1939).
525. Jacqueline Canetti (1921–1971), Uncle Joseph's oldest daughter.

526. Elias signed a contract for the second German edition of *Die Blendung* with the Munich publisher Willi Weismann in February 1948. It appeared at the end of that year. Weismann also published an edition of the *Komödie der Eitelkeit* in 1950 in a printing of six hundred copies, only some of which were bound. On the collaboration between the Canettis and Weismann, cf. *Broch—Canetti—Jahnn. Willi Weismann und sein Verlag 1946–1954*, edited by Jochen Meyer, *Marbacher Magazin* 33 (1985), pp. 27–45.
527. Emil Ludwig, the pen name of Emil Cohn (1881–1948), *Geschenke des Lebens: ein Rückblick* (The Gifts of Life: A Retrospective) (Berlin, 1931). Elias had met Ludwig, the successful author of several biographies of historical figures, at the home of the Benedikts in Vienna. In *The Play of the Eyes*, he mocks Ludwig for boasting about his meetings with Mussolini (*Memoirs* 781, IX 240 f.).
528. The Canettis had known the physician Fritz Jerusalem (later known as Fritz Jensen, 1903–1955) since their days in Vienna.
529. A visual pun. *Fröhliche Weihnachten* = Merry Christmas (*Weihnachten* = literally "holy nights"). *Weinen* (to weep) is not etymologically related. [DD]
530. Charles Chaplin's black comedy about an unemployed bank clerk who marries and then murders rich widows to support his crippled wife and children. Although Chaplin considered it his most intelligent and brilliant film, when it premiered in 1947 it was disliked by both the press and the public and was even banned in Memphis, Tennessee.
531. Eponymous hero of Voltaire's 1759 novel *Candide ou l'optimisme*, who believes he lives in "the best of all possible worlds."
532. The text from "clemency" to this point is typed in red.
533. The phrase between quotes is in English in the original.
534. *Recommandé* = registered.
535. Not completely legible. Perhaps *Couvert* (envelope).
536. Instead of the three lectures originally planned, Elias gave an "introductory lecture" entitled "Proust—Kafka—Joyce" at the summer school in Bryanston, Dorset, in August 1948. It was first published, together with a German translation by Karen Lauer, in 2005 in X 9–48.
537. Cf. Elias's vituperations against T. S. Eliot (1888–1965) in *Party in the Blitz*, pp. 2–3, 5–7, 31, 58–61; *Party im Blitz*, pp. 8–9, 12–14, 40, 70–73.
538. The Jesuit writer and philosopher Martin d'Arcy (1899–1976) was the best-known English apologist for Roman Catholicism and inspired Evelyn Waugh, among others, to convert.
539. At Maida Vale 187. In May 1951, Elias autographed a photograph for his landlady "To Frau Professor Fischel, the only person who ever gave me a home."

540. His mother's sister.
541. Probably Bellina Arditti.
542. An official, such as a sheriff, entitled to collect royal revenues.
543. Town in Norfolk, about ninety-five miles northeast of London. The country estate Sandringham House belongs to the British crown.
544. Queen Elizabeth (1900–2002), wife of King George VI.
545. Queen Mary (Mary of Teck, 1867–1953), widow of King George V.
546. Princess Margaret (1930–2002), younger daughter of George VI and Elizabeth.
547. Princess Elizabeth (born 1926), from 1952 Queen Elizabeth II.
548. Cissy Arditti, cousin of Elias and Georges.
549. Jacqueline and Edith.
550. *Sic*, in English. [DD]
551. That is, with Marie-Louise von Motesiczky.
552. See note 332 above.
553. *Haushälterin* = housekeeper; *aber ich bitt Sie* = I ask you now.
554. French: "in spite of, not because of."
555. Franz Baermann Steiner (1909–1952), lyric poet and ethnologist, had known Elias since 1937. He emigrated to England in 1938.
556. In English in the original.
557. Cf. *Crowds and Power* 26–27; III 26–28.
558. "That you had a drink." Veza uses the wrong past participle *gesauft*, then corrects it to *gesoffen*. The German in her postwar letters is in fact not only sprinkled with English words and phrases but also often employs phraseology more typical of English than German. [DD]
559. Perhaps Emanuel Hirschtritt.
560. French, "In search of gained time." A play on Proust's *A la recherche du temps perdu* (In Search of Lost Time).
561. On the verso of pages one and two (original and carbon copy):

    Dramatis personae of *The Wedding*
    Chief Building Officer Segenreich, father of the bride
    Johanna, mother of the bride
    Christa, the bride
    Karl, her brother in the third semester of university
    Mariechen, the youngest, fourteen years old

562. Paule Arhex.
563. French *putain* = whore. [DD]
564. Friedl Benedikt died of Hodgkin's disease in 1953.
565. The draft of a letter in Elias's hand has survived. It is written in English and was supposed to provide Nissim with a model for what to write for the English authorities:

My dear brother,

It is high time you come at last to see us. You have promised it for so long, and after all, it is nine years now since I saw you last. Georges is not at all well; he is still in the Sanatorium above Grenoble, and I think you ought to spend at <least> four weeks with him too; it would certainly improve the state of his health. You of all people ought to know how decisive the influence of emotional factors can be on a very sick person. You are my guest in Paris. There is enough room in my flat; and of course we shall be delighted to invite you for the time you are staying with Georges too. So do come, and don't worry about the financial side. I can't tell you how happy we shall be to have you as our guest in France, for two to three months at least. Everybody, the whole family, is looking forward to seeing you. So don't postpone it any longer.

Your loving brother.

566. Probably Franz Baermann Steiner and H. G. Adler (see note 584 below), Steiner's friend and later his literary executor.
567. An untranslatable play on the words *Haushälterin* (housekeeper) and *Zuhälterin* (procuress). [DD]
568. On April 25, 1948, Nissim wrote a letter to Georges about Elias's visit:

> Elias is more likable than he used to be, because he really tries to be attuned to us. And yet I have to reproach him for his annoying tendency to be a parasite. It comes so naturally to him he doesn't even notice. The bygone days in Lausanne are over, when we longed for visits from relatives so we could take their money. But Elias thinks it's completely normal to accept advances and loans from all sides (and especially from relatives), yet he would have had no trouble financing his trip to France with an advance from his publisher.

569. See note 379 above.
570. Françoise, Nissim's first child by his second wife, had been born on April 4, 1948.
571. "Curriculum" and "negative" are the curriculum vitae and photograph for the publisher's publicity campaign. Cf. note 599 below.
572. Weismann in Munich.
573. Ménerbes, a medieval village in the Luberon mountains of Provence.
574. Marie-Louise von Motesiczky had invited Elias to Provence.
575. See note 280 above.
576. The French state examinations.

577. "Faulty action," in English in the original, is a literal translation of the psychoanalytical term *Fehlleistung*, a "Freudian slip" revealing subconscious desires. [DD]
578. The quoted sentence is in English in the original. [DD]
579. In English in the original. [DD]
580. A fictive report on the trial of Mussolini for war crimes: Cassius (pseudonym of Michael Foot), *The Trial of Mussolini, being a verbatim report of the first great trial for war criminals held in London sometime in 1944 or 1945* (London: Gollancz, 1943).
581. Veza quotes from the English translation of C. K. Scott-Moncrieff. The Canettis did not yet have access to a French edition of Proust (cf. p. 351). The passage occurs a few pages into "Swann in Love," Part 2 of *Swann's Way*.
582. In fact, Swann does not sleep with the maid, but does pose for her.
583. D. = Deutschland. Except for the first word, this sentence is typed in red.
584. The Prague writer Hans Günther Adler (1910–1988), imprisoned in a concentration camp from 1941 to 1945, moved to London in 1947. He is best known for the autobiographical works he began publishing in 1955.
585. UN Security Council Resolution 46 of April 17, 1948, demanded that all persons and organizations in Palestine forgo violence and "refrain from any political activity which might prejudice the rights, claims, or position" of either the Jewish or the Arab community.
586. See note 429 above. A sort of civil war had been raging since the adoption of the plan to partition Palestine by the UN General Assembly on November 29, 1947. The partition was opposed by extreme right-wing Zionist militias such as the Irgun, led by Menachem Begin, and Lehi (the Stern Gang), just as it was by Arabs fighting against the establishment of a Jewish state. The Zionist militias had carried out numerous attacks and bombings against Arab institutions and villages. From April 9 to 11, 1948, Irgun and Lehi units massacred approximately two hundred Arab civilians in the village of Deir Jassin.
587. In July 1947, Irgun had taken two British officers as hostages and hanged them when its demands were not met.
588. Founded in 1913 by Sidney and Beatrice Webb, George Bernard Shaw, and members of the Fabian Society, *The New Statesman* was published from 1931 to 1960 by Kingsley Martin. Virginia Woolf and T.S. Eliot were among its contributors.
589. *Sic* in the original. [DD]
590. The comparison with Moses' wife Zipporah from a Botticelli fresco occurs in the second part of *Swann's Way*.
591. See note 474 above.
592. Possibly a reference to Diogenes. [DD]

593. Original: *den Seinen gibt's der Herr im Schlaf*, "the Lord gives [bread] to his chosen while they sleep" (Psalm 127:2). In German, the proverb suggests undeservedly good fortune.
594. The twenty-fifth wedding anniversary of King George VI and Queen Elizabeth, the parents of Elizabeth II.
595. The Canetti brothers' father died of heart failure at thirty-one.
596. Proust, *Cities of the Plain*, Part 1.
597. "Inverted" added by hand as an afterthought.
598. Hans Henny Jahnn (1894–1959), German novelist and dramatist. [DD]
599. On April 27, Veza had written the publisher:

Dear Herr Weismann,

Canetti is going to send you an afterword for the *Hochzeit* on time. It will also contain his theories about modern drama. Unfortunately, he won't write a curriculum vitae. I had hoped that his scholarly brother would get him to write one, but he was unsuccessful. It is the one thing that I have difficulty doing, too, so I'm sending you the text from the American dust jacket which I've translated, in addition to correcting some inaccuracies in it . . . Here in England, the author's religion would never be mentioned, but Canetti is proud of being a Sephardic Jew. He is 42 but looks much younger and publishers are always pleasantly surprised to see an extremely attractive person standing before them instead of a grumpy scholar.

On May 6, Veza sent Weismann "this excellent curriculum vitae of Canetti, written by his brother." (Information supplied by Jochen Meyer, Deutsches Literaturarchiv, Marbach. The enclosure has been lost.)

600. In Ezekiel 38, Gog is a prince from the land of Magog whom God uses as an instrument to prove his power to the heathens. He plans to send him against Israel with a large army and then rain fire and brimstone down upon him.
601. French *car* = bus.
602. Probably the wife of the sanatorium's medical director (cf. pp. 313–314).
603. Veza is in error here: Søren Kierkegaard was twenty-nine in 1843 when he published *Either–Or*, his first great work, which included the "Diary of a Seducer." Kierkegaard came from a well-to-do family; while studying theology, he lived the life of a bon vivant, running up debts which his father paid. When his father died in 1838, Kierkegaard inherited a considerable fortune on which he lived until his death in 1855.
604. Experts in stenography have no trouble reading Elias's shorthand, which he himself referred to as secret writing. He used it for the first drafts of many of his works.

605. Don Quixote's beloved. Friedl is intended.
606. See note 595 above.
607. The Roman settlement on the site of present-day Vienna.
608. Probably Georges is meant, but possibly Francis Graham-Harrison, who had obviously flirted with Friedl Benedikt (cf. p. 358).
609. On May 14, 1948, the day the British mandate in Palestine ended, the Jewish National Council proclaimed Israel an independent state as of May 15, contrary to UN Resolution 46. The ensuing attack by Egypt, Transjordan, Syria, Lebanon, Saudi Arabia, and Iraq initiated the first Arab-Israeli War, which lasted until June 3, 1949.
610. After the Russian pogroms of 1881–1882, a group of young people founded the first Zionist movement for the emigration of Jews to Palestine.
611. The three alliterating adjectives are in English in the original. [DD]
612. That is, Endre Nemes (cf. note 422 above).
613. There's an untranslatable mixed metaphor here. *Sich jemandem an den Hals werfen* (to throw yourself at someone's neck) = to throw yourself at someone. But in his letter, Georges has apparently used *Kopf* (head) instead of *Hals* (neck). *Jemandem etwas an den Kopf werfen* (to throw something at someone's head) = to say something unpleasant without beating around the bush. Friedl was apparently capable of both. [DD]
614. The Austrian actress Helga Aichinger, twin sister of the writer Ilse Aichinger. Helga had a small role in Carol Reed's film *The Third Man* (1949).
615. In *The Fugitive*, Marcel receives a telegram from Gilberte which is signed "Albertine" due to a mistake of the telegraph clerk. The grandmother's death occurs in *The Guermantes Way*, Part 2, Chapter 1.
616. The painter Georges Arditti.
617. Bryanston.
618. Endre Nemes.
619. Probably Léon Pierre-Quint, *Marcel Proust, sa vie, son œuvre* (Paris: Sagittaire, 1925).
620. See previous note.
621. Illegible. Perhaps "Maud Wats" or "Marcel Weber."
622. Illegible. Perhaps "Angies."
623. Probably a misspelling of Italian *puttana* (whore). [DD] In Hindu mythology, Putana ("Putrefaction") is a demoness who was supposed to poison the infant Krishna with her milk. But as he nurses at her breast, Krishna sucks out all her life force and she dies.
624. Francis Graham-Harrison.
625. The three Western occupying powers had met without the Soviet Union in February and March. Then from April to June 1948 they met with the Nether-

lands, Belgium, and Luxembourg at the London Six Power Conference. On June 20, 1948, they carried out a currency reform in the Western occupation zones of Germany. The Soviet Union reacted on June 24 with a complete blockade of the Western sectors of Berlin. Great Britain began an airlift on June 28.

626. Emanuel Hirschtritt?
627. Typed in red from "about" to this point.
628. In Beaumarchais's comedy *Le barbier de Séville* (1775), Lindor is the alias under which Count Almaviva courts Rosina, who sends him a note.
629. See X 9–48 for both the lecture in its original English and a German translation by Karen Lauer.
630. William Glock.
631. The phrase between quotation marks is in English in the original. [DD]
632. In English in the original. [DD]
633. Friedl's pen name. [DD]
634. The proverbially wealthy British industrialist who built up a bicycle repair shop into the Morris automobile company.
635. Embarrassed to be with me in public.
636. These stories have been lost.
637. In English. [DD]
638. Here ends the packet of letters found among Georges Canetti's papers.
639. From 1954, the address shared by the Canettis in Hampstead, London.
640. Georges Canetti had just been named a Knight of the French Legion of Honor.
641. To the Hamburg publisher Claassen, which published *Masse und Macht* (*Crowds and Power*) in 1960.
642. "The Survivor," *Crowds and Power* 227–278; III 267–329. [DD]
643. The phrase between quotation marks is in English in the original.
644. Two or three illegible words.
645. *Crowds and Power* 434–462; III 516–549. [DD]
646. Elias was awarded the Nobel Prize for Literature in 1981.

BIBLIOGRAPHY

VEZA CANETTI

WORKS IN GERMAN

Der Fund. Afterword by Angelika Schedel. Munich: Hanser, 2001.

Geduld bringt Rosen. Munich: Hanser, 1992.

Die Gelbe Straße. With a foreword by Elias Canetti and an afterword by Helmut Göbel. Munich: Hanser, 1990.

Der Oger. Afterword by Elias Canetti. Munich: Hanser, 1991.

Die Schildkröten. With an afterword by Fritz Arnold and a biographical chronicle. Munich: Hanser, 1999.

WORKS IN ENGLISH TRANSLATION

The Tortoises. Translated by Ian Mitchell. New York: New Directions, 2001.

Viennese Short Stories. Translated by Julian Preece. Riverside, Calif.: Ariadne Press, 2006.

Yellow Street: A Novel in Five Scenes. Translated by Ian Mitchell. New York: New Directions, 1991.

SECONDARY LITERATURE

Veza Canetti. text + kritik. Munich, 2002.

ELIAS CANETTI

WORKS IN GERMAN

Aufzeichnungen für Marie-Louise. Edited and with an afterword by Jeremy Adler. Munich: Hanser, 2005.

Party im Blitz. Die englischen Jahre. Edited by Kristian Wachinger, with an afterword by Jeremy Adler. Munich: Hanser, 2003.

Werke in zehn Bänden. Munich: Hanser, 1992–2005:

I. *Die Blendung*, 1992.

II. *Hochzeit. Komödie der Eitelkeit. Die Befristeten. Der Ohrenzeuge*, 1995.

III. *Masse und Macht*, 1994.

IV. *Aufzeichnungen 1942–1985. Die Provinz des Menschen. Das Geheimherz der Uhr*, 1993.

V. *Aufzeichnungen 1954–1993. Die Fliegenpein. Nachträge aus Hampstead*, 2004.

VI. *Die Stimmen von Marrakesch. Das Gewissen der Worte*, 1995.

VII. *Die gerettete Zunge*, 1994.

VIII. *Die Fackel im Ohr*, 1993.

IX. *Das Augenspiel*, 1994.

X. *Aufsätze. Reden. Gespräche*, 2005.

UNPUBLISHED MANUSCRIPTS

ZB Elias Canetti's literary remains in the Zentralbibliothek Zürich. Numbering in the form "ZB 54" identifies the carton number.

WORKS IN ENGLISH TRANSLATION

The Agony of Flies: Notes and Notations. Translated by H. F. Broch de Rothermann. New York: Farrar, Straus and Giroux, 1994.

Auto-da-Fé. (First published in the United States in 1947 as *The Tower of Babel*.) Translated by C. V. Wedgwood. New York: Continuum, 1974.

The Conscience of Words. Translated by Joachim Neugroschel. New York: Continuum, Seabury Press, 1979.

Crowds and Power. Translated by Carol Steward. New York: Viking Press, 1963.

The Human Province. Translated by Joachim Neugroschel. New York: Seabury Press, 1978.

The Memoirs of Elias Canetti (The Tongue Set Free, The Torch in My Ear, The Play of the Eyes). Translated by Joachim Neugroschel. New York: Farrar, Straus and Giroux, 1999.

Notes from Hampstead: The Writer's Notes: 1954–1971. Translated by John Hargraves. New York: Farrar, Straus and Giroux, 1998.

Party in the Blitz: The English Years. Translated by Michael Hofmann. New York: New Directions, 2005.

The Plays of Elias Canetti. Translated by Gita Honegger. New York: Farrar, Straus and Giroux, 1987.

The Secret Heart of the Clock: Notes, Aphorisms, Fragments, 1973–1985. Translated by Joel Agee. New York: Farrar, Straus and Giroux, 1989.

The Voices of Marrakesh: A Record of a Visit. Translated by J. A. Underwood. New York: Continuum, Seabury Press, 1978.

Secondary Literature

Sven Hanuschek. *Elias Canetti*. Munich: Hanser, 2005.

Kristian Wachinger, editor. *Elias Canetti—Bilder aus seinem Leben*. Munich: Hanser, 2005.

PICTURE CREDITS

Photos 1, 2, 3, 4, 5, 6, 8, 9, 12, 13, 15: Estate of Elias Canetti, Zurich.

Photos 7 and 10: Fonds Jacques Canetti, Suresnes.

Photo 11: Marie-Louise von Motesiczky Charitable Trust, London.

Photo 14: Deutsches Literaturarchiv, Marbach.

Photos 16, 17, 18, 19: Zentralbibliothek, Zurich.

INDEX